THE CHURCH'S BOOK

The Church's Book

Theology of Scripture in Ecclesial Context

Brad East

WILLIAM B. EERDMANS PUBLISHING COMPANY
GRAND RAPIDS, MICHIGAN

Wm. B. Eerdmans Publishing Co.
4035 Park East Court SE, Grand Rapids, Michigan 49546
www.eerdmans.com

Book design by Leah Luyk

28 27 26 25 24 23 22   1 2 3 4 5 6 7

ISBN 978-0-8028-7815-1

Library of Congress Cataloging-in-Publication Data

Names: East, Brad, author.
Title: The church's book : theology of scripture in ecclesial context / Brad
     East.
Description: Grand Rapids, Michigan : William B. Eerdmans Publishing
     Co., [2022] | Includes bibliographical references and index. | Summary:
     "A study of the role that varied understandings of the church—explored
     through the work of noteworthy recent theologians—play in the doc-
     trine and interpretation of Scripture"—Provided by publisher.
Identifiers: LCCN 2021046131 | ISBN 9780802878151
Subjects: LCSH: Church—Biblical teaching. | Bible—Theology. | BISAC:
     RELIGION / Christian Theology / General | RELIGION / Christian
     Theology / History
Classification: LCC BS2545.C5 E27 2022 | DDC 262—dc23
LC record available at https://lccn.loc.gov/2021046131

Unless otherwise noted, Scripture quotations are taken from the New Revised Standard Version.

For Toni Moman,
"Miss Toni" to the countless children
who first heard the name of Jesus at her feet—
dedicated teacher, fellow theologian,
and lifelong lover of the church
and the church's book

Contents

CONTENTS

Foreword

"Intelligible disagreement is to be preferred by far to puzzled consternation" (p. 292). This conviction, with which no one can disagree, animates this very fine volume from Brad East. By the end of this volume East has clarified a host of issues, revealing that many of the central disagreements between practitioners of theological interpretation of Scripture can be made more intelligible by examining different doctrines of Scripture and how Scripture is related to ecclesiology.

Although some of my own work, as well as several recent contributions of others, has hinted at the importance for theological interpretation of understanding the interactions between doctrines of Scripture and doctrines of the church, no other volume makes this importance as clear as this one. Moreover, East is able to show some of the rich variety of ways in which "bibliology" and ecclesiology interact in the work of specific theologians.

East begins by noting that many of the early practitioners of theological interpretation during the late 1980s and early 1990s focused theoretical energy and arguments on matters of hermeneutics. For the most part, these scholars were trained in the practices of biblical studies and were arguing for a place within a landscape dominated by historically governed modes of exegesis. Only more recently have theologians entered these discussions by pointing out the conceptual and theological priority of doctrines of Scripture. Once this is recognized, matters of ecclesiology follow naturally, because no matter how one conceives of their relationships, one cannot say "Scripture" without implying "church," too. Of course, there is no single doctrine of Scripture and no single ecclesiology and no single way of relating them. Nevertheless, East has brought us to the heart of the matter.

The core of this volume is its detailed discussions of John Webster, Robert Jenson, and John Howard Yoder with regard to bibliology and ecclesiology. East chooses these three theologians for two basic reasons. First, each of them is, in his own way, deeply influenced by Karl Barth. East makes a strong case for Barth being the generative force for almost all types of theological interpretation of Scripture. Second, Webster, Jenson, and Yoder respectively represent the ecclesial traditions of the magisterial Reformation, Catholicism (broadly conceived), and the radical Reformation. East also includes a very thoughtful apology for the use of Yoder while also seriously reckoning with Yoder's history of abusive relationships with women.

The virtue of these discussions is East's commitment to reading each of these scholars with the utmost charity. I believe each of them would recognize themselves in East's treatment of their work. As a result, East is able to display the internal coherence between the ways each understands Scripture and its place in the life of the church. Quite frankly, if I were trying to teach students about the importance of interpretive charity, I might well assign them to read these chapters in this volume. Intelligible disagreements depend on the various parties being able to recognize themselves in others' accounts.

Despite their common heritage in Barth, Webster, Jenson, and Yoder have strikingly different "bibliologies" and relate Scripture to the church in different and incompatible ways. This is not to say that scholars within these distinct traditions cannot engage in common tasks of scriptural interpretation. Rather, it is to recognize that when intractable interpretive stances emerge, the issues may have far less to do with hermeneutics and more to do with how each comes to the interpretive task, relying on differing approaches to the nature of Scripture and its relationships to the church. In the final chapter East actually shows how this works in relation to specific scholars and specific scholarly disagreements.

I do not mean to give the impression that Brad East is simply a very able expositor of others' views. All of the discussions in this book display East's analytical rigor and theological sophistication. As one of the subjects under discussion in this book, I will speak for all of us and say that there are many times East is able to do more for and with our work than we did ourselves.

East's close attention to the work of others can tend to deflect from the ways he genuinely clarifies and advances discussions in theological interpretation. I look forward to seeing how future theological interpreters take these advances and work with them to push theological interpretation in new and promising directions.

Stephen E. Fowl

Acknowledgments

It has been a long road from the initial idea for this book to its being published. A full decade, in fact. I have lost count of the number of versions it has gone through, and I am sure I have forgotten to list half the people whom I owe a debt of gratitude. I cannot list them all by name, much less say what they have meant to me. If you helped along the way, know that I am thankful.

As for the named: I ought to begin with my brother, Garrett, who floated the concept of this book to me in the fall of 2011. Thanks to him and to my other brother, Mitch, for their friendship, their support, and their theological minds. Also to Stacy and Allison for their relaxed toleration of their husbands' weakness for the *rabies theologorum*.

This book is a major revision of my dissertation in the Department of Religious Studies at Yale University, which was submitted and approved in 2017. Thanks first of all, then, to my advisor, Kathryn Tanner, for constant encouragement, aid, wisdom, insight, and (what is not native to me) love of concision and economy of prose. Thanks as well to the rest of the committee: Miroslav Volf, David Kelsey, and Steve Fowl. I could not have dreamed of a more fitting, or a more formidable, group of readers for a dissertation on this topic (they quite literally wrote the books on it, after all), and their kindness, generosity, and feedback meant a great deal. Thanks, finally, to the other faculty from whom I learned or with whom I worked during my time at Yale, in particular Christopher Beeley, Adam Eitel, John Hare, Jennifer Herdt, Dale Martin, Linn Tonstad, and Denys Turner. If I learned anything during my studies, I learned it primarily by osmosis from these brilliant scholars.

Thanks to other teachers and mentors: Felix Asiedu, David Fleer, Randy Harris, Tim Jackson, Luke Timothy Johnson, Ben Langford, Steffen Lösel, Ian McFarland, Don McLaughlin, Carol Newsom, Glenn Pemberton, Jeanene Reese, Tracy Shilcutt, and Wendell Willis.

Thanks to colleagues, friends, and erstwhile fellow students: Awet Andemicael, Liza Anderson, Matt Anderson, Richard Beck, Justin Crisp, Ryan Darr, TJ Dumansky, Jamie Dunn, Matt Fisher, Andrew Forsyth, Janna Gonwa, Todd Hains, Laura Carlson Hasler, Justin Hawkins, Wes Hill, Zac Koons, Andrew Krinks, Mark Lackowski, Liv Stewart Lester, Mark Lester, Samuel Loncar, Ryan McAnnally-Linz, Jimmy McCarty, Ross McCullough (in more than one sense: *nemo nisi per amicitiam cognoscitur*), David Mahfood, Jake Meador, Stephen Ogden, Kester Smith, Bradley Steele, John Stern, Myles Werntz, Lauren Smelser White, and Leonard Wills. Thanks also to those I came to know because of this project: Lee Camp, David Congdon, Chris Green, Peter Kline, Kris Norris, Kendall Soulen, Tyler Wittman, and Steve Wright. Thanks to all those named above who read and commented on the manuscript, as well as Darren Sarisky, Lacey Jones, and Stanley Hauerwas; thanks especially to Stanley, the late Robert Jenson, and the late John Webster, all of whom took the time to encourage this project and my work in general.

A special word of thanks to the numerous colleagues and friends who helped me think through the moral, theological, and scholarly questions surrounding the inclusion of Yoder in the manuscript: first at a meeting of the Yale Ethics Colloquium in 2015, then in the summer of 2020 via a series of revisions to the excursus that now precedes chapter 5.

Thanks to my graduate assistant Luke Roberts for his labors in helping to prepare the bibliography. Thanks as well to my colleagues in the CBS at ACU: my deans, Ken Cukrowski and Chris Hutson; my chairs, Rodney Ashlock and David Kneip; those with whom I've discussed the matters of this book, especially Fred Aquino, Cliff Barbarick, John Boyles, Steve Hare, Vic McCracken, Amanda Pittman, and Jerry Taylor; and last but not least, Carlene Harrison, who makes the world go round.

Thanks to Spencer Bogle, who is the reason I am in this business in the first place; to the Christian Scholarship Foundation and the Louisville Institute for support at just the right time; and to James Ernest, for giving this newly minted PhD a chance. It is an honor to publish with Eerdmans. I hope he agrees that what I have written is in fact a book, not the other thing.

Thanks to my parents, Ray and Georgine East, who have never flagged in their support of or faith in me. Thanks especially to my mother, who over the years has read a steady stream of theology supplied by her eldest son. Apart from her, I doubted that this work would be read by someone not paid to do so; now, I suppose, actual living readers will presumably pay to have the honor. Though they'll have to get in line behind her.

Thanks to Toni Moman—"Miss Toni"—to whom this work is dedicated, a lifelong servant and lover of God's children. All ministers are theologians, and only God knows how many children have had their first dose of theology from Miss Toni. They are all of them better for it, as am I. Years ago I told Miss Toni that, if and when I had the chance to write a book, I would dedicate it to her. Well: it's finally here!

Thanks to my children, Sam, Rowan, Paige, and Liv, all of whom were born during my work on this book, and who make it all worth it. Every day, it seems, a package arrives at our door, and they roll their eyes in unison: "Another book for Dad." I look forward to opening a new package and showing them a book with Dad's name on the cover—if only for another, altogether spirited eyeroll.

Thanks, finally, and most of all, to my wife, Katelin, who has been my partner, companion, and best friend for more than seventeen years. We have traveled from central to west Texas; to Atlanta, Georgia; to New Haven, Connecticut; and back again. I cannot imagine doing so without her. Under God, I owe everything to her.

Soli Deo Gloria.

Brad East
Feast of St. Benedict of Nursia, 2021

PART I

Whose Book?

History, Academy, and Church

CHAPTER 1

Fault Lines

*Theological Interpretation of Scripture
and the Place of Ecclesiology*

Scripture's *sitz im leben* is being heard, in synagogue and church.

—Christopher Bryan[1]

All accounts of Scripture are inseparable from accounts of the church.

—Angus Paddison[2]

Advocacy for theological interpretation involves a series of loosely "postmodern" riffs on Barth-inspired themes.

—Daniel Treier[3]

Holy Scripture is the word of the Lord Jesus Christ to and for his body, the church. This is the bedrock confession of the church in its liturgy. When and where the people of God assemble in the Spirit, and the words of the prophets and apostles are read aloud in their midst, the only fitting response is acclamation of the risen Christ's living speech to his beloved, in the present tense. Scripture's reading is housed in worship and met with praise. For the witness of the canonical texts is not merely the record of past events or of the thoughts of the long since departed. It is the medium of the triune God's address to his covenant community, the sign and instrument of divine revelation. What is spoken and heard comes

1. Bryan, *Listening to the Bible*, 124.
2. Paddison, *Scripture*, 21.
3. Treier, "What Is Theological Interpretation?," 152.

3

from God, *through* his servants, *to* his people. Indeed, these holy texts—sanctified by the Holy Spirit for a people called to be holy as the Lord is holy—arose throughout the life of God's people. They did not come first, either under the old covenant or under the new. Rather, the people preceded the canon and gave rise to it. This is not to say that the people were the ultimate source of the canon: Scripture is the word of the Lord because, and only because, the Spirit of the Lord inspired its words to be the vehicle of God's saving and sovereign speech. Nor is this to deny the priority of Israel's scriptures to the church's founding: their antecedence is a nonnegotiable fact of the church's life. Exodus and Sinai come before Easter and Pentecost, and in their absence the gospel would fall to the ground, lifeless.

No, the significance of the precedence of God's people to God's word written is threefold.

First, the election and consecration of a people of God's possession, the object and witness of God's gracious will and presence in the midst of a fallen world, holds primacy over the canon. This people's mission, their very existence, is the great divine work in history, the goal and inner rationale of creation. Scripture is secondary to this primary work. It serves, enables, and empowers it; the canon is for the church, not the church for the canon.

Second, the texts of canonical Scripture were composed, edited, distributed, used liturgically, copied, transmitted, received, and interpreted by and among the children of Abraham. If Abraham's children never existed, there would be no Law or Psalms, Gospels or Epistles. Holy Scripture consists entirely of covenant writings; that is to say, of documents and testaments of those who lived as heirs to Abraham's friendship with the one true God. Members of Abraham's family wrote them, revised them across time, read them in public worship and private devotion, and republished them for future generations. The proximate source or creaturely origin of these texts, therefore, is not generically human; it is covenantal. The author of the canon is the Israel of God.

Third, if Scripture's context is salvation history, in which God calls a people to be his own among the nations, and if Scripture has its birth in the life of that people, then Scripture's purpose is nothing but the upbuilding of the same. Put differently, the particular texts that constitute the church's canon are not an accident of history; they were chosen by the church for the furtherance of a particular end: the proclamation of the good news of Christ until his return. In acting to enshrine the testimony of the prophets and apostles to the gospel, the church thereby ensured that it would hear not only their human voices but also, through them, the voice of Christ guiding, rebuking, teaching, forgiving, commanding, and sending his followers in their mission to the nations. Thus the reading of the scriptures in the liturgy; thus the ensemble of ritual actions surrounding it, above all the cry of thanks to God. Gratitude pours forth because it is not merely God's word, but God's word *for* God's people. Like the *meth' hēmōn* of Immanuel or the *pro nobis* of the creed, that little word "for" makes all the difference. It is a microcosm of Scripture's being and ends—a word of consolation and presence, the gospel in a preposition—that tells us everything we need to know.

This book is about that "for." It is about the relationship of Scripture to the church. It is also about the *doctrine of Scripture*, or bibliology, in relation to the *doctrine of the church*, or ecclesiology. This study is a very small sample of bibliology: namely, theological reflection on the nature, authority, purpose, and interpretation of the church's sacred canon. Notice that hermeneutics, or the question of how the church ought faithfully to read Scripture, is but one among many aspects of the doctrine of Scripture—and in my ordering here, last. Interpretation concludes the series rather than beginning it because how one reads the text depends on what the text is and what it is for, as well as why one is reading the text and in what context. The central context has already been specified: the mission and worship of the community of Jesus Christ. Hence the connection to ecclesiology, or theological reflection on the church. Conventional commitments in bibliology cut across ecclesial divisions, but the very nature of those divisions means that ecclesiology will look quite different depending on the particular church in view (which is to say, since theology is not free-standing but a discursive practice embedded in lived traditions, the differences will depend on the church to which the theologian in question belongs). For example: Is the church indefectible? Is its teaching infallible? Is its primary task the administration of the sacraments, the instruction of the faithful, the evangelization of the lost, the rectification of injustice? Does it expect a hearing in the halls of power, or does it assume marginal status, even persecution? Does it anticipate broad-scale improvement in the welfare of human societies, or the perdurance of sin's corrupting power, however subtle? Does it see proper development in its own life, or is it watchful of a kind of perpetual temptation to outgrow (and thus leave behind) the founding witness of the apostles and the early church?

It is easy to see how these and other questions bear directly on the doctrine of Scripture. For example, if Scripture is authoritative, how is its authority exercised, and by whom? May the church read Scripture in such a way that the reading thereby produced is itself authoritative on a par with Scripture? Or are all churchly readings fallible and therefore in principle revisable? Who says which interpretation takes the day? Or what of doctrinal elaboration that emerged in the centuries following the apostles? Is there such a thing as dogma? If so, what is its status as an authority and how is it related not only to Scripture's authority but also to its interpretation? Finally, what of questions that have been raised in the ongoing life of the church's mission, questions about which the canon is silent or, where it has something to say, underdetermined? What of episcopal succession, relics, the intercession of the saints, the veneration of icons, the adoration of the Eucharist? What of nuclear war, animal testing, genome editing, abortion, democracy, human cloning, extraterrestrial life?

In short, how one answers questions about the nature, authority, and interpretation of Scripture follows from and depends on one's understanding of the nature, authority, and mission of the church. Just as church and Scripture are intertwined, so too are the doctrines thereof. They are reciprocally conditioned and mutually determined. If Holy Scripture is the church's book, then it makes sense that the church would call for a theological account alongside or prior to a theological account of the book as such.

In recent centuries, however, the status of the Bible as the church's book has come into question, or at least become something less than axiomatic. The fragmentation of the theological disciplines in the academy combined with historiographic study of the biblical texts has, as it were, shifted the burden of proof: the church must make a claim to these texts, justifying before the bar of scholarship its possession of them and its traditional ways of reading them.[4] In disciplinary and sometimes ecclesial practice, the following premise is not merely stipulated but presumed: namely, that each of the canonical texts is first of all a discrete historical artifact, best investigated by those trained in the relevant specialties (philology, history,

---

4. In this book I use "history" to designate whatever happened in the past; "historical" to modify entities, persons, events, beliefs, or practices that in one way or another pertain to the past (or to the ongoing sweep of human affairs); "historiography" to denote scholarly investigation into the past; and "historiographic" to modify varieties of such intellectual inquiry.

text criticism, anthropology, sociology), and best understood, if at all, in its originating context. By contrast, ecclesial contexts—the church's sacred tradition, dogmatic teaching, canonical collection, and liturgical assembly—are understood to be secondary, optional, negligible, fanciful, burdensome, and/or scandalous in relation to the task of understanding the text. It is important to see, moreover, that this situation was not imposed from on high, but rather was acquiesced to and even perpetrated by the leading lights of theological thought and ecclesiastical leadership. It was not the "secular" academy that did this, in other words, but seminaries, Christian scholars, and pastors. The result, at least in the Western world, has been a continued diminishment of confidence in Scripture's identity as the church's book and the Lord's living word to the church, as well as in the church's dogmatic and exegetical traditions. After all, what are those traditions if not well-intended but ultimately failed attempts to grasp what only we, now, by the proper methods, understand?

This is only the briefest sketch of the fate of Scripture during and after the Enlightenment, a potted history and a biased one.[5] Such stories are often inattentive to the role of Scripture in actual churches and in believers' ordinary lives, focusing as they do on elite scholars, thinkers, and movements whose influence sometimes went unrecognized or took generations to go into full effect. To be clear, the church never *lost* the Bible. There was always resistance to the trends outlined above, both in scholarship and in the liturgy. Simply put, so long as Scripture is read in the congregation and recognized "as what it really is, the word of God" (1 Thess 2:13 RSV), it remains the church's book. Nevertheless, the trends outlined above were real and readily identified. They called for action. Organized resistance sought to hold the line against encroachments on the church's confession, its deed and title to the scriptures of old. This resistance could take less than healthy forms, such as fundamentalism, but even at its best it was usually defensive in posture.[6] One can under-

---

5. See further Legaspi, *Death of Scripture*; Reventlow, *Authority of the Bible*; Sheehan, *Enlightenment Bible*; Preus, *Spinoza*; Hahn and Wiker, *Politicizing the Bible*; Morrow, *Theology, Politics, and Exegesis*; Hahn and Morrow, *Modern Biblical Criticism*; Harrison, *Rise of Natural Science*.

6. As Hans Frei writes, "It cannot be said often and emphatically enough that liberals and fundamentalists are siblings under the skin in identifying or rather confusing ascriptive as well as descriptive literalism about Jesus at the level of understanding the text, with ascriptive and descriptive literalism at the level of knowing historical reality" (*Types of Christian Theology*, 84).

stand why. How faithfully to defend continued recourse to Scripture as the Lord's word in the "modern" world—one founded on so much rejection of the old and so much innovation in knowledges and forms of life—without becoming nostalgic, reactionary, or fundamentalist?

Karl Barth had one answer: stop beating a retreat and stage an offensive. And so he did, from the end of the Great War to the height of the Cold War. It is fair to say that, for the last century or so, theology in the West—Catholic and European but especially Protestant and Anglophone theology—has lived in Barth's shadow. This is certainly true for theological reflection on Scripture and its interpretation. The major shifts and movements undergone by both the doctrine of Scripture and biblical hermeneutics in the half-century since Barth's death bear his unmistakable imprint (if not his imprimatur). Everywhere one looks, one sees one more branch of the Barthian tree.

This is not a book about Barth. But it does concern his lasting legacy in the field, specifically regarding the question of Scripture's relationship to the church and how best to depict that relationship theologically. Rather than answer that question directly, I pursue it through engagement with three primary figures: John Webster, Robert Jenson, and John Howard Yoder. In one way or another, all three are students of Barth, bearing the impact of his thought on their own while repurposing it in different ways. These theologians both articulate and illustrate the centrality of a particular account of the church for the doctrine of Scripture and its interpretation. Furthermore, each of them speaks out of and on behalf of a distinct strand of Christendom in its divided state: magisterial reformation, catholic, and radical reformation. Close attention to their theological systems offers concrete examples not only of material proposals worth taking seriously, but also of the doctrinal logics animating such proposals.

I address all this in detail in the coming chapters, and I say more at the end of this chapter about the structure and rationale of the book. For now I want to clarify why it is that I am focusing on the topic of Scripture's relationship to the church as well as its dogmatic overlay, the role of ecclesiology in bibliology. Instead of beginning with Barth and moving to the present, I want to start *in medias res*, with where we find ourselves at the moment, before looking backward and asking of Barth's influence. Specifically, I want to discuss what has come to be called "theological interpretation of Scripture" (TIS). Both the origins and the primary features of TIS will orient us to the state of the question—that is, the proper reading of Scripture as the church's authoritative canon in the overriding context of the church's history, tradition, and worship. In addition, TIS will illuminate a lacuna in the literature that this book seeks to identify and, in part, to address. This lacuna helps to explain what I understand to be an impasse in the field, which in turn is the impetus for this study.

Theological Interpretation of Scripture

In the last two decades there has been a veritable explosion in publications with TIS[7] as their subject or method: essays and articles, edited volumes, books,[8] journals, dictionaries, commentary series[9]—the "movement," such as it is, has become a minor publishing industry in and of itself. Why such popularity, both for scholars and for their read-

---

7. Throughout the book I use "bibliology" and "TIS" to denote two different things, though at times, especially in this chapter, they may seem interchangeable. Bibliology is the larger category, meaning Christian theology of Holy Scripture; whereas TIS refers to the specific quasi-movement, discussed below, of "theological interpretation of Scripture" that has developed and expanded over the last two decades. The latter term is thus encompassed within the former; the two are not synonymous.

8. See, e.g., the pieces gathered in Fowl, *Theological Interpretation of Scripture*; Sarisky, *Theology, History, and Biblical Interpretation*. See also Adam et al., *Reading Scripture with the Church*; Allen, *Theological Commentary*; Davis and Hays, *Art of Reading Scripture*; Gaventa and Hays, *Seeking the Identity of Jesus*; Ford and Stanton, *Reading Texts, Seeking Wisdom*; Bartholomew and Thomas, *Manifesto for Theological Interpretation*; Paddison, *Theologians on Scripture*. For a sample of important monographs, see Sarisky, *Scriptural Interpretation*; Young, *Art of Performance*; Byassee, *Praise Seeking Understanding*; Cunningham, *Scripture in Barth's Doctrine of Election*; Wood, *Theology of Henri de Lubac*; Greene-McCreight, *Ad Litteram*; Levering, *Participatory Biblical Exegesis*; Paddison, *Scripture*; Swain, *Trinity, Revelation, and Reading*; Volf, *Captive to the Word of God*; Treier, *Theological Interpretation*; Leithart, *Deep Exegesis*; Chapman, *1 Samuel as Christian Scripture*; Billings, *Theological Interpretation of Scripture*; Green, *Practicing Theological Interpretation*. For books either sympathetic or adjacent to TIS, but focused on a historical period or directed to the guild of biblical studies, see Young, *Biblical Exegesis*; Peeler, *Epistle to the Hebrews*; Davis, *Opening Israel's Scriptures*; Pierce, *Divine Discourse*.

9. See, e.g., the *Journal of Theological Interpretation*, whose inaugural issue was published in 2007; Vanhoozer et al., *Dictionary for Theological Interpretation of the Bible*. As for commentary series, see the Brazos Theological Commentary on the Bible, The Two Horizons OT/NT Commentary (published by Eerdmans), and the T&T Clark International Theological Commentary.

ers? Doubtless it is something of an academic fad, and advocates ought to be wary of the faddish vices: self-aggrandizing narratives of decline and recovery; locating oneself at the end of (scholarly) history; obsessing over the smallest matters of disagreement; supposing contemporary challenges and solutions will persist indefinitely; forgetting the wider historical backdrop, in relation to which one's own moment is a small and probably insignificant detail.[10] Granting those dangers, it seems to me that the popularity of TIS owes itself to an attempt to make good on a long-sought promise: releasing Scripture from its captivity to historical criticism, thereby breaking down the wall between theology and exegesis. Old habits die hard, after all, as do disciplinary divisions. TIS suggests that these disciplinary divides can finally be put behind us. Christian theologians can therefore return, without looking over their shoulders or supplying exhaustive methodological justification, to the principal source and sustenance of their work—Holy Scripture. Christian exegetes can likewise read the Bible as more than an ancient historical document, with more in mind than probabilistic facticity, hypothetical reconstruction, and antecedents, analogues, and audience.[11]

But what does it mean to read Scripture theologically? How do practitioners define and practice TIS? How has it evolved, what does it look like, and what are its major features? Instead of surveying the field, I want to focus on a single figure, Stephen Fowl, who is arguably the one most responsible for ushering in this cavalcade of activity. Having set the scene with Fowl, we will be in a position to note the cracks beginning to show in the foundation of TIS, and the role that ecclesiology has to play in both diagnosing and responding to the problem.

10. Practitioners of TIS should keep in mind that the issues around which the Biblical Theology Movement—a long defunct precursor—rallied are quite similar to those that characterize the so-called renewal of TIS. In Brevard Childs's account (*Biblical Theology in Crisis*, 32–50), these issues included: the theological dimension of the Bible; the unity of the whole Bible; the revelation of God in history; the distinctive biblical mentality; and the contrast of the Bible to its environment. Rephrase the last two—say, as the Bible's "unique witness" and "countercultural vision"—and the description is not far off the mark.

11. I do not want to overstate the case, as if there were no contemporary theologians before TIS, or none outside of TIS during the last three decades, using the Bible in materially normative ways in their work. There are numerous counterexamples: among many others, see Charry, *By the Renewing of Your Minds*; Gunton, *Introduction to Christian Doctrine*; McClendon, *Doctrine*; McFarland, *Divine Image*; O'Donovan, *Desire of the Nations*; Sonderegger, *Doctrine of God*; Williams, *Christ on Trial*.

Fowl initiated a new discourse in academic theological engagement with Scripture. But how did he arrive at a point where he could do so? As he tells the story:

> Early in my graduate studies I became very frustrated with what I took to be the hermeneutically unsophisticated and theologically arid state of biblical studies. I and many others my age found great encouragement in the writings of Brevard Childs and Anthony Thiselton. These two scholars in particular made it seem possible to combine serious philosophical and theological concerns with critical sophisticated study of the Bible. . . . As a result, when I got the opportunity to study in Sheffield with Anthony Thiselton, it was an easy choice to make.[12]

Using speech-act theory, Fowl wrote his dissertation on Paul's use of hymnic language about Christ.[13] But dissatisfaction persisted.

> As I completed that project it appeared to me that although it had been a good form of therapy for my views about language, speech-act theory would be of only limited use in interpreting texts. Further, it seemed to me that the real significance of combining hermeneutics and biblical studies would appear in matters around the use of Scripture in ethics. This led me to the work of Alasdair MacIntyre, and then to Stanley Hauerwas, and finally to my erstwhile colleague, L. Gregory Jones. I realized that my focus on ethics as an outworking of an interest in hermeneutics and Scripture was too narrowly conceived. Christian ethics is inseparable from theology.[14]

This nexus of influences and concerns led Fowl to begin writing the essays and articles that would eventually be collected in his 1998 book *Engaging Scripture: A Model for Theological Interpretation*. There Fowl argues

---

12. Fowl, *Theological Interpretation of Scripture*, xiii.
13. Fowl, *Hymnic Material in the Pauline Corpus*.
14. Fowl, *Theological Interpretation of Scripture*, xiii–xiv. He goes on to describe his initial sense that philosophical hermeneutics would be the way to bridge the divide between biblical scholarship and theology, before deciding against this in favor of "understand[ing] the ends and purposes of the Christian life and Scripture's role in achieving those ends," along with "ecclesiology and specific ecclesially based practices" (xiv). Theology, in other words, not ethics or philosophical hermeneutics, has to govern and inform what it means to read the Bible theologically.

that, in reading the Bible, Christians' "primary aim in all of [their] different settings and contexts is to interpret scripture as part of their ongoing struggles to live and worship faithfully before the triune God in ways that bring them into ever deeper communion with God and with others. This means that Christians are called not merely to generate various scriptural interpretations but to embody those interpretations as well."[15] Given this aim, Fowl's overarching proposal is that "Christian interpretation of scripture needs to involve a complex interaction in which Christian convictions, practices, and concerns are brought to bear on scriptural interpretation in ways that both shape that interpretation and are shaped by it. Moreover, Christians need to manifest a certain form of common life if this interaction is to serve faithful life and worship."[16] Against formal theories that seek to fix this interaction in advance, Fowl claims "there is no theoretical way to determine how these interactions must work in any particular context," which means that "Christians will need to manifest a form of practical reasoning" that will guide them in making wise judgments about how to read, what to do, what to believe, and when and how any one of these factors should bear on the others.[17]

Fowl's book proposes (and enacts) a transition from biblical theology to theological interpretation.[18] He engages this transition on a number of fronts. Hermeneutically, he demonstrates the bankruptcy of ostensibly

15. Fowl, *Engaging Scripture*, 3.

16. Fowl, *Engaging Scripture*, 8. The "if" in the last sentence is easily overlooked, but it is significant nonetheless: faithful life together in the church is not a precondition of interpreting the Bible well; both virtuous non-Christians and vicious Christians do it all the time. But the fruit of such interpretation is liable to "serve faithful life and worship" only *if* "Christians . . . manifest a certain form of common life."

17. Fowl, *Engaging Scripture*, 8–9. The book goes on to make a number of discrete arguments in support of this overall purpose: in favor of underdetermined interpretation (in lieu of indeterminate or determinate interpretation); against the claim that texts "have" ideologies; regarding the active role of the Holy Spirit in reading Scripture (sometimes contrary to what the text was once taken to mean); how Christians can read the Old Testament in light of their convictions without falling into supersessionism; how theological interpretation can use (ad hoc) the work of historical criticism; what the role of the church's life and authority have to play in scriptural interpretation; and more. These topics broadly encompass the central foci of the six chapters that make up the book.

18. See the subheading midway through the introduction: "Theological Interpretation rather than Biblical Theology" (Fowl, *Engaging Scripture*, 13). For a sharp critique penned a generation earlier, see Gilkey, "Travail of Biblical Language." See also Bartholomew, "Biblical Theology," which brought Gilkey's article to my attention.

neutral approaches to biblical exegesis. Morally, he shows the intrinsic role that virtue and moral formation play in interpretive judgments. Ecclesiologically, he explores the relationship between Scripture and church and the ways in which each is bound up with the other. Theologically, he reveals the unavoidable—indeed, positively necessary—function of beliefs and convictions about God in understanding what the Bible is and how to read it. Historically, he corrects the tendency in biblical scholarship to presuppose views about the text that effectively disqualify the church's tradition of reading practices. Practically, he resituates the location of reading Scripture in the ordinary life of actual churches: such that, on the one hand, the Bible's role and authority are no longer abstract matters for scholars to dispute but pragmatic questions of immediate relevance; and, on the other hand, issues of existential or ethical importance (say, nonviolence or sexuality) must be resolved in the complex communal negotiation of exegesis, life together, and discernment of the Spirit's leading. Such a task is impossible if the texts of Scripture are truly accessible only for the specialist with the relevant expertise.

Fowl wants, in short, to reintegrate the fragmented disciplines of Christian theology, a reintegration centered on what had once classically united them: Holy Scripture. Exegesis is not the first step in a sequence, nor is theology a move away from the Bible; following the premodern tradition, "Christian interpretation of Scripture [is] a type of theology."[19] That is, theology takes the form of reading Scripture,[20] in particular contexts with particular interests in mind, with a dense web of convictions and practices operative in the reading process, in light of a particular theologically articulated telos: ever greater fellowship with the one and undivided Holy Trinity in and with the one holy catholic and apostolic church. To put it mildly, this is a substantially different account of the shape and significance of biblical exegesis than the account offered in the guild or in many seminaries. So be it: Fowl rightly insists that there is no "pure" hermeneutical procedure that thereupon leads, perhaps by the bridging discipline of biblical theology, to Christian doctrine. The disciplinary divisions—and they are just that: divisions—between text,

---

19. Fowl, *Theological Interpretation of Scripture*, xiv. Cf. the opening comments in Fowl, *Idolatry*, 1-2.

20. See R. R. Reno's comments in his essay, "Biblical Theology and Theological Exegesis": "Theology is . . . a form of reading Scripture" (400); "Theology is a practice of reading. It is not a conclusion drawn from reading" (403).

tradition, doctrine, and ministry are artificial and therefore unhelpful for Christian engagement with Scripture. They do not serve Christians' ends in reading Scripture. It is these ends, moreover, that should determine how Christians read the Bible, not historical or hermeneutical judgments about how to read texts in general.

At the time, Fowl's proposal was both a sign of what was already happening around him and itself an inauguration of a sea change in the field. Only twelve years later Miroslav Volf could write the following:

> In my judgment, the return of biblical scholars to the theological reading of the Scriptures, and the return of systematic theologians to sustained engagement with the scriptural texts—in a phrase, the return of both to theological readings of the Bible—is the most significant theological development in the last two decades. Even if it is merely formal, it is comparable in importance to the post–World War I rediscovery of the Trinitarian nature of God and to the resurgence of theological concern for the suffering and the poor in the late sixties of the past century. . . . True, because the Bible can be misused and because it has been badly misused over the centuries, the value of rediscovering the theological reading of the Bible will ultimately depend on how well it is read. But . . . its being read well depends on its being read in the first place.[21]

Volf's observation puts the matter just right. Whether or not TIS is a movement, and whether or not it will continue as such, is neither here nor there. It may very well fade away as quickly as it came on the scene. The immediate point is to note the sheer amount of work being devoted to the subject across the theological academy. The broader, more lasting point—what Volf allows may be "merely formal"—is that a shift has occurred in academic engagement with the Bible, on the part of both biblical scholars and theologians. A concomitant effect of this shift is the relative sidelining of historical criticism as *the* dominant and defining methodology for biblical exegesis (in this case, whether one be a scholar, a theologian, a pastor, or a layperson).[22] So long the *sine qua non*

---

21. Volf, *Word of God*, 14–15. I have removed the emphasis from the last clause in the first sentence.

22. There are other causal factors: the emergence of emancipatory reading strategies (liberation, black, feminist, womanist, queer, postcolonial), the hermeneutics

of "serious" or "responsible" exegesis, historical criticism no longer carries the day as a matter of course; where it still holds sway, the onus has shifted to those who continue to assert its status as "the" proper mode of understanding biblical texts.[23] The question now concerns the role of historical-critical methods *within* broader interpretive paradigms, usually discussed as a matter of proportion, ad hoc utilization, or prolegomena.[24] It will be interesting to see what happens in the coming years, not least since disciplinary divisions may become either more elastic or more entrenched depending on scholars' convictions, institutional identities, and the fragility of Christian higher education.[25]

As for TIS, when I use that term in this book I mean the following: *an approach to Christian reading of the Bible as canonical Holy Scripture that relativizes historical-critical methods, foregrounds theological convictions and interests, and assumes a scripturally mediated communicative relation between the triune God and the church.*[26] The term is descrip-

---

of suspicion, postmodern hermeneutics, critical theory, the decline of the mainline churches and their seminaries, the rise (and recognition) of Christianity outside the West, the uptick of non-Christian and non-religious biblical scholars, dissatisfaction with the "assured deliverances" of historical criticism, and so on.

23. See, e.g., Collins, *Bible after Babel*; Collins, *Encounters with Biblical Theology*. Cf. the insightful review essay of *Bible after Babel* by Michael C. Legaspi, "What Ever Happened to Historical Criticism?"

24. Although one still never fails to encounter the hasty caveat that historical criticism remains "necessary" at some stage of the interpretive process. See my counterargument in East, "Hermeneutics of Theological Interpretation."

25. I want to be clear that these questions—whether or not a tipping point has been reached, whether or not historical criticism is or will soon be on the wane, and whether or not a majority of biblical scholars agree that historical criticism should no longer be the one methodology to rule them all—are all immaterial to my argument. It does not matter *for my argument* whether or not the guild is in agreement with me or with the broader TIS coalition. Too often academic narratives of renewal or declension place argumentative weight on the contingent fact of consensus or majority-agreement, as if that had any bearing on the correctness or fittingness of one's own position. My aim in framing the story this way is only to say that we find ourselves in a transitional moment, both for historical criticism, which is on the defensive, and for alternatives (like TIS), which are on the offensive. This state of affairs does not necessarily reflect which party is "right" or "better" and which is not. But it does mean, for someone who affirms TIS against historical criticism as I do, that there is an opportunity, at once both intellectual and institutional, for countering the status quo.

26. Here are two other definitions for TIS. First, Stephen Fowl: "Scripture needs to be understood in the light of a doctrine of revelation that itself flows from Chris-

tive: I intend this definition to capture accurately the broad contours of the big-tent quasi-"movement" of TIS as it has developed over the last two decades. Two parts of the definition are worth elucidating before moving on. First, by "as canonical Holy Scripture," I mean to connote the whole complex of traditional Christian beliefs about the Bible that fund its designation as "Holy Scripture," a complex that is ultimately a theological judgment, or confession, about the canon as a whole. Further, I mean to specify that the church is the primary context for reading and understanding Holy Scripture in this way. Second, by "theological convictions and interests," I mean that theological interpretation of Scripture is a two-way street: even as, in reading, Christians are shaped by Scripture, they in turn bring practices and convictions to bear on their reading that shape it accordingly. Not only is this unavoidable, hermeneutically speaking, it is also desirable and fitting, theologically speaking. By including this phrase in my shorthand definition, then, I mean to exclude those ways of approaching the Bible's interpretation that seek to be purely "excavatory." Excavation as it were breaks down the hermeneutical circle and hammers it out into a single linear line, an arrow pointing out of the text through the reader and into the world. Whether such a view is defensible is beside

---

tian convictions about God's triune life. Scripture is a gift from the triune God that both reflects and fits into God's desire to bring us into ever deeper fellowship with God and each other. . . . [T]heological interpretation of Scripture will involve those habits, dispositions, and practices that Christians bring to their varied engagements with Scripture so they can interpret, debate, and embody Scripture in ways that will enhance their journey toward their proper end in God" (*Theological Interpretation of Scripture*, 13–14). Second, John Webster: "What is theological interpretation of Scripture? Answer: interpretation informed by a theological description of the nature of the biblical writings and their reception, setting them in the scope of the progress of the saving divine Word through time. Theological interpretation can take many forms, some commentarial, some in other genres; not all theological interpretation is immediately recognizable as such. . . . It is more a way of reading which is informed by a theologically derived set of interpretive goals, which are governed by a conception of what the Bible is: Holy Scripture, God ministering his Word to human beings through human servants and so sharing with them the inestimable good of knowledge of himself" (*Domain of the Word*, 30). In an important sense, TIS has yet to be fully defined, as its present formal-material openness is part of its appeal. In this way practitioners, in their first-order practice and second-order reflection, adjudicate its meaning collectively. For defense of continued theoretical reflection on these questions, see Sarisky, *Reading the Bible Theologically*, as well as East, "What Are the Standards of Excellence?"

the point here; TIS, in my descriptive usage, does not encompass persons holding this position.[27]

Theological Interpretation, Ecclesiology, and the Interlocutors of This Book

As the term suggests, TIS is about *interpretation* first of all. And as I said above, questions of interpretation are only one element of the doctrine of Scripture, which is itself inseparable from the doctrine of the church. Hence, in seeking to reclaim Scripture for the church through theological interpretation, TIS has, in a manner of speaking, gone about the task backward. This can be seen by asking about the role of the church, especially particular ecclesial traditions or denominations, in theological interpretation.

At first glance, for instance, it is not clear what makes the participants in the newfangled movement of TIS *into* a movement. In its sheer sprawl of authors and publications, TIS is marked by a striking theological and ecclesial pluralism, having drawn within its orbit a whole host of theological thinkers across varying disciplines. Writing about this diffuse character, Daniel Treier notes that, at a minimum, "advocacy for theological interpretation involves a series of loosely 'postmodern' riffs on Barth-inspired themes."[28] Elaborating on the rough sketch outlined above, then,

27. There are many conservative and evangelical Christian biblical scholars whose theory and practice, it seems to me, diverge on just this question. That is to say, it is evident that they do indeed bring all manner of theological convictions to their reading of the canonical texts, yet for the most part they undertake their scholarly work and submit it to evaluation by the guild as if that were not the case. I do not mean they bracket such convictions in a methodologically agnostic manner; I mean it is clear that such convictions are operative in a material way that informs their hermeneutical judgments. Such a procedure is perfectly legitimate, both academically and theologically, but it ought to be acknowledged rather than denied or obscured. For an articulation of the frustrations that result among non-Christian scholars, see Davies, *Whose Bible Is It Anyway?* For sensitive attention to the issues, see Bockmuehl, *Seeing the Word*; Moberly, *Bible, Theology, and Faith*.
28. Treier, "What Is Theological Interpretation?," 152. See also Treier, *Theological Interpretation*, 11-36, for a detailed narrative of the origins and direction of TIS with which my own account is in substantial agreement. In discussing Catholic and Orthodox biblical hermeneutics, Treier (an evangelical) also touches briefly on "the hermeneutical importance of ecclesiology" (33). As he writes, "we might ask whether, or, in what sense and to what extent, non-Catholic Christians can pursue biblical interpretation that fully participates in God's creating and redeeming activity, given

we might understand the formation of TIS as a kind of pincer movement, beginning with Barth and centered on Yale Divinity School. From the side of biblical studies, Fowl represents Barth's indirect influence via both Brevard Childs and Stanley Hauerwas.[29] From the side of theology, Hauerwas represents those identified with, or who learned from, the so-called Yale School of postliberal theology. The Yale trio of Hans Frei, George Lindbeck, and David Kelsey mediated a particular postmodern reception of Barth to an entire generation of theologians, not least regarding how the Bible should be theorized and interpreted.[30] From both directions, therefore, there is a kind of scholarly convergence on the possibilities of theological interpretation without, however, a common motivating factor, much less a shared theological account of the Bible, the church, or the nature and ends of exegetical reason.

How are practitioners of TIS bound together, then? They are united, negatively, by their dissatisfaction with the institutional, intellectual, hermeneutical, ecclesial, and theological shortcomings of regnant bib-

---

the church's claims. For all church contexts, ecclesiology proves to be a crucial issue regarding theological interpretation of Scripture" (32).

29. The idea that American biblical scholars in the 1970s through the '90s encountered Barth largely indirectly through Childs (among others) comes from personal correspondence with Fowl. For the major works of Childs, see his *Biblical Theology*; *Old Testament as Scripture*; *Old Testament Theology*; and *New Testament as Canon*. Other notable works of Childs include *Isaiah as Christian Scripture*; *Church's Guide for Reading Paul*; "Speech-Act Theory and Biblical Interpretation"; and the early, influential essay "*Sensus Literalis* of Scripture." See also Noble, *Canonical Approach*, and his essay "Jowett, Childs, and Barr." For critique, see Barr, *Holy Scripture*, esp. 49–104; Johnson, "Crisis in Biblical Scholarship." Finally, for Hauerwas, see *Matthew*; *Peaceable Kingdom*; *Unleashing the Scripture*; *Without Apology*; "The Moral Authority of Scripture: The Politics of and Ethics of Remembering" in his *Community of Character*, 53–71; and "Why 'The Way the Words Run' Matters: Reflections on Becoming a 'Major Biblical Scholar,'" in his *Working with Words*, 94–112.

30. For systematic analysis and critique of the Yale School, see DeHart, *Trial of the Witnesses*; cf. Tanner, *Theories of Culture*. For relevant primary texts that touch on either Barth, the Bible, or both, see first Kelsey, *Proving Doctrine*; *Eccentric Existence*. Second, Frei, *Doctrine of Revelation*; "Scripture as Realistic Narrative"; *Identity of Jesus Christ*; *Eclipse of Biblical Narrative*; "'Literal Reading' of Biblical Narrative"; and *Types of Christian Theology*, esp. 56–69. Third, Lindbeck, *Nature of Doctrine*; "Scripture, Consensus, and Community"; "Story-Shaped Church"; "Postcritical Canonical Interpretation"; and "Barth and Textuality." Lindbeck's use of Barth has been criticized by, e.g., Ronald Thiemann ("Response to George Lindbeck"), George Hunsinger ("Truth as Self-Involving"), and John Webster (*Word and Church*, 62), who goes on to critique Frei's interpretation of Barth on the next page.

lical scholarship; and, positively, by their desire to retrieve practices of scriptural reading from bygone eras, whether patristic, medieval, or reformational. Such practices include spiritual interpretation, figural reading, allegory, moral sense, *lectio divina*, trinitarian hermeneutics, christological exegesis of the Old Testament, commentary disburdened of historical reconstruction, multiplicity of meanings, identification of God as the principal author of Scripture, and so on. The resulting disciplinary and denominational diversity matches the sheer range of possible topics of interest. Guild exegetes, ethicists, liturgists, systematicians, homileticians, patristic scholars, medievalists, and Reformation historians (whether Calvinist or Orthodox, Catholic or Baptist, Anglican or Anabaptist) all want to reclaim the church's book—and the church's practices of reading it—over against the reductions and simplifications of historical-critical biblical scholarship, whether or not such scholarship is produced by Christians.[31]

In this way TIS is at once ecclesiocentric and ecclesially divided. In a recent work, Fowl draws a key conclusion from this conjunction: "after participating for fifteen or more years in debates and arguments over theological interpretation, I am beginning to wonder if some of the current argument over methods and theories arise more from confessional differences than methodological differences."[32] Treier makes similar comments, noting the implicit and increasingly explicit bibliological disagreements between practitioners of TIS that have their roots in ecclesiological differences.[33] Treier's point is intended only as an observa-

---

31. Consider the range of disciplines, backgrounds, and ecclesial traditions represented by only a handful of entries in two different commentary series. First, Belief: A Theological Commentary on the Bible, which includes Jennings, *Acts*; De La Torre, *Genesis*; and Long, *1 & 2 Timothy and Titus*. Second, the Brazos Theological Commentary on the Bible, which includes Pelikan, *Acts*; Hauerwas, *Matthew*; and Jeffrey, *Luke*.

32. Fowl, *Theological Interpretation of Scripture*, 73-74. He goes on: "This is not all that surprising. One might well expect that formation within a particular ecclesial tradition would then influence one's approach to theological interpretation in a variety of ways. . . . At the moment, however, there does not seem to be any easy way to bring [such] confessional differences into the arguments over methods of theological interpretation" (74).

33. Treier, "What Is Theological Interpretation?," 145, 153-61. See his opening comments:

> To define "theological interpretation," one might adopt various strategies. . . .
> The following article proposes a more circuitous, ultimately *ecclesiological* route. To begin, we need a more descriptive effort, specifying what those who

tion, not a judgment, though he does see it as bearing potentially fruitful ecumenical consequences.

In any case, Fowl's and Treier's suggestion about ecclesiological fault lines in TIS is correct, but it calls for further investigation. That is the aim of this book. I want to use their suggestion as a stimulus to explore the relationship between bibliology and ecclesiology, both in general and in particular theological systems. For the connections are direct and materially operative, and only more so when they remain implicit and thus unexamined. Every account of the Bible both assumes and implies an account of the church, and vice versa; the lines of influence are reciprocal and circular.[34] Scripture is always the church's book, the church always the community under the Word. The welter of ecclesially divided yet ecclesiocentric reflection on Scripture therefore calls for taking a step back and drawing the (usually unremarked) substantive connections between doctrines of Scripture and doctrines of the church. As we have seen, self-described practitioners of TIS are united largely by what they stand against; where they are united by positive aims or convictions, these are usually of a highly formal nature—unless, that is, their ecclesial commitments overlap in substantive ways. Identifying ecclesiological premises in distinct bibliologies, or vice versa, sheds light on the relation between the two and the work each does in relation to the other.

---

already use the terminology of "theological interpretation" are groping to say, for, while it may (aspire to) be a perennial practice, theological interpretation has contemporary appeal in a context of perceived neglect regarding particular classic possibilities. After understanding this, we may then conclude more constructively that this apparently providential possibility for church renewal has entailments for what "theological interpretation" can—and cannot—mean. The descriptive effort proposed here involves, in the first section of the article, constructing a coherent narrative framework that associates major players in the conversation with the respective strategies above, offers a consensus account of the interpretative practices in question, and proposes a genealogy, suggesting that "theological interpretation of Scripture" qualifies as a "movement," rather than merely being a matter of coincidental vocabulary or diffuse conversation. Yet, in a second section, key disagreements emerge among its participants via a kind of "ecclesiological reduction," so that the descriptive starting point surfaces dogmatic implications. In particular, strong parallels surface between the fortunes of "theological interpretation" and another essentially contested concept—"postliberal" theology. (144–45)

34. As Angus Paddison writes in one of the epigraphs quoted above, "All accounts of Scripture are inseparable from accounts of the church" (*Scripture*, 21).

To be sure, bibliology need not and must not become an exercise in, or be annexed to, ecclesiology. In one sense that is just the problem at hand, for all too often there is not enough conceptual separation between the two to draw the necessary connections between them. In this respect, as I said above, there are two levels of theological analysis at work: on the one hand, the relationship between the church and the Bible; on the other hand, the relationship between *the doctrinal loci* of ecclesiology and bibliology. The latter relationship is, as it were, a theology of theology; which is to say, a meta-theological treatment of topics that are themselves theological treatments of concrete matters. The argument of this book is that theological treatments of Scripture and church are disordered, when they are disordered, in part due to second-order disrepair in coordinating these two doctrinal loci in relationship to each other. Even when these theological treatments are not so disordered, the lack of explicit coordination between them makes disagreement over aspects of both bibliology and hermeneutics inadjudicable, especially when those disagreements are in fact rooted in opposed accounts of the church, not of Scripture. Throughout this book, then, I will be commenting on both levels: first, at the level of what to say theologically about the Bible vis-à-vis the church; and, second, at the level of what to say about a well-ordered *theological presentation* of that relationship.[35]

The plan of this book is not to speak in general about theological systems and doctrinal logics but to engage the proposals of three particular theological thinkers: John Webster, Robert Jenson, and John Howard Yoder.

None of these scholars is still with us. Although Webster passed away before Jenson, he was a generation younger than both Jenson and Yoder. His mature work was therefore contemporaneous with TIS, and his relationship to the movement accordingly more direct than theirs. By contrast, Yoder died in 1997, so he did not live long enough to see the movement take shape and begin to attract practitioners. As for Jenson, in virtue of his training, interests, and age, he straddled the worlds of systematic theology and the doctrine of Scripture and its interpretation. Beginning with Yoder and moving in chronological order, I will now offer

---

35. One recurring metaphor that I will use to describe the theological systems under analysis is taken from Williams, *Architecture of Theology*, which is an exemplar of the sort of study I have in mind.

brief sketches of their respective careers and approaches to bibliology in Barth's wake as well as explain my rationale in selecting them.[36]

John Howard Yoder (1927-1997)[37]

Yoder earned his ThD at the University of Basel in the 1950s, where he studied under Barth, Oscar Cullmann, Walther Eichrodt, and Karl Jaspers, among others.[38] When he returned to the US, he taught at Goshen Biblical Seminary and Mennonite Biblical Seminary from 1958 to 1961, and again from 1965 to 1984. Having begun to teach classes at Notre Dame in 1967, he was appointed Professor of Theology in 1977 and taught there until 1997, the year of his death. Trained as a historian of the early radical reformation, he wrote in the fields of social ethics, ecclesiology, ecumenism, peace studies, New Testament, missiology, and more. His early seminal work, *The Politics of Jesus*, although materially an argument for ecclesial pacifism grounded in Christ's normative example, is formally a sustained exegetical engagement with the New Testament in general and with the Gospel of St. Luke in particular. Yoder never departs from this approach in the course of his career. His method, if he has one, is to turn to the Bible with the expectation that, if read critically but plainly in the context of the church's life and with a healthy respect for the historical distance between "then and there" and "here and now," the biblical text will have something to say of direct import for life and faith in the world today. Put simply, Scripture for Yoder is historical, political, and ecclesial. It is rooted in times and places other than our own. Its origin and end are this-worldly affairs caught up in God's creation and the calling of a people set apart from the world. To read Scripture well for Yoder entails reading it with these features to the fore. Yoder terms this approach "biblical realism," a position he says he received from his teachers, such as "Hendrik Kraemer, Otto Piper, Paul Minear, Markus Barth, and Claude Tresmontant."[39] The Bible, in his view, is first and fore-

---

36. I will refrain from citing their voluminous publications except where I quote from them or citation is called for by more than cursory reference.

37. I discuss Yoder's history of abuse in the excursus that precedes chapter 5 below.

38. For biographical information, see McClendon, "John Howard Yoder"; Nation, *John Howard Yoder*, 1–29; Goossen, "'Defanging the Beast.'"

39. Yoder, *Politics of Jesus*, x. For more on "biblical realism," see vii–xi, 4; in greater detail, see Yoder, *To Hear the Word*, 58–76, 155–77. In the foreword to the latter volume, Michael J. Gorman identifies "five pairs of adjectives" to describe Yoder's understand-

most a moral-pastoral document—"mostly narrative in framework and doxological in tone"[40]—that serves the function of norming the community of faith as that community encounters new challenges that force it to reckon with acceptable change and continuity of identity.[41]

Yoder's bibliology thus occupies that liminal time after Barth but before the emergence of TIS. The time of Childs, in other words, when the shadow cast by the great German "biblical theologies" (e.g., those of Gerhard von Rad and Rudolf Bultmann) still lingered, and questions about methodology and anxieties over fundamentalism kept theologians skittish about exegesis and biblical scholars in thrall to historical criticism. The combination of Yoder's German training and Mennonite identity seems to have inoculated him against this fraught period of disciplinary demarcation; he was trained in the "reputable" methods of scriptural interpretation, but he went on, with no signs of angst, to use the Bible in making normative claims about christology, ecclesiology, and social ethics. In this way he was both a man of his time and something of an outlier, which well reflects the different sides of his public career. Though "successful" in the field from an early time, he nonetheless remained at the margins of the academic mainstream—teaching at Mennonite seminaries, publishing in obscure places,[42] appearing as a prominent name largely within ethics and peace circles—until the last decade of his life. His work thus serves as, among other things, a window into the development and practice of bibliology between Barth and TIS.

Robert Jenson (1930–2017)

Jenson's career runs closely parallel to Yoder's, though on decidedly different tracks. Born in 1930 (three years after Yoder), Jenson studied

---

ing of "biblical realism": "canonical and 'post-critical'"; "narrative and coherent"; "pastoral and missional"; "ecclesial and eschatological"; and "creative and critical" (xvi–xvii, emphasis removed).

40. Yoder, *To Hear the Word*, 88.

41. See Yoder, *To Hear the Word*, 102–19.

42. As Hauerwas writes in his foreword to Nation, *John Howard Yoder*: "Yoder's published work is but the tip of the iceberg. He wrote constantly and in an extraordinary variety of venues. Indeed, much of his work is still not published. I once thought no one could publish more obscurely than I have. But [now] . . . I know my claim to obscurity to be sheer pretention. Of course, John had an advantage. He was a Mennonite, and Mennonites have a gift for in-group publications" (x–xi). Cf. Hauerwas, "Foreword," in Carter, *Politics of the Cross*, 9–11.

in Heidelberg in the late 1950s, learning from such luminaries as Peter Brunner, Edmund Schlink, Gerhard von Rad, Günther Bornkamm, and Hans von Campenhausen. He wrote his dissertation on Barth and met with him in Basel to discuss it, sitting in on a seminar he led.[43] Though trained and rooted in modern philosophy, Jenson was a systematic theologian par excellence, writing on every topic under the sun: sacramentology, christology, pneumatology, ecumenism, Lutheranism, religion, the arts, politics, and much more. The three great topics on which he expended the most energy in the final decades of his life were the Trinity, the church, and the Bible. That trajectory intersected with bibliology after Barth in noteworthy ways.

On the one hand, Jenson's turn to the Bible was a late development; most of his important essays and articles on the subject, as well as two biblical commentaries, were published after his sixty-fifth birthday. On the other hand, Jenson's direct engagement with the Bible, and willingness to read it theologically, was a distinctive feature of his work from the beginning. This was due partly to a kind of self-conscious escape from what he perceived early in his career to be recondite and parochial arguments among Lutherans about inspiration and biblical authority. Jenson found in historical criticism a tool with which to read the Bible with intellectual seriousness that did not require jettisoning his faith, while he found in Barth and some of his teachers a way of reading the Bible with an edge "more critical than the critics," taking it seriously as the church's Scripture and as theology's chief source and measure.[44] His writing in the late 1970s and early 1980s on the sacraments, trinitarian doctrine, and dogmatics more generally is characterized by constant and explicit attention to Scripture, engaging in close biblical exegesis where it is called for, and continual conversation with the latest in (usually German) historical-critical scholarship.

Jenson's "turn" to the Bible as an object for theological reflection came in the late 1990s, around the time of the publication of his two-volume systematics.[45] Here we find Jenson's mature bibliology. As he puts it, the Bible is first and foremost the church's book. It exists nowhere else than in

43. For biographical information, see Jenson, "Theological Autobiography"; Jenson, "Reversals," 30–33; Braaten, "Robert William Jenson"; Braaten, "Personal Tribute"; Blanche Jenson, "You Shall Love the Lord"; Fryer, "Robert W. Jenson."

44. See Jenson, "Theological Autobiography," and his foreword in Byassee, *Praise Seeking Understanding*, x–xii.

45. In 1997 and 1999, respectively.

the church and to no other purpose than the church's in putting it together. Apart from the church's particular mission, "the binding of these particular documents between one cover becomes a historical accident of no hermeneutical significance."[46] Moreover, "the church" is not temporally constricted: the Christian community that reads its Scripture today is one and the same community as that of the apostles (and of the church fathers, the scholastics, the reformers, and so on). There is therefore real cultural and historical distance between "then and there" and "here and now." But it is not the hermeneutical distance of a *different* community—perhaps irrevocably lost to us or infinitely far from us—than the present one, since what is in view in the biblical texts is the very same community of which Christians today are members.[47] Hence it can truly be said that "our common life is located *inside* the story Scripture tells."[48]

Jenson's bibliology thus resides on the catholic, ecclesiocentric side of TIS, combined with an unruffled acceptance of many postmodern hermeneutical claims; though he never wholly spurned his use of and affection for historical criticism, it is severely qualified and made entirely subordinate to the church's interpretive aims, interests, and judgments. In this way his position might be described as a catholic radicalization of Barth—or, alternatively, a de-Protestantization of Barth—emphasizing the church over against the Bible considered in itself.[49] Such a view cuts hard against the grain of those like Childs who want to maintain the disciplinary and conceptual distinction between biblical exegesis and Christian dogmatics for the sake of an "integrity" ascribed to the Bible that must not be imposed upon or made into a wax nose. For Jenson, there is no such thing. Churchly creed and dogma are not impositions on or obstacles to the biblical text being read well; they are the Spirit's own tools, given to us for accomplishing the task. Just so, apart from those tools, Scripture will inevitably be misread, even with the best of intentions.

---

46. Jenson, "Hermeneutics and the Life of the Church," 89–90. See also Jenson, *Triune Story*, 59–69, esp. 59.

47. See the discussions in Jenson, *Triune Story*, 61–62, 66–69, 100–103, 114–16.

48. Jenson, *Triune Story*, 114.

49. If this sounds like Stanley Hauerwas, that is because it is. See Jenson, "Hauerwas Project"; cf. Jenson's comments in *Systematic Theology*, 2:209n114: "Although my understanding of ethics is not to be fathered on Stanley Hauerwas . . . his work provides the template for the following and is at all times in the back of my mind" (see also 144n64; 209n112). Cf. Hauerwas's essay "Only Theology Overcomes Ethics," in *Trinity, Time, and Church*, 252–68.

John Webster (1955-2016)

Webster studied at Cambridge in the late 1970s and early 1980s, and he wrote his doctoral thesis on Eberhard Jüngel.[50] By the late 1990s, Webster established himself as a premier exponent of Barth, which in turn led him to consider more classical dogmatic topics, such as the doctrine of God, christology, ecclesiology, and bibliology. In each of these areas his proposals are identifiably Reformed but nonetheless constructive, marked by emphases that swim against the tide of much modern theology (which for Webster are represented by correlationist liberalism, "Yale School" postliberalism, and "radically orthodox" postmodernism).[51] Webster's thought is theocentric to the core; any theological position that seems to relocate the center of gravity elsewhere—in the culture, in the church, in the person—is immediately suspect. Following this line, the Bible, as God's inspired and sanctified instrument of ruling and instructing the church—as the means of the Lord Christ's speech to his people—is not an immanent feature of ecclesial life, a community-authored/authoring document subject to interpretive caprice. In contrast to prevailing views in comparative religion and postmodern hermeneutics, Webster asserts that the Bible has an "ontology." That is, the church does not *make* the Bible to be something or construe it *as* something; it *is* something and has a given nature: Holy Scripture. The Bible is Holy Scripture not inherently, of itself, or as a natural property, but in virtue of God's action, as an element in the economy of grace. Webster thus, like Barth, both relativizes and prioritizes Scripture: the former by setting it in the larger context of divine revelation and the triune God's works of creation, reconciliation, and consummation; the latter by identifying it as principally a product and instrument of God's will and action rather than as a common element of human social and religious life.

50. For biographical information, see Webster, "Discovering Dogmatics." See also Davidson, "John"; Allen, "Reading John Webster."

51. A wry broadside comes in one of Webster's minor essays: "One of the most striking features of current doctrinal theology is the quite extraordinary way in which ecclesiology has become 'first theology,' that is, doctrinally basic. One could trace this not only in contemporary Roman Catholic and Anglican ecclesiologies, but also in Lutherans like Lindbeck and Jenson, Free Church theologians like Volf, right through to the pan-eucharistic metaphysics of *Radical Orthodoxy* (a book whose title is a textbook example of catachresis)." See Webster, "Goals of Ecumenism," 10–11.

Webster therefore occupies, vis-à-vis Jenson, an opposing pole on the TIS continuum. His work sets Scripture firmly over the church, emphasizing time and again its spiritual character and its origin in God's self-communicative presence and acts. Webster, downstream from Yoder and Jenson, is the most explicitly "Barthian" of the three, at least in his bibliology and ecclesiology. He also wrote at a somewhat different moment in the life of academic systematic theology, in which the kind of classical dogmatics he esteemed and emulated was not seen as problematic in the way it might have been in the 1960s, '70s, and '80s (especially in the United Kingdom). Where Yoder and Jenson show signs, even where they lack methodological anxiety, of feeling the need to justify their work by answering the challenges of historical criticism, Webster's writing is entirely free, confident, and forceful in its irreducibly theological description of the Bible and of the exegetical task.

In relation to the sort of middle position represented by Fowl, furthermore, Webster is appreciative but critical. In his view, such approaches tend to construe the canon apart from prevenient divine action, to overdetermine its nature by ecclesial supervision, and/or to prioritize hermeneutics to ontology. To the extent that they do so, Webster judges them to be failures precisely as attempts at *Christian theology* of Scripture. As he writes,

> The Bible, its readers and their work of interpretation have their place in the domain of the Word of God, the sphere of reality in which Christ glorified is present and speaks with unrivaled clarity. . . . Bibliology and hermeneutics are [therefore] derivative elements of Christian theology, shaped by prior Christian teaching about the nature of God and creatures and their relations. . . . [And] bibliology is prior to hermeneutics, because strategies of interpretation will be maladroit unless fitting to the actual nature of the text which they seek to unfold.[52]

Here is neither Childs, nor Jenson, nor Fowl:[53] Barthian in descent, "after" liberalism *and* postliberalism yet resistant to ecclesiocentrism,[54] Webster's position remains one of the premier proposals on offer in TIS today.

---

52. Webster, *Domain of the Word*, viii.
53. Neither (Stanley) Fish nor (Stephen) Fowl?
54. See here Webster and Schner, *Theology after Liberalism*, and Webster's essay therein, "Theology after Liberalism?," 52–61. See also Webster, "Ecclesiocentrism."

Critical Reception

None of these figures has yet to receive extensive critical treatment on the topic of Scripture.[55] Mature reception of Yoder[56] and Jenson is still in its early stages, and although they have alike exerted enormous influence on the field, surprisingly little secondary literature has addressed bibliology in their work. As for Webster, who tragically and unexpectedly passed away at the height of his career, the time is ripe to begin to receive his work in a way that is more than merely appropriative.[57] Nor

55. As with their primary works, I will refrain from citing the relevant secondary literature until their respective chapters. Let me mention, however, two new works that came into my hands in the final days of preparing this manuscript that bear directly on the matter of this book. First is Seitz, *Convergences*, which compares the work of Brevard Childs with that of Paul Beauchamp, SJ, a French scholar of the Old Testament; Seitz is interested in, among other things, the role of ecclesial tradition in both divergences and convergences in late-twentieth-century approaches to interpreting the Bible that remain sensitive to historical-critical methods. Second is Taylor, *Reading Scripture as the Church*, which is a revision of his dissertation at Duke University. It features Webster, Jenson, Hauerwas, and the field of missional theology as conversation partners with Dietrich Bonhoeffer's account of discipleship. Not only do its interlocutors overlap with mine, it asks a similar question at the outset:

> Ecclesiology has obviously carried great weight in recent conversations about theological interpretation, but rarely has ecclesiology itself become an object of theological focus within them. When we say that Scripture is the book of the church, what do we mean by *church*? Which church do we have in mind? As much as this question remains unaddressed, ecclesial hermeneutics remains ecclesially ambiguous. In this book, therefore, I ask an ecclesiological question as a means of answering a hermeneutical one. I set out deliberately to consider what it means to read in, as, and for the church. Which aspects of the church are hermeneutically salubrious? What practices come embedded within it? And how does this influence the shape and ends of faithful interpretation? (9)

The direction in which Taylor takes the project runs parallel to and at times diverges from that taken in this book; whereas he is interested in a practical hermeneutics of discipleship rooted in a proper doctrine of the church, I am interested in theological accounts of Holy Scripture and the role played within them by opposing ecclesiological commitments.

56. Since Yoder's death in 1997, there have been at least a dozen books published posthumously in his name. So although he had a great deal of acclaim in his lifetime, and therefore ongoing critical interaction with his work, interpretation of his thought as a whole or thematic engagement with a single issue in his entire oeuvre has not truly been possible until now.

57. See now Allen and Nelson, *Theology of John Webster*.

have these three theologians yet been brought together as they are in this book, owing perhaps to their inhabiting somewhat distinct (though certainly overlapping) theological subcultures. Part of the force of this book's contribution will thus be displaying the productive nature of putting them into conversation.[58] As mutual interlocutors, they highlight gaps and supplement problems in one another's theological proposals, thereby contributing to an overall account of Scripture that follows their lead but lacks some of their shortcomings.

Indeed, the differences between Yoder, Jenson, and Webster present opportunities for productive discussion in two respects. First, the substantive distinctions between their positions concern disputed issues that have been widespread in theological reflection on Scripture over the past century. These include topics such as the Bible's nature or ontology, its authority in and over the church (and vice versa), and how to read it rightly or faithfully. This set of questions will be to the fore in my explication of Yoder, Jenson, and Webster's bibliologies, and will help to coordinate their positions in relation to others in the field.

Second—and here is the decisive difference—each of the theologians in view represents one of the three major strands of the global church: catholic (Jenson),[59] magisterial reformation (Webster), and radical reformation (Yoder).[60] At the level of their individual positions, then, these

58. Notably, there is very little direct interaction between them in their writings. Jenson (positively) reviewed *Barth's Moral Theology* (in *International Journal of Systematic Theology* 2 [2000]: 119–21) and contributed to his *Festschrift* with his essay "Thomas Aquinas's *De ente et essentia*," but otherwise did not directly engage him in print. Neither Jenson nor Webster engages Yoder in print except for the occasional footnote, nor did Yoder write of either of them. Webster, for his part, does take Jenson as a somewhat regular interlocutor—though almost always as a foil. See, e.g., Webster, "Systematic Theology after Barth," 255–58; "'In the Society of God,'" 211–12.

59. I am stretching on this characterization, since Jenson was (an ordained) Lutheran. I will justify identifying him as a catholic in chapter 4; suffice it here to say that his theology, and his theology of Scripture, are consonant with and faithfully represent the broad approach to the canon common to Rome and Constantinople. At the level of autobiography, Jenson, in the three closing paragraphs of his essay "Reversals," poses and somewhat elusively answers the question why he (and his wife Blanche) never swam the Tiber.

60. Each man, in fact, was ordained: Jenson in the Evangelical Lutheran Church of America, Webster in the Church of England, Yoder in the Mennonite Church USA (if somewhat against his wishes, given his critical views of ordination; he forfeited his credentials in the last years of his life, during the church disciplinary process in which he was involved). Their ecclesial commitments are thus neither nominal nor

differing ecclesial commitments serve as a key site for locating disagreements, and the reasons animating those disagreements, between their theologies of Scripture. This brings us back to an observation I mentioned above. The connection between bibliology and ecclesiology highlights a lacuna in contemporary theological treatments of Scripture, an oversight that suggests an instability in the surface unity between theological interpreters of the Bible. Recall Fowl's query whether "some of the current argument over methods and theories arise more from confessional differences than methodological differences."[61] This book is an exercise in following that hunch to its logical end. The means by which I do so is the exposition of these three theologians. To be clear, ecclesiology plays an important role, but the inquiry starts from and returns to bibliology. That is, the primary doctrinal locus from whose vantage point I ask about the relationship between theology of Scripture and theology of the church is the former. That focus governs and guides the discussion. This book is therefore not a work "in" or "of" ecclesiology, except in a derivative and highly qualified sense.

The book's argument is not, I hasten to add, that contemporary bibliologies or theological interpreters of Scripture ignore or neglect to speak of the church. On the contrary, bibliology in the last two decades has been marked by an especial interest in the church. Rather, I am making the point that *the theological connections between* the nature, purpose, and identity of the church—topics traditionally addressed in ecclesiology proper—and the nature, authority, and interpretation of Holy Scripture are typically ignored or only given superficial treatment. Moreover, it is all too rare for theological claims, or rather premises, in the one doctrinal locus to be made operative, in an explicit way, in the discussion of the other. Motives and commitments that might make all the difference end up remaining concealed rather than brought out into the open. That is the issue I hope to address.

Furthermore, and finally, even if it were the case that, on the whole, bibliologies today did not overlook these connections or leave them implicit (and I think they do), I am interested in a theological analysis of those connections. This project is therefore a sort of theological analogue to David Kelsey's procedure in *Proving Doctrine*. There Kelsey looks to

---

adventitious to their theology; as those who regularly preached and presided, their work reflects this essentially ecclesial habitat and horizon.

61. Fowl, *Theological Interpretation of Scripture*, 74.

analyze the logical relations between "church," "scripture," and "authority" in the usage of theologians from a linguistic-conceptual vantage point—that is, as a study in *method*.[62] In contrast, my aim is to identify and explore the *theological* connections between (theology of) Scripture and (theology of) church as a second- and third-order study of doctrine in which, as a "theology of theology," dogmatic judgments are operative rather than bracketed.[63]

Returning to our theologians: If theological subculture and ecclesial identity, not to mention their substantive positions, separate them in the ways I have described, then what unites them? More than anything, and to bring matters full circle, what connects them and makes them of common interest is the person and work of Karl Barth.[64] In the coming chapters, however, Barth is not prominent in the argument. His work is front-loaded here and in the next chapter primarily as preparation for the rest of the book. That is: Having situated what comes after Barth in genetic and historical relation to his thought, his presence in what follows is more implicit—structural and subterranean—than explicit. He is

62. In this way, *Proving Doctrine* is a sort of meta-methodology: "a study in theological methodology" (5). In Kelsey's words: "Strictly speaking, I suppose this is not a theological essay at all; it is *about* theologies. It does not make theological proposals to the Christian community as such" (9).

63. See Kelsey's comment late in the work: "'The Bible is the church's book' makes what is apparently an accurate *historical* claim; but 'Biblical texts are the church's scripture' makes an important *conceptual decision* (i.e., self-involvingly to adopt a certain concept 'church'), and 'Scripture is authority over the church's life' makes a *conceptual claim* that is analytic in the foregoing conceptual decision" (*Proving Doctrine*, 177).

64. In Basel Yoder studied with Barth and appreciatively engaged his work throughout his career. See, e.g., the unofficial second dissertation he wrote and presented to Barth shortly before the defense of his actual dissertation: *Karl Barth and the Problem of War*. Jenson similarly learned from Barth firsthand, published two books on his theology (*Alpha and Omega*; *God after God*), and continued to engage Barth as an essential theological interlocutor in all his writings. For example, more than thirty-five years after submitting his dissertation on Barth, Jenson's two-volume systematics contains no fewer than sixty-eight citations of Barth in the index—surpassed only by St. Augustine, St. Thomas, and Luther. At the same time, see Jenson's comment on "never [being] a proper Barthian" in "Theological Autobiography," 49–50, as well as the anecdote recorded in one of the last things he published: "D. Stephen Long's *Saving Karl Barth*." As for Webster, at the time of his death he was one of a handful of the most respected interpreters of Barth in the world. Across his career, for example, he authored four books on Barth and edited *The Cambridge Companion to Karl Barth*. His Barthian bona fides are therefore unimpeachable.

the fountainhead from which a prominent stream of current theological reflection on Scripture flows, and Yoder, Jenson, and Webster at once receive his influence and redirect it in new and important ways. Barth thus circumscribes the inquiry, in shape and in content, by setting the table—the questions pursued and the terms of pursuit—for those after him. In chapter 6 I reflect on where and how Barth's influence was felt in the foregoing chapters, and what that might mean for Barth's legacy in Christian theology of Scripture.

Before turning to Barth and thence to our primary figures, however, let me say a word about the understanding of ecclesiology that informs my analysis in the coming chapters. It trades on a typology of church division that guides my treatment of their thought and structures my use of their ecclesial commitments to stand in for a fractured Christendom. A brief explanation is therefore in order prior to beginning chapter 2.

Catholic, Reformed, Baptist: A Typology of Church Division

Typologies of the church are a regular feature of ecclesiology. They may be biblical, historical, prescriptive, or ideal. Perhaps the simplest typological approach is found in a recent introduction to evangelical theology, which lists nine varieties of Christian faith, life, and thought: Orthodox, Catholic, Lutheran, Reformed, Anabaptist, Anglican, Baptist, Wesleyan, and Pentecostal.[65] Such a list is rooted in historical developments and attentive to subtle disagreements (say, between Protestant groups) without multiplying the categories to a number that would prove unworkable. And it is true that all these traditions, and more besides, have a contribution to make to the witness of the church universal.

Having said that, the differences between, for example, Lutheran, Reformed, and Wesleyan doctrines of Scripture are miniscule. They are matters of the finest detail and of interest only to participants in dialogue between those traditions. Each of them confesses *sola scriptura* in the robust manner of magisterial Protestantism. What divides them is how they read the text, not their construal of it.[66] Moreover, such a list leaves

---

65. See Treier, *Introducing Evangelical Theology*, 245–72. For comparison with classic exercises in the genre, see Niebuhr, *Christ and Culture*; Dulles, *Models of the Church*, esp. 7–25.

66. Consider, e.g., Johann Gerhard's sustained polemic against "the Papists" in his

out less institutionalized sub-movements, such as Pietists, Puritans, and Stone-Campbellites,[67] not to mention African-American churches, non-denominational churches, and newer churches that have arisen in the global south in the last century.[68] It further ignores non-Western ecclesial communities separated from both Constantinople and Rome, such as the Oriental Orthodox and the Church of the East. The goal of such a list, then, ought to be either comprehensiveness at the level of historical, global, and institutional detail, or a conceptual framework that gathers together the manifold styles of being, doing, and thinking church into ideal types that incorporate any number of concrete communities and traditions old and new. This book opts for the latter approach.

It seems to me that what I will call fundamental ecclesial logics—embodied and theorized ways of enacting and understanding what it means to be the church of Jesus Christ in the world—come in three major forms: catholic, reformed, and baptist.

By "catholic" I mean the episcopally ordered liturgical, sacramental, and conciliar tradition of doctrines and practices common in the East and West prior to the sixteenth century, and still found among the Orthodox, Roman Catholic, Oriental Orthodox, Coptic, Eastern, and (I would argue) Anglican churches. These traditions account for more than two-thirds of global Christians today.[69] They ordain priests who administer the sacraments that ground and govern the devotional life of the baptized. These priests, together with the bishops of whom they are delegates, form a divinely willed order of authority and charism in the church. This authority, which stretches back to the church's founders and first teachers through apostolic succession, is a gift of the Holy Spirit, by

---

1610 "On Interpreting Sacred Scripture," pausing to dispute with "the Calvinists" only on the question of eucharistic doctrine and the words of institution. See *On Sacred Scripture*, 2.11.172–79.

67. See, e.g., Hatch, *Democratization of American Christianity*; Winship, *Hot Protestants*; Hall, *Puritans*; Hughes, *Reviving the Ancient Faith*; Williams, Foster, and Blowers, *Stone-Campbell Movement*.

68. See, e.g., Stanley, *Christianity in the Twentieth Century*; Sanneh, *Disciples of All Nations*; Jenkins, *Next Christendom*; Battle, *Black Church in America*; Warnock, *Divided Mind of the Black Church*.

69. See the report published in 2011 by The Pew Forum on Religion and Public Life as part of the Pew-Templeton Global Religious Futures Project; the report is titled "Global Christianity: A Report on the Size and Distribution of the World's Christian Population" and is available at https://assets.pewresearch.org/wp-content/uploads/sites/11/2011/12/Christianity-fullreport-web.pdf.

whose presence the risen and ascended Christ guides the church across time. Such authority lends itself, on occasion, to decisive and even infallible judgments regarding matters of acute controversy, questions of biblical interpretation, and issues unaddressed in the canon of Scripture.[70]

By "reformed" I mean those magisterial churches that trace their lineage, doctrines, and liturgical practices to the Protestant reformations as led by persons such as Martin Luther, Philip Melanchthon, Huldrych Zwingli, John Calvin, Martin Bucer, and Heinrich Bullinger. These churches by and large reject the status of the pope; the authority of tradition; apostolic succession through the office of bishop; the veneration of Mary; the sacrament of holy orders; the intercession of the saints; the writing of icons; and indeed the whole conciliar and sacramental system of hierarchy, lay piety, and impetration that reigned in medieval Christendom. By contrast, reformed traditions—found among Lutherans, Presbyterians, Wesleyans, and others—emphasize the supreme authority of Scripture alone; the priority of grace in salvation; the importance of God's gift of faith; the sovereignty of God in every sphere of life; the fallibility of postapostolic tradition; the centrality of the proclaimed word; simplicity in common worship; the exclusivity of Christ's role as priest and mediator; and the plurality of legitimate modes of church organization. Like the catholic tradition, reformed theology sees a role for the church in the affairs of the state; yet merely human law in either civic or ecclesial spheres cannot and must not bind the conscience of the faithful regarding matters of salvation. Put differently, reformed thought denies the doctrine of the two powers: one (the king) to rule secular affairs, one (the pope) to rule spiritual affairs. For Christ rules his people through his written word; he alone is the head of the church.[71]

By "baptist" I mean those largely autonomous and independent traditions of "free church" Christianity that share as exemplars and predecessors, if not always as progenitors, populist renewal movements such as those led by John Wycliffe, Jan Hus, Menno Simmons, Conrad Grebel, John Smyth, Roger Williams, Philipp Spener, Richard Allen, and Alexander Campbell.[72] I adopt the catchall designation "baptist" for these tra-

70. See, e.g., Kereszty, *Church of God in Jesus Christ*; Sertillanges, *The Church*; Levering, *Introduction to Vatican II*; Ratzinger, *Church, Ecumenism, and Politics*; Ware, *Orthodox Church*.

71. The doctrine of the church in Calvin is unsurpassed; see book 4 of the *Institutes*.

72. Richard Allen could well be placed under the reformed type; it depends, it seems to me, on whether one places emphasis on the man himself or on the ecclesial

ditions from James William McClendon, a capital-B Baptist whose work sought to incorporate the insights of these "low church" traditions as well as to inject them into academic discourse as serious proposals for theological consideration. Sometimes they are grouped together under the heading of the radical reformation, although strictly speaking only those who trace themselves to the Anabaptists of the sixteenth century qualify for that label. In any case the family resemblance between them is clear. They are neither catholic nor magisterial in church polity; whether or not they ordain, their communities are "free" in the sense of autonomy and self-determination. They are "free," furthermore, in their relationship to the governing authorities; they presuppose a strong separation between church and state, and they do not support the formal establishment of any denomination or religion, including their own. Their acceptance of sacred tradition is far more tenuous than reformed churches; even if they profess a creed or maintain confessions, which they often spurn anyway, these hold little sway next to the canon. "No creed but the Bible" is the hallmark here. A certain doctrinal minimalism and even heterodoxy *as judged by catholic and reformed standards* mark baptist faith and practice. Finally, this multilayered freedom is found perhaps above all in the emphasis placed on personal conversion and the uncoerced nature of coming to faith. The baptist tradition is thus known also as the believers church, for its ranks are filled, at least ideally, only by those whose faith is living, active, and sincere. Believers baptism, or the restriction of baptism to those able to count the cost and confess personal faith in Christ, is the telltale sign of this conviction.[73]

No typology is perfect, and every type cuts corners in its capacity to hold together all that is assigned to it. Nonetheless, it seems to me that both historic and global Christianity finds concrete expression, to varying degrees, in one of these forms. Some communities straddle the line—for example, Anglicanism can be found in catholic, magisterial, and charismatic forms, not only in different countries, but even within the same city. American Baptists, for their part, can trend in a reformed direction, depending on their judgments about Calvin, their relationship

---

tradition he founded. In a way, this ambiguity reveals the ambiguity of Wesleyanism: is it high church or free church, magisterial or baptist? The precise answer to that question may well depend on region, local or national culture, and congregational leadership.

73. See, e.g., the three volumes of *Systematic Theology* by James William McClendon Jr., titled *Ethics; Doctrine; Witness.* Cf. Ferguson, *Church of Christ.*

to the creed, and the "height" of their liturgy.[74] Innovation in polity, explosive evangelization, and non-institutional forms of Christian faith in the global south raise still more questions for how to categorize ecclesial forms and logics as Christianity enters its third millennium.[75]

Caveats aside, these three types—catholic, reformed, and baptist—guide the discussion in the coming chapters. Indeed I take them for granted. Where I do not intend to refer to one of these ecclesial logics or ideal types, either the wider context or the capitalization of these terms (i.e., Catholic, Reformed, Baptist) should alert the reader to my meaning.[76]

Let me close with a question and with a promissory note. The promissory note is that these three types return to the surface in chapter 7, following the exposition of our three primary figures and the ways in which they represent and embody discrete theological logics regarding the role of Scripture in the church. There I offer a second typology, a sort of overlay onto the one offered here, regarding how each church-type construes Scripture in light of the nature, mission, and authority of God's people.

As for the question: The dividing line in ecclesiology is typically drawn between Roman Catholic and Protestant (or, in my terms, between catholic and reformed) understandings of the church and therefore of Scripture's authority within it. My inclusion of the so-called baptist type is meant to trouble this default dichotomy.[77] Theologians

---

74. See now Harvey, *Baptists and the Catholic Tradition*.

75. For rich reflection, see Leithart, *End of Protestantism*; Sanneh, *Whose Religion Is Christianity?*; Jennings, *Christian Imagination*. See also, e.g., Martin, *Pentecostalism*. I may be mistaken in classifying Pentecostal churches under the "baptist" heading; perhaps these churches ought to constitute their own grouping. I am disinclined to do so given the definitions offered above and their only partially historical rooting. These three theological types are meant to gather together disunified and often disorganized communities and traditions under a common label, a label intended to signify a family resemblance. If the heuristic works to that extent, it has succeeded; if not, so much for the heuristic.

76. "Reformation" will be capitalized when I mean to refer to the whole complex phenomenon of sixteenth-century Protestantism, considered in all its diversity as a single event; the term will be lowercase when I mean to refer either to movements within the whole (radical reformation, magisterial reformation, etc.) or to call attention to its plural and diffuse character (as in reformations). Reference to "reformers" will be lowercase throughout, on a par with prophets, apostles, bishops, priests, church fathers, medievals, and moderns.

77. See Yoder's reflections on the implicit bilateralism of ecumenical dialogue and

from baptist backgrounds often find themselves on the outside of these discussions, though in terms of sheer numbers they represent more believers than theologians from reformed traditions. That exclusion is sometimes self-imposed, but it is worth amending in theological discourse nonetheless. That said, the reader will notice the substantial overlap between the reformed and baptist approaches to the Bible and, in certain respects, to the church. This overlap will only become more apparent as we set the three theologians alongside one another in the book's final two chapters. The question, then, is whether the baptist type or logic *rightly* drops out of the picture, because for all intents and purposes its commitments, together with its protests against the catholic tradition, are one and the same as those of the reformed; or whether the baptist position ought instead to remain a constant, unassimilable third party in these conversations. That is not a question I answer outright, however. I leave it to readers, and particularly to members of baptist traditions, to decide for themselves.

Outline of the Book

My aim in what follows is at once genealogical, expository, diagnostic, and constructive. Having already framed the inquiry, in the present chapter, with the state of TIS and Stephen Fowl's observations about its burgeoning divisions, the rest of Part I continues to set the scene by turning to Barth and unfolding his programmatic treatment of Scripture's nature and authority in the church (chapter 2). Part II offers a series of close engagements with Webster, Jenson, and Yoder (chapters 3–5, respectively), presenting their work as paradigmatic of distinct modes of coordinating the doctrines of Scripture and church (along with other dogmatic loci) while observing both the virtues and the vices of their substantive proposals. Pulling the threads together, Part III draws normative conclusions for theological reflection on these topics. Chapter 6 unpacks the lessons imparted by these three major figures, noting their transmission and revision of Barth's legacy, before proposing a theological account of Scripture that learns from but goes beyond them. Chapter 7 expands on the second-order doctrinal analysis of bibliology and ecclesiology under-

---

what he understands to be the third way represented—but almost always ignored—by free church traditions, in *Royal Priesthood*, 221–320, esp. 277–88.

taken in Part II, with a view to the implications for theological scholars speaking across church divisions.[78]

The resulting intervention, if one could call it that, is a mild one. I want to call attention to the logical connections between these all-important doctrinal topics, and to show how such attention can bypass or overcome gridlock in certain disagreements over Scripture and its interpretation. Such deadlock presents as disagreement over the Bible when, often enough, it is rooted in disagreement over the church. Realization of this situation, and continuing the conversation within the ambit of a different doctrinal locus, may do little more than shift focus onto a different, equally intractable dispute. But intelligible disagreement is a worthy achievement in any discourse, including theology. It is better to know what we are divided over, and why, than to keep spinning our wheels in ignorance of the deeper issues in play.

78. Because the book has multiple aims in mind, readers, if such there be, may find different paths through it. Beyond a linear path (reading start to finish), some readers may focus on the limited genealogy that runs from chapter 1 to chapter 5; others may home in on Part II or even a particular figure explicated there (for I do mean each of those chapters to constitute discrete contributions to the secondary literature); others may jump from this chapter to the constructive arguments found in Part III. I even imagine certain readers will want to read the excursus following chapter 4 first, for reasons largely distinct from the doctrinal interests of the book.

CHAPTER 2

Karl Barth

The Witness of Scripture in the Protestant Church

American Protestants, to whom the thought of Karl Barth was transmitted usually half a generation late and often through the filter of American controversies he did not mean to speak to, and then evaluated more as a philosophy than as proclamation, can hardly sense how simply fitting and how widely true is the statement that a generation of pastors were compelled by his work to rethink their faith, and to preach it, in the light of the overwhelming difference it makes if God has really spoken.

—John Howard Yoder[1]

It seems to me that Barth's biblical exegesis is a model of the kind of narrative reading that can be done in the wake of the changes I describe in this book.

—Hans Frei[2]

What we pursue is Evangelical and Reformation exegesis of the reality of the Church.

—Karl Barth[3]

It is as easy to overstate as to understate the importance of Barth's theology of the Bible. On the one hand, in the expanse of his work's context,

---

1. Yoder, *Karl Barth and the Problem of War*, 3.
2. Frei, *Eclipse of Biblical Narrative*, viii. Cf. Frei, *Types of Christian Theology*, esp. 38-46, 78-94.
3. Barth, *Church Dogmatics* I/1, 100. Hereafter, citations of the *Church Dogmatics* in this chapter will be abbreviated *CD*.

from the beginning of his career in the aftermath of the First World War to its conclusion in the midst of the Cold War, it is fair to say that his understanding and use of Scripture were revolutionary and epochal: a flash of lightning in the night sky.[4] As Yoder writes in the excerpt cited above, it is difficult to capture the impact of the unabashed proclamation that "God has really spoken," and the manifold consequences for human life and thought. The beating heart of Barth's dogmatics is indeed the undeterred conviction that in Jesus Christ God has spoken once for all, and reality is determined by the fact. His insistence, extension, and explication of this claim was as radical as it was unstinting, and he pressed it to every friend, enemy, and would-be alternative. Moreover, since God has spoken and the Bible mediates this speech by bearing witness to it, the only possible course of action for the Christian in general and the theologian in particular is: "Exegesis, exegesis, and yet more exegesis!"[5]

On the other hand, as unconventional and innovative as Barth was in both his bibliology and his exegesis, he did not appear out of nowhere: his context shaped him in important ways. Like all thinkers he was partly beholden to forms of thought from which he sought to disburden himself. And Barth did not languish in obscurity, left to his devices as a solitary prophet whose message fell on deaf ears.[6] To state the obvious, Barth did not invent the commentary with his *Römerbrief*—even if he did reinvent the genre, at least partially. He neither coined *sola scriptura* nor, like a modern Josiah, hauled it out of deep storage, rescuing it from the ruins. He did not repudiate historical criticism, though he did relegate its status to a sort of exegetical propaedeutic, thereby mitigating its influence on the interpretive task. Finally, he was surrounded and accompanied at all times by an academic culture that very rarely strayed far from its gravitational center—the study of the Christian Bible—a culture popu-

---

4. To use an early favorite image of Barth's. See, e.g., Barth, *Romans*, 331: "In the Gospel, in the Message of Salvation of Jesus Christ, this Hidden, Living, God has revealed Himself, as He is. Above and beyond the apparently infinite series of possibilities and visibilities in this world there breaks forth, like a flash of lightning, impossibility and invisibility, not as some separate, second, other thing, but as the Truth of God which is now hidden, as the Primal Origin to which all things are related, as the dissolution of all relativity, and therefore as the reality of all relative realities."

5. Barth, *Das Evangelium in der Gegenwart*, 17; cited in Donald Wood, *Barth's Theology of Interpretation*, viii.

6. See, e.g., Busch, *Karl Barth*; Webster, *Cambridge Companion to Karl Barth*; Dorrien, *Barthian Revolt*; Dorrien, *Kantian Reason and Hegelian Spirit*; Balthasar, *Theology of Karl Barth*; McCormack, *Critically Realistic Dialectical Theology*.

lated by figures such as Eduard Thurneysen, Emil Brunner, Rudolf Bultmann, Dietrich Bonhoeffer, and Hans Urs von Balthasar, all of whom devoted themselves to the careful interpretation and application of Holy Scripture.[7]

Perhaps the best way to capture Barth's achievement with respect to the Bible, at least in terms of his aim and the reception of his thought, is to see it as a work of *dogmatic liberation*. That is, what Barth began with his Romans commentary and continued with the *Church Dogmatics* was one long process of wresting the Bible out of the critics' hands, returning it to pride of place in the church's pulpit, and stepping back to let it speak for itself. Which is to say, to listen to what God would do and say through it. In the proximate context of the church and the ultimate context of God's saving and communicative acts, the Bible could be heard again as a fresh word too long suppressed by reading habits more akin to archeology than to sitting at a teacher's feet. In Barth's hands the Bible ceased to be an inert object patient of mastery and expertise, and became instead a living, irrepressible subject—or, better, an instrument in the hands of the Living One, the Word of God—that went to work on *oneself*. Thus freed and thus resituated, the Bible could be seen no longer as merely the artifact of an antique religious culture, or primarily the purview of the academy, or the distillation of principles for high civilization, or the raw materials for reconstruction of an original pure message of morality.[8] Barth and those after him could read and theologize the Bible for what it was: Holy Scripture, the witness of the prophets and apostles, and so the church's authoritative book through whose testimony resounds the gospel word of Father, Son, and Holy Spirit.

What, more specifically, are the features of Barth's bibliology? In the following I discuss his account of the nature and authority of Scripture, prefaced by a discussion of revelation as the Bible's founding and encompassing sphere. Barth's ecclesiology emerges in the process, inasmuch as his treatment of Scripture entails a treatment of the church as at once set under Scripture's authority and established in its own relative authority in the life of obedient freedom. Let me say at the outset, as well, that in what

---

7. Cf. Barth and Thurneysen, *Come, Holy Spirit*; Thurneysen, *Sermon on the Mount*; Brunner, *Revelation and Reason*; Balthasar, *Word Made Flesh*; Bultmann, *Theology of the New Testament*; Bonhoeffer, *Discipleship*.

8. See, e.g., Harnack, *What Is Christianity?* Cf. the essays by Spinoza, Strauss, Troeltsch, Bultmann, and Ebeling collected in Sarisky, *Theology, History, and Biblical Interpretation*, 11–217.

follows my aim is simple: to present Barth's thought on these issues, with clarity and in as much detail as I can offer without swamping the exposition or the chapter as a whole. I am neither recommending nor criticizing what Barth says. Barth's thought is crucial context for understanding the developments in bibliology after him and thus for engaging the work of Webster, Jenson, and Yoder. But it is not necessary to agree with him or his proposals. So while I am certainly *interpreting* his work in this chapter, and as charitably as I can, I mostly avoid signaling when I or others find his arguments questionable. To do so would double the chapter's length and take us on an unnecessary detour.

That said, let us turn to Barth's doctrine of the Word of God.

The Word of God[9]

For Barth, the doctrine of Scripture is a function of the doctrine of revelation, which in turn is a function of the doctrine of God the Holy Trinity. Each is nested within a larger doctrinal context, which gives shape and content to the derivative doctrine contained therein. This is why the first volume of the *Church Dogmatics* is titled *The Doctrine of the Word of God* and, as prolegomena to the larger theological project, begins with confession of the triune God, whose revealing word dogmatics seeks to explicate.

To begin at the beginning, then. The God of Christian faith is the Trinity: Father, Son, and Holy Spirit. "The doctrine of the Trinity is what basically distinguishes the Christian doctrine of God as Christian," and so "the doctrine of the Trinity" stands "at the head of all dogmatics."[10] To be sure, "the doctrine of the Trinity is a work of the Church," but it is so as "an interpretation" of Scripture, "translat[ing] and exeget[ing] the [biblical] text" (*CD* I/1, 308)—and it is "a good interpretation" at that (310). One cannot, however, discuss the Bible's nature, that is, "what is distinctive for the holiness of this Scripture if first [one does] not make it clear . . . who the God is whose revelation makes Scripture holy" (300).

---

9. For relevant secondary literature, see esp. Frei, *Doctrine of Revelation*; Hunsinger, *How to Read Karl Barth*; Hunsinger, *Disruptive Grace*; McCormack, *Orthodox and Modern*; Sykes, *Theological Method*; Sykes, *Centenary Essays*; Biggar, *Reckoning with Barth*.

10. *CD* I/1, 301, 300. Subsequent page citations from *Church Dogmatics* I/1 appear in parentheses.

But just what is the relationship between revelation and the triune God? In point of fact, "revelation is the basis of the doctrine of the Trinity; the doctrine of the Trinity has no other basis apart from this" (312). Barth does not mean that claims about God's triunity have their source in divine revelation, though that is true. He means that the doctrine itself arises from the nature and structure of revelation.

"*God* reveals Himself. [God] reveals Himself *through Himself.* [God] reveals *Himself*" (296). Thus the event of revelation is itself trinitarian: "the subject, God, the Revealer, is identical with His act in revelation and also identical with its effect"; therefore "we must begin the doctrine of revelation with the doctrine of the triune God" (296) who "in unimpaired unity yet also in unimpaired distinction is Revealer, Revelation, and Revealedness [*der Offenbarer, die Offenbarung und das Offenbarsein*]" (295). Barth's language here is liable to the interpretation that he is making a claim about history or about logical necessity: either that the doctrine of the Trinity arose out of analysis of revelation or that it must do so if it would be faithful.[11] I think it best to take him to be saying this: Revelation is the unique and inimitable act of God by which humans come to know God as God is. God is the living and active Lord at every stage of this event—and, importantly, for Barth it is an event—which means that *God* reveals *God* through *God*: the agent, action, and effect all remain wholly and singularly divine. The theological implication is twofold: on God's side, it is in fact *God*, as God is, who is revealed; on our side, there is no aspect of the event or part of the process that is ceded to us, in which we "take over," filling in the gaps left by God. This account of revelation entails—that is, assumes and confirms—the historic Christian confession of the Trinity because each of the three "sites" of God's self-revealing action is appropriated to one of the three hypostases of the Trinity; in this way the doctrine of revelation and the doctrine of God are mutually supporting. Barth is explicit about trinitarian doctrine proceeding from biblical exegesis. What he is saying here is that what revelation reveals is the Trinity, and it does so trinitarianly.

So God is the revealer, the triune revealer. What is revelation? Revelation is the Word of God, that is, "revelation denotes the Word of God itself in the act of its being spoken in time" (118). Specifically, "revelation

---

11. See the insightful analysis of Rowan Williams, "Barth on the Triune God," first published in 1979 and now collected (alongside essays on Lossky, Hegel, and Balthasar) in Williams, *Wrestling with Angels*.

... does not differ from the person of Jesus Christ nor from the reconciliation accomplished in Him" (119). Thus: "God's revelation is Jesus Christ, the Son of God" (137); "to say revelation is to say 'The Word became flesh'" (119).[12] Revelation is essentially christological in form and content, for *what* is unveiled is nothing other than "God's turning to man" (179), and this is, from all eternity, God's Word to humanity. Barth goes on to discuss the Word of God as speech (132–43), act (143–62), and mystery (162–86). The emphases here concern the character of God's Word as active, dynamic, and free, issued by a sovereign subject—a Speaker—whose speech is, by virtue of whose it is, sui generis and entirely efficacious. God's Word does what it says, effects what it signifies, and accomplishes the message it bears to its listeners. It is God's action, in speaking, to decide *for* us and to bring us to a moment of absolute decision, seized by a terrifying address utterly outside and beyond us that is nevertheless the announcement of our salvation, of our being rescued from the catastrophe into which we have gotten ourselves, and of the judgment of grace. In thus addressing us God remains Lord, and so we have not comprehended or grasped God in his turning to us in mercy; faith, as "acknowledgement of the mystery of God's Word," consists not in God "giving Himself... into our hands but [in] keeping us in His hands" (176). God remains transcendent even in the incarnation; God remains hidden even in revelation.[13]

In sum, for Barth revelation is the total singular event of the advent of Jesus Christ—his person and work distinct yet inseparably united in the incarnation—through which event the triune God has spoken and continues to speak to humanity his Word of grace. This Word, as God's own sovereign action, is at once efficacious (eliciting faith) and mysterious (repudiating attempts to domesticate or naturalize it). Following this account, then, how does humanity hear God's Word? How do people encounter divine revelation?

Barth's answer to these questions is what he calls the threefold form of the Word of God. The explication above is of the first—principal and antecedent—form: revelation proper.[14] But revelation, according to Barth, "never meets us anywhere in abstract form. We know it only indirectly,"

---

12. *CD* I/2, 483: "Now revelation is no more and no less than the life of God Himself turned to us, the Word of God coming to us by the Holy Spirit, Jesus Christ."

13. For Barth's discussion of this dialectic, see *CD* I/1, 304–33.

14. "The Word of God Revealed," *CD* I/1, 111–20.

that is, mediately, "from Scripture and proclamation. The direct Word of God meets us only in this twofold mediacy" (121). Revelation is always mediated, which is to say, it is always mediated *by* some *to* others.[15] Thus the other two forms of revelation are alike instances of attestation—testimony, commentary, pronouncement—*concerning* revelation, and just so God's Word is heard through their heraldry. The second form is Holy Scripture. The third form is church proclamation. But this is misleading, since "proclamation" encompasses both forms. Church proclamation, on this schema, is the church's unending task, commissioned by the risen Christ, to preach the Word of God. This charge is constitutive of the church's life and work. By God's free grace, indeed, "the Word of God preached means . . . man's talk about God in which and through which God speaks about Himself" (95). That is, in and through the all-too-human, fallible, and fallen speech of ministers and priests, preachers and evangelists, God himself speaks his own Word, the good news of Jesus Christ, and—by sheer miracle—people repent and believe.

The point to note here is that, on the one hand, God's Word is not merely a past event ("there and then") but one that happens, as an event, in the present ("here and now"); and, on the other hand, although God's Word is mediated by human speech, it is nonetheless still God's Word, divine revelation, because it is God who elects to speak it in and through human words. The emphasis, therefore, is less on the occasional or unpredictable nature of God's speaking through human speech, and much more on the fact *that* it happens and that it is *God* who makes it happen.

What, then, of the Bible? The Bible, according to Barth, is prophetic and apostolic witness to divine revelation in Jesus Christ. In the threefold form of God's Word, it occupies the second place, bearing witness to the first form (revelation) and issuing in the third form (church proclamation) as a privileged species of the latter.[16] Like ordinary church preaching, that and how and when the Bible may be said to "be" God's word is a matter of God's gracious action and free will, and so of its being in becoming. Which is to say, the Bible is the Word of God to God's people, the church, not in and of itself due to properties it bears as a special text nor due to the fact that Christians subjectively experience it to be such. Rather, the Bible is the Word of God when it objectively *becomes* God's Word

---

15. For clear statements in this regard, see *CD* I/2, 463, 492. See also the extensive discussion in Hunsinger, *How to Read Karl Barth*, 76–151.

16. For the following, see *CD* I/1, 99–111.

as an event of God's freely chosen loving condescension: God elects to speak to the community of faith; when this happens it does so through this book, the Bible, and its singular content is the eternal Word of God, Jesus Christ himself.[17]

Barth is explicit that the Bible is "a Church document, written proclamation," and therefore both the Bible and preaching "may thus be set initially under a single genus, Scripture as the commencement and present-day preaching as the continuation of one and the same event," namely, the church's proclamation of God's Word (102). But between the two there is "a dissimilarity in order, namely the supremacy, the absolutely constitutive significance of the former for the latter" (102). The logic motivating this claim is ecclesiological: "We must begin exegetically, conscious that what we pursue is Evangelical and Reformation exegesis of the reality of the Church" (100). What does such exegesis discover? Answer: "The Church is not alone in relation to God's Word" (100). That is, the church is not "engaged in dialogue with itself," not "left alone and referred to itself, to its own vitality" (105), "not left to itself in its proclamation" (101): the source and object and criterion of proclamation comes not from itself but "from elsewhere, from without . . . in all the externality of the concrete Canon as a categorical imperative which is also historical, which speaks in time" (101). The biblical canon thus "constitutes the working instructions or marching orders by which not just the Church's proclamation but the very Church itself stands or falls" (101). Accordingly, the content of the canon is none other than Jesus Christ (107)—in fact, the Bible is nothing less than "the book of Christ" (109)[18]—and just so "Scripture with this content must confront the life of the Church . . . as a criterion which cannot be dissolved into the historical life of the Church" (108).

17. See CD I/1, 110: "The statement that the Bible is God's Word is a confession of faith, a statement of the faith which hears God Himself speak through the biblical word of man. . . . We do not accept it as a description of our experience of the Bible. We accept it as a description of God's action in the Bible. . . . The Bible, then, becomes God's Word in this event, and in the statement that the Bible is God's Word the little word 'is' refers to its being in this becoming. It does not become God's Word because we accord it faith but in the fact that it becomes revelation to us." The echoes of eucharistic change are unmistakable, whether or not Barth intends the analogy.

18. See the later comment in CD I/2, 513: "If the Church lives by the Bible because it is the Word of God, that means that it lives by the fact that Christ is revealed in the Bible by the work of the Holy Spirit."

The Nature of Scripture[19]

In volume I/2 of the *Church Dogmatics* Barth takes up this topic again, and at length: "Chapter III: Holy Scripture" includes §§19–21 and stretches to nearly three hundred pages. Barth had written in the previous part-volume that "revelation engenders the Scripture which attests it" (*CD* I/1, 115), evoking the specifically theocentric (and not merely ecclesiological) logic of a full account of the nature of Scripture. Now he aims to provide such an account. I will limit my engagement to §19, titled "The Word of God for the Church." Of the many noteworthy features of Barth's extensive discussion there, I want to lift up five for discussion.

First, Barth begins this way: "The Word of God is God Himself in Holy Scripture. For God once spoke as Lord to Moses and the prophets, to the Evangelists and apostles. And now through their written word He speaks as the same Lord to His Church. Scripture is holy and the Word of God, because by the Holy Spirit it became and will become to the Church a witness to divine revelation" (*CD* I/2, 457). Scripture is what it is—holy and God's Word—in virtue of the divine will and action. The Bible does not escape the axiomatic rule of Barth's thought: God (graciously) determines all that is and how it is. To inquire into the Bible means to ask after God's gracious action, to refer the Bible to God's almighty and merciful will.

Second, there is no other ground or external basis apart from the Bible on which to stake the claim that it is God's Word. For "the statement that the Bible is the Word of God is an analytical statement, . . . grounded only in its repetition, description and interpretation, and not in its derivation from any major propositions. It must either be understood as grounded in itself and preceding all other statements or it cannot be understood at all" (535). The only basis for the claim "that the human word of the Bible is the Word of God . . . is that it is true" (535–36).[20] As such, "this one ba-

---

19. For relevant secondary literature, see the works cited above and below regarding Barth's doctrine of revelation and theological exegesis; see also Runia, *Karl Barth's Doctrine of Holy Scripture*; Hunsinger, *Thy Word Is Truth*; Yuen, *Barth's Theological Ontology of Holy Scripture*; Watson, "The Bible"; Thompson, "Witness to the Word"; McCormack, "Being of Holy Scripture"; MacDonald, *Karl Barth and the Strange New World*; Bender, *Confessing Christ for Church and World*, esp. 21–205.

20. See the summary claim at the beginning of the next section: "The truth and force of Holy Scripture in its self-attesting credibility is itself . . . a single and simultaneous act of lordship by the triune God, who in His revelation is the object and as such the source of Holy Scripture" (*CD* I/2, 539).

sis" becomes "the basis of the Church" insofar as the church continues to acknowledge and accredit it (536). Barth believes this to be a necessary admission for Protestant theology and, more broadly, for Christian faith, because it is simply the nature of the case; following Calvin, he suggests "we might just as well ask where we can base the distinction of light from darkness, of white from black, of sweet from sour" (535). That the Bible bears witness to, attests, mediates, signifies, and even "becomes" God's own Word is as sheerly true as it is indemonstrable apart from itself, as it elicits, effects, and produces the knowledge of itself in its hearers. This is part of the mystery of God's Word, of God's decision to use the feeble and errant words of human beings as a medium to serve the divine self-communication; but, just so, it is fitting to God's own being and act, a sort of hermeneutical or bibliological analogue to Barth's polemic against natural theology. God is known through God; God alone communicates the knowledge of himself. God is *not* known *apart* from his own purposive and personal act of self-revelation. In the same way Scripture, which testifies to and, by grace, is God's Word, is known through itself; it is not known as what it is apart from God's unconditioned and gratuitous act to *make* it known. "The Bible must be known as the Word of *God* if it is to be *known* as the Word of God" (535).[21] Just as one does not reason oneself up to the knowledge of God—to God's existence, attributes, will, or acts—so the Bible does not admit of epistemic possession or comprehension (works righteousness of the mind, natural theology of the book): it sets the terms and establishes the result of the encounter, and only thus does one come to know it for what it is.

Worth noting, third, is Barth's use of agential language for the Bible. This is evident throughout his writings, but one especial place this is apparent is his discussion of the canon. "What is it," Barth asks, "that makes the Bible of the Old and New Testaments the Canon?" His answer: "the Bible constitutes itself the Canon," that is, "it is the Canon because it imposed itself upon the Church as such, and continually does so" (CD I/1, 107). To use a measure by which to gauge the legitimacy of purported canonical documents would be to set up a norm over that

---

21. As Barth also states: "That the Bible is the Word of God is not left to accident or to the course of history and to our own self-will, but to the God of Abraham, Isaac and Jacob, the triune God as Him whose self-witness alone can and very definitely does see to it that this statement is true, that the biblical witnesses have not spoken in vain and will not be heard in vain" (CD I/2, 535).

which norms but is not itself normed; it would be to subject the church to self-dialogue. "No, the Bible is the Canon just because it is so. It is so by imposing itself as such" (107). In conjunction with the previous point, that there are no extra-biblical epistemic grounds for the knowledge of the Bible as God's Word, how should we understand Barth's language here? He does not mean, as he might be taken to mean on a flat-footed reading, that the "Bible"—this bound book of typeset pages sitting on my desk—"does" something or "acts" as a person or subject in the world. Nor does he mean that human agency is uninvolved in the reception of the Bible, in the event, as it were, of "being imposed upon" by the Bible. His point, rather, is twofold.

On the human side, there is real agency, actual action, but it is *receptive* action, "active passivity" in the Lutheran sense.[22] As with all of God's works, so with Holy Scripture: what humans do (and are to do) is receive, listen, attend, acknowledge, confirm, repeat, reiterate. The point is to emphasize divine action, freedom, and grace. Barth's talk of the Bible "doing" this or that is theological shorthand for the larger claim that, through the Bible, *God* does this or that. Understanding this shorthand is important for interpreting Barth well in light of later hermeneutical debates that identify problems in Christian attribution of agential language to the Bible and, correlatively, of description of Christian interpretation as "merely" listening to or reading what the text plainly "says."[23] Whatever Barth's shortcomings, he is not prone to naturalizing the Bible's meaning or power, as if one could simply point to what is "there" in the text and expect unanimous agreement. Just as what the Bible "is" is perceived spiritually—which means both in excess of its natural properties and by the power of the Holy Spirit—so what the Bible "does" is spiritually described, recognized, and accomplished.[24]

22. For an analysis of the subtle distinctions between Barth's Reformed emphasis on "active" agency over against Lutheran emphasis on "passive" agency, see the two essays that conclude Webster's *Barth's Moral Theology*, titled "'The Grammar of Doing': Luther and Barth on Human Agency" and "Justification, Analogy and Action: Barth and Luther in Jüngel's Anthropology" (151–214). See further Mangina, *Karl Barth on the Christian Life*.

23. See here Martin, *Sex and the Single Savior*, esp. 1–35.

24. Barth discusses the Word of God as "Subject" further, in extensive detail, in *CD* I/2, 660–85, esp. 683–85. See, e.g., 685: "the Word is first the Subject and only then the object of history." The term "history" here encompasses all human operation "on" and use "of" the Word. Barth is insistent that he is speaking of "the Word of God *in the form of Holy Scripture*" (685, my emphasis). The options for interpreting

A fourth notable feature in Barth's account of Scripture is where Barth modifies or departs from the tradition, meaning the Reformed tradition of bibliology.[25] Two decisive places where we witness this are, first, Barth's distinction of the Bible-as-witness from that to which it witnesses, the Word of God; and, second, Barth's denial of biblical inerrancy. In both cases it is less clear than might be desired just how different Barth's account is from typical Reformed affirmations, since Barth's goal in each case is to retain the upshot of the traditional claim while excising what he takes to be unhelpful or problematic. With respect to the Bible as God's Word, his use of "witness" is meant to cut the Gordian knot of identification between human texts and the Word of God. The eternal Word of God is not a predicate of any merely created entity;[26] moreover, recall

him, then, are: (1) his account is nuanced enough to allow for this sort of Scripture-as-instrument-of-the-Word flexibility; (2) there is simple conceptual slippage in his language; or (3) the claim, read in its plain, prima facie sense, is incoherent. I opt for (1) allowing for moments of (2).

Also relevant to this discussion is Barth's treatment of Christ's prophetic office in *CD* IV/3.1, esp. §69. Consider some of the representative claims he makes there: "the covenant of God with man and man with God as fulfilled in Jesus Christ is not a dumb fact but one which speaks for itself. The reconciliation of the world with God accomplished and consisting in Him is revelation in its very reality" (165); "it is first Jesus Christ Himself in His person and action who declares Himself to be the Reconciler and as such also the Revealer, and then, on the basis of the latter aspect, there is human *kerygma* and apostolate and *didaskalia* in the Gentile world" (11); "Where God is present as active Subject; where He lives, as is the case in the life of Jesus Christ, life is not just possibly or secondarily but definitely and primarily declaration, and therefore light, truth, Word, and glory. A mute and obscure God would be an idol. The true and living God is eloquent and radiant" (79); "Th[e] prophetic and apostolic mode of thought is the norm in the Canon of Holy Scripture. Applied in detail, it is the school where we are taught how the statement that Jesus Christ is the one Word of God is to be properly understood and legitimately made. As we go to this school, we learn to think and make it humbly yet boldly before God and man" (92).

25. For samples of the mainstream tradition on these matters, see, e.g., Calvin, *Institutes*, 1.6–8; Gerhard, *On the Nature of Theology and Scripture*, 1.1.1–3.51, 17.362–23.493; Turretin, *Institutes of Elenctic Theology*, 1:2.1–6, 16–21; Warfield, *Inspiration and Authority*; Bavinck, *Reformed Dogmatics*, 1:323–494. Cf. Muller, *Post-Reformation Reformed Dogmatics*, esp. 2:147–388.

26. See *CD* I/2, 513: "There is only one Word of God and that is the eternal Word of the Father which for our reconciliation became flesh like us and has now returned to the Father, to be present to His Church by the Holy Spirit. . . . That the Bible is the Word of God cannot mean that with other attributes the Bible has the attribute of

that revelation is coterminous with the person and work of Jesus Christ. So the Bible is identical neither with God's eternal Word nor with revelation as such. Therefore the Bible is *mediated revelation*, a witness *to* God's Word, and so (but only so) the means *of* God's self-communication. In this nonidentical unity between God's Word and the Bible, Barth believes he can affirm the church's traditional emphasis on the nature and authority of Scripture while escaping problems at once theological, historical, and hermeneutical. In other words, Barth wants to maintain Scripture's *vere homo* alongside its *vere deus*: truly written by humans, truly attesting God's Word and work.

This concern is even more evident in Barth's comments about biblical fallibility. He writes: "the prophets and apostles as such, even in their office, even in their function as witnesses, even in the act of writing down their witness, were real, historical men as we are, and therefore sinful in their action, and capable and actually guilty of error in their spoken and written word" (*CD* I/2, 529). Barth sees in the tradition a constant, inevitable slippage toward an implicit communicability between divine and human attributes, such that for the Bible to bear God's Word it must become something other than human—something other than what humans *are*—receiving predicates that are proper to God alone, that is, non-communicable divine attributes such as infallibility and inerrancy. Earlier in the same part and volume of the *Church Dogmatics*, Barth discusses *sarx* as what humans contingently are and what Christ became: fallen existence, weighed down by sin and death, not simply that which is finite or creaturely.[27] Read in this connection, Barth's argument here is that the Bible, even in its status as Holy Scripture and witness to revelation, nevertheless remains *sarx*. The Bible is not quasi-divine; the Bible is therefore best understood as a miracle: "That the lame walk, that the blind see, that the dead are raised, that sinful and erring men as such speak the Word of God: that is the miracle of which we speak when we say that the Bible is the Word of God"; "the truth of the miracle [is] that here fallible men speak the Word of God in fallible human words" (529). Consequently, and finally:

---

being the Word of God. To say that would be to violate the Word of God which is God Himself—to violate the freedom and the sovereignty of God. God is not an attribute of something else, even if this something else is the Bible. God is the Subject, God is Lord. He is Lord even over the Bible and in the Bible."

27. See *CD* I/2, 132–71, esp. 147–59.

To the bold postulate, that if [the prophets and apostles'] word is to be the Word of God they must be inerrant in every word, we oppose the even bolder assertion, that according to the scriptural witness about man, which applies to them too, they can be at fault in any word, and have been at fault in every word, and yet according to the same scriptural witness, being justified and sanctified by grace alone, they have still spoken the Word of God in their fallible and erring human word. (529–30)

As in soteriology and epistemology, so in bibliology the justification of sinners by grace alone applies to every doctrine; none is excepted. The Bible is therefore "like the water in the Pool of Bethesda"; "the presence of God's Word in the Bible [is not] an attribute inhering once for all in this book as such" (530), but rather, in the freedom of the divine decision, God graciously condescends to stir the waters of these texts with his healing, powerful, unpossessable communicative presence.[28]

If the prior move regarding Scripture's non-identity with revelation operates at some distance from the mundane practicalities of interpretation, this latter claim about biblical fallibility would seem in principle to imply that exegesis will identify theologically relevant errors, mistakes, untruths, and/or contradictions in the text. But, again, it is not clear what material force this formal claim has on Barth's actual interpretive practice, and so to what degree his disagreement with the tradition is a substantive one.[29]

Fifth and finally, Barth insists that the biblical canon is not closed but open. This may come as a surprise, given his emphasis on the Bible's divine provenance and instrumentality. But it follows logically, first, from his rejection of any intrinsic or self-evident properties that might confirm, to the naked or natural eye, the Bible's status as Holy Scripture; and, second, from his dismissal of the description of the church's confession of this truth as anything like the bestowal or granting of authority, preferring instead talk of the church's recognition and reception of divine action and authority. Furthermore, Barth takes himself to be

28. "The revelatory event and experience is not only unitary but infallible, God guaranteeing the divinity of his Word, miraculously grasping man through the uncertain medium of worldly happening and bringing him into the single true event of the divine being. It is Calvin's irresistible grace rendered into epistemological terms" (Rowan Williams, "Barth on the Triune God," 115).

29. For sharp dispute along these lines, see Rogers and McKim, *Authority and Interpretation*; Woodbridge, *Biblical Authority*.

following the lead of the Protestant reformers, many of whom (on his reading) expressed doubts about certain biblical texts, implicitly proposing that they be deemed non-canonical. To be sure, on the one hand, Christians "have the right and duty to accept [the church's] answer as good and sufficient" regarding what texts constitute the canon of Holy Scripture—that is, which texts faithfully testify to divine revelation (476). But there is no "absolute guarantee that the history of the Canon is closed" (476), and so "we cannot rule out a consideration of the possibility of an open alteration in its constitution," whether "a narrowing . . . or an extension" (478). Thus, on the other hand, "the individual in the Church certainly cannot and ought not to accept it as Holy Scripture just because the Church does. He can and should himself be obedient only to Holy Scripture as it reveals itself to him and in that way forces itself upon him, as it compels him to accept it" (479). Barth qualifies this rather startling assertion of individual private judgment by saying, first, that Scripture exists in and for the church, and so it is only within the church that the believer will properly hear its message and discern whether it is in fact testimony to divine revelation; and, second, that the believer must listen to the church's "so far unaltered judgment" about the Bible,[30] which "radically precedes as such the judgment of the individual" (479).[31] Nevertheless, Barth does not retract his statement. For it accords with the broad features of his overall stance: that the church has no authority over Scripture; that the church's historic judgment *may* be mistaken; that the canon is therefore open to alteration (by subtraction or addition of texts); and that individual Christians ought not to affirm the existing

---

30. This is something of a dodge, since Christendom's divisions include differing canons. Perhaps Barth means to say that the churches' judgment about those books that ought unquestionably to be received as canonical, at least in the last millennium once doubts about works like the Apocalypse died away, is unaltered? And that those texts that may or may not be canonical (Tobit, Wisdom of Solomon, etc.) do not call this primary judgment into question? If so, that is quite the qualification.

31. Further: "Therefore we hear the judgment of the Church, but we do not obey its judgment, when we accept the settlement which the Church has, of course, made. In and with the Church we obey the judgment which was already pronounced, before the Church could pronounce its judgment and which the Church's judgment could only confirm. Just as the question of the witness of revelation can only be a question of faith, so too the answering of that question can only be a knowledge of faith. When we adopt the Canon of the Church we do not say that the Church itself, but that the revelation which underlies and controls the Church, attests these witnesses and not others as the witnesses of revelation and therefore as canonical for the Church" (*CD* I/2, 474).

biblical canon merely because the church does so but only to the extent that they hear God's Word addressed to them in and through it. They will read and hear the Bible as it stands, in the sphere of the church, with the undoubted expectation that it is and will be Holy Scripture. But some of it may turn out not to be.

In conclusion,[32] Barth sets his theology of the Bible in the larger context of his treatment of divine revelation, which in turn is set in the ultimate context of the doctrine of God. Within these nested doctrinal contexts, the Bible is understood as Holy Scripture, that set of texts engendered *by* divine revelation that attests *to* divine revelation as its witness. As Scripture testifies to revelation—the Word made flesh, Jesus Christ—it mediates and just so becomes God's Word in and to the church. It does this by God's own free will and act; it is known as such of itself and on no other basis. It is uniquely effective in virtue of its relation to God as his chosen instrument through which to mortify and vivify lost sinners, to convict of sin and awaken to faith. Scripture remains human (fleshly) without qualification, neither becoming divine nor assuming divine attributes; and the collection of texts that constitute it is, although prima facie trustworthy, not fixed but open inasmuch as the church is fallible in its discernment of God's Word. This, according to Barth, is the nature of Scripture. What, then, is its authority?

The Authority of Scripture

Barth moves directly from discussion of Scripture's nature to discussion of its authority:[33] §20, "Authority in the Church," consists of two parts,

---

32. One important piece of Barth's presentation I leave undiscussed here is his emphasis on the two-testament character of the Bible; that is, Christian Holy Scripture consists of Old and New Testament together, which as a single canon testifies to the one Lord Jesus Christ. See CD I/2, 70–121, 481–85. This is a hugely important point in itself (in its explicit denial of Marcionism) and in its original context (given the tendency in German biblical scholarship to discount the validity or enduring value of the Old Testament for Christian faith and theology), but it is not immediately relevant for our purposes here. For, happily, the point is widely agreed upon in the tradition and by the primary figures considered in this book. For Barth's discussion of the relationship between Israel and the church and of the Old Testament's witness to Christ, see CD II/2, 195–305, 354–409, respectively.

33. The formal arrangement of paragraphs 20 and 21 is between "objective" and "subjective," that is, Barth's desire "to distinguish between . . . an outer and an inner deter-

"The Authority of the Word" (*CD* I/2, 538–85) and "Authority under the Word" (585–660), before moving on to §21, "Freedom in the Church," comprising "The Freedom of the Word" (661–95) and "Freedom under the Word" (695–740). The present discussion regarding biblical authority will focus on the first part in each paragraph (§20.1 and §21.1), especially the former.

Stepping back for a moment, it is important to see the interlocking pieces at work here. In bibliology authority is a function of nature, because what the Bible is determines what it is for and how its purpose is properly to be achieved. What the Bible is, however, is "Holy Scripture," which for Barth denotes its status as witness to revelation in and for the church. Its "nature" thus has to do not with properties inhering in it (divinely given or not), but with God's action to set it apart (just as it is) for a particular service: that of testimony to the gospel. Its authority follows from this appointment, which adds nothing to its being as a human artifact, but rather places it in a particular context for a particular end, while directing others to comport themselves to it as an authority. Moreover, for Barth the Bible's authority is inherently an ecclesiological question, because—*as* church proclamation set apart for mediating God's Word to God's people—"Holy Scripture is the Word of God *to* the church and *for* the Church" (475, my emphasis). It has its place and fulfills its end in the sphere and life of the church; whatever authority it has is exercised in and over the church. It is here that bibliology and ecclesiology are most intertwined, though the relationship can be determined in either direction or dialectically. We will see in what follows that, for Barth, whereas the "arrow" of authority goes from Scripture to church, the direction is reversed with regard to the doctrinal loci: ecclesiology governs bibliology, insofar as what the church is and can be determines what Scripture is and is for. (Recall the quote cited above: proper bibliology follows from "Evangelical and Reformation exegesis of the reality of the Church.")[34] And this, in turn, is because Barth places both doctrines in subordinate relation to the doctrines of God and revelation, such that the "lines" of theological movement go at once from God through Scripture to church and from God through church to Scripture.

---

mination of this obedience" (538). This leads to assigning authority to the former and freedom to the latter, which Barth takes up in order as the Word's authority and freedom, and secondarily the church's authority and freedom established and limited thereby.

34. *CD* I/1, 100.

What does this look like in detail? To begin, the whole of Barth's discussion of the Bible's authority is an explication—hermeneutical, historical, and ecclesiological—of the claim that "Holy Scripture is the authority of Jesus Christ in His Church" (CD I/2, 585). The authority of the Bible as such is therefore christologically determined. For Jesus Christ is the Lord and head of the church, and Scripture is his appointed herald and witness through whose testimony he speaks and rules, is heard and obeyed. The church "is related to Him as the human nature which He assumed is related to His divinity. . . . The Church would not exist without Him, just as the creature would not exist without the Creator. It is the same relation as that of the Creator and creature which exists between Him and His Church. . . . The relation between Jesus Christ and His church is, therefore, an irreversible relation" (576).

On one side, this means that the church is *ruled* by Scripture, or rather, that Scripture is the instrument of Christ's rule of the church. "To say that Jesus Christ rules the Church is equivalent to saying that Holy Scripture rules the Church" (693). The mediacy of the Bible does not "imperil the immediacy of the relation between the Lord and His church," but rather "constitutes the true immediacy of this relationship" (694). On the other side, the church's relationship to Scripture can be summarized in one word: obedience. "The Church really is the Church" where "it finds itself in a known and therefore real relationship of obedience to what constitutes its basis and nature and therefore to Jesus Christ the Word of God" (542). There is, according to Barth, an "antithesis" between two partners, God and humanity: "One of them, and only one commands. The other has to submit to this command—just to submit" (542). We see this relationship in exemplary form in the prophets and apostles, the original and authoritative recipients of revelation. The point is crucial: "The existence of the Church of Jesus Christ stands or falls with the fact that it obeys as the apostles and prophets obeyed their Lord. It stands or falls with the known and actual antithesis of man and revelation, which cannot be reversed, in which man receives, learns, submits and is controlled, in which he has a Lord and belongs to Him wholly and utterly" (543). "Obedience" is a moral-spiritual epitome of the being, life, and witness of the Christian church as the body of Christ and hearer of his Word.

At least three concerns are to the fore in Barth's discussion here. First, just as Scripture ensures that the church is not in dialogue with itself,[35]

---

35. For Barth this is finally a soteriological claim: "the final positive meaning of the

so it also rules out any possibility of the church's being self-governed. Barth believes that "the self-government of the Church is the admitted essence of both Catholicism and also Neo-Protestantism" (575), whereas self-government is a non-communicable property of God, "indeed it is the great prerogative of God" (575). Self-government is as such the refusal to obey, and the self-governing "church" therefore "makes itself like God" and just so "ceases to be the Church" (575). Christ and Christ alone governs the church through Scripture; obedience to Christ through Scripture, then, just is the refusal of self-government because it is consent to *being* governed by another—this One, the sovereign and gracious Lord enthroned in glory but present in power to his people.

Second, Barth simultaneously affirms Scripture's mediateness—its irreducibly "temporal, historical and human" character (540)—and closes off any suggestion that this entails a relativization of its authority. If, contrary to fact, it were the case that "like all other authoritative powers in the Church," Scripture could "only *represent* the divine authority," then it would follow that the church may and should "appeal from Scripture . . . to a true and original Word of God . . . beyond the representative and preliminary judgment of Scripture to the supreme and real Judge and Lord" (541, emphasis mine). But if, as is the case, Scripture is the instrument of Christ's rule of the church, if its authority is transparent to Christ's own authority so that the church is obedient to Christ to the extent that it is obedient to Scripture, then there is no shortcut, no workaround, no bypassing the mediacy of the Bible for a surer, more immediate audience with the Lord. The Bible is the only court of appeal. For in the witness of the prophets and apostles

> the Church itself has to do personally with its Lord. Therefore in the *per se* mediate, relative and formal quantity of Scripture, in which their witness is presented to us, it has to do with the self-subsistent and self-maintaining direct and absolute and material authority, with its own existence, nature and basis. Consequently the Church cannot evade

Evangelical decision" is that "it is taken in the thankful recognition that the Church is not alone, that it is not left to its own discussions and especially that it is not left to itself. . . . From [the] misery of the solitariness of the creature fallen in sin and death the Church is snatched away by the fact that God in Jesus Christ is present and gracious to it in concrete authority, which means in an authority which is different from and superior to its own. It is the Word of God as Holy Scripture which puts an end to this misery" (*CD* I/2, 584–85).

Scripture. It cannot try to appeal past it directly to God, to Christ, or to the Holy Spirit. (*CD* I/2, 544)

If the book rises and the letter speaks, if the book is read and the letter understood, then with them the prophets and apostles and He of whom they testify rise up and meet the Church in a living way. It is not the book and letter, but the voice of the men apprehended through the book and letter, and in the voice of these men the voice of Him who called them to speak, which is authority in the church. (*CD* I/2, 581)

The church is itself as it obeys the voice of the One who speaks in the voices heard in Scripture; there is no other possible relation than obedience, no other form of obedience than this one, through this ordered line of authority.[36]

The third concern Barth has in this section is arguably the precipitating cause for the whole discussion: the church's *own* authority. As with so much in Barth regarding divine and human action and relation, the logic is clear: the principal and universal authority in the church is Holy Scripture—as "an authority *in* the Church which is also an authority *over* the Church" (574)—and just thereby "the definite authority of the Church itself is established and limited" (539). Scripture upholds the church and so generates its genuine authority, even as it constrains it by setting itself over it. "Holy Scripture is the ground and limit of the church, but for that very reason it constitutes it" (539). The Word of God is to the church as God's creative and saving acts are to rebellious creatures: their source, terror, sustenance, and salvation. Scripture's authority "does not destroy but defines" the church's authority (574). But the order of authority and the relationship it entails—Christ's command and the church's obedience—is both asymmetrical and unyielding: "The grace directed to the Church cannot be transformed into a possession and a glory of the Church" (577). The temptation to annex to itself what is solely and properly Christ's is perennial for the church, even "strangely irresistible" (578). That is why the church must be ever vigilant, and Protestant dogmatics must unfailingly press the issue. To the question, "What is it . . .

---

36. See *CD* I/2, 580: "In the Church the tradition of the Word of God, obedience towards Jesus Christ and subjection to His authority are not an open question but are ordered and regulated from the very first and for all time by the existence of the apostles and prophets."

that concretely prevents this [transfer] and makes it impossible?" (578), Barth replies that the "only [answer can] be the simple one that this concrete necessity is the fact of Holy Scripture" (578–79). This is "the Evangelical decision" (578) issued by the sixteenth century.[37] The church must never falter in confirming this decision, lest it cease to be the church at all. Regarding ecclesial authority, it follows that "all other authorities in the Church are themselves conditioned by the fact that they are subordinated to [the] word [of Scripture] as the concrete form of the Word of Christ and only to that extent are they authorities in the Church" (580).

A twofold picture emerges of the role and exercise of scriptural authority in the church's life. On the one hand, Scripture "is always His Word as against its word" (579). That is, Scripture is adversarial:[38] it con-

---

37. See here Barth's extensive small-print discussion of the respective authorities of Scripture, tradition, and the church, contrasting the *evangelische* church of the reformers with Roman Catholicism on the one hand and Neo-Protestantism on the other; CD I/2, 544–72. See also Barth's programmatic statement at the outset of this discussion:

> The Word of God in the revelation of it attested in Holy Scripture is not limited to its own time, the time of Jesus Christ and its Old and New Testament witnesses. In the sphere of the Church of Jesus Christ it is present at all times, and by its mouth it wills to be and will be present at all times. *This is the Evangelical confession of faith.* In this confession of the vitality and therefore of the presence of the Word of God as already actualized and to be actualized again and again *there is included the Church's confession of itself*, i.e., of its institution and preservation by the Word of God for the authority entrusted to it and the mission enjoined upon it. (573, emphases mine)

Barth's phrasing here could not be clearer regarding the inseparability of confession of, as well as theological reflection upon, Scripture as the Word of God and the church as the people of God, that is, the people defined and ordered by the Word of God.

38. It is also adversarial with the world: see Barth's discussion of Scripture's "power" in CD I/2, 674–85, where he writes, "The real world is attacked by Jesus Christ and the testimony of Jesus Christ. It is victoriously attacked. . . . [I]n the Word of God [the world] is now confronted by a superior power. . . . Scripture confronts the world with faith in God's revelation in Jesus Christ . . ." (680). It is worth noting that for Barth this implies not the sword but the cross, since the announcement of the gospel elicits hatred, rejection, and violence and those who announce it "have to bear the cross like their Master." As for those who attack the Word itself, "it has the power to maintain itself in face of the . . . attacks made upon it." Therefore: "The maintaining of the Word of God against the attacks to which it is exposed cannot be our concern, and therefore we do not need to worry about it. . . . [Indeed,] there is nothing about

fronts the church, stands over against it, challenges and provokes and accuses and judges it—from without, from a distance, independently, autonomously (579–80). It is other, alien, enemy, judge. It is the sword of the Spirit (Eph 6:17), double-edged, able to pierce between bone and marrow (Heb 4:12). Its written nature in particular (581–82) fixes it, not in a controllable stability, but rather as an essentially non-plastic entity, an unassimilable but permanent element in the church's life, which never ceases to goad, prod, and question it.

On the other hand, it is this very character that makes Scripture the condition of the possibility of the church's reform:

> if behind every alleged or genuine oral tradition, over and above every authority in the Church, there is a Holy Scripture, and if this Holy Scripture is as such recognized as the judge by which from the very outset all ecclesiastical tradition has to be judged and to which all ecclesiastical judges have always to listen, then that means that the Church is not left to its own devices, that the source of its renewal is open, and therefore that it itself is open to be renewed and reformed in the light of its origin and object. (582)[39]

In the hand of Christ, in the Spirit's power, the word of Scripture both slays and makes alive, mortifies and vivifies. The church is ever threatened by its relentless interrogative presence, even as this seemingly hostile presence is also a plenteous giver of life and renewal. This encapsulates the *evangelische* ecclesiological paradox stemming from the Protestant affirmation of *sola scriptura*: The church is ineliminably defectible—in fact the church has fallen, forsaken its identity, and become non-church at locatable times and places in history—yet Christ's promise stands that the gates of hell shall not prevail against it (Matt 16:18). Barth's presentation stands in deep continuity with this tradition. Scripture is at once that which accuses an erring or fallen church before the Lord and that

---

whose solidity we need be less troubled than the testimonies of God in Holy Scripture. For a power which can annul these testimonies is quite unthinkable" (681).

39. See Barth's immediately preceding comments: "[Scripture's] written nature guarantees its freedom over against the Church and therefore creates for the Church freedom over against itself. If there is still the possibility of misunderstanding and error as regards this sign in virtue of its written nature, there is also the possibility of being recalled by it to the truth, the possibility of the reformation of a Church which has perhaps been led into misunderstanding and error" (CD I/2, 582).

which keeps the church from straying to the right or to the left. Like the Johannine description of the Holy Spirit, Holy Scripture both convicts of sin and guides into all truth (John 16:8, 13).

In short, "Holy Scripture alone has divine authority in the Church" (581), for "the authority of the sign . . . is given with the revelation itself" (580). It bears the authority of the Lord Christ himself as his chosen instrument for ruling, governing, and guiding his body, the church. The response it establishes and sustains is one of humble obedience, as the church hears and heeds the living and powerful speech of its sovereign Lord, the body's head. Within this ordered relationship of superior and subordinate, the church has its own authority, relative but real. This authority is absolutely distinguished from Scripture's authority, around or beyond which the church may not maneuver or appeal. Scripture is not an obstacle to the church's personal knowledge of and relationship with the Lord; it *is* this knowledge and relationship, the form that it takes by the Lord's own will and institution. Scripture is not church, nor church Scripture: the relationship parallels that of body and head (though only analogously), and the asymmetry goes all the way down. Scripture is the church's sustenance to the extent that it is not assumed as part of the church—to the extent, that is, that it remains church proclamation *set apart from* all subsequent proclamation as the latter's fixed foundation and measure. Thus and only thus will Scripture be itself and the church itself, for the life, faith, and mission of God's people rest entirely on the independence and unobstructed authority of God's Word.

Précis: Ten Themes in Barth's Theology of Scripture

So much for Barth's bibliology. The following chapters take up what emerged in its wake. As a segue, this chapter concludes with a summary of the issues and themes that Barth passed on to those who came after him. First, though, I want to offer a brief comment on Barth's interpretation of Scripture. The comment is brief for the simple reason that Barth's exegetical method is far less influential, precisely in its details, than his theology of Scripture. Within that theology, what has proven influential for other theologians is (1) the sheer *fact* of his relentless multivalent attentiveness to the biblical text as the source, impetus, and criterion for his dogmatic proposals; and, as the form that fact takes, (2) the specific interpretive *posture* he takes up when he turns to read the Bible theologically. It is therefore these formal features, rather than the method or the matter, of his approach to scriptural exegesis that are of interest to us.[40]

Consider Francis Watson's global observation about Barth's *Church Dogmatics*: "From beginning to end, [it] is nothing other than a sustained meditation on the texts of Holy Scripture." In this way "Barth's biblical interpretation is not a particular item [on his agenda], but the foundation and principle of coherence of his entire project."[41] With respect to exegesis, moreover, Barth was not beholden to any one method; as John Webster writes, Barth's actual

> exegetical practice in the *Church Dogmatics* is quite varied . . . and unsystematic. Sometimes he gives lengthy exegetical treatment to specific passages; sometimes he generates catenae of biblical quotations with little comment. He produces extensive restatements of biblical stories, arguments, themes, or concepts. At some points his interest is more directly applicative, and at other points scriptural citations are analyzed in the course of seeking warrants for theological proposals. Moreover, the presence of Scripture in the [*Dogmatics*] is as much in its saturation by biblical allusion, citation, and paraphrase as it is by explicit exegesis.[42]

For us who would read Barth reading Scripture, then, Webster suggests that the *Church Dogmatics* "is best read as a set of conceptual variations upon scriptural texts and themes, sometimes explicitly tied to exegesis, sometimes more loose and indirect, but always attempting to indicate what is already proclaimed in the prophetic and apostolic witness."[43]

To indicate what is already proclaimed in the biblical witness: that is probably as compact a summary of Barth's modus operandi in scriptural interpretation as one can find. Barth's own second-order reflections are expansive, though his procedures, as Watson and Webster suggest, are varied and do not follow the seemingly straight line of *explicatio-medi-*

---

40. For secondary literature, see esp. Wood, *Barth's Theology of Interpretation*; Greene-McCreight, *Ad Litteram*; Cunningham, *What Is Theological Exegesis?*; Gignilliat, *Barth's Theological Exegesis of Isaiah*; Burnett, *Karl Barth's Theological Exegesis*; Congdon, "Barth and Bultmann on Scripture"; Frei, "Scripture as Realistic Narrative"; Hunsinger, *Disruptive Grace*, 210-25; Ford, *Barth and God's Story*.

41. Watson, "The Bible," 57.

42. Webster, "Barth, Karl," 84.

43. Webster, "Barth, Karl," 83.

tatio-applicatio.[44] Some of Barth's most potent and searching remarks on hermeneutics come early in his career: in his preface to the second edition of *Romans*, for example, and in his lectures on the Fourth Gospel. The former is famous for clarifying his appreciation of historical-critical tools as necessary but wholly preparatory to the true task of hearkening to God's living word.[45] The latter, for its part, contains some striking claims regarding what Barth calls the *objectivity* of Christian theological reading. For instance, not only is the sacrament of baptism not a threat to the objective character of biblical interpretation; it is, together with prayer,[46] a necessary (though never sufficient) condition for a truly objective engagement with the text.[47] That is because the text, as an artifact of apostolic and prophetic proclamation of the gospel, speaks of God in the midst of and for the sake of God's people, the church, which in turn is constituted by baptism and the confession that attends it. If one would encounter what the Bible speaks of, given what the Bible *is*, then what alternative is there? As Barth puts it: "I answer [my opponents' objections] by asking quite simply whether, if the [text] is to be treated seriously at all, it is reasonable to approach it with any other assumption than that God is God."[48]

---

44. See *CD* I/2, 695–740. Darren Sarisky has appropriated this schema for his own constructive proposal for theological interpretation in *Reading the Bible Theologically*, 284–327.

45. Barth, *Romans*, 2–15. See further McCormack, "Karl Barth's Theological Exegesis." Cf. Webster, "Karl Barth." I do not discuss Barth's deployment of the *analogia fidei* in this chapter. For recent engagement, see Hector, *Theology without Metaphysics*; Spencer, *Analogy of Faith*; White, *Analogy of Being*.

46. *CD* I/2, 684: "we cannot read and understand Holy Scripture without prayer, that is, without invoking the grace of God." Cf. Gerhard: "Even though [the divine mysteries] are set forth externally, one still cannot grasp their salutary and complete meaning apart from the internal illumination and light of the Holy Spirit. . . . Prayer is necessary for us to receive the divine and supernatural light of the Holy Spirit. . . . This full illumination of the Holy Spirit is necessary for a salutary understanding and interpretation of Scripture as a whole and all of its parts. This is why all readers and interpreters of Holy Writ need to pray that they would receive such illumination of divine light—and these prayers should be in earnest" (*On Sacred Scripture*, 2.4.49–51).

47. Barth, *Witness to the Word*, 1–9. Cf. *CD* I/2, 684. See the helpful discussion in Webster, "Witness to the Word." See also Miller, *Seeing by the Light*, 73–149. Miller offers a rich exposition of the hermeneutic at work in Barth's exegesis of the Fourth Gospel, an exposition I regret I did not have at hand until after the completion of this chapter.

48. Barth, *Romans*, 11.

Exegesis, in short, is intrinsically theological, indeed confessional. Reading the Bible is a dogmatic affair through and through. The canon of Holy Scripture calls for a particular configuration of hermeneutical relations: Christian readers with Christian convictions[49] reading the Bible as Christian Scripture in the Christian church. Prolegomena have their place, but exactly as *fore*-words to the main event.[50] To suggest otherwise would be to deny the objective spiritual nature either of Scripture or of the church that gathers around it to hear God speak. Anyone is free to make such denials, but it would be odd and self-defeating for theologians, or Christian readers in general, to do so.

Thus it is Barth's exegetical *posture*, and not his interpretive methods, that stamped itself on future theological generations. And though he was far from alone in this regard (for example, Bultmann towered over the field as well),[51] many of the most significant ideas and arguments in bibliology that arose in the latter half of the twentieth century were united as responses to, extensions of, or departures from Barth's proposals. Let me conclude by noting at least ten such issues raised by his work.

1. *Christology.* Jesus Christ is the content and hidden logic of Scripture; either Scripture is understood as a function of and witness to the person and work of Christ or it is not understood (theologically) at all.

2. *Revelation.* Scripture testifies to and thus proclaims the saving gospel Word of God, which is nothing less than the revelation of the incarnate God with us, present to speak, judge, and redeem. Far from being merely an ancient document fit for historians, Scripture is a function of living divine speech addressed to us here and now, in the present tense.

3. *Witness.* On the one hand, Scripture is not identical with the Word but testifies to it, which opens up all kinds of avenues for revision of received doctrines (restraint in predicating properties of the text; admission of error in the text). On the other hand, Scripture is the appointed witness to the Word and therefore demands of the church absolute and unqualified subordination, submission, and obedience: Scripture bears divine authority.

4. *Postmodern.* If Scripture is a medium of divine speech, as its witness, then no longer should either the church or dogmatics follow Protestant

---

49. Convictions, note, not only about matters such as God, self, and world, but also about the Bible itself.

50. See *CD* I/2, 464–72, 722–36.

51. For recent magisterial and appreciative treatment of Bultmann, see Congdon, *Mission of Demythologizing*.

liberalism in placing contemporary mores next to or above Scripture; in that sense, Barthian bibliology is "post"-modern inasmuch as it is an attempt to move past the posture of modernity setting itself up over against Scripture as its enlightened judge.

5. *Exegesis*. Given this status accorded Scripture, if dogmatics would be faithful it must consist of nothing so much as unending, unexhausted interpretation of the Bible; theology, thunders Barth, that is not exegetically funded and determined from start to finish is no theology at all.

6. *Church*. The Bible is Holy Scripture in and for the church, and so essentially a churchly document, with the people of God as its primary audience. It is therefore in and for that community that the Bible is principally to be read, however scholarly that reading may seek to be.

7. *Historical criticism*. Because the Bible is a historical document and because the Bible speaks of historical happenings, inquiry into these historical features ought as a matter of course to be brought to bear on its interpretation. But historical criticism as such hardly comprehends, in truth it scarcely begins, the task of exegesis, and when viewed as the sole or primary work of interpretation it corrupts and occludes the true calling of the church's readers and hearers.

8. *Narrative*. As a historical book composed of two parts, one leading to and one following from its central event, the career of Jesus of Nazareth, the Bible is best read as a single, though complex, story. From creation, fall, and the calling of the covenant people Israel through the climax of the incarnation of the Word, including his death, resurrection, and ascension, to the gathering and sending of the church at Pentecost, Scripture is the great drama of the triune God together with humanity and should therefore be read as such.

9. *Israel*. The covenant did not begin with the annunciation but with Abraham,[52] nor is the New Testament the whole of Scripture, for the Law, the Prophets, and the Psalms preceded the apostles. Accordingly, neither Israel nor the Old Testament is peripheral to or superseded in the gospel, the church, and the Bible; both, rather, are an integral and abiding part of all of them.[53]

---

52. Though the calling of Abraham has the annunciation as its telos from the beginning. After all, "the scripture . . . preached the gospel beforehand to Abraham" (Gal 3:8; cf. Rom 10:4).

53. My summary account belies the complexity and indeed the failure of Barth's position on these matters. For the dialectics of Barth's stated views, see the compressed account in his *Dogmatics in Outline*, 72–81. Cf. Sonderegger, *Karl Barth's*

10. *Premodern.* It follows from the above affirmations that modern theology's rejection or skepticism of the premodern hermeneutical tradition is both unwarranted and unavoidably damaging to Christian faith and dogmatics. This tradition repays close study, one result of which is a reclamation of figural reading of Scripture; that is, reading for more than the plain sense, for meaning apparent only to the eyes of faith, spying divine resonances and evocations across the Testaments, not only retrospectively but prospectively as well.

These themes reappear in the coming chapters, and Part III takes stock of their influence in the thought of Webster, Jenson, and Yoder. We turn now, though, to these primary figures themselves, engaging each of their respective theologies considered in its own right.

"*Doctrine of Israel*"; Wyschogrod, *Abraham's Promise*, 211-24; Lindsay, *Barth, Israel, and Jesus.*

PART II

Which Church?

Division, Authority, and Catholicity

CHAPTER 3

John Webster

The Holiness of Scripture in the Reformed Church

Scripture is not the church's book . . . what the church hears in Scripture is not its own voice.[1]

The *Wissenschaftlichkeit* of exegesis is its orientation to Scripture as the church's book, that is, a text which has its place in that sphere of human life and history which is generated by God's revelation. To read it otherwise is not to read *it*, but to misread it by mislocating and therefore misconstruing the text.[2]

The question . . . is whether it is more appropriate to speak of the people of the book or the book of the people.[3]

Rejection of *sola scriptura* in favor of Scripture *and* tradition is . . . a corollary of a rejection of the ecclesiological implications of *solus Christus*.[4]

John Webster was a theologian's theologian.[5] Although his initial theological training did not prefigure it, Webster's professional trajectory was

---

1. *Confessing God*, 189. Citations in this chapter will include authorial attribution only for authors other than Webster.
2. *Word and Church*, 100.
3. *Word and Church*, 24.
4. *Word and Church*, 25.
5. Webster died on 25 May 2016, less than a month before his sixty-first birthday. A *Festschrift* in his honor published a year prior contains a rich selection of essays expounding topics related to his work: Nelson, Sarisky, and Stratis, *Theological Theology*. For obituaries and remembrances, see the "Editorial Announcement" in *International Journal of Systematic Theology* 18 (2016): 359; Davidson, "In Memoriam: John

marked by an ever-increasing appreciation of the classical intellectual heritage of the Christian tradition and, in particular, the integrity and dignity of the office of theologian. His public profile was quiet and unimposing, but his theological journey was far from static. After study of Barth ("the grand old man of Basel") rescued him from the methodological navel-gazing, as he saw it, of doctrinal criticism and modern philosophy,[6] he continued to move forward by looking further and further backward: to Reformed divines, to Lutheran scholastics, to the whole premodern inheritance of the church, not least such patristic and medieval masters as St. Augustine, St. Gregory the Great, and St. Thomas Aquinas. There he found a rich storehouse of penetrating perception of what he understood to be the great theme of Christian dogmatics: the singular perfection of God the Holy Trinity.[7]

Webster"; Allen, "Toward Theological Theology"; East, "John Webster, Theologian Proper." W. Travis McMaken has gathered more than two dozen links to online tributes at http://derevth.blogspot.com/2016/05/tributes-to-john-webster-index.html; and *Sapientia*, periodical of the Carl F. H. Henry Center for Theological Understanding, conducted a year-long tribute to Webster featuring one piece per month written by colleagues, students, and friends of Webster's, including Joseph Mangina, Fred Sanders, Stephen Holmes, and Kevin Vanhoozer: http://henrycenter.tiu.edu/2016/08/john-webster-1955-2016-theologian-essayist-and-friend-a-year-long-tribute/. Most recently, the first issue of volume 21 of *International Journal of Systematic Theology* (2019) featured five articles by senior scholars (Fred Sanders, Katherine Sonderegger, Ian A. McFarland, Darren Sarisky, and Oliver O'Donovan) engaging Webster's thought (1–92). Finally, two books authored by Webster have been published posthumously: *The Culture of Theology* (edited by Ivor J. Davidson and Alden C. McCray) and *Christ Our Salvation: Expositions and Proclamations* (edited by Daniel Bush).

6. "Discovering Dogmatics," 129–30.

7. See *Domain of the Word*, ix. In two newly republished editions of previous collections of essays, Webster has this to say (writing in January 2015): "Re-reading earlier work is, I suspect, often a discomfiting exercise; certainly there are things here which now I would say differently, or not at all. There are historical judgments to which I no longer subscribe, such as the criticisms of post-Reformation Protestant scholasticism. More importantly, there are dogmatic matters which in hindsight I would handle differently. The essays are relatively light in their treatment of God's immanent life and operations, partly because of an implicit, and again, characteristically modern, anxiety that talk of God apart from his transitive works opens the door to generic theism, and partly because when I wrote the essays I had yet to come to understand how God's inner perfection and bliss apart from creatures is the very ground of his relation to them. . . . Further, . . . I do not now think that theological talk of virtues and practices is necessarily excluded. The dangers of immanentism are best met by

Whatever the locus of doctrinal discussion, Webster believed that everything in theology turns on the one and only God, replete in himself, complete in beatitude, alone without want or need because full without measure.[8] Where theology forgets to begin and end with this One, declines to gaze in his direction with endless delight, and neglects to feast on him with inexhaustible adoration, theology has lost its way. For theology without the Lord at its center is theology unworthy of the name.

We come to know this God as he gives himself to us. Thus the doctrine of Scripture is ingredient within the dogmatic corpus. In addition to theology proper and christology, Webster devoted himself to the doctrine of Scripture with unflagging zeal across his career. When engaging Webster on this topic it will do the reader well to bear in mind the shifts in sources and modes alluded to above. For the most part I interpret Webster's writings as all of a piece, but occasionally I make a point to note where the Barthian register is more pronounced in his earlier as compared to his later work.[9] Scott Swain is right to call Webster's thought

---

attending to the structure of Christian teaching about creation, especially about God as the one who moves and perfects creaturely movements" (*Word and Church*, xi–xii). And second, echoing that last comment: "the account of the difference between God and the world would be less abstract and more persuasive, as well as more relaxed, if it were articulated through a doctrine of creation: as it stands, it risks a certain abstractness, and is dominated too strongly by the desire to run counter to naturalism" (*Confessing God*, x).

8. *Confessing God*, 1. See further Allen and Nelson, *Companion to the Theology of John Webster*; Fischer, *Preparing the Way*; Allen, "Theological Theology"; Wittman, "John Webster"; East, "Theology of John Webster."

9. See, e.g., *God without Measure*, 1:56–57, which discusses Barth's christocentrism; or the brief comment that Barth's "worry is . . . misplaced" regarding the doctrine of inspiration ("Inspiration of Holy Scripture," 246). It is notable that Webster only rarely criticized Barth in print; his shift away from Barth was no dogmatic patricide, throwing off the yoke of the outgrown teacher. It was the modest but real recognition that Barth's theology was not spotless; that some of his innovations were unnecessary, some of his rejections too speedy; and that, perhaps most damningly for the Barthian to admit, Barth was not the means of theology's deliverance from modernity's straitjacket. Hence the irony of D. A. Carson's line, in a review of Webster's *Holy Scripture: A Dogmatic Sketch*, that "Webster is more Barthian than biblical" ("Three More Books on the Bible," 11). Ivor Davidson shares a relevant anecdote: "'That's the Barthian view, I guess,' I once heard a speaker comment in reply to John's case about something; unsurprisingly when the 'B-' adjective is so deployed, the assessment was not meant as a compliment. 'I'm not interested in whether it's Barthian or not,' fired back John. 'The question is: Is it biblical?'" ("John," 32).

"dogmatic theology in a . . . Reformed and Thomistic key."[10] To whatever extent it remains Barthian, it is always Reformed and, by the end, tracks quite closely with the summative scholastic approach represented by St. Thomas and his heirs (not all of them Catholic).[11] Furthermore, it is worth mentioning that Webster was a British theologian ordained as a priest in the Church of England. He regularly preached the word and presided at the sacrament.[12] Yet he undertook his work in a national-cultural context of both formal establishment and post-Christian secularism.[13] This is distinct from the American contexts inhabited by Jenson and Yoder, even as Webster occupied the somewhat overlooked Calvin-friendly wing of that rambunctious communion called Anglicanism.[14] Finally, Webster's modus operandi as a theologian, not least with respect to modern and postmodern anxieties about method, was simply to get on with it.[15] In his words, "description is a great deal more interesting and

10. Swain, *God of the Gospel*, 7. See also Webster's late reflections in "Recent Developments in Dogmatics."

11. Consider two of Webster's late essays on moral issues, now collected in *God without Measure*, 1:5–27, 87–102. The first ("Where Christ Is") treats christology and ethics through commentary on St. Paul's Letter to the Colossians; the second ("Courage") more or less straightforwardly follows "Ambrose, Augustine, and Gregory, but most of all [Thomas Aquinas]" (89). Both essays, in other words, are contemporary glosses on ancient theological authorities, with Scripture having the priority. That, in a nutshell, is Webster's theological method.

12. See the two collections of his sermons: *Grace of Truth* and *Christ Our Salvation*.

13. I use this last term merely descriptively to denote widespread lack of commitment to or involvement in formal organized religious communities and their practices, beliefs, and traditions.

14. See, e.g., his "Ministry and Priesthood"; "Lambeth: A Comment"; "The Goals of Ecumenism"; "*Ut Unum Sint*."

15. See his comment in *Holiness*, 21: "[Theology] will . . . be characterized by a focused intensity; by getting on with its job, politely ignoring the dissuaders, declining pressing invitations to involve itself in all sorts of intramural work, and instead giving itself single-mindedly to building the walls of the city of God." See also *Holy Scripture*, 125–26: "Though Christian theology will certainly want to have its say in the conflict of the faculties, it will by no means feel itself compelled to wait for the resolution of that conflict before it can proceed. Rather than engaging in too much skirmishing about the nature of reason and its operations, an authentic Christian theology will simply go about its task with a measure of quiet determination, working under the tutelage and for the well-being of the spiritual community of which it is part and seeking thereby to fulfill its office." See finally "David F. Ford," 559: "This kind of theology [the kind commended by Webster] would require of the theologian a kind of ascesis, a laying aside, an *inattention* to all sorts of stimuli, and a dogged persistence in attending to a set of given

persuasive than apology." He thus "work[ed] on the assumption of the truthfulness and helpfulness of the Christian confession, and [did not] devote too much time and energy developing arguments in its favor or responses to its critical denials."[16] As fresh and emboldening as readers find this approach to be (and I am among them), we will see below that it is simultaneously Webster's greatest strength and his greatest weakness.

This chapter consists of three sections, a pattern that holds for the next two chapters. First, bibliology: Webster's theology of Holy Scripture as the sanctified instrument of the risen and ascended Lord Christ to teach, rebuke, enliven, and judge the church in its dispersed life among the nations. Second, ecclesiology: Webster's theology of the church as the creature of the divine Word, constituted by the divine address, and wholly recipient in the gift of faith confessed by the community across time. Third, analysis: here I unpack Webster's arrangement of the relevant dogmatic loci, focusing in particular on his coordination of the relationship between the doctrines of God, church, and Scripture. Explication and critique are interwoven in what follows; comparison with Jenson and Yoder must wait until Part III.

Bibliology: The Holiness of Scripture

This section takes up Webster's theology of Scripture. I consider, in sequence, the nature or ontology of Scripture, its character as a medium of Christ, and its reception in the church via canonization and interpretation. Close exposition of Webster's texts will give way to critique as the section moves toward ecclesiology. This shift is not an accident. There are serious issues with Webster's surprisingly contrastive depiction of divine and human agency, and these are felt most acutely when he turns

---

problems which at first sight are not very attractive or interesting or fruitful, but will in the end break our wills and so teach us true joy. Might it not be that such a theology—a bit stiff, a bit formal at times, clumsy and gauche to the cultural élite—will turn out to be not just edifying for the church but also for the church's conversation partners?"

16. "Discovering Dogmatics," 130. See also *Word and Church*, 10–11: "The account which follows is frankly dogmatic. It assumes the truth of the church's confession of the gospel, regarding that confession as a point from which we move rather than a point towards which we proceed. Readers disposed to anxiety about the viability of such an exercise will find little here to still their hearts. *Theologia non est habitus demonstrativus, sed exhibitivus.*" Cf. Griffiths, *Intellectual Appetite*, 1–6.

to ecclesial activity in relation to the canon of Scripture. The question this problem raises for us is whether the sort of thick account of divine action articulated by Webster must generate, or degenerate into, a thin ecclesiology. Or can it be retained without curtailing the full-bodied and mediating action of the church?

The Nature of Scripture

Webster's doctrinal matryoshka doll is both classical and Barthian. It begins with the doctrine of God the Trinity, whose life *in se* is perfect, simple, and complete, infinitely replete with fullness of life, beauty, goodness, and peace. God is *a se*; he needs neither to create nor, having created, to save fallen creatures. Yet this very fact is the condition of the possibility for salvation history: divine aseity is the ground of divine grace.[17]

The doctrine of the Trinity includes an account of the divine works both *ad intra* (the eternal processions of Son and Spirit) and *ad extra* (the temporal missions of Son and Spirit in the incarnation and the outpouring at Pentecost). Talk of the divine sendings leads, in turn, to discussion of the economy of grace, that is, the whole movement of God's free turning to fallen humanity, in which God communicates the fullness of himself in mercy and love to restore and elevate sinful and rebellious creatures to unbreakable fellowship with himself. As an element within this gracious movement, Holy Scripture serves and attests the self-communicative presence of God, through which God speaks, as from a human temple, the good news of the gospel of Christ.[18] Which is to say, through Scripture God the Word speaks the word of God.

How does Webster understand revelation? As he defines it, "revelation is the self-presentation of the triune God, the free work of sovereign mercy in which God wills, establishes and perfects saving fellowship with himself in which humankind comes to know, love and fear him above all things."[19] God is at once revelation's wholly free agent and

17. See here especially *God without Measure*, 1:13–28. With respect to Scripture, see "The Domain of the Word" and "Principles of Systematic Theology," in *Domain of the Word*, 3–31, 133–49. For broader comments on methodology, see "Introduction."

18. Webster takes this image from St. Augustine, *Teaching Christianity (De Doctrina Christiana)*, Prologue.6.

19. *Holy Scripture*, 13 (emphasis removed from the whole quotation). My next sentence draws on *Holy Scripture*, 13–17.

its content; the matter of revelation is nothing other than God's triune being in spiritual self-presence, initiated by nothing other than God's gracious will, and as such is a mystery. Furthermore, "revelation is purposive,"[20] it has a telos: the restoration of our nature, the establishment of fellowship, the perfection of our life with God. The work of revelation is one and the same as the work of reconciliation. God reveals as God saves, for "God's action towards the world is personal: not merely the operation of a causal force, but intentional action which establishes relations and proffers meaning."[21] "Revelation is [therefore] the corollary of trinitarian theology and soteriology."[22] In short, though talk of revelation may deal secondarily with questions of epistemology, or of faith and theology's sources and norms, "its material content . . . is the sovereign goodness of Father, Son and Spirit in willing, realizing and perfecting saving fellowship."[23]

From revelation Webster turns immediately to christology and bibliology, doctrinal loci bound together by one of the most dominant themes of his thought: "The gospel's God is eloquent: he does not remain locked in silence, but speaks."[24] More specifically, "God speaks as in the Spirit Jesus Christ speaks."[25] How so? Webster writes:

The eternal Word made flesh, now enthroned at the right hand of the Father, is present and eloquent. His state of exaltation does not entail his absence from or silence within the realm within which he once acted in self-humiliation; rather, his exaltation is the condition for and empowerment of his unhindered activity and address of creatures. This address takes the form of Holy Scripture. To accomplish

20. *Holy Scripture*, 15.
21. *Domain of the Word*, 7–8.
22. *Holy Scripture*, 17. See further the comment in *Word and Church*, 25n41: "Properly speaking, revelation is not a 'doctrine,' and certainly not a separate dogmatic *locus* (its separation is, in fact, part of the pathology of modern theology). Appeal to revelation is more like a *modus operandi* which pervades the entire dogmatic corpus, and which is a corollary of other primary doctrines (notably, the doctrines of Trinity and salvation)."
23. *Holy Scripture*, 17. One work (recently published at the time) in the background is Abraham, *Canon and Criterion*. Webster comments on the book a few pages later (24n22). See further his "Canon and Criterion."
24. *Grace of Truth*, 11. Cf. *Christ Our Salvation*, 155: "God is communicative . . . God isn't mute . . . God is a speaking God."
25. *Domain of the Word*, 8.

his communicative mission, the exalted Son takes into his service a textual tradition, a set of human writings, so ordering their course that by him they are made into living creaturely instruments of his address of living creatures. Extending himself into the structures and practices of human communication in the sending of the Holy Spirit, the divine Word commissions and sanctifies these texts to become fitting vehicles of his self-proclamation. He draws their acts into his own act of self-utterance, so that they become the words of the Word, human words uttered as a repetition of the divine Word, existing in the sphere of the divine Word's authority, effectiveness and promise.[26]

A number of things are worth drawing out further here.

First, the Bible is what it is—Holy Scripture—in virtue of divine action. Strictly speaking, this is universally true: everything that exists is what it is—insofar as it is created, sustained, ordered, and directed in being—in virtue of divine action, for this is only to say that God, as Creator, is providentially sovereign over creation. But the Bible is not what it is in the same way that, say, *The Iliad* and *Macbeth* are the texts that they are. God has a unique relationship to the texts of the biblical canon, such that together they *are* Holy Scripture: the servant of the divine address to intelligent creatures. "Scripture has its being in its reference to the activity of God"; apart from this reference, "it becomes reified into an independent entity whose nature and operations can be grasped apart from the network of relations in which it is properly located."[27] Such reification is a product not only of naturalist and non-theological approaches to the Bible; it happened first of all in "the gradual assimilation of Scripture into theological epistemology in the post-Reformation period,"[28] and can be seen as well in ostensibly "theological" proposals for interpretation of Scripture that strain to justify the presence of the modifier. For talk of God and God's action is not much in evidence.

Second, it follows that the Bible is not an end in itself,[29] nor should second-order consideration of how to read it overtake the principal object of theology's concern: namely, God and all things in God. Thus: "bibli-

26. *Domain of the Word*, 8.
27. *Word and Church*, 28.
28. *Word and Church*, 28.
29. Like the church, the book itself is only the proximate *res* of bibliology; the ultimate *res* is God in God's outer works of saving mercy. See *God without Measure*, 1:177–78.

ology is prior to hermeneutics," and both "are derivative elements of Christian theology."[30] Proper "depiction" of Holy Scripture therefore requires that one "deploy language of the triune God's saving and revelatory action."[31] Why? Answer: "The ruler and judge over all other Christian doctrines is the doctrine of the Holy Trinity,"[32] for "all other Christian doctrines are applications or corollaries of the one doctrine, the doctrine of the Trinity."[33] Within a different doctrinal locus, that of soteriology, Webster insists that the doctrine of justification is not, as Luther called it, the *articulus stantis et cadentis ecclesiae*, nor *rector et iudex super omnia genera doctrinarum*. Such claims attest the pathology of a (typically modern) dogmatic vision that subordinates aseity to promeity.[34] So with Scripture: it is not a free-standing or anthropocentric topic, but ordered to, and thus a subset of, the doctrine of the triune God.[35]

Third, dogmatics is, for Webster, "the servant of exegesis."[36] Bibliology, "as a piece of dogmatics," is therefore "wholly subordinate to the primary work of the church's theology, which is exegesis."[37] In this way the task of bibliology is doubly circumscribed: on one side by its theoretical subordination (to the doctrine of God), on the other by its practical subordination (to the task of exegesis). Theology of Scripture is a work of dogmatic *assistance*: it "cannot presume to anticipate or control exegetical work, to which it is an ancillary science," but assists exegesis "by portraying the field of exegetical activity, the divine and human agents in that field, the actions undertaken by these agents, and the ends which they serve. In this way it acts as an auxiliary to exegetical labor," helping "Christian exegetes [to] understand their place in the divine economy and so more fittingly perform the task to which they are appointed."[38] Exegesis is therefore "the theologically primary act,"[39] in the service of which dogmatics seeks to articulate theological knowl-

30. *Domain of the Word*, viii.
31. *Holy Scripture*, 1.
32. *God without Measure*, 1:159.
33. *Holy Scripture*, 43.
34. See "*Rector et iudex super omnia genera doctrinarum?* The Place of the Doctrine of Justification," in *God without Measure*, 1:159-75.
35. Cf. the discussion in *Domain of the Word*, 7, 145-46.
36. *God without Measure*, 1:168.
37. *Confessing God*, 36.
38. *Confessing God*, 36-37. See also *Holy Scripture*, 107-35; *Holiness*, 17-21.
39. *Domain of the Word*, 130.

edge with conceptual rigor and analytical clarity. This knowledge should inform, even as it is judged by, further exegesis of particular scriptural texts.[40] Moreover, dogmatics—including dogmatics of Scripture—does not improve upon the text.[41] The words of Scripture are, to be sure, subject to the reality they bear witness to, but dogmatic concepts are in turn subject to those words. The Bible's role for theology, as for faith, is less Wittgenstein's ladder than Jacob's: for the perpetual ascending and descending of contemplation and action, not for kicking away once the top is reached.[42]

Fourth, in virtue of divine action, the Bible has an ontology: it *is* something concrete and determinate because God wills to make it so.[43] That something is Holy Scripture, the instrument of the risen and ascended Christ's speech to the church and the world. The prophets and apostles "are an embassy of God's eloquence. . . . [And] Holy Scripture is the textual settlement of this embassy."[44] This settlement is a matter of God's determination, apart from and prior to our affirmation and reception of it, which follows upon, acknowledges, and confirms what God has in fact done in prevenient grace. Texts are creatures,[45] and the canonical writings comprise those textual creatures uniquely and definitively caught up in the wake of Christ's reality-determining death and resurrection as servants and auxiliaries of the proclamation of the gospel. In this way they are "eschatological signs,"[46] that is, signs bent and ordered to a horizon—the inbreaking reign of God—beyond the merely immanent or

40. *Domain of the Word*, 130–31.

41. *Domain of the Word*, 131.

42. Or, perhaps, only to be kicked away by God in the eschaton. (One also thinks of the eighth chapter of *Moby-Dick*, in which Father Mapple mounts the "very lofty" pulpit not by stairs but by "a perpendicular side ladder, like those used in mounting a ship from a boat at sea." Upon finishing his climb, the preacher drags the ladder up to himself, "leaving him impregnable in his little Quebec." The ladder, in short, descends and ascends solely for the occasion of the proclamation of the word of God. See Melville, *Moby-Dick*, 43.)

43. Webster repurposes the term from the critique of Wilfred Cantwell Smith, *What Is Scripture?*, 237: "*There is no ontology of Scripture.* The concept has no metaphysical, nor logical, reference; there is nothing that scripture finally 'is.'"

44. *Domain of the Word*, 120–21.

45. Not *living* creatures, which the term popularly conjures up, but, as inanimate, creatures nonetheless. By analogy, consider liturgical talk of the eucharistic elements as "creatures."

46. *Domain of the Word*, 39.

historical, even as they remain, like all signs, created, contingent, natural, temporal. "In sum: the biblical text *is* Scripture; its being is defined, not simply by its membership of the class of texts, but by the fact that it is *this* text—sanctified, that is, Spirit-generated and preserved—in *this* field of action—the communicative economy of God's merciful friendship with his lost creatures."[47] How best to describe the character of this ontology-bestowing divine work?

Webster's proposed term is *sanctification*. By this he means "the act of God the Holy Spirit in hallowing creaturely processes, employing them in the service of the taking form of revelation within the history of the creation."[48] Put differently, "sanctification refers to the work of the Spirit of Christ through which creaturely realities are elected, shaped and preserved to undertake a role in the economy of salvation: creaturely realities are sanctified by divine use."[49] Why does Webster choose this term, what does it entail, and how does it relate to other bibliological terminology?

More than anything, sanctification is Webster's attempt to avoid the Scylla of naturalism and the Charybdis of supernaturalism, which he sees as the besetting temptations of Christian bibliology. (The analogy to christology, regarding Christ's human and divine natures, is suggestive, but it fails in important ways.)[50] Perennially, approaches to understanding and reading the Bible construe it *either* as "a book like any other," divorced or abstracted from its location within the wider economy of revelation and redemption, and so reduced to the natural-historical processes of authorial text-production common to all cultures, times, and places;[51] *or* as a book liberated of creatureliness, elevated to heavenly status, denuded of historical particularity, human authorship, contingent cultural features, and the like.[52] A properly Christian theology of Scripture, according to Webster, must find a way to describe the Bible's sui

---

°

47. *Holy Scripture*, 29.

48. *Holy Scripture*, 17–18.

49. *Holy Scripture*, 26.

50. See Webster's brief critique in *Holy Scripture*, 22–23; *Domain of the Word*, 13. Cf. Work, *Living and Active*; Castelo and Wall, *Marks of Scripture*.

51. See Jowett, "On the Interpretation of Scripture." Cf. Morgan with Barton, *Biblical Interpretation*.

52. This approach is revealed more in practice than in theory, at least in academic scholarship on the contemporary scene, but samples of this tendency may be found in Reventlow, *History of Biblical Interpretation*, vol. 2.

generis character relative to other texts, as a product and vehicle of divine action and use, without sacrificing its creaturely character as a result. Sanctification is his attempt to chart that middle path.

The many reasons for Webster's choice are themselves rooted in Scripture. Sanctification is a divine act ("for I the Lord, I who sanctify you, am holy"; Lev 21:8), and traditionally appropriated to the Holy Spirit (cf. Rom 15:16). Holiness is an essential attribute of God, but is nonetheless the high calling of God's people: "You shall be holy, for I am holy" (Lev 11:45; 1 Pet 1:16). It is therefore one of the four classical marks of the church ("one holy catholic and apostolic"), understood not as an innate property but as the gracious act of God in the creation of a people for himself, such that "holiness" both names God's *gift to* Israel/church and is *synonymous with* its existence as a people in the world. This is because its peoplehood is one and the same as its identity as having been set apart from the world by God's acts of deliverance and mercy in exodus and resurrection, at Sinai and Pentecost. Jesus prays to the Father, "Sanctify them by the truth; your word is truth" (John 17:17 RSV). The Holy Trinity sanctifies a people for himself, the church (1 Pet 2:9), through the work and presence of the incarnate Holy One and his Holy Spirit (Acts 2:14-36; Heb 13:12; 1 Cor 6:11), in the sanctifying power (1 Tim 4:5) of his "holy word" (Jer 23:9), attested and heard in Holy Scripture—which, by God, is itself set apart for the church's ongoing holiness, faithfulness, and righteousness (2 Tim 3:16). Sanctification is thus a densely packed biblical term at the cross-section of a number of important and relevant theological matters, including the Trinity, divine action, divine attributes, the church, mission, salvation, revelation, and the Holy Spirit. No term is perfect, as Webster readily admits; "all that matters is [its] fittingness for the task of orderly explication of the matter itself."[53] But given the options available, sanctification is his preferred alternative.

How does sanctification relate to inspiration, the more traditional affirmation of Scripture? Just as sanctification is set within the larger scope of divine revelation, so inspiration is set within a wider account of God's action to sanctify the biblical texts. That is to say, inspiration is one among many aspects of Scripture's sanctification, making the latter the more general and the former the more specific term. In this way sanctification includes all "the processes of the production of the text—not simply authorship . . . but also the complex histories of pre-literary and

___

53. *Holy Scripture*, 10.

literary tradition, redaction and compilation," and further extends "to the post-history of the text, most particularly to canonization . . . and to interpretation."[54] Sanctification is therefore at once a completed act and an ongoing process, akin to the sanctification of the church and of individual believers. Scripture *is* holy, even as it *is being made* holy in the life of the church, as the church receives, acclaims, translates, publishes, reads, reasons about, disputes over, listens to, contests, wrestles with, exposits, comments on, contemplates, and proclaims the inspired text, in the illuminating power of the Holy Spirit.

What then of inspiration? Whereas sanctification has to do with the whole sweep of Scripture's history, formation, and reception considered *sub specie spiritus sancti*, inspiration concerns the Bible's textuality: the production, by the Holy Spirit through human persons and communities, of *this particular text*, with a view to its author(s), content, and verbal form. Indeed, the doctrine of inspiration is but a conceptual explication of the apostolic claim that "all Scripture is inspired by God" (2 Tim 3:16), for "no prophecy of scripture . . . ever came by human will, but [human beings] moved by the Holy Spirit spoke from God" (2 Pet 1:20–21). Inspiration says: Holy Scripture, though human-authored, is somehow or other also, and primarily, caused or authored by the Holy Spirit. Much could be said of Webster's account of the "somehow or other," but, given its continuity with the Reformed orthodox and Lutheran scholastics, the details need not detain us.[55] Suffice it to say that, qualified by concerns about over-inflating inspiration to the point of its becoming the principal topic of bibliology rather than being merely one element of it, Webster affirms the divine work of the Spirit's inspiration of the scriptures. According to this work, the canon's human authors freely willed to write what God sovereignly willed that they write, so that both the form and the matter of the biblical texts are the product of God's action, neither more nor less than what God desired them to be.[56]

What of inspiration's upshot? Having earlier asserted that "God speaks as in the Spirit Jesus Christ speaks," Webster now, following this

---

54. *Holy Scripture*, 30.

55. For the details, see his late essay "Inspiration of Holy Scripture."

56. This late affirmation is somewhat at odds with his earlier unease with strong scholastic accounts of inspiration. This section and the next seek to represent the scope of Webster's written work as it stands, while noting (mostly in the footnotes) where there is discrepancy or a change of mind. See my similar comment below about ecclesiology and the cultivation of virtue through habitual action.

understanding of inspiration, revises the claim to say that "God speaks *as inspired Scripture speaks.*"[57] Holy Scripture's inspiration means "that the Spirit teaches discursively, *through these words.*"[58] And so:

> The words which the Spirit provides and employs are a *settlement* of the divine Word. This is not meant in the sense that Scripture constitutes a deposit of "inspiredness" which does its job in isolation from God's continuous relation to it. . . . Rather, with God's breathing of Holy Scripture, a stage is reached in the self-publication of the divine Word from which all subsequent reception of the Word will derive and by which it will be determined. After inspiration, there is for creatures *in via* no further—clearer, more immediate, more expansive—communication of the Word of God. At least in the temporal economy, the prophets and apostles will not be superseded, as if they were merely stages on the way to a more comprehensive revelation. After inspiration there comes, not more inspiration, but hearing, receiving, contemplation of the Word which *has been* uttered; what comes next is *lectio.*[59]

Inspiration is a kind of eschatological closure, a provisional but definitive act of divine communication in the time between the times. What comes next is neither more prophets nor more apostles, but reading what the prophets and apostles have written, once for all.

Together, sanctification and inspiration are Webster's two most emphatic moves in describing Scripture's ontology. The result is a salutary proposal for avoiding the two dangers identified above; dangers that lead to either the human or the divine element crowding out the other. Some theologians draw an analogy to christology at this point, seeing a correspondence between the natures of Christ and the attributes of Scripture. Webster is right to hesitate before that analogy and to pursue instead an alternative conceptual strategy. In what follows I explore this strategy and how it seeks to strike a balance between two positively correlated affirmations of Holy Scripture, which we might combine in this way: the canon (1) is united in and by Christ (2) as a medium distinct from him. Which is to say, the Bible mediates the revelatory presence of Christ without rendering it immediate.

---

57. *Domain of the Word,* 16 (emphasis mine).
58. *Domain of the Word,* 17 (emphasis mine).
59. *Domain of the Word,* 17.

Scripture as the Medium of Christ

As "high" a doctrine of Scripture as Webster proposes, it never elides the distinction between revelation proper and the biblical text,[60] which he describes variously as revelation's servant, auxiliary, and instrument. Revelation is one and the same as Jesus Christ, the eternal Word of God become a human being in our midst, who suffered, died, was buried, rose again, ascended into heaven, and is seated at the right hand of God the Father. Scripture is a double-edged sword in the hand of Christ to rule, slay, and redeem. It is not Christ himself, now become text.[61] Rather, it is what the prophets and apostles were when alive, only in textual form. Nobody confuses the servant for the master, the embassy for the king, the sent for the sender. So too for Scripture: though it bears the Word, it is not itself the Word; though it testifies to the Lord, it is but the finger of the Baptist, not the One to whom his finger points; though it speaks the truth, tells of the way, and communicates life, it is not itself the Way, the Truth, and the Life. Encounter with the word of Scripture is not unmediated encounter with that word's speaker; it is an encounter, to be sure, but it is a *mediated* encounter. Desire for immediacy is either eschatological hope—desire for the beatific vision, unattainable this side of death—or sinful presumption—desire for more than what God has deigned to give, something other than what we in fact have.

Webster frames this concern by reference to what he calls "the pathos which necessarily attends all theological work," part of which is "the fact that we are instructed to receive the divine Word in these contingent forms—to hear, not God's own voice in unmediated force and power to persuade, but God's voice as it has been heard and then repeated by other creatures." The "enduring struggle for . . . [Christian] theology of Scrip-

60. Which is not to say that it does not come close. In *Domain of the Word* he writes of "the Word of God" as "revelation in its presence as Holy Scripture" (139). In the same volume, however, he is crystal clear: "God gives his Word to the prophets and apostles, but God does not become their words" (13). In any case, the consistent point for Webster regarding Scripture's "mediateness" is not that it *separates* or *distances* Scripture from revelation, but rather that it names the proper *relationship* between the two. It is forgetting or overlooking that relationship, or that there is a relationship in the first place (rather than simple identity), that Webster is concerned to counter.

61. Stated clearly, though as an exposition of Barth: "Scripture is witness: it is not identical with revelation, but that instrument through which the testimony of the prophets and apostles is set before us" (*Word and Church*, 95). See the continued discussion following this quotation in 95-98.

ture," accordingly, is "coming to terms with revelation's embeddedness in the realm of temporal forms, including linguistic and literary forms." Try as it might, "theology cannot resolve scriptural mediacy into revelatory immediacy; and it must not simply bear with it or kick against the goads, but learn to profit from it as that which God has designed. The divine Word speaks as this form."[62] Consequently, "There is no straight line from the text to the speech or Word of God, and its human language is not something of which divine speech can be unambiguously predicated. Here God speaks in a veiled form, sacramentally."[63] In the reading and hearing of the text, "God's agency is real and effective and yet indirect";[64] and it is that indirectness that gets at the heart of Webster's emphasis on Scripture's irreducible mediateness.

Scripture is mediate because it is a medium of Jesus Christ. In all their diversity, the texts of Scripture are a unified instrument of the risen Lord's self-presentation. That they are one is Christ's work just as much as their being Scripture at all: ontology and unity, nature and attribute, are two aspects of the very same divine action. The picture of Jesus found in the finale of St. Luke's Gospel is to the fore here: Jesus, risen in hidden glory, opening up the scriptures, interpreting them with unique authority, and revealing "what was said in all the scriptures concerning himself" (24:27 NIV; cf. vv. 13–35).[65] Therefore, what makes the disparate texts of Scripture a unity—which is to say, a unified medium of Christ—is what might be called their christological ontology: their provenance, production, and purpose have Christ alone as their source, agent, and end. Scripture's *res* is nothing other than "the mystery of the gospel,"[66] glossing "the gospel" as "the good news of Jesus Christ, who is its sum and substance."[67] As "a creaturely auxiliary of the exalted Lord's self-proclamation,"[68] Scripture is one in virtue of Christ's action through the Spirit, as he authors it, sanc-

---

62. *Domain of the Word*, 9.

63. *Word and Church*, 73. In his earlier formulations, Webster used the language of "sacramental" action as the proper register for understanding the relation of Scripture to divine speech (see further on 74, where it is positively recommended). He seems to have left this behind, however. See the brief critique in *Holy Scripture*, 24–25. See also, however, his remarks about "mediated divine action" and Scripture in *God without Measure*, 1:191.

64. *Word and Church*, 74.

65. See esp. Webster's comments in *Domain of the Word*, 38–41.

66. *Domain of the Word*, 61.

67. "What Is the Gospel?," 109.

68. *Domain of the Word*, 38.

tifies it for a particular end, and orders every jot and tittle to himself. "In him all things hold together" (Col 1:17)—including the Bible.

The result is at once christological, ecclesiological, and hermeneutical: "The biblical texts . . . are acts of communication in the present," whose "communicative agent . . . is the risen Jesus Christ."[69] To be sure, "the original communicative agents (writers/tradents/recipients) are not displaced, but rather become relative to Jesus Christ who is now *auctor primarius* of the texts' address. As the risen one takes Scripture to himself and deploys it to speak of himself and of all things in his light, he reorders its reference so that by Scripture we are directed to his present word as that in which these past acts of communication are brought to fulfillment."[70] In short, the biblical "texts are servants [of] the eternal Son," and "by him they are held together . . . as a company of emissaries appointed to do his bidding as the history of his revelation to creatures unfolds."[71]

Webster's bibliology is centered on Christ because it is centered on God, and it is this bifocal approach that both permits and necessitates the emphasis on mediateness. It is permitted because Webster's christological maximalism entails that Christ's status and action are not undermined by a text that remains truly human, unelevated to quasi-divine status. And it is necessitated because to make Scripture less than creaturely, "more" divine, and therefore immediate *would* undermine Christ's status and action, in the sense that it would render Christ impotent, inert, inactive relative to a text into which he, or his role, had been assimilated, emptied out, exhausted. (In his *kenosis* Christ remains what he was, and so do the canonical texts.) Revelation would no longer name the omnipotent living Lord who reigns from heaven, speaking through Scripture as from a human temple. It would be convertible without remainder with this set of texts, bound in a book grasped by mortal hands;

---

69. *Domain of the Word*, 42. See also *Grace of Truth*, 77, 80, 87, 153, 221.

70. *Domain of the Word*, 42–43 (the original has "tridents" [*sic*]). The tense of the verbs used of Christ here raises the question of time and chronology. Does Christ "take up" and "reorder" the texts of Scripture *consequent* to their production, after their having come to be? If not—if Christ commissioned and directed their production from the beginning, by the Spirit—then why do they need "reordering"? What does such an action accomplish? Why do they not already bear christological meaning and reference "prior" to the risen Christ's taking them up? On their face, Webster's claims are ontological, not epistemological, but I doubt retrocausality is in view.

71. *Domain of the Word*, 18.

a kind of textual incarnation, the written Word of God *simpliciter*. For Webster, the Bible must never become this, as it has at times for Protestants since the Reformation. Twofold emphasis on Scripture's mediate character and on its christological ontology—its having, as all reality has, Christ as its Alpha and Omega—is Webster's way of avoiding divinizing Scripture without naturalizing it as a result.

That Christ is simultaneously Scripture's primary speaker and its principal referent—its *auctor primarius* and its *res*—grounds and confers its unity, which in turn is one of Scripture's chief attributes. Such attributes are properties of Scripture that result from its unique status in the divine economy. Classical discussion of these features arose in post-Reformation Protestant doctrines of Scripture. Though we need not enter into extensive engagement with Webster's account of Scripture's attributes,[72] two are worth discussing: authority and canonicity. These will serve as a bridge to the next section on Webster's ecclesiology. For the authority of Scripture is directly related to its ends, and is therefore intimately connected to the church. As we have seen, for Webster talk of Scripture's nature precedes talk of Scripture's function in the life of the church, just as talk of God *in se* and of God's works of love *ad extra* ground and frame talk of Scripture itself. Having done this necessary preliminary theological work—examining Webster's understanding of what Scripture is in relation to the triune God, his will and action, and the economy of grace—we are now in a position to turn to Scripture's ends, as Scripture is received in the church in the form of a sacred canon bearing divine authority in its midst.

The Reception of Scripture

Though we are in the realm of the church, we remain in the locus of the doctrine of Scripture. Why? Because, as Webster insists, the hearing and reading of Scripture is not, simply in virtue of its being human activity, thereby transferred from the prevenient and saving sovereignty of divine activity. The life of the church is not a sphere of merely human, social, or phenomenal activity, such that description of it in non-theological terms would be sufficient to the task. Its special character means that

---

72. Such an account emerges ad hoc across Webster's essays, with the exception of clarity: see, e.g., *Confessing God*, 33–68; *Holy Scripture*, 91–106.

Scripture's place within it calls for irreducibly theological description, beginning with its authority.

"The authority of Scripture," writes Webster, "is its Spirit-bestowed capacity to quicken the church to truthful speech and righteous action."[73] It is Spirit-bestowed because it is a function of divine action and self-presence, and because it is not conferred by the church on Scripture but is antecedent to the church's reception or use thereof. Authority names the kind of rule Scripture has in the church; such rule, far from being isolated or an end in itself, "is an aspect of God's [own] saving rule."[74] Scripture's authority is thus "its power to command thought, speech and action by virtue of the fact that it brings to bear upon its hearer the purpose of the one who presents himself through its service."[75] That purpose is, most of all, soteriological: "the content of Scripture [is] the gospel of salvation and [therefore] the directedness of Scripture [is] towards the enabling of life in truthful fellowship with God through the ordering of the church's speech and action."[76]

Scripture's authority, in sum, is ordered to the saving work of the triune God. Its business consists entirely in being the means of Christ's conduction, by the Spirit, of reconciled sinners from all manner of folly and ruin into covenant fellowship with, and saving knowledge of, God the Father. This soteriological telos follows the logic of Webster's christocentric account, and brings with it an important implication for understanding the status of Scripture's ordered authority in the church. If "the authority of Scripture is the authority of the church's Lord and his gospel," then it "cannot be made an immanent feature of ecclesial existence." Here is Webster's polemical point: "Scripture's authority *within* the church is a function of Scripture's authority *over* the church."[77] Over against functionalist, sociological, and postmodern accounts of religious

73. *Holy Scripture*, 52. Cf. *Word and Church*, 224.
74. *Domain of the Word*, 19.
75. *Domain of the Word*, 122.
76. *Holy Scripture*, 56.
77. *Holy Scripture*, 56. This sentence is almost verbatim what Barth writes in *Church Dogmatics* I/2, 574: "the Evangelical confession of the Word of God includes a confession of the authority of the Church. . . . But before we say a single word about the authority of the Church—and this is the parting of the ways where the Evangelical decision is ineluctably and irrevocably made—we have to insist that there is an authority *in* the Church which is also an authority *over* the Church. This authority is itself the basis of all authority in the Church": namely, the authority of the word of God in Holy Scripture.

textual authority as being the community's own authority "invested" in its sacred text(s),[78] Webster argues that the Bible's authority precedes and conditions the church's recognition of its divinely authored authority. He does not deny that, in its role as authoritative text, the Bible has been abused (which is to say, has been used to hurt people). But he does deny that making it "a function of [ecclesial] society"[79] is the way to solve the problem, for the problem remains: the community's contingent whims and mores go on arbitrarily harming people, now with the cover of a text it stands over, rather than beneath.[80] "What is needed . . . is a dogmatic move: the reintegration of the authority of Scripture into the doctrine of God, . . . removing [the] affirmation [of Scripture's authority] from the sphere of the politics of invention, and restricting the church's office to the pedagogical one of confessing or attesting that Scripture's authority flows from its given place in the economy of grace."[81]

Webster argues that, if the church is conceived in strictly social terms, it absorbs Scripture into itself, thereby denuding its authority. Scriptural authority becomes a function of ecclesial authority: Scripture speaks when, where, and what the church speaks; Scripture's voice becomes the church's voice, no longer the voice of its head and Lord. *Sed contra*, says Webster: "Scripture is not the church's book,[82] something internal to the community's discursive practices; what the church hears in Scripture is not its own voice. It is not a store of common meanings or a Chris-

---

78. See the classic statement in Kelsey, *Proving Doctrine*.

79. *Holy Scripture*, 54.

80. The contested question here is whether the Bible "itself" is a harmful document, that is, a text conducive to or responsible for harmful consequences wrought in people's lives. There are two common responses to an affirmative answer. On the one hand, an anti-essentialist objection contests the notion of texts as agents capable of action or culpability, as though texts can "do" anything at all apart from human beings who read them and put them to particular uses (for good or ill). On the other hand, a theological objection asks whether, if the canon of Holy Scripture is in itself and as such a harmful document, the church ought to revise, reorganize, or reject it. Webster is amenable to the first response, theologically modified by an account of divine agency, and follows the *reductio* of the second response by disputing the premise.

81. *Holy Scripture*, 54-55.

82. Though see the differently inflected use of this phrase in *Word and Church* regarding Bonhoeffer's approach to biblical interpretation: "the *Wissenschaftlichkeit* of exegesis is its orientation to Scripture as the church's book, that is, a text which has its place in that sphere of human life and history which is generated by God's revelation. To read it otherwise is not to read *it*, but to misread it by mislocating and therefore misconstruing the text" (100).

tian cultural code,"[83] "not . . . simply one more aspect of the ordered statutory life of the community."[84] Furthermore, just as the church is understood, on the scheme being criticized here, in terms of other social groups, so the Bible comes to be understood in terms of other texts. Whatever sociological, philosophical, and hermeneutical analysis suggests texts-in-general are, and in particular what they are in the context of communities-in-general, is thereby applied without qualification to what the texts of Scripture must be in the community of the Christian church.[85] The specifically *theological* mistake here, according to Webster, "is the dogmatic mislocation of Scripture in ecclesiality," rather than in the doctrine of revelation, itself rooted in the doctrine of God the Trinity. A dogmatically mislocated account of Scripture, "by treating Scripture as a semiotic *positum* in the culture of the church as visible social entity, . . . risks severing the transcendent reference of both church and Scripture."[86] Bibliology must, therefore, insist on Scripture's authority *over* the church lest it be subsumed into the church's own life, thus robbing the church of its very being and sustenance, converting communication into solipsism.

Given this account of Scripture's authority in the church, what of its reception? How does Webster describe the process of canonization, the practice of interpretation, and the human and ecclesial activities involved in both?

That Holy Scripture is a canon means, in the formulation of David Kelsey, that the body of texts that constitute the church's scriptures is not merely a collection of authoritative texts, but an authoritative collection of texts.[87] For Webster, the canon is, as with all else in the doctrine of Scripture, a matter of divine action. The "dogmatic mislocation" mentioned above "occurs when the Christian theology of Scripture is transplanted out of its proper soil—essentially, the saving economy of the triune God—and is made to do duty as a foundational

---

83. *Confessing God*, 189.
84. *Holy Scripture*, 48.
85. *Holy Scripture*, 48-49. See the comment in *Word and Church*: "Dogmatic portrayal of the canon . . . involves a good deal more than offering an ecclesial gloss to a sociology of texts and their uses" (25). Webster has in mind the work of, e.g., Jeanrond, *Text and Interpretation*; Jeanrond, *Theological Hermeneutics*; Green, *Imagining God*; Green, *Theology, Hermeneutics, and Imagination*; Smith, *Fall of Interpretation*.
86. *Holy Scripture*, 49.
87. See Kelsey, *Eccentric Existence*, 132-56.

doctrine."[88] The consequent shift, made partly in response to resulting destabilizations in the doctrine of Scripture, to make ecclesiology "first theology"—to shift, that is, the foundation from text to community—does not improve the situation. The texts that make up the canon are not there by accident; their collection is not the arbitrary or random product of human caprice and they did not receive, as it were, the divine stamp of approval only after the fact: as if, once the church closed the canon, God seconded the opinion. Rather, canonization is an element, like inspiration, of the divine work of Scripture's sanctification, in which "the texts are segregated by a divine decision to play a role in the divine self-manifestation."[89] Humanly speaking, canonization is "akin to a muddled set of interwoven processes,"[90] in which the church acted to include or exclude certain texts as its sacred writings. "What is needed," then, is not a denial of such human decision-making, but "a theological account of the church's action at this point."[91]

The work of Christ and the Spirit saturates Webster's account of canonization. Webster follows Calvin's rhetoric in describing the church's canonizing acts as approving, receiving, recognizing, assenting, confessing, and submitting, rather than authorizing, bestowing, judging, or asserting.[92] Canonicity, Webster writes, is finally unexempt from the central truth of every "other element in the church," namely, that it "is a matter of grace, of a divine promise attached to a creaturely reality."[93] By the Spirit's energizing aid, the flock of the church hears and recognizes the voice of its shepherd in these and not other texts, and gladly, gratefully acknowledges the fact.

The question for us to consider is whether Webster has overcompensated, correcting primary emphasis on human activity by creating an imbalance in the other direction. Lewis Ayres argues that he has. Re-

---

88. *Word and Church*, 9.

89. *Word and Church*, 31.

90. *Holy Scripture*, 58n32.

91. *Holy Scripture*, 58.

92. *Holy Scripture*, 61–66 (passim): As "an act of approval," it is "a receptive rather than an authorizing act." It is recognition, not bestowal; "Spirit-guided assent," not "self-derived judgment"; "normed compliance," not autonomous assertion. It is an act of confession that is, finally, "an act of submission before it is an act of authority," for it identifies "a set of human activities, attitudes and relations which refer beyond themselves to prevenient divine acts of speaking and sanctifying."

93. *Holy Scripture*, 66. Again, Webster's language is fundamentally sacramental.

garding Scripture's canonization, Ayres writes that "Webster so carefully separates the authority of scripture from the Church ... expressly in order to preserve God's freedom in action," since, in reformed traditions, "to emphasize the role of the historical community of Christians in forming the canonical scripture is to undercut the true relationship between God's giving of the canon and the church's acknowledgment and reception of that divine gift."[94] To this, Ayres offers two comments in response.

[First:] To see the Church as *given* its ability to distinguish the canon of scripture from other texts that might have been included, may be understood as God's gracious giving to humanity of free and appropriate actions that serve the unity of the body of Christ as a faithful, contemplative and speculative community. Viewing the actions of those drawn into the body of Christ as necessarily in competition with the "direct" action of God, is not a road we need travel if we also have an account of redemption in which human beings are drawn by grace into true freedom. ... [Second:] the very project of separating so clearly the gift of scripture and human recognition of that gift becomes much more complex once one recognizes that scripture grew more and more fully into being what we may call classically scripture not simply when it was "recognized" but when the Church learned how it was to be read. Church and scripture once again become deeply interwoven.[95]

Ayres sees the problem clearly. If Webster affirms the judgment that divine action and human action are not, in principle, competitive with each other—and he does—then there is no reason why he cannot affirm what Ayres suggests here: namely, that just as the Spirit's inspiration elicits free agency in human authors writing what God desires to be written, so the Spirit's presence in and to the church graces it with the ability to discriminate *between* those texts that are inspired (and so fit for service as instruments of divine speech) and those that are not (however edifying they may nonetheless be).[96] Not only is this picture theologically at-

94. Ayres, "Reading Allegorically," 624.

95. Ayres, "Reading Allegorically," 624-25. Cf. Matthew Levering's similar critique in his *Christ and the Catholic Priesthood*, 144n50; cf. 29n22; 137n42.

96. The Spirit surely continues to enable and empower the church's ongoing interpretation and embodiment of Scripture; whether or not this should be called "inspiration," or whether that term should remain technical, as a specific description of the process of the canonical texts' occasions of inscription, is an open question. Jenson,

tractive, it is surely closer to what actually happened: Christian believers discussing, disputing, and discerning which texts should be counted as trustworthy, as *graphai hagiai*, such that they could be read with confidence and trust in local church communities. Such processes involved much labor, energy, ambiguity, and self-assertion. Doubtless they admit, on the whole and retrospectively, of being described as something like an extended movement of reception or submission to God. But if such description has little purchase on the actual beliefs, motives, attitudes, and actions of the people involved, and if that bundle of human emotions and activities is not somehow theologically problematic, it stands to reason that Ayres's account is more compelling, inasmuch as it accounts for the process of Scripture coming to be recognized *as* Scripture in a way fitting to both human and divine activity, without subjecting the latter to the former, or dominating the former by the latter.

It is important to see that this is not an extrinsic critique of Webster's project, but proceeds on his own terms. Divine action is aboriginal and sovereign, but neither cancels nor mitigates creaturely action; divine action is the wellspring of creaturely action, that which makes it more alive, more powerful, drawing it to its final cause in irresistible grace. On such a schema creaturely action cannot threaten divine action, whether in reality or at the conceptual level. Yet there remains in Webster a reticence here, something like a theological anxiety, as though to offer a three-dimensional portrait of canonization as consisting of wholly human (though not solely human) acts would qualify divine action, or make it redundant. This anxiety appears in the realm of hermeneutics, too.

Webster frames exegesis, as he does canonization, by the prevenient works of Son and Spirit, in the context of the economy of grace, in the social space of the community of the Word. Exegesis is "the fundamental

---

as we shall see in the next chapter, opts for the former. I side with Webster in opting for the latter option, finding his use of "sanctification" for the entire sweep of Scripture's life (from beginning to end) to be more helpful as an overarching category. For particular moments within that sanctifying movement, Paul J. Griffiths (*Song of Songs*, xxiii–xxxiv) applies the eucharistic term "confection" to denote that set of temporally extended corporate ecclesial actions whereby Scripture comes to be in its fullness: from inscription through preservation and liturgical use to reception, translation, and formal approval. In a similar vein, I find it fitting to apply the term "chrismation" to denote the closure of the canon by the church's authorized leaders: the sacramental seal that confirms and declares the fact and the scope of the Spirit's unique work upon and within this collection of texts—and no other. See further East, *Doctrine of Scripture*, 32, 60.

theological responsibility."[97] Theological reason is therefore "exegetical reason," which issues from a "hermeneutical conversion" on the part of the Christian reader, a conversion wrought by the Spirit's power.[98] The result is regenerate readers who "read Scripture with faith," which means that they "read Holy Scripture as those who acknowledge that they are within the reality of saving grace."[99] Exegesis is thus "an episode in the history of sin and its overcoming," and "can only occur as a kind of brokenness, a relinquishment of willed mastery of the text,"[100] compelling the reader to a kind of exegetical epiclesis: that is, to "invocation of the Spirit, which is the basic act of existence in Christ. Christian reading is thus, very simply, a *prayerful* activity."[101] Conversion to faith, the encompassing reality of grace, confession of sin, and appeal to God embody the shape of faithful Christian life in general, and just so embody the shape of faithful exegesis of Holy Scripture.

It is for this reason that "the historical, literary and speculative virtues of exegetes and dogmaticians are . . . subordinate to spiritual graces."[102] Of the former—that is, of the "historical and literary arts"—"much is to be expected, but only as an instrumental and subsidiary good," for "the text is *signum*, not *res*."[103] To read the Bible in faith, then, is at once an intelligent and a spiritual activity (albeit as the former is ordered to the latter), because it is simultaneously a "following [of] the words of the text"[104] and "a hearing of the Word."[105] Webster is keen to incite confidence on the part of the church and its theologians that, granting the Bible's complexities and the knowledges and practices that may and should inform good readings, they will not be disappointed in turning to Scripture; that, indeed, they are "entitled to expect divine instruction,

---

97. *Holiness*, 18.

98. *Holy Scripture*, 88.

99. *Domain of the Word*, 27. The quote continues: ". . . and who know that an end has been made of mistrust, fear and evil detachment. For such readers, interpreting Scripture is a literary and historical enterprise which is at the same time a mode of living in the presence of God."

100. *Holy Scripture*, 87–88.

101. *Word and Church*, 83. The quote continues: "Prayer constitutes and accompanies Christian reading . . . [as] the humbling and reorientation of our agency, which now finds its end in hearing God's Word."

102. *God without Measure*, 1:80.

103. *Domain of the Word*, 29.

104. *Domain of the Word*, 130.

105. *God without Measure*, 2:5.

and so . . . may with good cause count upon being directed to a conclusive word."[106] This is a matter of hope, grounded in the divine promise, and in such hope Webster recurs to the Reformation maxim: *sacra scriptura locuta, res decisa est.*[107] The inculcation of such an expectation will require, in the end, that faithful readers of Scripture be not "masters but . . . pupils in the school of Christ."[108]

So far, so good. The problem lies not in anything Webster says but rather in what he does not say. Although his wide-angle description of the exegetical task is superlative, he never zooms in to take a closer look; and on the rare occasions when he does, his comments are surprisingly vague and uncharacteristically vacuous. This is true both when he discusses scriptural hermeneutics in a general way and when he treats the nature of the Christian reader.

By what interpretive strategies, after all, may the church faithfully engage Scripture? This is a pressing question, historically and theologically. Much of the energy of the Reformation had to do with a critical transformation of the way that Christians read Scripture, not merely the content or result of their reading. Discussion of this question has been rich and extensive in recent decades, not least due to the writings of figures like Henri de Lubac, *ressourcement* theology, and revisionist revivals of certain strands of patristic and medieval theology.[109] Yet regarding spiritual, figural, allegorical, tropological, anagogical, christological, ecclesial, and other reading strategies, Webster writes little to nothing.[110] In one of the few places where he does address the question, Webster says that "the principal task of theological reason is figuring out the literal sense, that

---

106. *God without Measure*, 2:5.

107. Webster regularly adverts to this common Protestant slogan: see *Holy Scripture*, 57; *Confessing God*, 34; *Domain of the Word*, 122.

108. *Holy Scripture*, 101.

109. See, e.g., de Lubac, *Medieval Exegesis*; Balthasar, *Mysterium Paschale*; Ayres, *Nicaea and Its Legacy*; Anatolios, *Retrieving Nicaea*; Young, *Biblical Exegesis*; Levering, *Scripture and Metaphysics*; Levy, *Introducing Medieval Biblical Interpretation*; Dawson, *Christian Figural Reading*; Turner, *Eros and Allegory*.

110. Webster is not often an interpreter of the Old Testament, which is usually the proving ground for answering these hermeneutical questions. The relevant exceptions come in his sermons, where he preaches on the Psalms and the Prophets: see *Grace of Truth*, 53-61, 75-108, 119-54, 167-86, 197-206; *Christ Our Salvation*, 6-12, 19-40, 98-120, 149-64. His sermon on one of the servant songs of Isaiah (52:13-15, in *Grace of Truth*, 77-83) comes the closest to articulating an explicit Christian hermeneutic of Israel's scriptures.

is, what the text says. This would be an absurdly naïve claim if the literal sense were thought of merely as information to be retrieved from an inert source in which it has been deposited. But the prophets and apostles are *alive*, their texts are their *voices* which herald the *viva vox Dei*."[111] As a theological claim, this last sentence is puzzling. It is doubtful Webster means to refer to the souls of the prophets and apostles in heaven, in the communion of saints. I can only surmise that he wants to indicate the unique manner in which the living Spirit uses their words, deposited in texts (texts that are, in themselves, surely without life?), as an instrument of the Lord's living speech. It is unlikely Webster means to imply that the souls of Moses and Isaiah, St. Peter and St. Paul *also* speak from heaven when and where their words are read in the Spirit. In any case, at the hermeneutical level, "what the text says" is a decidedly unhelpful gloss on the literal sense. As a recommended reading strategy, it falls into tautology: what Christians ought to read the text for is what it says, and what it says is what it says.

Perhaps we might pursue an alternative interpretation of Webster's reticence. Let us suppose his theological worry concerns shutting down or foreclosing the exegetical event by specification of so many rules, guidelines, and procedures that, far from aiding exegesis to hear the voice of God, invariably deaden and mechanize it—as though cranking the right interpretive lever will generate the right propositional-doctrinal content. That is a fair enough worry, not least in an academic and theological culture that for some time has prized certainty, demonstration, method, and assured results. It would benefit Webster's reader, however, for the worry to be made explicit.

More to the point, though, discussion of how to go about certain ecclesial and theological tasks, above all biblical exegesis, is far from out of bounds. Consider St. Augustine, among Webster's most-cited authorities. One of his most influential works, *De Doctrina Christiana*, is simply a handbook on biblical interpretation. In it Augustine offers quite direct answers to ordinary questions about exegesis: how best to read, what the meaning of a scriptural text is, how many meanings biblical texts can have, the relation between the church's authority and Scripture's, the extent to which (divine and human) authorial intention matters, and much more. Webster's bibliology offers no concrete help in this regard, and,

---

111. *Domain of the Word*, 130. As ever, Webster is following in Calvin's train on hermeneutical questions.

more often than not, implies a dismissal of the set of questions raised by it.[112]

The issue, to be clear, is not that Webster does not address everything; it is that his inattention to or deflation of human-ecclesial action has a distorting effect across his work. This is evident not only in the short shrift he gives to hermeneutical questions but also in his account of Christian interpretive activity as such, particularly in its temporal, habitual, and learned aspects.[113] As Angus Paddison writes, Webster's "account of Scripture's relationship to the church [is] frustratingly disembodied and set at a distance from the church's dense, timeful practices." This raises, as a consequence, "the specter of *episodic* accounts of Scripture's action on and among us: such accounts are insufficiently wedded to

---

112. For similar comments, see Wesley Hill's review of *Domain of the Word*, published in 2016.

113. This is not unrelated to Webster's onetime antipathy to the language of habit and of moral self-improvement (for which see, e.g., *Word and Church*, 47–110; though see now his later moral essays for a substantive shift, esp. *God without Measure*, 2:49–102, 123–40). For example, regarding "habits of mind and heart" such as "love of the gospel, docility in face of our forebears, readiness for responsibility and venture, a freedom from concern for reputation, a proper self-distrust," Webster writes: "*None of these things can be cultivated*; they are the Spirit's gifts, and the Spirit alone must do his work. What we may do—and must do—is cry to God, who alone works great marvels" (*Confessing God*, 83, emphasis mine). It is unlikely Webster would have affirmed this claim in the last years of his life, but it bears repeating, not only because of its importance for his earlier thought but also because its simplicity may mask just how radical it is: "None of these things can be cultivated"—that is, believers' cultivation of spiritual habits of faithful and loving orientation to God and neighbor is impossible. Concerning the larger ecclesiological picture, Webster acknowledges that the church is a creature of history and historical process, but heavily qualifies this by dogmatic description of its identity: "[That the church has a given nature] does not make the church *less* than a historical project; what it does suggest, however, is that the project that the church is, is more than a rather indeterminate set of cultural negotiations in which the church figures out some kind of identity for itself. The church is not finished; it learns itself over time; it does not possess itself wholly, because its source of life is the infinity of God. But God's infinity not only opens up a historical horizon that the church fills with social forms; it is the *law* of churchly action, giving direction and shape. The church is not an indefinite or arbitrary social-cultural assembly, but is shaped by the divine plan, and its history unfolds as that plan moves toward fulfillment" (*God without Measure*, 1:190–91). One can hear in this language echoes, in critique, of Tanner, *Theories of Culture*. Elsewhere he writes similarly, repudiating the notion of "the church as a process of ongoing negotiation" (*God without Measure*, 1:69). See further East, "Undefensive Presence."

the horizontal time which we inhabit and so make it hard for the church to see how Scripture and God's action *consistently* relate one to another through and in time."[114] The problem is ecclesiological, as is the solution: "To avoid this episodic language—correlative with a punctiliar account of God's action on Christians—Scripture's life needs to be located very firmly within the life of the people of God."[115] Scripture (proximately) comes from and is oriented to the historical church, the concrete church in time; it must be located there and made sense of there, even in bibliology, if it is to be understood well. The consequences for exegesis are similar, according to Paddison. Webster focuses disproportionately on divine action in human interpretation, even preferring the term "reading" to "interpretation" because, in his view, the latter unduly magnifies the human agent's self-importance. Paddison rightly objects: "Surely this is to imply that interpretation cannot itself be sanctified by God, in the same manner that the human texts of the Bible are enlisted into the service of the gospel?" In conclusion, "By hindering his readers from exploring how we *learn* to read Scripture through the time God gives us, Webster ends up not sufficiently protecting himself from the risks of a one-sided account of interpretation. In other words, Webster falls into the same trap he . . . warn[s] against, of pitting human agency in competition with divine agency."[116]

Paddison thus arrives at the same judgment reached above, that Webster emphasizes divine agency to the detriment of human agency in the reception of Scripture. This is ironic, given Webster's rehabilitation of Barth's account of human agency against his critics.[117] Webster's theology of interpretation turns out to be but an inversion of the more common disproportion in the field of biblical scholarship, rather than an orderly corrective that gives priority to God without drawing a contrastive relation between divine and human action. The result is a magnificent vision of Scripture's relation to God and of God's activity in Scripture's reception in the church. But little remains that is material, practical, or specific

---

114. Paddison, *Scripture*, 20. Webster resists this implication (see esp. *Confessing God*, 182–83), but the difficulty remains.

115. Paddison, *Scripture*, 21. Indeed, Paddison here states well the principle under investigation in this book: "All accounts of Scripture are inseparable from accounts of the church."

116. Paddison, *Scripture*, 22. See further Bowald, *Rendering the Word*.

117. See Webster's *Barth's Ethics of Reconciliation*, esp. 59–98; *Barth's Moral Theology*, esp. 99–123, 151–214.

on the human, interpretive side. Webster is not wrong to cut against the grain of contemporary obsession with interminable adjudication over indeterminate texts and their pervasive interpretive pluralism.[118] It is doubtful, however, that the patient survives the cure.

Ecclesiology: The Hearing, Holy Church

Christian theology consists of variations on common themes. What makes one theologian or system distinct from another is not always a substantive difference; often it is the eloquence or beauty on display, or the particular articulation of a doctrine, or an especial emphasis on a certain aspect of the whole rather than another. Ecclesiology is no different. There are many ways to describe the church in theological terms. Like all theologians, Webster sees the church from an angle, giving weight to certain features over others. In this section we gaze at the church with Webster, from his vantage point, lingering over what he observes as well as noticing what he overlooks.

We turn first, then, to a brief sketch of his ecclesiology, followed by reflection on the task of the doctrine as he understands it; second, to Webster's constructive theology of the church as the creature of God's Word; and third, to tendencies toward abstraction in his description of a kind of *ekklēsia asarkos*.

Principles of Ecclesiology

The church of Jesus Christ is the creation of the triune God. It is the product of the loving will and reconciling acts of God the Father through the external missions (1) of the eternal Son of God, incarnate in and as Jesus of Nazareth, who was crucified, rose from the dead, and ascended to heaven; and (2) of the eternal Holy Spirit, poured out at Pentecost on peoples from every nation, sent to set apart, equip, and indwell a people of

---

118. See, e.g., *Domain of the Word*, 122, 169–70; *God without Measure*, 1:79–80. Webster does add nuance to this concern, writing of our sinful disregard for prophets and apostles (*Domain of the Word*, 12) mere pages before he allows that conflict over interpretation is one of the ways "in which God keeps the church in the truth" (31). The phrase "pervasive interpretive pluralism" comes from Christian Smith, *Bible Made Impossible*.

God's own possession. Christian theology of the church has these divine works and their creaturely counterpart as its subject matter. Accordingly, it must be fitted to this subject matter as an exercise in theological reason, following upon faithful confession: *one God, the Father . . . one Lord, Jesus Christ . . . the Holy Spirit . . . the one holy catholic and apostolic church.* The church, too, is a matter of confession, as a community brought into reality by the Father, sustained in being by the Spirit, and charged with a mission by the risen Son. It thus requires dogmatic description, no less than Scripture, faith, or Jesus. Webster, as we have seen, resists the move to place the church alongside everyday sociopolitical entities, as if its identity or life were patient of such analysis. No, to properly understand the church requires operative talk of God, God's works, and the economy of grace, for the church is ultimately the creature of the Word, who rules it in royal freedom, with omnipotent grace, for the glory of his name and the salvation of the world. The principal means of his rule is Holy Scripture.

Webster outlines this vision of ecclesiology in programmatic fashion: "Dogmatics talks of the church by talking about God and God's works, and it does so as its first and governing descriptive act."[119] Indeed, he goes on, "dogmatics arrives at the doctrine of the church by Trinitarian deduction," because, like every Christian doctrine, "a doctrine of the church is a function of the doctrine of the Trinity."[120] How so? Because it "is to be traced back to the immanent perfection of God's life and his free self-communication in the *opera dei exeuntia.*" Therefore "a theology of the church is not simply a phenomenology of ecclesial social history but an inquiry into that history's ontological ground in the being and works of the church's God." This need not involve denial of the social and historical features of the church; rather, per Webster, it qualifies right perception of them by prior understanding of their true source and sustenance. Thus, the church's "natural and historical properties . . . only become objects of intelligence (rather than simply of phenomenal regard) when they are understood as elements in the saving transit of creatures from their origin to their end in God's society."[121] Ecclesiology therefore "has a proximate and a principal *res*": the former, the church's social and historical characteristics, practices, beliefs, form of life, and so on, whether

---

119. See the original article containing this sentence "'In the Society of God,'" 205 (now excised in the version gathered in *God without Measure*, 1:177-94).

120. *God without Measure*, 1:181, 177.

121. *God without Measure*, 1:177.

normative (how and what they ought to be) or descriptive (how and what they are in fact); the latter, "the temporal processions of God and the eternal processions from which they are suspended."[122] Grounded in and generated from these processions, in turn, are the church's creation, vocation, identity, and mission.

Does this proposal tend toward idealism? Such idealism is precisely what has led in recent decades to renewed emphasis on the concrete church's visibly identifiable features; since the church exists in neither the human nor the divine mind alone but in the world, should not ecclesiology direct its gaze there, toward the church's tangible social features?[123] Webster grants the concern but denies its application for two reasons. The first is critical-doctrinal: "ecclesiology may not become 'first theology'; the ecclesiological minimalism of much modern Protestantism cannot be corrected by an inflation of ecclesiology so that it becomes the doctrinal *substratum* of all Christian teaching."[124] To do so begins the move toward "some of the dogmatic distortions found in nineteenth-century theologies of moral community," distortions that enervate resistance against "the drift to naturalism" and "immanence."[125] Put differently, such an "ecclesiology can so fill the horizon that it obscures the miracle of grace which is fundamental to the church's life and activity."[126] The second reason for denying the charge of idealism is a kind of theological counter-principle. Against the animating conviction "that the real is the social-historical,"[127] Webster follows St. Thomas in understanding the being and acts of God as supremely real, for they are the ground and reality of all other being and acts.[128] Theologians ought to know better than to suppose that visibility or availability to empirical reason is the hallmark of the real: "Time and society are derivative realities, and that derivation is not simply a matter of their origination; it is a permanent mark of their historical condition." Thus, to make ecclesiology "a matter of historical sociology or practical reasoning," as so many in modern theology want to do, "is to neglect the principle that all creaturely being is

122. *God without Measure*, 1:177, 178.
123. See the excellent treatment, then considered follow-up, in Healy, *Church, World, and the Christian Life*; Healy, "Practices and the New Ecclesiology."
124. *Confessing God*, 155.
125. *Word and Church*, 18.
126. *Confessing God*, 155.
127. *God without Measure*, 1:178.
128. *God without Measure*, 1:179.

grounded in God, and by reason of that neglect to misapprehend the kind of historical society that the church is. . . . Put simply: ecclesiology and ecclesial action are creaturely realities, to be set under the metaphysics of grace."[129] Ecclesiology must conform itself to its object, in this case a community, but a community of a specific kind; inquiry into it should therefore be fitting to what it is: a creature of grace.

The Creatura Verbi Divini

Ecclesiology seeks to answer, or at least to offer an adequate account in response to, a set of perennial questions: What is the church? What is its essence, being, or irreducible identity? What features most determinately mark out its life in the world? What are its characteristic actions? What is its charge or mission?[130] What are faithful forms of its organization? What are dangers, threats, or temptations to which it is liable, of which it should be cognizant and wary?

Webster's most common and, arguably, his controlling image for the church is that of the *creatura verbi divini*: the creature of the Word of God.[131] By this image, of Reformation provenance, Webster means to say that "the church is that human assembly generated and kept in life by the continuing, outgoing self-presentation ('Word') of Jesus Christ."[132] More succinctly: "To be the church is to be spoken to by Jesus in the Spirit."[133] The church as *creatura verbi* is fitting for Webster because it encapsulates so many of his emphases. The church is a *creature*: neither

---

129. "'In the Society of God,'" 203 (another sentence slightly altered in the later version presented in *God without Measure*, 1:179–80).

130. An observation I lack the space to discuss in detail in what follows is the absence of a theology of mission in Webster's doctrine of the church. The church as a *missionary* community, a people *sent* by Christ—with a concrete positive charge, as opposed to the negative condition of exile or the neutral experience of diaspora—is wholly lacking in his thought. When the notion does appear in his writing, it is under-theorized, rendered in passive language, or indistinguishable from dispersion. For example, his proposal in one sermon, that the church fulfill its mission by "sticking to its post" (*Christ Our Salvation*, 104), is representative: the image is of someone standing still.

131. Webster repeatedly cites with approval Christoph Schwöbel's essay "Creature of the Word."

132. *Word and Church*, 196.

133. *Grace of Truth*, 159.

self-made nor self-realizing but created, a product of divine action and therefore neither reducible to, nor exhausted by, the observable features on the surface of its social existence. The church is a creature of *the Word*: though properly a work of the undivided Trinity, here the church's creation is appropriated eminently to God the Son,[134] the capstone to whose salvific work in becoming incarnate, dying, rising, and ascending is the outpouring of his Spirit on Pentecost, which event precipitates the creation—*ex nihilo*, according to Webster[135]—of his body, the church. The identification of the church as a creature of *the Word* suggests at least two further resonances. First, the gracious source of the church's existence: God's saving speech is no different than God's creative speech, in that it is sheerly gratuitous, unmerited, and wholly derived from God's good pleasure. Second, the importance of Scripture: the Word speaks through the word, that is, Christ, the head of the church, speaks to it through the biblical witness; this witness therefore precedes and sustains the church's life. Where and as the church hears the voice of its Lord and maker in Holy Scripture, there it is most truly itself, the sanctified creature of God's holy Word.[136]

---

134. See here "Trinity and Creation" in *God without Measure*, 1:83–98, for talk of eminent appropriation.

135. See, e.g., *Domain of the Word*, 44: "The gathering of the saints is Christ's election and calling *ex nihilo*." Cf. *Holy Scripture*, 71; *Christ Our Salvation*, 174: "[the apostles] are a pure miracle; they're made out of nothing." How to make sense of this claim? Surely it can only be an analogous use of the term "*ex nihilo*," for it is not literally the case that there is not anything from which God creates the church (much less the apostles). Not only are there human beings, but there are *believing* human beings, persons faithful to the Lord, before, during, and following his earthly advent. Moreover, the "nothing" in Webster's formulation comes much too close to erasing Israel as a relevant ecclesiological factor; one would be better to say that God creates the church *out of* Israel-and-the-gentiles. Or even that it is not an act of creation at all, but an act of covenant liberation: God opens up Israel *to* the gentiles, so that God's elect covenant people now—precisely as a fulfillment of God's promises to Abraham—include both those who descend from Abraham according to the flesh and those who do not. Cf. *Christ Our Salvation*, 83: "Jesus [is] reconstituting the people of God, starting the covenant afresh. Henceforth, because of his call, the people of God will be *God's* people because they are *his* people, those who hear *his* summons."

136. "The church is not called first of all to live and proclaim the gospel, but to *hear* the gospel. . . . What is involved in hearing the gospel? The church hears the gospel as it reads Holy Scripture in the context of the assembly of the people of God who gather to praise the Lord Jesus in sacrament, fellowship and service. . . . The church hears the gospel in the repeated event of being encountered, accosted, by the word

In sum, and in Webster's most technical formulation, "the church is the human assembly which is the creaturely social co-efficient of the outer work in which God restores creatures to fellowship with himself."[137] The risen and ascended Lord Jesus "gathers a congregation around himself" as "the creaturely counterpart of his risen presence."[138] As such the church is "the audience of revelation,"[139] for the risen One addresses it in power, grace, and truth. Hearing this address is a matter of fellowship. The church is not merely a consequence of or a bystander to Christ and his work of reconciliation; it is, by grace, "a creaturely counterpart *to the fellowship of love which is the inner life of the Holy Trinity*," which is to say, "fellowship with God is . . . the mystery of which the gospel is the open manifestation."[140] God speaks, and in speaking saves, and in saving restores to fellowship. The church is the social shape taken here and now by this fellowship-restoring, saving speech—the name of which is Jesus Christ—on the way to its final perfection by the Spirit.

Even if the church's creation is appropriated to the Son, it remains the work of the whole Trinity. For "the Word" of which the church is the creature "refer[s] to God's self-communication, the revelatory self-gift of the triune God which directs the creation to its saving end," and "in the space which is made by [this] Word," "the church exists."[141] How does Webster describe the church's life in terms of the works of Father, Son, and Holy Spirit?

Often it comes through a sort of extended gloss on St. Paul's Letter to the Ephesians, which speaks of the inseparable yet distinct triune works of electing, reconciling, and perfecting a people for God's own sake.[142] Each of these works finds eminent expression, respectively, in the eternal subsistent relations of Father, Son, and Holy Spirit; the origin,

---

of the gospel as it meets us in the reading of Scripture in the midst of the community of faith and its worship. Hearing the gospel in this way involves repentance and faith, that is, constantly renewed abandonment of what the gospel excludes and embrace of what the gospel offers. Such hearing can never be finished business. Hearing the gospel is not a skill we may acquire nor a material condition in which we may find ourselves, but a spiritual event which happens in prayer for the coming of the Holy Spirit, and in which we are always at the beginning" ("What Is the Gospel?," 109–10).

137. *God without Measure*, 1:177.
138. *Domain of the Word*, 43.
139. *Domain of the Word*, 44.
140. *Confessing God*, 153 (emphasis mine).
141. *Holy Scripture*, 44.
142. See, e.g., *Holiness*, 52–76; *God without Measure*, 1:183–88.

creation, and temporal life of the church are in this way indexed to the inner perfection, completeness, and fecundity of the Holy Trinity. Such an account of the church pushes against certain trends in contemporary ecclesiology, such as ethnography or practical theology.[143] By contrast to such approaches, Webster describes his own proposals as "exercises in 'negative ecclesiology,' in that [they] try to win back to Christology"— and, ultimately, to the doctrine of God the Trinity—"territory which has been annexed by accounts of ministry, liturgical action, morals or spirituality; and thereby [they] make a claim about the permanent centrality of the divine Word (self-communicative presence) for an understanding of the church and its action."[144] We saw above in the discussion about scriptural authority that Webster's ecclesiology mounts a protest against this doctrinal territorial annexation, as it were. What more specifically does Webster have in mind here, and why does he see it as a problem?

The ecclesiological currents in view are those associated with the names of (inter alia) George Lindbeck, Stanley Hauerwas, and John Milbank, according to whose depiction the church is a polity among polities—indeed, intending the evocation, a polity *of* polities—and a community set apart from others by its social norms, habits of speech, and material practices.[145] Though these theologians and those they have influenced think that the church is unique due to its relation to God, one of their animating goals, speaking broadly, is to portray the church as socially and politically relevant, especially in terms of the critical purchase it has, or should have, on other communities and the wider society. This goal leads them to emphasize those features of the church that are directly analogous to other social groups. At times, argues Webster, this emphasis can lead to ecclesiological discussion in which talk of God is functionally inoperative, merely overlaid onto more determinate human practices, or even absent. The upshot, or at least the impression given, is a picture of parallel polities:[146] the *civitas*

---

143. See, e.g., the essays in Ward, *Ecclesiology and Ethnography*; Fulkerson, *Places of Redemption*; Watkins, *Disclosing Church*; Branson and Martínez, *Churches, Cultures, and Leadership*; Miller-McLemore, *Companion to Practical Theology*.

144. *Word and Church*, 3.

145. See Lindbeck, *Nature of Doctrine*; Hauerwas, *Christian Existence Today*; Hauerwas, *In Good Company*; Milbank, *Being Reconciled*; Milbank, *Word Made Strange*; Milbank, Pickstock, and Ward, *Radical Orthodoxy*; Cavanaugh, *Torture and Eucharist*. See also volume 2 of Jenson, *Systematic Theology*.

146. See Nathan R. Kerr's critique of Hauerwas on this score in his *Christ, History, and Apocalyptic*, 93-126.

terrena and the *civitas dei*, side by side, the latter of which finally bests the former for reasons readily discernible to non-theological analysis. On this view what outbids the world is something proper to the church, native or immanent therein.[147]

Against this, as we have seen, Webster counters that the church is first of all an *opus dei*, the product of a wholly gratuitous and uncontrollable divine act. Therefore a properly theological account of the church requires dogmatic speech prior to moving to the level of the social-historical.[148] "The church is known as God is known": through faith.[149] That the church is the body of Christ and the temple of the Spirit, created at Pentecost and sent by God into the world, is not available as such to the grammar and methods of the sociologist or the political theorist (why, Webster insists, would any Christian theologian think it was?); the church is a matter of divine workmanship, and therefore *talk* of the church requires unmitigated talk of both God and God's action.

As with Scripture, then, what the church is is not available to natural apprehension; it is spiritually perceived, because the church's visibility is *spiritual* visibility.[150] This notion of the church as "spiritually visible" is central to Webster's ecclesiology. In arguing for it, though, he is alert to the force of the Catholic charge of Nestorianism in Protestant ecclesiology such as his own. Such a charge consists of at least two facets: extrinsicism and Docetism. The first sees a tendency to make the church "a wholly human reality . . . exterior to the mystery to which it witnesses,"[151] the mystery being divine grace; the second, relatedly, sees an analogy to a deficient christology, wherein the church, like a Jesus who merely

---

147. To be clear, this move is not always a naturalizing one; it is sometimes a hyper-supernaturalizing move, in which the church is spoken of in quite transcendent terms. Here the problem, for Webster, is the way this crowds out Christ's sovereign authority and presence in the church. The church remains a spiritual-theological entity, but, at least descriptively, since Christ has as it were emptied himself into it, the church assumes to itself roles, titles, and activities that are proper to God alone. This is less Lindbeck or Hauerwas, more Milbank and Jenson. The reason for including them here is that the end result is often the same: a focus on the church as an entity unto itself, naturalist sociology having been transfigured by theology, all the while remaining at the level of the concrete community constituted by its internal life of social practices.

148. See again "'In the Society of God.'"

149. *Confessing God*, 182.

150. See *Holy Scripture*, 47–50; *Confessing God*, 174–91.

151. Comité mixte catholique-protestant en France, *Consensus oecuménique et différence fondamentale* (1987), nr. 14; cited in translation in Jenson, *Unbaptized God*, 125.

"appears" to be flesh-and-blood, only "appears" to be a truly human, historical community, whereas in fact the "true" church is pure, ideal, heavenly, untainted by the world of fallen, finite human beings.[152] Both tendencies treat the concrete church here and now as effectively empty of theological content: the former because it is devoid of abiding divine presence and action; the latter because the church's essence is so assigned to the spiritual as to rebuff all meaningful temporal analysis. In both of these aspects the church triumphant is the only relevant object of ecclesiology. These charges are serious because Webster affirms the truths animating them: (1) that the church is a site of grace, a place in which and a people in whom God abides, moves, and acts; and (2) that the church is undeniably a social group akin to others, made up of actual human beings, with a history that is *real*, and often less than savory. His response is not to deny these truths but to qualify them, and further to offer a theological redescription, according to which the church, in all its sordid and terrestrial historicity, is fundamentally a reality created and sustained by God, and whose identity is centered in Christ and maintained, unconquerably, by the Spirit. Like Scripture, again, the church has a sort of ontology, christological because trinitarian. And just as with Scripture's own natural history, Webster insists that this claim entails no denial of sociality or historicity, but is rather "a way of identifying the *kind* of social history that the church is, namely, a social history that is one long reference to its origin in God's goodness."[153]

The Incarnate Body of Israel's Messiah[154]

What ought we to make of the foregoing? Recall my comments above regarding Webster's inadequate treatment of canonization, rooted in a deflation of human-ecclesial action and authority. As we observed there, so also here: the proof of the pudding is in the eating. If it were the case that, alongside Webster's rich and irreducibly theological depiction of the nature and ends of both Scripture and church, he also provided an

152. For further discussion of these christological analogies in ecclesiology, see Jenson, *Unbaptized God*, 125–28. Also see again Healy, *Church, World, and the Christian Life*. Webster comments favorably on Healy's work in *Holy Scripture*, 50n13.

153. *God without Measure*, 1:181 (emphasis mine).

154. What follows is in part adapted from East, "John Webster, Theologian Proper," 345–49.

equally dense account of the church in its human, historical, and social aspects, then that would render his counterproposals far more plausible. It would answer in advance the very charges he seeks to discount, namely an idealism or Nestorianism endemic in ecclesiology stemming from the magisterial reformation. Unfortunately, Webster's so-called negative ecclesiology functions also as a kind of negative anthropology; consequently, the problems that arise here are not accidental but cut to the heart of Webster's project.[155]

The problems can be traced to a certain tendency to abstraction in Webster's writing.[156] I do not mean that he talks about difficult topics, like divine simplicity, or non-empirical matters, like moral ontology. I mean that, regarding certain issues, there is a lack of *texture*, a propensity to deploy personified concepts, dogmatic synecdoches, and sweeping generalities that elide important ethical and theological questions. For example, Webster often refers to humanity as Adam's children, and to Adam as the first human being, created good but fallen.[157] It is unclear from Webster's writings, however, what historical or theological force this is meant to have. Was there "an" Adam? Or is "Adam" a trope, a stand-in for our evolutionary ancestors? Are the doctrines of original sin and justification affected by evolutionary biology? What about traditional ways of reading the book of Genesis? So far as I can tell, Webster trades on the biblical and classical understanding of Adam without registering his judgments regarding debates from the last two centuries about Adam, Genesis, evolution, and historical criticism. To be clear, I am not pre-judging the kind of answer he might have given. I am signaling this kind of avoidance as a problem, one intimate with the apolitical character of his theology.[158]

For a more detailed example of the kind of abstraction I am talking about, consider Webster's account of salvation history. He regularly tells

---

155. For a thorough positive assessment, see Allen, "Toward Theological Anthropology."

156. Others have criticized Webster's ecclesiology in particular on this point. See, e.g., Brittain, "Reply to John Webster."

157. See, e.g., *Domain of the Word*, 16, 18, 131, 188, 190; "Perfection and Participation," 394; *God without Measure*, 2:147, 184.

158. Another example is the absence of any discussion of hell, reprobation, or universalism in Webster's work. At most, "hell" denotes either the sentence of damnation of which believers have been acquitted (*Christ Our Salvation*, 7, 68, 72) or the mess we sinners have made of the world ("Hell is everywhere: in sickness, in worry, in loss of hope, in loneliness and guilt"; 72).

the scriptural story from a "God's-eye view" that, however accurate in the broad strokes, distorts his representation of Scripture's total narrative. That is, he focuses so exclusively on the "moments" of the specific divine works (creation, reconciliation, redemption) and of the divine missions (the incarnation of the Son, the outpouring of the Spirit) that he crowds out not only the details of those works and missions, but also much else that is not included in them. A typical instance is Webster's summary description of what he calls "the history of fellowship between God and creatures." He writes:

> This history is the long, complex, yet unified movement of God's giv-ing, sustaining, and consummating created life. Created reality is as it participates in this history with God. It is a history with three prin-cipal moments, which correspond to the three great external divine works. There is, first, the moment of creation; God the Father, maker of heaven and earth, brings creatures into being out of nothing and bestows on them their several natures. To human creatures he gives a nature which is not fully formed, one which unfolds over time, which is enacted. There is, second, the moment of reconciliation. Human creatures reject the vocation that their given nature entails, and seek to be what they are not: self-originating, self-sustaining, self-perfecting. Yet such is the goodness of the creator that creatures are not permitted to ruin themselves. God destines the creature for perfection, and God is not hindered. In the history of covenant grace, at whose center lies the incarnation of the Word and which embraces creatures now in the Spirit's quickening power, God arrests the creature's plunge into de-struction and turns the creature back to himself. And so there is, third, the moment of consummation, inaugurated but awaiting completion, in which the creator ensures that creatures attain their perfection.[159]

Granted the formal, compressed, and synoptic character of this ac-count, it is consistent with the rest of Webster's oeuvre in that it makes no mention whatsoever of, for example, the people Israel or the earthly career—specifically, the ministry of healing and teaching—of the human Jesus.[160] It is worth pausing here to linger on what should be rather shock-

---

159. From "On the Theology of the Intellectual Life," in *God without Measure*, 2:143. Similar condensed summaries may be found throughout Webster's writings.
160. As will become clear, I am not saying Webster never *talks* about Israel, much

ing: a Christian theologian's scripturally grounded summary of "the history of fellowship between God and creatures" that does not include the names "Israel" or "Jesus."[161] *Is* there such a history of fellowship that does not have the people Israel as its condition of possibility? Yet this aporia is present across Webster's many works. Though he occasionally mentions Israel, the calling, life, and mission of the Jewish people—and the obverse, the identity of God *as* the God of the Jews—play no material role in Webster's theology.[162]

For example, Webster writes about law and transgression in a late essay on the doctrine of justification. At one point he even writes, "To reject the law of God is to reject God."[163] Yet nowhere do we read of Israel or its Torah—the Law of Moses and Sinai given for the holy life of God's elect people, the Law that Jesus came not to abolish but to fulfill (Matt 5:18),

---

less Jesus. It is the substantive role played by them in his theology, and the sort of attention given to them there, in which I am interested. For a brief discussion of Israel, in the context of interpreting Hebrews, see *God without Measure*, 1:63–65, as well as the footnote above regarding Webster's exegesis of, and hermeneutical approach to, the Old Testament.

161. Not that absence of the name of Jesus is a dominant feature of Webster's work; see, e.g., his clear treatment of this very point regarding the particularity of the gospel mandated and epitomized by Jesus's name in "What Is the Gospel?," 113. At the same time, it seems to me, as I spell out below, that it is an open question whether the particularity not merely of the name of Jesus but of his earthly career—the happenings and doings and sayings and sufferings narrated by the canonical Gospels—becomes overshadowed in Webster's later work through almost exclusive attention to the triune persons in their antecedent eternal divine plenitude. Cf. Webster's two most explicit reflections on, as he puts it, the theological character of theology: first, "Theological Theology" in *Confessing God*, 11–31 (this was his inaugural lecture as Lady Margaret Professor of Divinity, delivered at Oxford in October 1997); second, "What Makes Theology Theological?," in *God without Measure*, 1:213–24 (originally published in the *Journal of Analytic Theology* in 2015). Mapping the continuities and discontinuities of these two essays would call for an investigation unto itself. I will only observe that, in the former, Webster writes that "the object of theology is nothing less than the eschatological self-presence of God in Jesus Christ through the power of the Holy Spirit" (1:26). In the latter, he writes: "The object of Christian theology is twofold: God the Holy Trinity and all other things relative to God" (1:213). Notably, in the later essay the name "Jesus" does not appear, nor "Christ" except in a minor allusion to 1 Corinthians 2: "we have received the Spirit, we have the mind of Christ" (1:217). See below for my critique of this apparent shift from concreteness to abstraction.

162. Though an exception may be found in Webster's comments in his essay on the exordium to Hebrews, "One Who is Son" in *God without Measure*, 1:59–80, at 63–66.

163. *God without Measure*, 1:172. Cf. *Christ Our Salvation*, 6–31, 119–20.

the Law that St. Paul called "holy and just and good" (Rom 7:12)—only "law" in general. "God's law," Webster clarifies, "is best thought of as God's personal presence . . . God's gift of himself . . . the claim that God makes upon us as our Maker and Redeemer." Preaching on Psalm 119, the height of affection for the particularity and gracious donation of the Torah of Moses in the biblical writings, Webster glosses "the law which is celebrated all through" the psalm as "our vocation to be human . . . the form of life with God, the path of real human flourishing."[164]

Something is amiss here. The problem, to be sure, is not limited to Webster; Israel's erasure from Christian theology is a long and lamentable story, one fortunately on the mend in recent decades.[165] But it must be noted where it occurs, along with the problems of which it is a symptom. The primary problem here is an overly schematic, generalized, and *uncarnal* account of God's presence and action to bless and to save God's human creatures. And the problem reappears in Webster's christology.

Webster greatly admired Barth's doctrine of reconciliation. In particular he lavished praise on what he called Barth's "massive descriptive expansion of the person and works of the central subject in the history of reconciliation: Jesus."[166] Indeed, "Barth's doctrine of reconciliation is . . . striking above all for its *narrative density*, its ceaseless vigilance against conceptual takeover," for the history of Jesus is irreducible; it is neither more nor less than this man's "historical progress from Bethlehem to Calvary."[167] Webster has Barth in mind when he turns to criticize Eberhard Jüngel's depiction of the crucified Jesus:

> Jesus' death is expounded [by Jüngel] in an almost context-less way, in relative isolation from the life which he lived. In the Gospel drama, the death of Jesus has its full weight of meaning as an event which,

---

164. *Christ Our Salvation*, 9. Given the rest of his thought, it is jarring to find in Webster this unqualified move to departicularize and universalize—even to translate, for cultured despisers and skeptics, biblical language into liberal idiom—what ought to remain a *skandalon*: the election and covenant of Israel, not only through Abraham, but through Moses at Sinai.

165. See, e.g., Soulen, *God of Israel*; Kinzer, *Post-Missionary Messianic Judaism*; Braaten and Jenson, *Jews and Christians*; Yoder, *Jewish-Christian Schism Revisited*; Tapie, *Aquinas on Israel and the Church*; Levering, *Christ's Fulfillment of Torah and Temple*.

166. *Barth's Ethics of Reconciliation*, 82.

167. *Barth's Ethics of Reconciliation*, 83–84.

even in its sheer pointlessness and waste, is the culmination of the life of the one who dies. Calvary "sums up" the life of Jesus, not as a symbol which allows us to pass over or dispense with all that has gone before, but as that which is the culmination of his life of willed obedience. Though one could expect Jüngel to have an interest in this feature, he shows little sense of its importance, and it may be interesting to speculate why this is so. In part it is that his Christology, oriented to the speech-event of Jesus' proclamation, does not attach much significance to the dramatic features of Jesus' life as the Gospel narratives unfold it: Jesus is less a character with dispositions than an eschatological voice. Partly it is because, in stressing that the cross is an event in the being of God, Jüngel may run the risk of losing its human specificity. . . . None of this is to accuse Jüngel of idealism; but it is to say that the "unsubstitutable" character of Jesus, his resistance to mythologization, demands that a good deal of attention be paid to the concrete, if his particularity is not to be overwhelmed by interpretative concepts.[168]

Almost context-less . . . a symbol which allows us to pass over what has gone before . . . less a character with dispositions than an eschatological voice . . . losing its human specificity . . . overwhelmed by interpretative concepts: these words apply uncomfortably well to Webster's christology. And this, not because Webster's doctrine of Christ is "too high," but because it does not come "down" from the heights (of divine aseity, preexistence, generation, sending) into the first-century sociopolitical Jewish world of Roman-occupied Palestine, into which the eternal Son of God was sent and born—*born*, it bears emphasizing, of a woman, Mary, under the Law, Torah, to a people, Israel, aching for deliverance, for a Messiah, for a kingdom. (Not for nothing did the apostles ask the risen Jesus, "Lord, is this the time when you will restore the kingdom to Israel?" [Acts 1:6].) Webster's christology and his summary of salvation alike lack the same thing: narrative density, the textured human carnality of the fully human man Jesus of Nazareth, the particularities of whose life—his disputes, teachings, actions, healings, parables, signs, miracles, sufferings—are the flesh and bones of an orthodox doctrine of Christ. Abstraction from these particularities leaves Christ emaciated, ghostly, disembodied.[169]

---

168. *Word and Church*, 174-75.
169. It is possible that Webster's eventual systematics would have corrected for

Christian faith and theology rightly teach that Jesus was and is the eternal Logos, *unus ex trinitate*; but it is Jesus, Mary's son, with his flesh and his people and his obtrusive narrative identity in their midst, who is the Logos incarnate. Christology comes up short if it fails to reckon with this One, in all his carnal specificity. The same goes for ecclesiology, which is the doctrine of his body, and bibliology, which is the doctrine of his saving speech. For a church without flesh cannot be the body of Israel's Messiah; an *ekklēsia asarkos* would mean a *logos asarkos*. But the Word became flesh and dwelled among us, and dwells among us still in the gathering of his sacramental body to hear and receive his live-giving word. Ecclesiology must account for this community, the people of God incarnate, or beg off the task altogether.

A se, ab extra, extra se: Exegeting the Reality of the Church

In this section I step back and analyze the architecture of Webster's theological reflection on Scripture and the church. By tracing the lines connecting the dogmatic loci in play, we will be in a position to see how certain doctrines apply pressure on others, which will in turn clarify the decisions Webster makes—decisions that are often invisible but are deci-

---

this problem. For example, in his unpublished Kantzer Lectures at Trinity Evangelical Divinity School in 2007, titled "Perfection and Presence: 'God With Us' According to the Christian Confession," Webster says of Jesus that his "human history takes place within Israel, within the covenant. Jesus is a Jew at that late and degenerate stage of the history of God's dealings with the people of God which stemmed from the patriarchs but which has now stumbled into its climactic episode. Jesus's human history is both the fulfillment of the covenant and its re-inauguration." In the same lecture (the fourth, titled "Immanuel") he also says that a "theology of Immanuel such as I have sketched would need to be filled out by an account of Jesus's human life, passion, and death. . . . Such an account would, in essence, be an exegesis of the writings of the Evangelists and the other apostolic interpreters in the context of the canon as a whole: *exegesis*—not the reconstruction of the history of early Christian traditions or worship or culture but the explication of the texts in which Christ, now present to the church, elucidates himself." To which one can only say: Amen! It is notable, however, that even within this lecture, even when he undertakes to summarize what "such an account [might] show about the human history of Jesus," the plane never leaves the runway; it taxis indefinitely, always deferring liftoff to some later more opportune time. Clearly Webster would never have opposed the sort of sustained, textured exegesis to which I refer above and of which he speaks here. But for whatever reason, he is never quite able to get around to it himself.

sions for all that, contingent and therefore never per se necessary. Before I turn to such analysis, however, let me preface my approach to analyzing Christian doctrine in this way.

Theological reflection may be thought of as consisting at three levels or orders.[170] At the first or primary level are ordinary believers in church communities talking, thinking, and deliberating about theological matters. At the second level are theologians and scholars writing, teaching, and disputing with one another about *how to think and talk about* those first-order theological matters. At the third or meta level is discourse that reflects on talking-about-talking-about-theological-matters—that is, this third-order discussion considers theologians' dogmatic endeavors at a level removed from the back-and-forth of constructive proposal, critique, and disputation by looking at the whole *as a discourse*, observing patterns, argumentation, arrangement, and the like. One can simply call this the level of methodology, but often methodology is heavily engaged in the constructive, second-order level of making proposals and criticisms based on judgments about how things should go. I mean to understand this third level as somewhat "above the fray," seeking simply to understand what is happening at the second level, though not without theological commitments and judgments of its own. Third-order dogmatics remains dogmatic, and hence is a kind of "theology of theology," subjecting second-order proposals to close analysis for the sake of consistency, coherence, and better understanding.

In what follows, and in the coming chapters, this threefold understanding of theological reflection will be in the background of the discussion, not the foreground. Too heavily thematized, it becomes clunky and obstructive to analytical clarity, rather than conducive to it. My language will thus be more colloquial: I will speak, for example, of looking at Webster's or others' theology "from one angle/perspective" or another. I want to highlight the formal distinctions now, however, in order to introduce and frame my approach at the outset, while dispensing with as much jargon as possible in the move to substantive engagement.

Returning to Webster, then, our task is to consider those elements in his system that, at one level, receive priority or exert pressure on others, yet do not do so at another level. Three such elements populate and require fitting coordination in Webster's bibliology: God, Scripture, and

170. See the helpful discussion by Kelsey in his essay "What Kind of Project Is This?," in *Eccentric Existence*, 12–45.

church. Regarding the relationship between the latter two—considered at the second-order level—Webster expresses his central concern well when he asks "whether it is more appropriate to speak of the people of the book or the book of the people."[171] The first phrase is an identity-constituting encapsulation of Webster's ecclesiology, whereas the second phrase reflects the dogmatically confused mislocation of emphasis that, in Webster's view, improperly shifts the center of gravity from God and God's Word to God's people who possess or define God's Word. We have also seen the way in which Webster relates and orders Scripture and church respectively to God. Neither Scripture nor church ever has priority over against God in the arrangement and content of dogmatic description. Scripture does, under God, have priority over against the church, and when the sequence runs God–church–Scripture, the church lacks any meaningful priority over Scripture, for the precedence of God as living subject qualifies the church's agency relative to Scripture, while Scripture-as-object remains inalienably a source (from which to receive) and an instrument (through which another agent works). In Webster's doctrinal schema, in short, the church remains subordinate even as a subject, patient even as an agent.

In this Webster exemplifies the ecclesiological emphases of the reformed tradition. The church, in being removed from center-stage, as it were, does not cease to be part of the act; book 4 of Calvin's *Institutes* is sufficient evidence of that. The church nevertheless becomes a permanently qualified element of Christian dogmatics, set forever under the sign of the sovereignty and prevenient grace of the triune God. And it is doubly qualified by the authority and centrality of Scripture, apart from which the church has neither life, nor legitimacy, nor authority of its own, nor even relation to God. Scripture is the stable element in this arrangement, whereas the church represents the unstable element. If the church has stability at all, it is the kind of stability had by an infant in his mother's arms—utterly dependent on his superior, totally lacking any ability to sustain himself, wholly at the whim (not capricious, but loving, kind, and gracious) of another. To continue the metaphor, if the mother is God, then Scripture is the milk on which the infant-church feeds (itself a biblical image),[172] and apart from which it can neither live nor grow into

---

171. *Word and Church*, 24.

172. See 1 Cor 3:2; Heb 5:12–13, 1 Pet 2:2. Figural commentary, preaching, and poetry from patristic and medieval texts make much of this imagery as well. See, e.g.,

maturity. Nor can that which enlivens and sustains the infant be detached from the one who provides it; they are inseparable and alike necessary for the child. There is not one without the other. To look elsewhere for nourishment is to miss the point: the milk just is the means by which the mother feeds, nourishes, and nurtures her child. To wish it were otherwise would amount to simple denial or, what is worse, a refusal of the very intimacy and form of relation that is proper to these two, a mother and her infant son.

Such, at least in metaphorical form, is Webster's view of God, Scripture, and church, regarding their proper coordination and dogmatic elaboration. This ordering of priority is fitting, in that it models or reflects at the level of theological proposal what it recommends for the practice of daily life: that the actual church be set under the actual Bible, as a mode or embodiment of its subjection (along with the Bible) to the actual, living God.

Comparison with the catholic and baptist traditions represented by Jenson and Yoder will have to wait until chapter 6, but it is important to see that the theological decisions Webster makes here are just that: decisions. They are not self-evident or obvious, even if they prove to be on the mark. To be sure, Webster is not inventing his claims whole cloth; they have a history, and he is seeking to be faithful to a particular tradition: the reformed theological tradition. But his claims nonetheless remain his own, and his specific way of making them, formulating them, and presenting them should be received and analyzed with respect to him as their author, not others as their influence. What might such analysis conclude?

It is clear that certain beliefs about God stand at the head of all the other theological claims Webster makes, including bibliological and ecclesiological claims. Certain of these claims are bedrock for Webster, and determine everything else one might say about the Christian confession. In brief, these include the identity of the one true God as Father, Son, and Holy Spirit; his infinite and immutable perfection; his goodness extended to creatures through his sovereign acts to create and redeem in the economy of grace; his antecedent and omnipotent will to execute salvation for sinners through the missions of the Son and the Spirit; his absolute and unshared efficacy in accomplishing these works; his sanctification of

---

Turner, *Eros and Allegory*; St. Gregory of Narek, *Festal Works*, 112; St. Ephrem the Syrian, *Hymns*, 100, 370–71; St. Bernard of Clairvaux, *Song of Songs I*, 53–60.

a people for himself from all nations as the domain of his mercy and of the human praise of his glory; and his unrivaled rule over the world and guidance of his people by the powerful presence of the Spirit, sent by the risen Christ who is seated at the right hand of the Father.

Scripture and church find their place within and following these prior commitments. That is why Webster insists so fervently that doctrinal loci be traced back to the doctrine of God the Trinity, and further that judgments about God and the gospel issue in judgments about other theological matters, such as Scripture or church, and thereby inform how those matters are understood, approached, and engaged.[173] In other words, Webster abjures all biblical scholarship—which, often enough, is undertaken in a Protestant or evangelical mode—that seeks to approach the Bible "without presuppositions," as if such presuppositions might "impose" upon or "do violence" to the text. By contrast, Webster believes that the only way rightly to understand the Bible is to interpret it in light of and subject to judgments *about* the Bible informed by the gospel of God—not least the commitments outlined above (however articulated, in whatever form).[174] As he writes, responding to those who deem historical criticism the principal way of reading the Bible and who therefore see readings not determined by its methods as deficient, "Scripture has its historical properties by virtue of its relation to the divine Word. . . . Scripture can no more be read in isolation from the divine Word than the history of Jesus can be grasped apart from or prior to its relation to the eternal divine Logos."[175] Theological interpretation—which is just to say Christian interpretation—of Scripture is interpretation that presupposes the widest context of meaning, the most expansive frame of reference, and reads accordingly. So too for bibliology and ecclesiology: framed by the proper commitments, these are dogmatic endeavors that will not (or, at least, need not) err to the right or the left, inasmuch as they are rooted

---

173. See, e.g., his "definition" of theological interpretation in *Domain of the Word*: "interpretation informed by a theological description of the nature of the biblical writings and their reception, setting them in the scope of the progress of the saving divine Word through time" (30).

174. The most basic outline is the Rule of Faith: see Ferguson, *Rule of Faith*.

175. *God without Measure*, 1:60. See also his comments in *God without Measure*: "The only historical Jesus there is is the one who has his being in union with the Son of God who is eternally begotten of the Father. Those who pore over the gospels searching for another Jesus (whether their motives be apologetic or critical) pierce their hearts with many pangs, for they study a matter which does not exist" (1:41).

in and guided by what matters most in Christian theology—God the Holy Trinity, living and existent *a se* and *in se*, in the perfect and loving divine movements *ad intra* and *ad extra*, which result in nothing less than the creation and salvation of the cosmos.

Scripture and church, I said, find their place within and following the theological commitments listed above. How so? As Barth so perceptively noted, reformed bibliology is an extrapolation of reformed ecclesiology.[176] The doctrine of Scripture, in other words, says what must be the case for Scripture *given what the church is*—having specified what the church is in light of what God, Christ, and his gospel are. This claim is ironic because it suggests that, while at one level claims about (God through) Scripture are what exert inter-doctrinal pressure on claims about the church, at another (prior or deeper) level it is the other way around, for claims about Scripture result from a proper understanding of what the church is.

This may seem confusing at first glance, so let me give an example of how it works. Webster often adverts to Reformation slogans as shorthand for his fundamental background commitments, and understanding their force and order can help to clarify his argumentation (as well as offer another window into the bedrock claims about God mentioned above and how they function). The dogmatic sequence of theological affirmations, both for the reformers and for Webster, runs this way: *solus deus, solus Christus, sola gratia, sola fide, solo verbo, sola scriptura*. Webster refers to all the slogans after *solus deus* as "extensions of [that] primary principle."[177] The emphases and priority are clear: absolute precedence belongs to (1) God and (2) Christ; then comes (3) God's sovereign agency in the work of salvation, which is utterly gratuitous, involving and requiring no human work to supplement or complete it; then follows (4) the human correlate to divine grace, faith, which is itself a divine gift, not a human accomplishment; next is (5) the word, the announcement of the gospel through the book of the gospel, the Bible, as the instrument of Christ the eternal Word; then, finally, and only at the end of this train of affirmations, we find the claim about (6) "Scripture alone." The resulting sense of the slogan is thus something like the following: Scripture is the (deputized and sanctified, primary and abiding) authority for the church's faith, morals, governance, and worship, *as an extension and digest of* the first

---

176. "What we pursue is Evangelical and Reformation exegesis of the reality of the Church" (Barth, *Church Dogmatics* I/1, 100).

177. *Word and Church*, 10. We might add *solus Spiritus*; cf. *Culture of Theology*, 89.

five affirmations, their material source and perpetual servant. Note well, then, that there is an embedded ecclesiology, or at least a set of direct ecclesiological consequences, contained in the first five affirmations—things that must, and must not, be true of a church that is faithful—of which *sola scriptura* is a kind of crystallization or précis. (This is why the slogan can serve as shorthand for all the rest, yet when uncoupled from them has such problematic potential.) The theological-methodological point should be clear: The doctrine of God, which here includes christology and soteriology, engenders and encompasses ecclesiology; bibliology follows ecclesiology, then redounds upon it.

We can trace the way in which Webster's ecclesiology follows from his theology proper and, in turn, determines what his bibliology must claim. Substantively, the argument runs like this:

(1) If God is that One whose life is *a se* and *in se*, who is wholly prior to, solely responsible for, and absolutely efficacious in creating, sustaining, justifying, and sanctifying fallen human creatures, then the church cannot be described in any way that would suggest that it is self-sufficient, acts apart from or alongside of God, participates in God's own being, will, or perfections,[178] co-constitutes or co-effects anything of salvific import, or even contributes toward the realization of God's purposes. These are all non-communicable, non-participable aspects of what it means to be the sovereign triune Lord. It is therefore a category mistake to assign, attribute, or predicate any of them to anything that is not God, including the church.

(2) If the church should not be characterized in any of these ways, but rather in the metaphorical imagery described above, namely of an infant held and fed at the breast (Scripture) of his mother (God), then other descriptions should be sought, descriptions that set God's people in contradistinction to God's existence. Thus the church's being is described as *extra se*, outside itself, rooted and located in God, not in itself.[179]

---

178. For, however, a shift in Webster's judgment on the propriety of the language of "participation," see *God without Measure*, 1:106-7.

179. See Webster's critical comment in his otherwise quite appreciative response to Pope St. John Paul II's *Ut Unum Sint*: "It is quite clear that in *Ut Unum Sint* there is no retraction of Christology and pneumatology, no immanentizing of the transcendent source of the church's life. Yet there is a certain tendency to de-eschatologize the life of the church by regarding ecclesial *koinōnia* as the fulfillment, not the anticipation, of the divine plan; despite all that is said about the need for constant renewal, there is a kind of assurance and density about the description of ecclesial existence which may deflect

(3) Exegeting this ecclesiological claim for bibliology, the word of Scripture is depicted as *ab extra*: not an immanent feature of the community's life, but alien, external, from the outside. Which is to say, from God, whence the church's being and identity are also sourced.

(4) Moreover, if this is what church and Scripture are, under God; and, further, if the church is not self-governing or self-determining, and certain forms of God's instrumental ruling of the church (such as magisterial or episcopal representation of Christ) are ruled out by prior commitments; then Scripture becomes the singular pivot and focal point of these concerns and claims.[180] Thus Scripture must be, relative to God, an instrument, means, witness, and servant of the divine self-communicative presence, through which God speaks, rules, instructs, and guides. In terms of its being and development, Scripture must therefore also be a product of—preponderant, overwhelming, or even exclusive—divine action: making, forming, sustaining, and sanctifying the canonical texts for the purposes just stated.

(5) Relative to the church, therefore, the dogmatic effect is a distancing, a sort of alienation. Yes, Webster grants, our forebears in the faith did, in fact, write, edit, gather, and canonize these texts. But, he continues, that is not the source of the texts' primary identity; nor does it determine their ultimate function and end. For the texts of Scripture are understood to be the conduit and locus of divine presence, speech, and governance, and hence of the church's being and identity; they constitute the temporal, tangible means of access to the "extra" in the church's essence, the place where the tangent line meets the circle's edge.[181] Consequently they assume crucial, necessary, and authoritative status relative to the church.

---

attention from the fact that the church owes its life at every moment to the work and word of God *extra se*" ("*Ut Unum Sint*," 41; see also his somewhat surprising openness to universal primacy, even if qualified, on the next page of that essay). The challenge for reformed ecclesiology here is the way in which the church is both fulfillment and anticipation simultaneously: it is not *nothing but* anticipation. Where one places the emphasis is doubtless a function of, as well as a contributing factor to, one's ecclesial home.

180. Webster hits directly on this point, and the logical connections between the loci, in his discussion of Roman Catholic ecclesiology (following a quote by Nikolaus Appel about the *totus Christus* and the canon): "Roman Catholic rejection of *sola scriptura* in favor of Scripture *and* tradition is . . . a corollary of a rejection of the ecclesiological implications of *solus Christus*" (*Word and Church*, 25). Cf. Congar, *Meaning of Tradition*; Florovsky, *Bible, Church, Tradition*; Behr, *Mystery of Christ*.

181. Barth, *Romans*, 30.

(6) It follows that such a status requires dogmatic grounding to warrant it, since such grounding does not come appended to the canon—that being the very absence at issue. And so bibliology is born, or at least bibliology of a certain kind: theological reflection that theorizes what Scripture's origin, nature, place, ends, and requisite attributes must be, *if* it would fulfill the role here assigned to it, *granted* the commitments about God, gospel, and church argued to be true and necessary by Webster, in line with the reformed tradition.

As he writes in appreciative but critical engagement with Yves Congar:

> In one highly important sense, Congar is entirely correct to set Scripture in the larger context of the history of God's self-communication. For a variety of reasons, Protestant dogmatics often lost the plot at this point, relocating Scripture away from soteriology into criteriology, with rather disastrous results. But I am not fully persuaded that the resultant extrinsicism can be adequately dealt with by Congar's folding of Scripture into the larger stream of the church's life. This is because Scripture's task as prophetic and apostolic witness to the divine Word can only be accomplished if it is in some sense an alien element in the church. Congar argues that Scripture is materially sufficient but formally insufficient. But without formal sufficiency, material sufficiency has no teeth. The sufficiency of Scripture (formal and material) does not, of course, mean that Scripture exists in abstraction from its presence to the church. But what kind of presence? Church and tradition, though they are the "space" in which Scripture is active as sanctified testimony to the *viva vox dei*, do not "fill out" Scripture or make good its insufficiency, any more than the servants of Jesus Christ fill out his lordship. *Sola Scriptura* does not extract Scripture from Christian history. But it does qualify that history as one which is addressed by an intrusive voice, the voice of the one who awakens the sleepers and raises the dead.[182]

At the material level, this is as clear and forceful a representation of reformed understanding of Scripture's relationship to the church as one can find. At the formal level, precisely because of its fidelity to this strand of reflection on Scripture and the church, there is a certain paradox and a

---

182. *God without Measure*, 1:209.

certain irony. The paradox is that the church is subordinate to Scripture (as the church's authority) and subject to it (as the chosen medium or mode of God's relation to the church); in these two ways, the church is set beneath or made secondary to Scripture. Yet, in reality, the church is immeasurably more *important* than Scripture, for it is the elect and justified people of God, the manifold company of human beings whom God has loved, saved, and sealed for eternal life. Scripture, like tongues and prophecies, will cease to be when it is no longer necessary; the church, like the theological virtues, will remain (cf. 1 Cor 13:7–13). In other words: believers, not the Bible, will inherit the kingdom. This paradox—of setting the lasting under the passing, the permanent beneath the impermanent—is reflected, as we have seen, even in the dogmatic order of priority. For, although dogmatics (at least in Webster's reformed hands) affirms Scripture's centrality and authority, it nevertheless does so *as a function of* its understanding of the church—even as that understanding is determined by the doctrine of God. Thus the irony. Not that, against his own intentions, Webster ends up doing what he opposes in others by annexing Scripture to the church; but rather that, *as* the doctrine of God runs *through* the doctrine of the church *to* the doctrine of Scripture, ecclesiology does end up determining bibliology. That is simply how the dogmatic lines get drawn, how one theological domino topples the others.

Given this nexus of theological claims about God, Scripture, and church, it is important to note that, although they are argued with reference to the Bible, the claims as such, especially those *about* the Bible, are not themselves "biblical." What I mean by this—and it is my point, not Webster's—is that "the Bible" per se does not have "a theology" "of" Scripture, because, as such, the Bible—the particular canon of texts constituting the church's Holy Scripture—knows no such thing. Even the last text written and included in the canon did not "know" and could not have "known" the entity subsequently called Holy Scripture by the church. That is *not* to say that God, through the texts of Scripture, could not or did not or does not have something to say about Scripture-as-a-whole, for God is not limited by time. Moreover, if judgments about Scripture-as-the-word-of-God are at times merely expansions of claims in canonical texts about the-word-of-God-*simpliciter*, there is nothing inherently (logically or theologically) problematic about that. Nevertheless the point stands: dogmatic claims about the Bible, theologies *of* Scripture, are not merely glosses on, meditations on, or paraphrases of what the Bible already says about itself as a totality, as Scripture. They are constructive proposals based on global readings of the whole canon—coordinated systematically to other doctrinal loci, in service of the church's faith, life, and knowledge—regarding what the Bible *must be* if it would faithfully fulfill what the church has come to recognize as its role and function *as Holy Scripture*, in response to what the church discerns as God's gracious, sovereign placement of this set of texts in the midst of its life. Dogmatic implications then ramify back outward to the doctrinal loci of God and church, in order to properly describe and situate them relative to what Scripture has come to be seen as.

Reformed bibliology, therefore, at least in Webster's hands, is not governed by what is sometimes called *nuda scriptura* or biblicism; as if what one may say, Christianly, about the Bible must already itself be said "by" the Bible.[183] Instead, theological judgments begin with exegesis of the Bible, and with the church's experience of life lived with and under the Bible's instruction and authority; those judgments then double back on biblical exegesis as well as biblical authority, informing and even determining how they should be understood, not least with respect to God's will and action.

The confidence of Webster's prose, underwritten by decisions and presuppositions that may be opaque to the reader, can suggest a kind of logical inevitability to his presentation. It can imply, that is, an absence of contingency: as though this just *is* the invariable shape of the doctrine of Scripture. As the next two chapters make clear, however, equally logical as well as traditional routes are available. It is up to the theologian to take them, or to chart others, and to do so by means of alternative configurations of the doctrines in question. Having seen one particular configuration in this chapter, emblematic of reformed understanding of Scripture and church, we turn in the next chapter to a quite different account, represented by the catholic theology of Robert Jenson.

---

183. For useful historical discussion, see Stanglin, *Letter and Spirit*, 130–32, 168–74, 222–25.

CHAPTER 4

Robert Jenson

The Drama of Scripture in the Catholic Church

Scripture is not a set of clues *from* which to figure out God, for the story it tells is *itself* the truth of God.[1]

The Christian Bible, Genesis to the Apocalypse, tells the one drama of Christ's coming.[2]

The Bible is the church's book, and . . . therefore the right rules for reading the Bible must be those that constitute the church's relation to this book.[3]

The Bible is the Spirit's book, who may do with it what he will; and the church as his prophet knows what that is.[4]

At the time of his passing Robert Jenson was arguably the English-speaking world's greatest living theologian. He successfully submitted his dissertation in 1959, one year before turning thirty; by 2017, at the age of eighty-seven, he had been writing and teaching theology on the international stage for more than half a century.[5] Not without reason did

---

1. "Scripture's Authority," 33. This and other essays by Jenson have now been gathered in *Triune Story* (quote on 117). Subsequent works by Jenson cited in this chapter will not receive authorial attribution.

2. "Strange New World of the Bible," 29 (emphasis removed from "Christian"); *Triune Story*, 160.

3. *Systematic Theology*, 2:277n24.

4. *Systematic Theology*, 2:276.

5. One year before Jenson died, Adam Eitel edited and published Jenson's lectures to Princeton undergraduate students as *A Theology in Outline: Can These Bones Live?* The slim volume is something of a valediction and a retrospective introductory

Wolfhart Pannenberg remark, in a 2000 review of Jenson's systematics, that Jenson's decades of work had "established him as one of the most original and knowledgeable theologians of our time."[6] Stanley Hauerwas later echoed the compliment, commenting that Jenson "has long been the 'best' theologian in America" (repurposing the accolade bestowed upon Hauerwas by *Time Magazine* in 2001).[7] In the last decade critical reception of his work has begun in earnest, with especial interest in his proposals in the areas of Trinity, time, and christology.[8]

If, as with Webster, the doctrines of Christ and the Trinity are the cornerstone of Jenson's thought,[9] the two "secondary" loci that occupied his attention in the final decades of his life are the church and its Scripture. With respect to these doctrines, it is important to see at the outset the ways in which Jenson's theology as a whole is simultaneously revisionary and traditional.[10] Revisionary, because the metaphysics presupposed by any one cultural epoch or ecclesial thinker is always subject to modification in light of the gospel; traditional, because there must be continuity

---

sketch of his thought. Both the tone and the style of the lectures call to mind Barth's *Dogmatics in Outline*, as the title suggests we are meant to do.

6. Pannenberg, "Trinitarian Synthesis," 49.

7. This quote by Hauerwas appears as a blurb on the back cover of Jenson, *Theology as Revisionary Metaphysics*.

8. See, e.g., Hunsinger, "Robert Jenson's *Systematic Theology*"; Farrow, Demson, and DiNoia, "Robert Jenson's *Systematic Theology*"; Swain, *God of the Gospel*; Stephen John Wright, *Dogmatic Aesthetics*; Rook, *Rhyming Hope and History*; Hart, *In the Aftermath*, 156–69; Gunton, *Trinity, Time, and Church*; Ochs, "Jewish Reading"; Cary, *Free Churches*; Lee, *Trinitarian Ontology and Israel*; Sholl, "On Robert Jenson's Trinitarian Thought"; Henry, *Freedom of God*; Green, *End Is Music*; Lincoln Harvey, *Jesus in the Trinity*. See also the two-part symposium on Jenson's theology in issues 2 and 3 of *Pro Ecclesia* vol. 28 in the summer and fall of 2019, respectively.

9. As early as the late 1960s both the doctrine of the Trinity and a church father like St. Gregory of Nyssa play a central role in Jenson's constructive thought. See *God after God*, 117–21 (for Gregory); cf. 122: "If we have an epochal task, it is to affirm the full significance of the doctrine of the Trinity. It is to carry through the attack on religion's understanding of what it means to be God, at last." See also *Triune Identity*; "The Triune God" and "The Holy Spirit," in *Christian Dogmatics*, 1:79–191; 2:105–85; cf. "Theological Autobiography to Date," 54. See finally his methodological ruminations in *On Thinking*, x: "only by reference to the specifically triune God is it possible to make these anthropological notions [freedom, death, consciousness, etc.] work well in thought. . . . [Readers] may come to say, at about the two-thirds point of each chapter, 'Here we go with the Trinity again!' I can only say, 'Well—Yes.'"

10. A. N. Williams skillfully describes this balance—and charts the resulting trajectory—in her essay "Parlement of Foules," which she wrote for Jenson's *Festschrift*.

encompassing discontinuity in the transmission of the good news from one generation to another. For Jenson, that is to say, some matters are not subject to revision; it is, rather, how we understand and articulate that which is fixed in the church's proclamation that is a matter of ongoing disputation in the conversation that is theology.[11]

As we saw in chapter 1, Jenson's ecclesial identity is complicated. His approach to ecclesiological questions is at once ecumenical and catholic. His longstanding participation in international dialogues solidified both his commitment to working for the unity of God's people and his appreciation for the vision of life, worship, and authority common to the church prior to the Great Schism and Protestant reformations.[12] Nothing doctrinal held Jenson back from communion with the bishop of Rome; he remained Lutheran, among other reasons, because he wanted to labor for the Spirit's gift of unity *with and beyond* the (providentially imposed?) divisions in Christ's one church.[13] His work on the Bible echoed and reiterated this commitment.[14] For the Bible, in

---

11. Cf. *Systematic Theology*, 1:3–41. For a more epochal, Protestant-revisionist interpretation of Jenson, see Hinlicky, "Theology after the Death of God."

12. "I have spent much of my career as a passionate ecumenist in the national Episcopal-Lutheran and the international Catholic-Lutheran dialogues: organizing conferences and study groups; speaking and writing on ecumenical matters; and co-hatching ecumenical schemes." As it happened, "ecumenical experience alienated me from extant denominational-territorial Lutheranism.... During ten years as permanent advisor to [the] third round of discussions [in the international Catholic-Lutheran dialogue], I was regularly appalled by Lutheran representatives' determination that nothing be proposed that would require actually changing anything in their churches' lives.... I was further appalled by the Lutherans' lack of theological imagination or nuance as compared with the other party—I had thought it was supposed to be the other way around" ("Reversals," 32). Jenson published the fruit of his ecumenical experiences in *Unbaptized God*.

13. See the concluding paragraphs of "Reversals," 33, beginning with, "For a long time I regarded a move to Rome as inevitable...." In many ways Jenson was a Protestant counterpart, lingering on the shores of the Tiber, to Joseph Ratzinger (now Pope Emeritus Benedict XVI). See the latter's reflections in 1986 (in *Church, Ecumenism, and Politics*, 134–36) on the state of the church's divisions as potentially a divinely wrought *felix culpa* through and beyond which the Lord might grace his people with unity.

14. Not least because it was mutually complementary with another shift in theology and ecclesiology: attention to the Jewish people. This is most clearly in evidence in two important essays: "Toward a Christian Doctrine of Israel"; "Toward a Christian Theology of Judaism"; see both essays now in *Triune Story*, 223–34, 251–60. See also Jenson and Korn, *Covenant and Hope*, esp. "What Kind of God Can Make a Cove-

Jenson's hands, is an ecclesial document through and through, rightly comprehended only in theological terms. With two commentaries on Old Testament texts, two books on (respectively) the doctrine and the inspiration of Scripture, and finally a posthumous collection of three dozen of his writings on the topic, Jenson solidified his contribution to the burgeoning field of theological interpretation and theology of Scripture more broadly.[15]

My treatment of Jenson will follow the pattern of the previous chapter. The first section takes up Jenson's bibliology, which construes the Bible as a narrative drama of the Trinity's creation and redemption of the world through the incarnation of Israel's Messiah, who as the drama's central protagonist speaks in and through the whole of the canon. The second section turns to Jenson's ecclesiology, which depicts the church as the prophet of God and body of Christ, filled with Christ's Spirit. The canon of prophets and apostles is therefore the church's book, and the church reads it aright when led by the Spirit. The third section considers the inner logic or dogmatic architecture that frames and structures Jenson's thought on these matters, exploring the ways in which he motivates his claims in one doctrine by premises found in another. Though idiosyncratic in certain respects, Jenson's theology of Scripture has as its rationale a catholic ecclesiology that informs and grounds those claims, usually unrevised, that he holds in common with the tradition.

---

nant?" and "Afterword: Where Do We Go from Here? Future Theological Challenges for Christians and Jews" (3-18, 284-88). Cf. Jenson and Korn, *Plowshares into Swords?*; Jenson and Korn, *Returning to Zion*. Finally, see the comments in *Systematic Theology*, 2:193 (in context of the full discussion, 167-210): "What is new in Christian theology is sustained attention to [relations between Christian and Jews, church and synagogue] and the need to use them with a certain bent, provoked of course by Europe's holocaust of Jews. Insight here has been demanded by guilt. . . . What the Holocaust has forced on our attention—besides the evil of which humans are capable—was the urgent need for the church to appreciate in practice and theology the in itself manifest fact that 'the Jewish way of life' did *not* in fact end [with the destruction of the temple and the expulsion of Jews from the land]." Jewish theologians like David Novak and Peter Ochs have repaid the favor; see Ochs, "Jewish Reading," as well as Novak, "Theology and Philosophy."

15. See *Song of Songs*; *Ezekiel*; *Canon and Creed*; *On the Inspiration of Scripture*. *Triune Story* includes the whole of *On the Inspiration of Scripture* (187-219) as well as the introductions to the two commentaries (127-40, 163-76). For further reflection on Jenson's hermeneutics that is somewhat at odds with my account, see Hinlicky, "How Theological Exegesis Disrupts Theological Tradition."

Bibliology: The Triune Drama of Scripture

In order to understand Jenson's theology of Scripture, one must first understand his account of theology. Theology is the necessary corollary of the nature of the message that founds the church, together with the mission that defines it. The church's mission, he writes, is "to see to the speaking of the gospel, whether to the world as message of salvation or to God as appeal and praise. Theology is the reflection internal to the church's labor on this assignment."[16] Further, because "the gospel always somehow makes the claim that Jesus is risen, the gospel is a message about an alleged event. That is, the gospel is a piece of *news*, even when we speak it to God; it belongs, insofar, to the same general class of utterances as 'there was an accident this morning on Main Street.'" Therefore the gospel and its speaking are inseparable from the tradition of its speaking and hearing: its "occurrence . . . depends on the chain of witnesses who have brought the news from the first witnesses to those who now hear." But this means that, as brought to us by a witness who herself first had it brought to her by a witness who . . . , the gospel is essentially and unavoidably mediated; there is no access to some original, pure, immediate *euangelion*, a mythic Ur-kerygma. Consequently, and stated most fully: "theology is reflection internal to the act of tradition, to the turn from hearing something to speaking it. Theology is an act of *interpretation*: it begins with a received word and issues in a new word essentially related to the old word. Theology's question is always: In that we have heard and seen such-and-such discourse as gospel, what shall we now say and do that gospel may again be spoken?"[17] Almost by way of addendum, he adds, "It is in the seam between these questions"—between what we have heard and what we shall say—"that there must be thinking, that theology is actual as 'hermeneutic.'"[18] As second-order hermeneutical

16. *Systematic Theology*, 1:11.

17. *Systematic Theology*, 1:14. Most succinctly: "Theology is thinking what to say to be saying the gospel" (1:32). See the similar formulation offered twenty-five years earlier: "Theology is the persistent and disciplined asking and answering of the question: Given that the Christian community has in the past said and done such-and-such, what should it say and do now?" (*Story and Promise*, vii). This, in turn, echoes the formulation of Barth forty years prior: "dogmatics as such does not ask what the apostles and prophets said but what we must say on the basis of the apostles and prophets" (*Church Dogmatics* I/1, 16).

18. *Systematic Theology*, 1:16.

reflection on what the church should or should not say if it would speak the gospel faithfully, theology "is best described as a sort of *grammar*," which "formulates the syntax and semantics of [the] language" of the church. Creed, dogma, confession, and doctrine "function as accepted rules of proper usage," whereas "theological opinions of individual theologians or schools are attempts to point out such rules."[19]

In what follows, then, we are observing one theologian's attempt to point out the rules governing proper Christian grammar of Holy Scripture and its place in the life of the church. This section discusses four features of Jenson's theology of Scripture: first, its status as a dogmatic decision of the church; second, its character as a unified narrative that tells the story of the triune God with us; third, the interpretive methods fitting to it as a divinely inspired text; and fourth, the problems that arise in Jenson's attempts at revisionary and moral exegesis.

A Dogmatic Decision of the Church

The first thing to say about the Bible, according to Jenson, is that it is a product of the church. This is true at every stage of the church's life: the prophets and apostles who originally authored and edited the biblical texts; their intended audiences; the subsequent maintenance, liturgical and pastoral use, and attentive reading of the texts; the texts' collection and republication; their eventual formalization in a canon; and the ongoing, endless activities of expositing, preaching, interpreting, and commenting on them. These and every other stage in the process that produced what the church recognizes as its Holy Scripture are functions of the life, faith, and worship of God's people, from Moses and David to Josiah and Isaiah to Jesus and St. Paul to St. Irenaeus and St. Athanasius and so on. God's people—which is to say, members thereof: leaders, servants, ministers, monks, and others—authored, received, replicated, assembled, authorized, published, translated, and printed the texts of the Christian Bible. It is, properly speaking, the church's book, whether considered historically, sociologically, or theologically. "For outside the church, no such entity as the Christian Bible has any reason to exist." The reason why this is so is bound up with the church's, and so the Bible's, ends, which are fundamentally missionary: "What Christians call the

19. *Systematic Theology*, 1:18.

Bible, or Scripture, exists as a single entity because—and only because—the church gathered these documents for her specific purpose: to aid in preserving her peculiar message, to aid in maintaining across time, from the apostles to the End, the self-identity of her message that the God of Israel has raised his servant Jesus from the dead."[20]

Two things require clarification at this point. The first is the conflation of "church" with "God's people," such that one can say that the church is the author, preserver, and publisher of the whole of Scripture. The second is the question of *God's* relationship to these texts, that is, of a specifically theological description of the church's Scripture. Let me take these up in turn.

For Jenson, the people of God is a single community extended across time, which encompasses both Israel and *ekklēsia*, beginning with Abraham and Sarah, opening up to the gentiles in the ministry of St. Paul, and continuing right up to the present; the communion of saints has among its population, inter alia, Moses, Hannah, Amos, Mary, Peter, Junia, Apollos, Macrina the Younger, Ephrem the Syrian, Julian of Norwich, David Walker, Sojourner Truth, Edith Stein, and Oscar Romero. There is no relevant difference *with respect to membership in God's single people* whether one is born before or after Christ, circumcised or uncircumcised, a subject of the Davidic dynasty or of the American imperium. It follows, moreover, that "not only is Scripture within the church, but we, the church, are within Scripture—that is, our common life is located *inside* the story Scripture tells. The Bible is not about some other folk."[21] Scripture is about the community of messianic faith reading and hearing it now, today. This matters greatly for how the Bible is read, for historical consciousness has taught biblical exegetes to say: "before we 'apply' a passage to ourselves, we first have to grasp it insofar as it is *not* about ourselves. We first have to understand a proposition of Paul's or a story about Samson in *its* community, specified precisely as *not our* community." To which Jenson rejoins: "The first part of that last sentence is true; the second is false."[22] For, as we have seen, "the church to which Paul

---

20. *Triune Story*, 112.

21. *Triune Story*, 114.

22. The idea being analogous to the Laodiceans and Colossians reading each others' letters from St. Paul: "And when this letter has been read among you, have it read also in the church of the Laodiceans; and see that you read also the letter from Laodicea" (Col 4:16). The letter to the Colossians was written for the Colossians, not the Laodiceans; but the community at Laodicea is one and the same as the community at Colossae: the *ekklēsia* of Jesus Christ.

belonged is the very same, diachronically continuous church to which we belong." Theologically stated: "if the church's claim to continue Israel is true, then the people of God who told Samson-stories are the very community to which Jews now belong by birth and into which baptized Gentiles have been grafted." To be sure, time has elapsed since the age of Samson and that of St. Paul to today, and so historiographic inquiry may provide significant service in understanding the context and culture of the texts that speak of them: "I do indeed need to build exegetical bridges between, say, Moses and Paul or between Paul and myself." The rebuttal does not concern historical knowledge as such, but rather predominant methodological frameworks and governing presuppositions that are at odds with Christian ecclesiology: for "there is no gap to be bridged between the unitary community of interpretation from which these documents come and in which we now work at reading them, since these are not two communities of interpretation but only one."[23] Thence comes a representatively Jensonian axiom about the church, which bears also on its canon: "The earthly *civitas dei*, if it exists at all, lasts from Adam to the eschaton."[24]

Part of an answer, then, has already been given to the second item regarding the theological aspect of this account of Scripture's production and character. For the ecclesiology that underwrites Jenson's bibliological claims is itself deeply theological; the church is no ordinary community that happens to have a founding charter, *even if* academics and exegetes outside the church should be willing to accept that minimal point in their dissections of the Bible. There is more to say, however. When Jenson emphasizes the ecclesial provenance of Scripture, he means to point out something "commonsensical," though often overlooked or forgotten. As he writes, "Protestantism emphasizes that these precise documents *impose* themselves on the church; Catholicism East and West emphasizes that it is the *church* that recognizes the exigency. I mean only to make the simple point presupposed by and included in both emphases: the collection comes together in and for the church."[25] Furthermore, to speak of the church's recognition, collection, and republication of the biblical texts is to speak at the same time of the Spirit's role in authoring

23. *Triune Story*, 115.
24. *Triune Story*, 116.
25. *Triune Story*, 59. From his essay "Hermeneutics and the Life of the Church," first published in 1995.

and animating the church's continuity of identity across time. On the one hand, then, with respect to the process of canonization, there is "a sense in which the church does not *make* the canon but rather *receives* it."[26] On the other hand, the reasons for the Bible's assemblage coincide with the Spirit's work in important ways. When the Lord tarried, at least longer than expected, the church required means whereby it could maintain the message that its founding leaders, the apostles, had delivered to it. This was crucial because, as we saw above, for Jenson "the church is a community of a *message*,"[27] the good news of Jesus's resurrection. The church thus "had to anticipate a future history . . . , in which institutions of historical continuity would be needed. At this juncture, the Spirit . . . granted touchstones of the true gospel and just so institutions of the community's historical self-identity."[28] These, according to Jenson, are Scripture, creed, and episcopate, the proverbial three-legged stool of church tradition, of which the principal authority is Scripture.

The church, like all living traditions, has questions and arguments that require adjudication. These may involve recourse to various kinds of authority. In gathering together a set of documents sufficiently "apostolic," the church thereby specified that *these texts* (and not others) are where such adjudication terminates: there is no superior or more reliable resource for resolving the question of whether this speech or that practice is a faithful saying or doing of the gospel; such questions have nowhere else to go for an answer.[29] "The canon of Scripture," accordingly, is "a dogmatic decision of the church."[30] For this reason the issue of the canon and scriptural authority is inseparably tied to the issue of dogma and ecclesial authority: For "if we will allow no final authority to churchly dogma, or to the organs by which the church can enunciate dogma, there can be no canon of Scripture. The slogan *sola scriptura*, *if* by that is meant 'apart from creed, teaching office, or authoritative

---

26. *Systematic Theology*, 1:27.

27. *Canon and Creed*, 3.

28. *Canon and Creed*, 5.

29. As witnesses to the resurrection, the apostles' living voice, in the form of the New Testament, authoritatively enables the church at once to identify the One it proclaims as risen and to unfold what that means—not by reproducing the apostles' arguments verbatim, but by following their example as models: "we turn to the apostolic church not for the certainly best thought-out instances of gospel-speaking but for unchallengeable instances" (*Systematic Theology*, 1:32).

30. *Systematic Theology*, 1:27.

liturgy,' is an oxymoron."[31] None of this is to say that the canon is an ideal list, whatever that might mean, or the list that critical scholarship would choose today. It is to say, rather, that "the canonical list is a historically achieved commendation by the church as community to the church as association of persons: here are documents in which to see how the church spoke the gospel while the church's reliance on the apostles was not yet problematic." If "the gospel is still extant," then "the canon is adequate" to its task. "And adequacy is, as with dogma, all that is required."[32]

No canon without dogma, no dogma without the church: the three are intertwined. Thus was it ever so, Jenson argues, even from the beginning: "The dogmatic imperative is congenital with the gospel, since a missionary faith necessarily lives from statement of the message to be brought and accepted. Claims to have 'no creed but Christ' either urge a tautology or are self-deception."[33] The church in its life comes, every so often, to climactic crossroads, where its answer to a question essential to the apostolic faith will decide its faithfulness to the gospel. The name for this answer is dogma: "A dogmatic choice is one by which the church so decisively determines her own future that if the choice is wrongly made, the community determined by that choice is no longer in fact the community of the gospel; thus no church thereafter exists to reverse the decision."[34] Dogma is therefore "an irreversible rule of faith."[35] After Nicaea and Constantinople, for example, there is no going back; either the church survived with its message intact or it vanished into the religious ether, leaving behind only a confused and altogether different community.

That is why not only dogma, but the authority of the church to issue dogma, is so important for Jenson. Dogma is what ensures that the church—the apostolic-gospel-message-announcing church—is self-

31. *Systematic Theology*, 1:27–28.

32. *Systematic Theology*, 1:28. The reference to the church as "association" and as "community" trades on "the notorious Weberian distinction of *Gemeinschaft* from *Gesellschaft*" (1:40n44).

33. *Systematic Theology*, 1:35. "I am aware that 'dogma' has acquired a variety of adventitious associations, most of them likely to put readers off. But there is no satisfactory other word to denote that small body of teaching that the church has formally determined is essential to the gospel. And it is a very small body of teaching indeed; it is certainly *not* the mass of what churches have mostly taught or 'theologians' opined" (*Theology as Revisionary Metaphysics*, 81n13).

34. *Systematic Theology*, 1:17.

35. *Systematic Theology*, 1:36.

identical across time, in the face of challenges from within and without. And the condition of the possibility of dogma is a church authorized to promulgate it. This entails both (1) that dogma is justified as a second authoritative element of tradition alongside Scripture, dogma being compressed, punctiliar interpretations *of* Scripture on this or that point, and (2) that there is a third authority: the church's teaching office, or magisterium. For Scripture and dogma are *texts*, which require living interpreters; they do not offer their sense of themselves. If, then, "the text itself is in any degree to adjudicate between proposed interpretations"—that is, to function *as* an authority at all—then "some living, personal reality must maintain the text's independence."[36] This is magisterial authority, "the church *as* church over against the church as a certain number of conjoined persons," in a succession of teachers who themselves "make one community with former teachers,"[37] thereby embodying a kind of "catholicity in time."[38]

The church's authorities are, then, Scripture, dogma, and magisterium,[39] which at once enable and constitute the church's diachronic self-identity and, to say the same thing, its fidelity to the message entrusted to it by the apostles. But I have left a key part out of the description so far, which Jenson does not: the Holy Spirit. For in fact *no* "structures of historical continuity merely as such can assure the integrity" of *any* community, including the church. "Thus neither Scripture nor creed nor liturgy nor teaching office, nor yet their ensemble, can as historical structures guarantee the fidelity of our proclamation and prayer to the apostolic witness." Trust that the church has not irrevocably erred at some point along its way is finally "faith that *God* uses the church's communal structures to preserve the gospel's temporal self-identity and so also the temporal self-identity of the gospel's community." Invocation of such divine action requires talk of the Spirit. So, stated with maximal theological precision, "Faith that the church is still the church is faith in *the Spirit's presence*

---

36. *Systematic Theology*, 1:39.

37. *Systematic Theology*, 1:40.

38. *Systematic Theology*, 1:41. This phrase comes from the Roman teaching office; see, e.g., Thurian, *Churches Respond to BEM*, 6:31-33 (cited in 1:41n46).

39. I have truncated Jenson's list, leaving out the liturgy and its institutions, which are an important part of his proposal, not least regarding theology's norms. Moreover, episcopacy and magisterium are not identical, though my account here might leave that impression. I trust my incomplete summaries will not be taken as misrepresentative of Jenson's larger picture: see *Systematic Theology*, 1:23-41, for the full discussion.

and rule in and by the structures of the church's historical continuity."[40] Scripture, dogma, and holy orders are the field of the Spirit's work: guarding the deposit of faith, building up the church in the knowledge of the gospel, empowering it for fidelity to its mission, granting it a share in the mind of Christ. In this respect, for example, to the question regarding "who is to defend the biblical text against its" possible misinterpretation, "the final answer is that the Spirit must do so."[41] As Jenson affirms and concludes, "At bottom, the chief thing to be done about the integrity of the church across time is to pray that *God* will indeed use the church's structures of historical continuity to establish and preserve it, and to believe that he answers this prayer."[42]

We have gone somewhat afield of Scripture; but only in appearance. For we have seen why, for Jenson, Scripture's authority requires churchly authority, lest either the sheer fact of Scripture's existence (the canonical decision *as* dogma) or its proper interpretation (epitomized and guarded by the creed; read and taught faithfully by the magisterium) be threatened. Yet these other authorities are finally subordinate to, because they are servants of, Scripture's own authority. For the canon alone remains the site of final recourse to apostolic teaching. It thus "has authority . . . over against any particular dogmatic proposal, magisterial *responsum*, or apparently mandatory liturgical order, if our perplexity becomes so extreme as to need such authority." So Jenson is happy to affirm the Protestant axiom that Scripture is "the *norma normans non normata*"—albeit with the exception that "other norms establish it in this position and . . . are necessary to its function in it."[43] I want to reiterate this last point. In continuity with the catholic tradition, Jenson argues that liturgy, creed, dogma, and magisterium (1) *establish* Scripture as the unmeasured measure of Christian speech, faith, worship, and life, and (2) *are necessary to its function in this capacity*. Scripture does not, indeed cannot, exercise authority in and over the church except by and through these other authorities, and not apart from them.[44]

---

40. *Systematic Theology*, 1:25 (emphasis mine in the last sentence quoted).

41. *Systematic Theology*, 1:40 (the "who" in this quotation is italicized in the original).

42. *Systematic Theology*, 1:41.

43. *Systematic Theology*, 1:26.

44. Notice the disjunction with Barth's comment quoted earlier in chapter 2: "the definite authority of the Church itself is established and limited" by "the authority of Holy Scripture instituted in the Church. . . . Holy Scripture is the ground and limit of

When it is exercised, though, how does Scripture's authority work?

Jenson answers: Scripture's authority is nothing other than its pride of place in the church to shape, goad, enlighten, and otherwise flummox its life and members. "Scripture's fundamental authority is simply the fact that its *viva vox* is present in the church, and so present as to shape her life." Stated as a charge: "*privilege* this book within the church's living discourse," that is, "let the Scripture be read, at every opportunity and with care for its actual address to hearers, even if these are only the reader." The test, then, for the healthy exercise of Scripture's authority in the church is not the amount of time or number of words spent talking *about* Scripture or its authority, but much more practical questions: "What stories, lines of argument, and turns of phrase actually come to furnish the minds of those supposedly instructed in the faith? When prayers and hymns are chosen or written, what vocabulary and what narratives of invocation and blessing come first to hand? Do we witness the preacher struggle to be faithful to the readings, whether successfully or not?"[45] Thus and not otherwise is Scripture's authority operative and successful. So that "the chief thing to do" if one wants to be "open to Scripture's authority" is to "hang out with it, on the corner labeled 'church.'"[46] Hang out with Scripture long enough, and its authority will work on you whether you like it or not.

The Triune Story

The category of "narrative" or "story" is central to Jenson's theology as well as his understanding of God, Scripture, and church. It is probably his central metaphysical concept. Consider the programmatic opening to his 1993 essay "How the World Lost Its Story":

---

the Church, but for that very reason it constitutes it"—and not the other way around—for "the truth and force of Holy Scripture in its self-attesting credibility is itself . . . a single and simultaneous act of lordship by the triune God, who in His revelation is the object and as such the source of Holy Scripture." See *Church Dogmatics* I/2, 539.

45. *Systematic Theology*, 2:273.

46. *Triune Story*, 120 ("To experience the authority of Scripture, this is the chief thing to do: Hang out with Scripture, on a particular corner, the corner where there is a little crowd gathered around someone telling about the resurrection"), 152 (from the essay "On the Authorities of Scripture"). Cf. 151–52 for a nice list of the various occasions on which Scripture exercises its authority, which is similar to the longer discussion at 215–19.

It is the whole mission of the church to speak the gospel. As to what sort of thing "the gospel" may be, too many years ago [in 1973] I tried to explain that in a book with the title *Story and Promise,* and I still regard these two concepts as the best analytical characterization of the church's message. It is the church's constitutive task to tell the biblical *narrative* to the world in proclamation and to God in worship, and to do so in a fashion appropriate to the content of that narrative, that is, as a *promise* claimed from God and proclaimed to the world. It is the church's mission to tell all who will listen, God included, that the God of Israel has raised his servant Jesus from the dead, and to unpack the soteriological and doxological import of that fact.[47]

The move to read Scripture as a whole in narrative fashion is a kind of formal implication of the contingent fact of the New Testament's supplementation to the Old. That God's ways with Israel and the world culminate in the career and happenings of the man Jesus requires narrative telling; the gospel is that telling; thus all that led up to Jesus in Israel and all that happened after him in Israel and the church's mission form a super-story or metanarrative encapsulating the complex though single history of God's faithful, saving, creative life with and acts for both God's people and the world.[48] That, in turn, requires attention to the narrative character of both human life and divine life, as well as to the implications for reading Scripture, *if* the canon would be read well qua narrative.[49]

If the Bible is a single great narrative, then it has more than a plot. It has characters. And if the story the Bible tells is not about some *other* community than the church (and the world in which it lives), then its characters include us—because they include all.[50] This is fitting if the biblical story is a universal story: excluding even a single person would restrict its scope. It follows, for Jenson, that the scriptural metanarrative is therefore

47. "How the World Lost Its Story," 19; now reprinted in *Revisionary Metaphysics,* 50–61, at 50.

48. See *Systematic Theology,* 2:274: "The gospel is a narrative, and this book is that telling of the narrative from which all others draw, quite apart from any need for their correction by it."

49. For sustained critique of reading the Bible as a single narrative, or rather according to a single narrative logic, see Kelsey, *Eccentric Existence.* See also Kelsey's latest book, which applies the same analysis of the braided narrative logics of Scripture to the doctrine of divine attributes: *Human Anguish and God's Power.*

50. See further along these lines Radner, *Time and the Word.*

not to be read as "a sort of reference volume about God," where God is an entity external to the story;[51] nor as a history-book about faraway ancient people other than ourselves; nor as a resource from which to marshal support for "some antecedent body of convictions."[52] No: "If we are in and not out of the story Scripture tells," the hermeneutical consequence for Christian interpretation is that "Scripture constrains our lives and thinking the way a play or novel constrains the lives and thinking of the characters." Scripture is a great drama, and we are the actors charged with its performance. "Note," however, "that this is so precisely *before* the play or novel is finished. . . . Let us say: Scripture is authoritative for us, as characters in the story that it tells, somewhat as the existing transcript of an unfinished play is determinative of what can be true and right for its characters in the part that remains to be written." And because this is a drama of which God is the author, it is not absurd—the divine playwright has both moral purpose and narrative intention—and it will be finished even if, for us in time, it has yet to be written.[53]

It is conceivable that characters in a story might be aware of the fact and wonder how to act in accordance with the story they are inhabiting. But Jenson doubles down on his analogy: *this* story includes its author *within* the story it tells, as one of its *dramatis personae*. Biblically and hermeneutically, this means that "the story is told not just as our story but fundamentally as God's story"; theologically and metaphysically it means that "the drama we inhabit with this omnipotent author constitutes his life as it affects ours."[54] This brings us to Jenson's particular spin on the doctrine of the Trinity, which radicalizes, by historicizing, God's life and being by identifying it entirely with God's life and acts with and for the world. So that, for example, the events of creation and exodus and crucifixion and resurrection just are the life of the triune God happening in created space and time, and just so they are for God his own happening eternally. Jenson means this as an expanded Barthian interpretation of God's gracious decision to be Immanuel, God with us, without remainder, and therefore as an anti-religious move: there is no God behind the

---

51. *Triune Story*, 115.

52. *Triune Story*, 116.

53. *Triune Story*, 116. Sometimes it appears that Jenson wants to go further and claim—or at least tease his readers with the possibility—that God *has not yet written it*, that somehow the transcript is unfinished also for God. But I may be misreading some of his more extravagant rhetoric on this point.

54. *Triune Story*, 117.

God revealed with and among us, no distance between us and the God so revealed. The God found in and as the man Jesus, with all the events leading up to him and all those that followed from him, is God-full-stop, all there ever is or was or will be of God the Father, Son, and Holy Spirit.[55]

This bears on our topic in a number of ways; I will discuss three. First, the unity both of God (of, that is, the triune *dramatis dei personae*) and of Scripture is christological: Christ is the hinge and center of all history, biblical or otherwise, created and uncreated. So, put simply, "the way the Christian Bible hangs together generally is as a single christological metanarrative,"[56] that is, "as a single dramatically coherent narrative of the coming of Christ and his kingdom."[57] Yet if this narrative is not one to which Christ is extrinsic, if "Scripture is not merely a record of divine-human history but a proclaiming of it, not merely an account of God's life with us to date but a voice in that life," then that voice bears a name, belonging as it does to a speaker who addresses us with it: "this voice is the Word of God, the Logos, the second identity of the Trinity." Per Jenson, this is not a disembodied voice or a fleshless speech but "the *incarnate* Word, the Word that God speaks as Jesus the crucified and risen Christ."[58] When the church reads and hears Scripture, then, whether it

---

55. More or less the whole of the first volume of his systematics is an argument for this point. For his specific treatment of time and God, see *Systematic Theology*, 1:207-23; cf. *God after God*, esp. 95-135; *Triune Identity*, esp. 57-187; *Unbaptized God*, 107-47; *Essays in Theology of Culture*, 190-201. For a useful examination of Barth on these themes, with a view to the influence or at least parallel trajectory of Hegel, see Eitel, "Resurrection of Jesus Christ." See also Schlesinger, "Trinity, Incarnation, and Time."

56. *Triune Story*, 159.

57. *Ezekiel*, 23 (*Triune Story*, 169). Cf. *Systematic Theology*, 1:58; see also *Triune Story*, 117: "Scripture is not a set of clues *from* which to figure out God, for the story it tells is *itself* the truth of God." Phrased more expansively, "The occurrence and plot of the life of God's people with God depends as a whole upon the occurrence and plot of the life of God with his people. It does so precisely as this one life is in both aspects constituted in the Father's originating, the Spirit's perfecting, and the Son's mediating of the two, and as it is *the whole reality of God* on the one hand *and of the creature* on the other" (*Systematic Theology*, 1:114, emphasis mine). God is himself a kind of story, constituted—"one with himself"—"by the dramatic coherence of his eventful actuality," as narrated in the church's Scripture (1:64). "As it is, God's story is committed as a story with creatures. And so he too, as it is, can have no identity except as he meets the temporal end toward which creatures live" (1:65). For critique, see Murphy, *God Is Not a Story*; Cumin, "Robert Jenson."

58. *Triune Story*, 118.

be Leviticus or Job, Joshua or Nahum, St. Mark or St. Jude, what it hears is the very voice of Jesus, the embodied Son of God, Israel's Messiah, crucified under Pontius Pilate and raised from the dead according to the scriptures.[59] And if Christ is the voice that addresses us in the words of the Bible, as a whole and in all its parts, then Barth was right to discover in the Bible a whole new world, the "real" world of which we are part.[60]

Consequently, second, "Scripture's story is not a part of some larger narrative; it is itself the larger narrative of which all other true narratives are parts."[61] For if it is the case that Scripture tells the one true story of God and creation, and therefore of all reality, then it is *within* this story that "all other presumptively true stories—from the quantum history of the cosmos to the story of your struggles with faith to the account of organic evolution to the history of the French Revolution to the story of someone's marriage, and so forth—must find their place and so their meaning, or otherwise be unveiled as illusion."[62] It must be emphasized that this hermeneutical framing is christological all the way down; there are not two (or more) worlds, the biblical and the secular (or whatever): "the Bible's world and this earth are one world, the world in Christ."[63] Moreover, the claim is not fundamentalist or biblicist, as though, to take his example, organic evolution cannot be credited because Genesis 1–2 does not mention it. The force of Jenson's point does, however, reveal his concerns and perceived opponents: not conservative evangelicals, but rather what he sees as the two chief influences on the liberal mainline church: Enlightenment modernity and nihilistic postmodernity, the former countenancing Scripture only to the extent that it accords with reason's dictates, the latter rejecting any and all claims to metanarratival truth. Given the live option of fundamentalism that would affirm Jenson's principle but put it to very different

59. The church fathers too saw the unity of the Testaments as a function of, and thus a testimony to, the unity of the triune God. Inspiration presupposed the truth of the scriptures: what it really secured was the self-identity of the deity responsible for inspiring prophets and apostles alike. See, e.g., Origen, *On First Principles*, Preface.1–10; 1.3.1; St. John Damascene, *Exposition of the Orthodox Faith* 4.17.

60. Given Jenson's sympathetic treatment of Origen throughout his career (beginning with *Knowledge of Things Hoped For*), it is worth noting the overlap between his mature position and that of Origen, at least as interpreted by John Behr; see Behr's "Introduction" to his two-volume edition of Origen, *On First Principles*, xv–lxxxviii, esp. his remarks on time, preexistence, and incarnation.

61. *Triune Story*, 117.

62. *Triune Story*, 150.

63. *Triune Story*, 160.

use, the question of how he would block that move is worth asking; we will come at least halfway to an answer below.

Third and finally, because Scripture is the single true narrative not only of the world but of God as well, Scripture has conceptual priority vis-à-vis received theological and philosophical ideas. In other words, Scripture revises what we thought we knew; it is not subject to revision based on our own reasoning. Here enters Jenson's project of "revisionary metaphysics," which is not a matter of pure reason distant from the biblical text but is itself a bibliological principle: "In my conviction, it must be a maxim of all Christian theology: if there is a clash between abstract notions of what is appropriate to God and scripture's story of the Lord's active presence in time, it is the former that must be rethought."[64] The specifics of Jenson's proposals on this set of issues (supremely the example above, God's relationship to time) are less relevant for our purposes than a twofold recognition: on the one hand, his revisionism is a product of his approach to biblical interpretation; on the other hand, his bibliology bears directly on his understanding of the normed character of the theological task.[65] Scripture's truth and authority as the one universal story of all that is, God included—as "a metanarrative that is 'meta' in superlative degree"[66]—generates a particular approach to cultural and intellectual inquiry. Whatever other stories (claims, doctrines, philosophies) about God there may be, and whatever they may say, they stand as worthy interlocutors for Christian theology. But they remain provisional, and therefore subject to the triune story that Scripture tells.[67] That which confirms, augments, or may find a place in that story, theology is wise to keep and use for its own purposes. That which does not, however august in reputation or ancient in provenance it may be, theology should be willing to revise or, should the belief or idea be so unscriptural as to be beyond recovery, reject outright.[68]

---

64. *Ezekiel*, 287.

65. See here Swain, *God of the Gospel*, 66–71. See also Jenson's comment in *Systematic Theology*, 2:65n50: "this work, like all serious theology, is metaphysically revisionary: it twists old language and invents new. But one does such things precisely with the language one already has from history; in Neurath's famous image, revisionary metaphysics is always a matter of repairing or remodeling a ship while sailing in her."

66. *Theology as Revisionary Metaphysics*, 64.

67. See Jenson's comments on philosophy in general and "Olympian-Parmenidean religion" in particular in *Systematic Theology*, 1:6–11; *On Thinking*, xi.

68. See, e.g., the representative claim in *Unbaptized God*, 120: "Christology is, or

Nicene Theory and Inspiration

It is a central feature of Jenson's mature theology of Scripture and its interpretation that the church's core doctrines—its liturgy, creeds, and dogmas—do not hinder faithful exegesis but rather assist and illumine it. Far from being an anachronistic imposition of later developments, the church's dogmatic tradition is a hermeneutical lens that brings what is obscure into focus, revealing what the text says rather than requiring it to say something other than its plain meaning. In fact, christological and trinitarian doctrine is not merely *a* hermeneutical lens, as if it were one among many equally viable options. It is *the* lens, *the* means by which Christian readings of the Christian Bible—the church's readings of the church's book—will be fitting, textually responsible, and theologically true. How does Jenson work out this claim?

The first move concerns the character of the church's historic doctrine. For that doctrine is not divorced from Scripture, a parallel stream as it were flowing backward to the apostles and forward to the kingdom. Church doctrine is exegetical in nature. It offers an interpretation of the biblical witness in response to contested questions that arise in the course of the church's life and mission. On questions of bedrock confession and identity, such as the divinity of Christ or the triunity of God, the very truth of the gospel is at stake. Jenson argues, therefore, that if such doctrines are untrue, then the gospel, and the church therewith, are lost in any case. Primitivism as a program is not an option; it fails both in theory and in practice. If such doctrines are true, however, then it follows that they are faithful (not to say exhaustive) interpretations of the canon. In which case the church's readers are wise to look to them as what they are: exegetical proposals. In their capacity as churchly authorities, moreover, they amount to a privileged hermeneutical lens for all subsequent engagement with Scripture.[69]

The second move follows from the first. Texts and their meaning are products of interpretive communities, uncontrolled by an original author's intention or an initial audience's understanding. This applies

---

should be, the thinking involved in *getting over* the self-evidencies about God that antecedent religion will in each case of the gospel's missionary penetration have hidden in the minds of this new sort of believers."

69. For further discussion, see *Systematic Theology*, 1:16–18, 35–41; 2:277–84; *Triune Story*, 112–20.

equally to the biblical texts as it does to all other texts. Such a claim is not perilous for the church's interpretation of the Bible, however. For unlike so many texts today, the canon of Scripture has a hermeneutical home: it belongs to the church and is understood fully and faithfully there and only there. Jenson then asks the relevant question: "Following *what* critical theory, and penetrating to *whose* agenda, should the church read its Scripture?" That is, given that every reading has a hermeneutic as well as some group's interests at stake (stated or unstated), what should these be for the Christian Bible? Jenson answers: "The community positioned to perceive what a scriptural text is truly up to is the church, and the creed is the set of instructions for discerning this agenda."[70] Elsewhere Jenson calls this approach, somewhat tongue-in-cheek, a "Nicene theory" of biblical interpretation.[71]

Such a hermeneutic is at home with figural, spiritual, and other "anachronistic" strategies of reading the Bible. What then of the "original" meaning of the texts? What role or relationship do they have vis-à-vis doctrine-guided readings? And what, in turn, of historical criticism, given that Jenson does not reject it in his affirmation of spiritual exegesis?[72]

---

70. *Canon and Creed*, 81. The quote continues: "The needed suspicious eye is the eye trained in the church to distrust all human religiosity, also as it may appear in Scripture. . . . And it is the triune God who is up to something with these texts, whose agenda is to be discovered, to be affirmed by the church and denounced by others." The wider context of Jenson's argument concerns the role of the Rule of Faith in reading Israel's scriptures and eventually the New Testament; this Rule of Faith became formalized in the Apostles' and Nicene Creeds, on which were based judgments about how best to read the whole canon as well as what to exclude from it; those who made these judgments were bishops in succession one from another. Hence the triumvirate explored in *Canon and Creed*, 1–76. For compendious historical and scholarly discussion, see Ferguson, *Rule of Faith*; Ferguson makes a stronger distinction than I do between the Rule and the creeds (whether inchoate or codified).

71. *Ezekiel*, 25. In context, Jenson writes: "I will make no room for the supposed contributions of the various critical theories currently on offer in academia and sometimes invoked to guide biblical and other exegesis—each projected from the viewpoint of a class, a gender, a race, and so on. Critique in the relevant late-modern sense is the effort to discern what a text 'really' says, as against what it may to unsuspicious eyes seem to say; and a labeled critical theory (e.g., feminist theory, postcolonial theory, queer theory) is a specific set of instructions for achieving such discernment. There is indeed a critical theory at work in this commentary, and it might be called 'Nicene theory'" (24–25; the quote also appears in *Triune Story*, 170).

72. See further Sarisky, "What Is Theological Interpretation?"

Regarding the first two questions, Jenson offers a direct answer, and I quote at length. "The trouble is," he writes, that

> when reading Old Testament texts christologically or ecclesially is contrasted with another reading which is said to take them "in themselves," or in their "original" sense, the churchly reading inevitably appears as an imposition on the texts, even if an allowable one. Christological or ecclesial readings will be tolerated for homiletical purposes, or for such faintly suspect enterprises as systematic theology, but are not quite the real thing. We need to question this all too automatic distinction. . . . It was . . . a function of the old doctrine of inspiration to trump the created author with prior agents, the Spirit and the Word, and to trump the alleged first readers with prior readers, with indeed the whole diachronic people of God, preserved as one people through time by that same Spirit. And then we may very well take the christological-ecclesial sense of an Old Testament text as precisely the "original" sense, the sense which it has "in itself," if in the particular case we have grounds to suppose that the christological-ecclesiological sense responds to the intention and reception of *this* primary agent and *these* primary readers.[73]

What are the theological grounds for this account of Scripture's inspiration and the church's interpretation? Late in his career Jenson sketched a proposal for a revised doctrine of inspiration that could affirm the Spirit-derived character of Scripture without being subject to what he took to be weaknesses in traditional accounts (such as literal dictation or propositional inerrancy). The heart of the proposal roots inspiration in the Old Testament—seen as a paradigm of the canon as a whole—and in the prophets—seen as emblematic of inspired speech. A prophet is made through union with the word of God by the indwelling of the Holy Spirit. In virtue of that union and indwelling, what the prophet speaks *just is* the word of the Lord: "The Spirit opens the person to receive the Word, the very Word who is the words the prophet is to speak, the Word who then speaks in those words."[74]

---

73. *Inspiration*, 31–32; *Triune Story*, 201–2. Note well Jenson's earlier allergy to Protestant accounts of Scripture's inspiration (and what he calls the error of inerrancy): see, e.g., Jenson and Gritsch, *Lutheranism*, 9–13. For later (brief) discussion, see *Systematic Theology*, 2:275–76.

74. *Inspiration*, 29; *Triune Story*, 200. For the full proposal, see *Inspiration*, esp.

At Pentecost the Spirit is poured out on the people of God as such. The church, accordingly, is not merely a community of prophets. It is a corporate prophet, the prophetic embassy of the kingdom. Pentecost is the event in and through which the church truly becomes the body of Christ, who is himself the church's head. The *totus Christus*, the whole Christ, is then God the Word *as* the final human prophet, including his many members, ordinary baptized believers stretching from that first momentous day in Jerusalem to kingdom come. What this community speaks is true prophecy, inspired by the Spirit; the content of its prophetic speech is the saving gospel promise of salvation in Christ. This feature of the church is not limited to the apostolic generation; it is part of the church's perduring constitution. The general work of the Spirit's inspiration of the prophetic community[75] therefore encompasses at once the writings of the apostles, their eventual reception and canonization in the episcopal church, and their magisterial interpretation in the selfsame church's liturgies, councils, and dogmas.[76]

In summary form: "The Bible is the Spirit's book, who may do with it what he will; and the church as his prophet knows what that is."[77] That Jenson here says "the Bible is the Spirit's book," and on the very next page says "the Bible is the church's book,"[78] is not incidental. This relation will occupy us in both the second and the third sections below.

The upshot for historical criticism is not wholesale rejection. Such scholarship was a boon to the early Jenson, and however strong his critique he is "unwilling to join those who now eschew historical-critical labors."[79] What he rejects is the *hegemony* of historical-critical methods, in the academy but especially in seminary and pastoral ministry. Their proper role, then, must not be to bridge (much less create) hermeneutical

---

14-47; *Triune Story*, 187-219, esp. 193-209. Cf. Abraham, *Divine Inspiration of Holy Scripture*.

75. In contradistinction to the special work of the Spirit's inspiration of specific prophets in old Israel.

76. *Inspiration*, 45-47; *Triune Story*, 208-9. Cf. Barth, *Church Dogmatics* I/1, 102: "The two entities [Scripture and church proclamation] may thus be set initially under a single genus, Scripture as the commencement and present-day preaching as the continuation of one and the same event, Jeremiah and Paul at the beginning and the modern preacher of the Gospel at the end of one and the same series."

77. *Systematic Theology*, 2:276.

78. *Systematic Theology*, 2:277n24. A few pages later he refers to the church as "the one community whose book this is" (281).

79. Foreword, in Byassee, *Praise Seeking Understanding*, x.

gaps between different communities. For, as we saw above, the covenant people of God is a single diachronic community. What historical criticism may and must do, instead, is identify and maintain, and just so render intelligible *to* us yet as distinct *from* us, the historical gaps between persons and time periods *within* the very same community and the single story to which it belongs.[80]

Just how this works in exegetical practice Jenson has exhibited in his own engagements with the text, especially in his commentaries.[81] The point to note in closing is that the "hegemony" against which Jenson is revolting, that of historical criticism, is not only a hermeneutical problem, but a theological one, and ecclesiological most of all. For "the error of almost all modern biblical exegesis is a subliminal assumption" about the church,[82] namely "that there is no one diachronically identical universal church," with the far-reaching upshot that "nearly all modern biblical exegesis in fact presumes a sectarian ecclesiology."[83] Contemporary theology of Scripture and its interpretation requires repair of defective ecclesiology.

Doctrine and Ethics in Exegesis

The great theme of Jenson's approach to questions of biblical interpretation is the church's freedom. The church, simply put, is free to read as it pleases. It is disburdened of anxiety or the need to justify itself, because no one and nothing—not the *Zeitgeist*, not the assured results of *Wissenschaft*, not even the Society of Biblical Literature—has authority over the church's reading of its own Holy Scripture. The Bible is the church's book, and therefore the church may put it to whatever uses in the service of its mission that it deems fitting and wise.

Such freedom is not autonomy, however; it is not anarchy or antinomianism. The church's freedom with Scripture is the freedom afforded it

---

80. Cf. *Systematic Theology*, 2:279: "Whatever hermeneutical gaps may need to be dealt with in the course of the church's biblical exegesis, there is one that must not be posited or attempted to be dealt with: there is *no* historical distance between the community in which the Bible appeared and the church that now seeks to understand the Bible, because these are the same community." See further *Triune Story*, 59–69, 112–20.

81. For discrete samples, see the essays collected in Part III of *Triune Story*, 221–341.

82. *Systematic Theology*, 2:279.

83. *Systematic Theology*, 2:280.

by the Holy Spirit. The church does not rule itself but is ruled by its head, the Lord Jesus. His word in the Spirit is the law of the church. And where such law binds, it binds with a view to freedom; it is, in Barth's phrase, divine grace in the form of an imperative.

Discovering the law of the Spirit in exegesis is the ongoing task of the church across time. The task is unfinished by definition; it will not conclude until the Lord's return renders questions of biblical interpretation moot. But it is a delicate undertaking because in the hermeneutical transition from receiving the gospel to speaking it, innovation not only will but must occur. It is the church's magisterial responsibility, led by the selfsame Spirit inspiring innovation where it is faithful, to oversee such hermeneutical development: to commend, to rebuke, to permit, to remind, to wait and see. One never knows in advance what newness will prove to be an organic and healthy growth in the knowledge and proclamation of the gospel, and what will turn out to be a dead end, a false start, or worse. The balance required is equal parts boldness and reticence, assertion and deference, courage and docility. In the moment, the church rarely gets it right. It is usually only after the fact, and by the Spirit's grace, that it manages to keep from tipping over and stumbling headlong into falsehood and foolishness.

Across his theological writings Jenson manages to strike this balance well enough, in the main and at the general level. Where he sometimes falters is in the details. Let me close this section by noting two areas in his account of churchly exegesis that fall short. Both are departures from the catholic tradition, and together they are related to, if not entirely explained by, a broader shortcoming in Jenson's bibliology.

Start with the shortcoming. What stands out in Jenson's writing on the Bible, not least after reading Barth and Webster on the same, is its displacement of God as the center of the doctrine, rooting it instead in the church. The challenge in bibliology is always a matter of finessing this relationship, and Jenson is right to center the church in one sense. But in the resulting account, the conclusion is unavoidable that, in Jenson's system as a whole, Holy Scripture is not firmly rooted in the doctrine of God and of God's will and action. Divine action is discovered, as it were, with a backward glance toward the presence of prophetic and apostolic texts in the liturgy of the church. Now there would be no problem if this were only in the order of knowing: doubtless such a description is apt to the historical record. But it is inadequate in the order of being, and in a full theological treatment of Scripture the former cannot be substituted for the latter. The Bible is the word of God because God wills for it to be so and acts in order to make it so. Such willing and action cannot be after the fact (although human cognition of such a reality is bound to be), which means that the canon of Holy Scripture is part of the design of God for his people from the beginning—indeed, from all eternity. Antecedent to Bethlehem and Pentecost, the Bible is in the works. How should theology depict such a process? What attributes result in a collection of texts thus confected? Jenson's system is perfectly capable of answering these questions, but for the most part he does not consider them. Perhaps a certain Protestant-scholastic stench still lingers in them. If so, more's the pity.

Distinct from this drawback in Jenson's account, though not unrelated to it, are two features of his exegetical practice that miss the mark.

First, as we saw above, Jenson argues that Scripture is read most faithfully when done under the hermeneutical tutelage of the creed and, more broadly, through the illuminating lens of the church's whole dogmatic tradition. This is a salutary and much needed intervention in contemporary exegesis. Where Jenson gets into trouble is that, when ostensibly reading Scripture through a creedal or dogmatic hermeneutic, he regularly substitutes his own theological proposals about, say, the doctrine of the Trinity, for what "the tradition" teaches about the Trinity. This means that when he gets to actual exegesis, the "critical theory" that serves his reading is not the church's tradition but his own controverted project. Now: to some extent this is inevitable, and inevitably what everyone does when reading Scripture. I have no access to some "pure" tradition of the church, and should I want to read Scripture in light of it, I will necessarily do so in light of my own understanding of that tradition. Even so, Jenson goes well beyond this common hermeneutical plight, and it would be rather easy for him not to do so.

Consider his proposals regarding time, impassibility, and Christ's risen body. They are all idiosyncratic—at times they approach being altogether exceptional—and Jenson is well aware of the fact. He is admirably sober regarding his own fallibility, which is a characteristic of all theological systems. He is unafraid to be bold because he knows he can afford to be: his trust is in God, not in his system of God. Nevertheless, time and again when Jenson reads Scripture "in light of the tradition," the tradition functions as a kind of Trojan horse by means of which Jenson reads Scripture through the lens of his own non-traditional proposals *with the implied authority* of church dogma.[84] I do not think it would be a

---

84. Let me instance two examples from his commentary *Ezekiel*: "It is a chief role

problem if Jenson simply read Scripture in revisionary fashion, according to his own theoretical lights (which he does to great effect in his systematics). The problem is when this is done under cover, as it were, of dogma's imprimatur. Incidentally, this is probably the feature of his exegesis that renders it the most implausible to those least inclined to judge it with charity, insofar as they see confirmed what they suspected beforehand: a reading of Scripture that validates Jenson's own system, because the system is what determines how Scripture is read. The hermeneutical circle remains virtuous within the historic church community, with its liturgy, dogmas, teaching office, and traditions of interpretation. Within particular theologians' systems, however, the circle becomes vicious all too quickly.[85]

The second problem concerns Jenson's account of Scripture's moral authority.[86] It is here where his Lutheran commitments make a difference. He takes for granted the distinction between "law" and "gospel," a dividing line not between the Testaments but, within each Testament, between that which binds and that which liberates by promise.[87] All Christian accounts of Scripture agree that some "law" no longer applies to the church, or does not apply to certain believers therein: for example, gentiles ought not to be circumcised. Similarly, for many traditions, women ought not to be ordained; for some, the ordained ought neither to marry nor to participate in warfare. These, however, are matters of cultic and canon law, if we may apply those later terms to commands found in the canon. What of moral law? Considering the Pastoral Epistles' guidelines for appraising candidates for church leadership (in this case 1 Tim 3:2), Jenson allows that a "mandate's sheer presence in Scripture cannot by itself make it binding for a different church than Timothy's."[88] This is a rule that Jenson in effect applies to the whole of Scripture: "The

---

of the doctrine of the Trinity to insist that the God who in his history with us casts down the high and raises up the lowly can do this because he is in himself just such a God—indeed, because this history with us is his own personal history" (143, on Ezek 17:22–24); "according to the doctrine of the Trinity, God's sharing of knowledge and intention belongs to his very being; the Son simply *is* God's knowledge and intention; and he is this *as* an other than the Father. Moreover, as it in incarnational fact happens, the Son is a human person; thus human sharing of God's knowledge and intention certainly is real in his case" (199, on Ezek 24:1–14). See also *On Thinking*, passim, esp. 9.

85. See further East, "Doctrine of the Trinity."

86. See *Inspiration*, 54–59; *Triune Story*, 212–15.

87. See further *Lutheranism*, 36–44; *Systematic Theology*, 1:14–16; 2:62–63.

88. *Inspiration*, 57–58; *Triune Story*, 214.

fundamental form of moral discourse [for biblical faith] is thus not deontological or consequentialist or the commendation of virtues. It is advice from the One who knows what we are, and our responding, 'We hear you.'"[89] This approach is of a piece, too, with Jenson's understanding of the church's mission: as the gospel encounters new cultures and contexts, the church's task is to *interpret* the antecedent habits and norms it finds there and so to fashion a properly enculturated ethic out of the encounter. The church's morals develop across time just as its doctrine does. Christians do not arrive on the scene with a readymade moral theory, since "the encounter between the church and any culture will be both appreciative and polemical. The church will find practices and ideas she can adopt and transform for her own, and others which she must combat. Neither the church nor the other culture will ever be the same."[90]

The Spirit inspires the *whole* of Scripture, in short, but not *each command within it* as perpetually binding on every member of the covenant community—even the moral commands. Yet Jenson recognizes the immediate problem: "our desire to be our own lawgivers may use" the fact that "inspiration is referred to Scripture as a whole . . . to relativize the actual biblical commands."[91] Jenson makes a valiant attempt to show by other means why certain commands remain binding (in this case, he finds permanent warrant in the opening chapters of Genesis for marriage between one man and one woman, since those chapters set the terms for the story that follows: to question those terms is to attempt to tell another story entirely).[92] But the attempt fails. Either his doctrine of inspiration needs to be strengthened, in order to shore up the moral force of Scripture's teaching; or his ethics must admit the possibility in principle of as much revision as his metaphysics. There is no third option.[93]

What is notable about the shortcomings I have just outlined is that they are instances of Jenson's *departure* from the catholic tradition: both in the case of the application of his revisionary metaphysics to exegetical practice and in the case of the Lutheran tradition's understanding of divine commands in Scripture, together funded by an innovative but nonetheless

89. "It's the Culture," 35; *Triune Story*, 344. Cf. *Systematic Theology*, 2:209–10.

90. *Triune Story*, 345.

91. *Inspiration*, 56; *Triune Story*, 213.

92. *Inspiration*, 56–59; *Triune Story*, 213–15; cf. *Triune Story*, 278–96, 327–34; *Systematic Theology*, 2:73–94.

93. For a different and quite stimulating meditation on a moral-ecclesial dilemma, see "Ethical Disagreement"; *Triune Story*, 327–34.

insubstantial account of inspiration that decenters God in bibliological description. Similarly peculiar, revisionary, and innovative ideas will not be far in our exposition of Jenson's ecclesiology. Yet at its heart is a deeply *un*original vision of the one universal church rooted in the episcopal, conciliar tradition common to East and West, and renewed in twentieth century theology: in the ecumenical movement, in multilateral dialogues, and especially in the second Vatican Council. To his version of that vision we turn next.

Ecclesiology: The Lord's Prophet

To get a sense of both the centrality and the radical character of ecclesiology in Jenson's project, consider a set of comments he makes about the structure of his two-volume systematic theology. He writes that he has followed traditional practice by dividing the books into treatment of God (volume 1: *The Triune God*) and of creation (volume 2: *The Works of God*). His twist is that "Christology and pneumatology, together with discussions of the historical Jesus, of the doctrine of atonement, and of the resurrection, are drawn back into the doctrine of God."[94] Traditionally, and wrongly in Jenson's view, "the doctrines of Christ and of the Spirit's coming appear . . . only in the parts devoted to *our* history, to what God does *to* and *for* us. The present work is structured to enable these doctrines to appear as teaching about God himself, as narrative of the history with us with which and by which he identifies himself."[95] When, in the second volume, Jenson comes to the doctrine of the church, he begins in this way: "It could be argued that in the system here presented, also ecclesiology belongs in the first volume." How could that be true? Answer: "There is a difference between the matter of this part and that of other parts of this volume, between the church's place in the gospel and that of the creation as such or even the creation taken finally into God." What is that fundamental difference? It is that "Christ is personally the second identity of God, and the *totus Christus* is Christ with the church; therefore the church is not in the same way an *opus ad extra* as is the creation, even when it is perfected in God."[96] Because, in other words, the church is united to Christ, the second person of the Trinity, it is conceivable to Jenson *to include the doctrine of the church in the doctrine*

---

94. *Systematic Theology*, 1:x.
95. *Systematic Theology*, 1:60.
96. *Systematic Theology*, 2:167.

of God, "to appear as teaching about God himself, as narrative of the history with us with which and by which he identifies himself."[97]

It would take us too far astray, and would in any case be a dead-end, to reflect on whether this constitutes a denial or blurring of the Creator-creature difference (which Jenson affirms and believes to be essential to Christian faith).[98] Rather, I begin in this way to show at the outset how important ecclesiology is to Jenson's theology. Moreover, it is at just this point that Jenson himself chooses sides, as it were: whether or not Christians "place our faith in the church" is, in his judgment, the ecclesiological dividing line between Protestants and Catholics. By affirming that they do, "this work takes the Catholic side" of that all-important question.[99] Thus, apart from the provocative suggestion that ecclesiology might be included in theology proper (and in the end, it is not), the impulse behind it is the fundamental judgment that the church is not only the object but in some way the subject, not only the recipient but somehow the mediator, not only "the fruit but nevertheless also the instrument of salvation."[100] This identification with "the Catholic side" was a shift, slow in development but in any case theologically substantive and therefore necessary for understanding Jenson's ecclesiology. In 1969 he could write of "Catholic" and "Protestant" "habits of mind" and then say "that this book will reflect a protestant mind—and will indeed be a sort of argument for its superiority as a pattern of believing reflection."[101] Later, in 2010, reflecting on changes in his theological journey, he calls attention to this passage (written by a four-decades-younger self) where "I had distinguished protestant and catholic 'sensibilities' and identified the former as my own," but then concludes: "now I would have to say the opposite."[102]

Whatever revisions Jenson might propose, then, however far-reaching they may appear to be, he self-consciously intends his theology of the

97. This is a function of Jenson's Lutheran understanding of the *communicatio idiomatum* of Christ, which in his thought migrates as a matter of course from christology to ecclesiology. For a compact treatment of what he calls his "hyper-Cyrillian" christology, see "How Does Jesus Make a Difference?"

98. See, e.g., "Creator and Creature," in *Theology as Revisionary Metaphysics*, 155–61.

99. *Systematic Theology*, 2:167.

100. *Systematic Theology*, 2:167n1, quoting J. M. R. Tillard, "We Are Different," *Mid-Stream* 25 (1986): 283. See the fuller discussion in *Unbaptized God*, 90–103.

101. *God after God*, 8. The alternating upper- and lower-case is original to Jenson's text.

102. "Reversals," 32.

church to be catholic in a strong sense.[103] As such, they are also meant to be ecumenical, in the twofold sense that they are offered to the ecumene and that they are in dialogue with, and held accountable to, international ecumenical efforts in the last century (especially after Vatican II) and the convergences and agreements that have been reached in the process.[104] Of the many proposals he makes that form his overall ecclesiology, my discussion in what follows is limited to those aspects that most acutely characterize his understanding of the church as well as those that are most relevant to grasping the relationship between Scripture and church in his theology. With that in mind, I focus on two features of Jenson's ecclesiology: first, the church in relation to the End, that is, the church as an eschatological detour in Israel's history; second, the church in relation to the risen Christ and his Spirit—that is, the church as the body of Christ, the *totus Christus* as Christ-with-his-body, and thus the church as a communal prophet, filled by the Spirit to speak the word of God in truth and with authority. Before turning to the chapter's final section, however, I offer a critical engagement with Jenson's ecclesiology, in particular his account of the Spirit in the church and the apparent indistinguishability of the Spirit's and the church's actions. Here the indictment of Webster in the previous chapter is reversed: instead of divine action swallowing up human action, here the two in effect become one.

But critique follows exposition, so let me turn there first. We begin with the End.

The Church, Israel, and the End

"Bluntly stated," writes Jenson, "God institutes the church by *not* letting Jesus' Resurrection be itself the End, by appointing 'the delay of the

---

103. To be sure, Jenson would not be Jenson without his Lutheran theological identity. Were the divisions in the church to be healed, Jenson would be a Catholic Christian in communion with the bishop of Rome whose christological and sacramental instincts would align most fully with Luther and Brenz, rather than St. Thomas or Pope St. Leo the Great, without such instincts rendering him anathema. For Jensonian reflections along these lines, see Long, "My Church Loyalties."

104. See *Systematic Theology*, 2:169: "the decisive interlocutors throughout this part [on the church] will be the second Vatican Council and the subsequent ecumenical dialogues with their theological enablers and commentators. Other thinking about the church will be recruited on a more ad hoc basis."

Parousia.'"[105] The church here is an eschatological entity, constituted by God's decisive act in Christ and the Spirit to inaugurate the Father's reign in the world, yet not itself the Eschaton or its imminent harbinger, but rather something short of it. This position is consonant with the formulation of "already/not yet" (that is, the kingdom is *already* inaugurated, but it is *not yet* consummated); but that is not where the emphasis lies. Rather, the rub is in the church's relation to Israel as much as its relation to the End. For to interrogate the church is immediately to raise the question of the people Israel: How does Israel relate to the church? Has Israel been replaced or superseded or fulfilled by the church? Does Israel have any continuing validity in its post-temple form as Rabbinic Judaism? If the gospel is true, argues Jenson, Israel cannot simply be done away with, nor can it be marginal to the picture; the answer to the question of the church must include an answer to the question of Israel.

Internal to Israel's calling as God's people was to bless the nations, and further, to receive their pilgrimage and worship of Israel's Lord as the one true God of all. Israel came, however, to see that this was an eschatological eventuation: it would only finally be fulfilled in a new age, consequent to climactic divine action to renew and establish Israel as God's covenant people. Had Jesus's resurrection been one and the same as this event, no gentiles would have been included in the kingdom's advent and the conversion of the old age to the new; one half of the promise would have been null and void. For Jenson, it follows that "the church is nothing other than an appropriate if beforehand unpredictable sidestep in the fulfillment of the Lord's promises to Israel. The church," in a word, is "an eschatological *detour* of Christ's coming." As such, "[she] is neither a realization of the new age nor an item of the old age. She is precisely an event *within the event* of the new age's advent."[106] The opening chapter of Acts confirms this account. When the apostles ask about the kingdom's coming (v. 6), now that Jesus is risen and revealed as Lord and Messiah, Jesus's response is that the promised *Spirit's* coming is imminent, which will then launch the mission to the gentiles: "and you will be my witnesses in Jerusalem, in all Judea and Samaria, and to the ends of the earth" (v. 8). It is then that Jesus is taken up from their sight by a cloud (v. 9): an anticlimactic scene, to be sure, for followers eager for the restoration of Israel. That it is the Spirit and the Spirit-wrought church of Jews-

---

105. *Systematic Theology*, 2:170.
106. *Systematic Theology*, 2:171.

plus-gentiles that comes after Jesus's death and resurrection is, Jenson argues, the Lord's eschatological detour that nonetheless will (and does) fulfill the promises to Israel. The detour will conclude with Jesus's return appearance; until then, "the straight line route to the Kingdom is broken, and a side trip through the church with its mission is ordained."[107]

This is the fundament of Jenson's ecclesiology; nearly everything that he has to say about the church follows from it. He elaborates by clarifying the nature of the church's "side trip." Because "the foundation of the church's being" is eschatological, "the church exists in and by *anticipation*."[108] Because, that is, "it is what creatures may anticipate from God that is their being," it is good theological grammar to affirm that "the church now truly *is* the people of God and the body of Christ and the temple of the Spirit"[109] (which are the three rubrics under which Jenson considers the church).[110] As "the church is grounded in God himself, the *Eschatos*," it is "doubly . . . moved" "by God to . . . fulfillment in him," insofar as the church is "one among God's creatures and . . . the creature that embodies that movement for others."[111] In other words, the church's life is sacramental; its very being as a community is constituted sacramentally. This is but another way of affirming the unique eschatological character of the church: "The fact that the church is not yet the Kingdom and that her life is what we call 'sacramental' are the same fact."[112] Jenson gets at the idea with a favorite adage of Luther's. The church is *the gate of heaven*, inasmuch as it gathers around the altar and lectern to see and hear God's word, the altar and lectern themselves being the gate of heaven for the church's members. "The church is a *moment* in the coming of the Kingdom, and just so is the gate of the Kingdom's *present tense* with God, that is, of heaven."[113]

The church anticipates the kingdom sacramentally; as the gate of heaven, it stands at the hinge, or overlap, between two realms. But these realms are not merely spiritual. They are filled with God's creatures, and

---

107. "Toward a Christian Doctrine of Israel," in *Triune Story*, 228. See further Ochs, "Robert W. Jenson."

108. *Systematic Theology*, 2:171.

109. *Systematic Theology*, 2:172.

110. See *Systematic Theology*, 2:189–227.

111. *Systematic Theology*, 2:172.

112. *Triune Story*, 233.

113. *Systematic Theology*, 2:172 (emphases mine). For critique of this construal of the church's participation in God, see Kline, "Participation in God."

so constitute societies. Glossing St. Augustine, what is in view is the polity of man and the polity of God.[114] The company of the baptized comprises the latter in the midst of the former; the church militant is therefore a kind of vanguard or embassy of the new age transposed by the Spirit into the old. It follows in turn that the particular form the church's polity takes is an important matter, and is far from indifferent to its sacramental character. Ecumenical communion ecclesiology arose during and after Vatican II in response to this question, and Jenson appropriates and extends it in order to articulate an account of eucharistic fellowship constituted at every level of the church's gathering.[115] The Eucharist, in this proposal, establishes church polity defined by a *koinōnia* at once horizontal (with one's fellow believers gathered in a single place) and vertical (with those called to oversee and administer the sacrament). But how is such fellowship to be effected in unity? And by whom? The question of polity, unity, and sacrament leads naturally to the question of holy orders.

The office of ordained pastor is crucial for the unity of the church's life as a fellowship, that is, for its unity across both time (backward to the apostles and forward to the End) and space (between believers in Rome and Beijing and Buenos Aires and Nairobi). This entails ordered succession of those ordained with this specific charism and charge, which is found in the episcopal office. For the bishop is both the individual and the institutional locus of unity at each level of the ecclesial pastoral hierarchy. And given that ordained pastors are assigned to different groupings or "levels" of church-collectivity, there is a highest level, that of the one catholic church constituted "in and out of" the many churches. This fellowship too has its own pastor, who in virtue of the office is a universal pastor: the bishop of Rome.[116]

The episcopacy is related to the canon of Scripture in two ways worth noting. First, ensuring faithful teaching is central to its pastoral task, that is, guaranteeing that what the church says and does is true to the gospel handed on by Jesus's apostles. This doctrinal task belongs to the teaching office or magisterium, which ordinarily leads the church in myriad

---

114. For Jenson's mature commentary on *The City of God*, see *Systematic Theology*, 2:76-85.

115. For the larger discussion, see *Systematic Theology*, 2:167-269; cf. *Unbaptized God*, esp. 17-103.

116. For discussion of each successive topic, see *Systematic Theology*, 2:228-34 (the charism of holy orders), 2:234-42 (the monarchical episcopate), 2:242-49 (the papal office).

unremarkable and mundane ways, but also, exceptionally, by dogmatic mandate. The magisterium, then, has final authority rightly to interpret Scripture for the community—not, that is, authority *over* Scripture, but authority *vis-à-vis the believing community* regarding *how to read* Scripture *as* the final authority on the truth of the gospel message.

Second, Jenson's justification for the magisterium is analogous to that given for the biblical canon. As he writes, "If the canon is divinely mandated, then something can appear in the already existing church's history and still be *iure divino*; if the Bible belongs to the church's foundation, then something can emerge in the already founded church and still belong to her foundation."[117] In this case, that "something" is the episcopate (along with the Rule of Faith codified in the creed), which Jenson argues is an irreversible work of the Spirit in the church's life to free it to be faithful to the gospel and to its mission of proclaiming it. What is important to see here is that, according to Jenson, if one rejects either the creed or the episcopate as lacking divine warrant for essential inclusion in the church's life, on the grounds that they were not there "from the beginning," one must for the same reason and with equal force reject the New Testament canon, which was written, collected, and certified long after Pentecost.[118]

Liturgy and episcopate, magisterium and tradition, dogma and even the canon all serve a single end: the proclamation of the gospel. But what is the gospel? And how does the church proclaim it? The answer lies in the sacraments, and in Jenson's Augustinian-Lutheran interpretation of them.

Sacramental Speech in the Spirit of Christ's Body

The church's mission is to speak the gospel to God, itself, and the world. The gospel is the news that Jesus is risen, in fulfillment of God's promises to Israel, and that the new age of the kingdom has begun in the outpouring of the Spirit on the church, which is the risen Lord's body in the world. The church exists in the time opened up by the Lord's ascension and "delay" in returning, a time in which the gentiles are welcomed into

---

117. *Systematic Theology*, 2:238.

118. Indeed, the office of *episcopos* and the *regula fidei* predate the canon and even the writing of certain canonical texts.

the covenant people as it undertakes its mission to the nations, announcing the gospel as it goes. The interrelations between these claims—about Christ, his resurrection, his body, the church, its mission, the gospel, its being spoken—are where Jenson works out his account of the sacraments and of the *totus Christus*.

Speech, for Jenson, is not a disembodied act.[119] It is necessarily bodily: speakers are themselves embodied, for to speak at all one must have a body to speak with. But speech is not limited to words, or rather, speech is not limited to *audible* words: speech encompasses gesture, symbol, drama, even the irreducibly nonverbal. The gospel is a word, a bit of news, a message about a body, the living body of Jesus of Nazareth. The gospel claims that this body, Jesus's body, is also and simultaneously the body of God. God, therefore, is not disembodied. He has a body, that of the first-century Palestinian Jew Jesus, which was tortured and executed and raised to new life in the Spirit. The mystery of God's embodiment, of the incarnation, is then internal to the gospel message: to talk about Jesus is to talk about the God who deigned to have a body like ours; about the God whose name is Immanuel; about the Spirit who worked the miracle of Jesus's conception in Mary; about the Word who became flesh. It is only fitting, then, that the telling of this mystery, the church's gospel-speech, be itself embodied. Just as the gospel's speakers are flesh and blood, so the words themselves become, by the Spirit's grace, flesh and blood (and other matter too). These are the church's sacraments.

The sacraments, or mysteries, of the church are, in St. Augustine's formulation (which Jenson follows closely), *visible words*.[120] The contrast is not the one that has latterly come to seem evident, words that are *visible* rather than *invisible*. Instead, the contrast is between *visible* and *audible* words: the latter are words we hear with our ears, because spoken by the mouth, whereas the former are words we see with our eyes, because spoken with rituals of hands, bodies, and creation's elements.[121] These visible words, the sacraments, *say* the gospel in a unique and necessary

119. For Jenson's treatment of language and embodiment, see especially *Visible Words*, 1–60; *Essays in Theology of Culture*, 117–31; *Systematic Theology*, 2:6–7, 35–38, 53–72.

120. "The Word comes to the element; and so there is a sacrament, that is, a sort of visible word"; cited in *Visible Words*, 3. See St. Augustine, *Tractates on the Gospel According to St. John* 80.3.

121. "We declare to you what was from the beginning, what we have heard, what we have seen with our eyes, what we have looked at and touched with our hands, concerning the word of life" (1 John 1:1).

way: sacramentality is essential to the church's being and life.[122] And we have just seen the reason: the particular God of the gospel is a God with a body, a God who does not despise the bodily or the material, a God who offers himself as an object for creatures to see, smell, touch, and taste, not only in the incarnation but also in the Eucharist, as well as in the whole sacramental life of the church.[123]

By catholic count there are seven sacraments.[124] But speaking more generally of the sacraments as the "mysteries" of ecclesial fellowship, Jenson argues that the total manifold activities of the church's life as a corporate body—"liturgical processions and blessings at family meals and signs of the cross and greetings in Christ's peace and invocations of saints and parental example in the faith and testimony before Caesar and kissing the crucifix and household reverence for the Book's place of honor"—though "not sacraments by any counting likely to be adopted ... are all minor or major mysteries of communion."[125] All the mysteries of the church's fellowship have as their source "the founding mystery of the church's communion," namely "the occurrence in her of the Word of God." This word is no disembodied occurrence, as we have seen: "The eternal *Logos* is God's *address* and not his mere meaning or intention; and in fact this address is Jesus of Nazareth."[126] That is to say, God's actual embodied speech, to himself and to us, is the whole life of the man Jesus. What Jenson means when he speaks of "the first and foundational mystery of communion" is "that the triune conversation"—as recorded, for example, in the Gospels' portrayal of the Father and the Son speaking to one another in the Spirit (cf. Mark 1:9–11; 9:2–8; John 12:27–32; 17:1–26)—"opens to creatures to be the converse of God within a historically actual human community." More concretely, "the primal

---

122. See *Visible Words*, 31–32: "it is a distinguishing mark of Christianity that it is decidedly and finally sacramental. If God is one thing humans have to communicate with one another, to the saying of which the word's embodiment is essential, God is the one thing Christians cannot cease to communicate. Insofar as our communities remain faithful to the specific gospel, we are bound to embodied discourse. All anti-sacramentalism in the church is forgetfulness of which God we worship; it is idolatry. The gospel wants to be as visible as possible."

123. See here *Visible Words*, 28–60; *Story and Promise*, 159–76.

124. See, e.g., the treatment of confirmation, penance, healing, and marriage in *Systematic Theology*, 2:261–65. For a lovely recent account of all seven from an Anglican priest, see Davison, *Why Sacraments?*

125. *Systematic Theology*, 2:260.

126. *Systematic Theology*, 2:270.

mystery of communion is . . . the *viva vox evangelii*, the event of living human persons speaking and showing God's word and so hearing and seeing it."[127] Most radically put: "The trinitarian speaker of God's word *ad extra* is the *totus Christus.*"[128]

Much follows from, or underwrites, this understanding of the church, its sacraments, and the visibility of both; it is a veritable metaphysical thicket. Let me lift up just three items.

First, Jenson repurposes St. Augustine's phrase in speaking of the *totus Christus*, the whole Christ, which means Christ along with the church. Just as a person is incomplete without head and body together, so Christ, eschatologically and therefore now proleptically in the anticipatory time of the *ekklēsia*, cannot be construed in full apart from believers. For the church really is—not metaphorically but ontologically—the body of Jesus Christ, just because he wills it to be so. Christ is one of the three whose mutual life is the eternal God ("God is what happens between Jesus and his Father in their Spirit");[129] therefore God has a body, and this body is, again, the ecclesial-sacramental community.[130] Salvation, in the End, will be communion in the communion that is the triune life; it will be a sharing in, a participation in, an entry and translation into, the perfect mutuality of Father, Son, and Holy Spirit, in and with the person of the Son, Jesus of Nazareth.[131] The sacramental life of the church is an anticipation of this eschatological eventuality, the name of which is the kingdom of God. The Lord's Prayer—to the Father in the Spirit with Jesus the Son—is the condensed epitome of the infinite conversant life of that final glorious reality. Which is to say: Following the life, death, and resurrection of Christ, which issues in what can only be called the ontological fact

---

127. *Systematic Theology*, 2:270-71.

128. *Systematic Theology*, 2:271. Although "the liturgical or devotional reading of Scripture is not 'a sacrament,' by any usual enumeration, [nevertheless] the coincidence of heaven and earth, future and past, sign and *res* is the truth of Scripture's role and power: Scripture is indeed a 'mystery'" (260).

129. *Systematic Theology*, 1:221.

130. So that Jesus, according to Jenson's metaphysically revisionary twist on Bultmann, was "risen into the church and its sacraments" (*Systematic Theology*, 1:229). For the full account, see 1:194-206, 227-30; 2:211-27; *Triune Story*, 223-34, 251-69; *Visible Words*, 28-50. See further Lee, "Eschatological Presence of the Risen Jesus," as well as Oliver Crisp's essay "Bodily Resurrection," in his *Analyzing Doctrine*, 217-35. These treatments of Jesus's resurrection bear not only on ecclesiology but also on the earlier discussion of the *logos asarkos*. Cf. McFarland, "Body of Christ."

131. See *Systematic Theology*, 1:224-36; 2:309-69.

that Christ's body is now the church, Christ cannot be considered apart from the church; the two are inseparable. And the next implication is one theological consequence of this commitment.

The church, as we have seen, is a single corporate prophet. This is a pentecostal reality, to be sure, a result of the fulfillment of the Lord's promise to pour out the Holy Spirit on all God's people, not just on specific individuals, thereby making the covenant people one great prophetic community. But it is also a christological reality, because the church is Christ's body, and Christ speaks in his members; in fact, Christ's living speech just *is* what is said in and by this community.[132] And the community knows what to speak as prophecy because its head is Christ and its Spirit is Christ's own. What it has to say is the gospel, and all concomitant interpretation thereof and commentary thereon.[133] This, in the end, is the strongest theological warrant for the church's authority to promulgate dogma, to certify creeds, to speak decisively in councils, to canonize texts as Scripture: that it speaks as Christ's body, indwelled by Christ's Spirit. Which raises the question, not unrelated to Scripture's power to judge and renew the church's speech: "Cannot the church speak wrongly? Cannot the church pervert the gospel?"[134] Jenson answers: "Certainly sermons and teaching and denominational proclamations and all the rest of the church's talking often pervert and sometimes actively oppose the gospel. But the church as one communal prophet living across time and through time cannot fatally err, not if the gospel itself is true. For it is promised" in Matthew 16:18, one of Jenson's favorite and oft-quoted passages, "that the gates of falsehood shall not finally prevail against the church, whatever may happen to particular epochs or cultures of the church."[135] We will have cause to reflect on this answer and on the issues it raises presently.

132. See *Systematic Theology*, 2:271: Christ "does not ... speak except by [his] body."
133. See *Systematic Theology*, 2:199: "As to what the church is to prophesy, the Word of the Lord has come to her once for all.... The church's prophecy is: 'Jesus is risen.' Her prophecy is that same message whose hermeneutic is the task of theology, the message labeled 'the gospel.' The church is to stand in the street or the temple or the palace, like Amos or Isaiah or Jeremiah, and state the truth of the present situation by speaking the Word that evokes the future: 'The one who inhabits and sends the future is this Jesus whom you crucified. What is to be expected is what may be expected from him. What may be done is what can be refined by his coming.'"
134. *Inspiration*, 43; *Triune Story*, 207.
135. *Inspiration*, 44; *Triune Story*, 207. This verse from St. Matthew's Gospel is very close to being the foundation stone upon which all of Jenson's theology, or at least all

Third and finally, though, we conclude with a similar observation to that with which we began this engagement with Jenson's ecclesiology: the church, or better, the body whose head is Christ, is the archetype, summary, and telos of all humanity, even of all creation. For the world was created for Christ—the whole Christ—and therefore for the church.[136] In short, "if the human creature has no other fulfillment than the vision of God, then the baptized person must be the only available paradigm of human personhood." That is to say: "Humanity within God's people is not a variety of humanity outside God's people; rather the latter is an abstraction from the former." In the final estimation, humanity—and therein each human being—"is an entity whose good is to belong to the *totus Christus* and who exists only in that he or she is directed to that good."[137] We are now in a position to see why Jenson was right to begin his systematic reflections on the church with a comment about its unique status relative to all other created works, as well as why it was thinkable to include ecclesiology in his doctrine of God. For the eternal God is incarnate as Jesus, and his risen body is the church, and the church is destined eschatologically for inclusion in the temporal infinity of the triune life. Rather than ask how or why the church could be included in theology proper, perhaps it is better within this schema to ask: Why not?

Indefectibility and the Spirit of Prophecy[138]

The freedom of the church in its reading of Scripture is, as I said above, the freedom bestowed on it by the Holy Spirit. That freedom is not license, however. It is the freedom of the body to obey its head, freedom,

---

his ecclesiology, is built. It appears everywhere in his work, as a kind of anecdotal warrant, rarely with explicit citation; see, e.g., *Systematic Theology*, 1:5; 2:88 (where Jenson applies Jesus's promise to both church and synagogue). For a defense of the notion of the divided church's "pneumatic abandonment," see Radner, *End of the Church*.

136. *Systematic Theology*, 2:4.

137. *Systematic Theology*, 2:289. Cf. *On Thinking*, 30: "So—what is it to be conscious? It is either to be one identity of the living triune God or to be one of the community for which this God makes narratively structured space in his life. That is to say, it is to participate in the life of the people of God, remembering that this participation need not be affirmative or immediate."

138. Parts of this section and the larger chapter were adapted for my contribution to *Pro Ecclesia*'s symposium on Jenson after his passing; see East, "Robert Jenson's Theology of Scripture."

by grace, to be faithful to Christ. The gospel would be false if the church could not be faithful—at least at the corporate level, over the long term—regarding matters that cut to the heart of the church's confession. But what about when the church is unfaithful at the local level or in the short term?[139]

We can formulate a critique of Jenson's answer by phrasing the question a few different ways. First: What does it mean to say that the church, because it is one with Christ and filled by the Spirit, therefore knows as a matter of course what to say and do, if it is admitted that the church, both communally and individually, errs and sins on a daily basis and with terrible, devastating effects? Second: Given this ecclesiology, in what way can Scripture function as an instrument of divine *judgment* on the church when it is unfaithful, particularly if the church's unity with Christ means not only that it knows what to say (the gospel) but also that it knows how to read? Scripture is the church's book, and the church is the Spirit's community. How then can the church—which, as the Lord's prophet, knows what the Spirit is saying to the church in Scripture, the Spirit's book—either err in its reading or, more to the point, *be corrected* in its (errant) reading? Third: Where, in this theological-conceptual picture of the church and Scripture, is the Lordship and agency of Christ vis-à-vis the church, particularly in its ongoing efforts to read and embody Scripture faithfully—efforts that, Jenson agrees, have often been pitiful, distorted, disastrous?[140]

What Jenson might say by way of response is the following. The church is finally indefectible with regard to the message it has to announce, and only at the outer limit of fidelity; dogma's adequacy is far from perfection. Moreover, entire communities or regions of the church may fall away, which is merely visible attestation that they are not of the single dia-

---

139. For recent reflection on these issues in relation to von Balthasar and in light of clerical sex abuse, see Lawson, "Apostasy of the Church."

140. Jenson often instances Chalcedon as the most theologically confused and potentially calamitous event in the church's early history. See *Systematic Theology*, 1:127–38. As he writes elsewhere of the Tome, having fitted its author St. Leo with the label "hyper-Antiochene": "If [he] were not a great pope, and a great teacher, one would simply [call him] 'heretical'" ("How Does Jesus Make a Difference?," 199; see also 400n37). Given that the Tome of Leo was quite literally canonized at Chalcedon, and therefore defines conciliar orthodoxy (rather than being subject to such definition from without), Jenson's willingness to suggest Leo was a heretic reveals something of the unreconstructed Protestant in him.

chronic people of God,[141] the one holy catholic and apostolic church. It is *this* community that will not fail to speak the gospel.[142] Which means also that particular individuals within it may fail and speak or act utterly unfaithfully; either they, like non-church communities, will fall away for good, or they will be reconciled to the church and re-enter communion with the one indefectible body. Furthermore, within the whole complex historical process of the church's life, individuals, groups, and movements will err in their speaking and in their reading of Scripture; but this too is internal to the dynamic of a forgiven people being sanctified across time by union with Christ. What the Spirit does is ensure that, when the time comes, on the whole and at crossroads moments, the church will be faithful in proclamation and interpretation. Jenson designates churchly reform as Christ's self-discipline—asceticism of the body enacted by the head[143]—but the thrust of divine agency is in the hands of the Spirit. For the Spirit, in Jenson's theology, so agitates the church that, on the one hand, it will *not*, in the end, fail to be true; yet, on the other hand, when matters come perilously close to sinking the ecclesial ship, the Spirit's presence will trouble the church into judgment, repentance, change— even division.[144] And so it is the Lordship of the Spirit that judges the

141. Perhaps this goes too far; perhaps Jenson would rather say that the passing-away of a regional or national church does not reflect on the faithfulness of all its local churches, only on the faithfulness of the whole. Or maybe even passing away before new growth and developments of the church in other places is not always necessarily a reflection of faithfulness at all, but part of the mystery of the gospel's progression and so of God's will.

142. Though one wonders how Rome fits into this (hypothetical) picture. If the one true church subsists in the Catholic Church in communion with and under the authority of Rome's bishop, could Rome—not merely the Pope himself—fall away decisively? If not, then Jenson has preserved part of the church militant from defectibility, rather than reserving indefectibility for the church triumphant.

143. See *Systematic Theology*, 2:212-15. Perhaps no claim of Jenson's has elicited more exasperated critique than this one.

144. I do not know whether Jenson would affirm this last work of the Spirit, although he never denied the justice of the sixteenth-century Reformation. It could certainly be handled biblically: through, say, figural reference to the division of the kingdoms of Israel and Judah, or through analogous use of the scriptural idiom of God's judgment of sin, which issues in God "handing over" the sinful individual or group to punishment, sin, the devil, and/or the logical consequences of their actions (cf. Rom 1:24; 1 Cor 5:4-5). After centuries of patience, did the Spirit hand over the church to its own wickednesses in the sixteenth century? See further Radner, *End of the Church*.

divided church, first, for being divided at all (since it had to come to that), and, second, for its manifold errors of exegesis, proclamation, and practice. The gates of hell shall not prevail against it, but they will test and lay siege to it, also from within. This promise is eschatological, and the unity and fidelity of the church in history, from the apostles to the Parousia, will be knowable only eschatologically. Until then, the church must simply trust in Christ's promise; like God's existence, if all one had to go on was the evidence of experience, one would have little reason for belief.[145]

Even if this is an accurate representation of Jenson's position, it nevertheless remains beset by problems that finally overrun his theology of the church as *totus Christus* and Spirit-filled communal prophet. Allowing as much as he does evacuates the content and so the force of his claims. For example, he asserts that, given the church's union with Christ by the Spirit, one need not ask how it knows what to say, because, as Christ's body, filled with his Spirit, it simply knows by virtue of its intimacy with him, by analogy to a husband and wife who finish each other's sentences, or indeed speak "for" each other.[146] That cannot be a sufficient explanation, however, if the question concerns, as it does in the context of his proposal, how we may understand, and so trust, that the texts of the Old and New Testaments are accurate in their presentation of the truth of God. In effect, his answer is: The canonical texts are accurate and worthy of trust due to the nature of prophecy; the prophet united to Christ speaks Christ's word by the Spirit as a matter of course, without extrinsic aid, just as the church as a communal prophet does as well—*except in the manifold cases in which it does not*. But why did the Spirit's general work of inspiration not fail in the past, with the texts that eventually became the Bible, when it has failed so often since?[147] Or, put better, since God the Spirit does not fail: If *human individuals and communities* filled with the Spirit

---

145. Jenson is fond of Luther's aphorism: *aut nullum esse Deum, aut iniquum esse Deum.* That is, *if* we merely surmised by looking around at the world and its presumed governance by a transcendent being, our conclusion would rightly be that "either God is not, or God is wicked" (quote from *De servo arbitrio* in *D. Martin Luthers Werke. Kritische Gesamtausgabe*, 18:784); see *Systematic Theology*, 2:4; *Ezekiel*, 77. In other words, apart from the revelation of the love of Father, Son, and Spirit in and through the cross and resurrection of Jesus, "theism" is a fool's game: "of all [philosophies] most to be pitied" (1 Cor 15:9).

146. *Inspiration*, 38; *Triune Story*, 204–5.

147. That is, if the Spirit's work of inspiration in the Bible's production is not different in kind from the Spirit's work of inspiration in the common life of the church since Pentecost.

have so often failed to speak the gospel faithfully since the Bible's composition, why did they not fail to do so in the biblical texts themselves?

Scripture, in Jenson's formulation, is the church's book and the Spirit's book, and the Spirit is the church's own communal spirit. It seems to me that one of the intimate relationships suggested by these three genitive constructions, forming a kind of closed triangle or unbreakable hermeneutical circle, must be loosened or qualified for some measure of critical distance between the church and Scripture to be a live possibility. The typical move, at least in Protestant circles, is to stretch the first relationship, so that Scripture is no longer the church's book but solely God's; hence the temptation, discussed earlier, to forget or elide the fact that the church (broadly construed) is the Bible's (created) author, collector, and hermeneutical home. My alternative proposal is to complicate the third, the Spirit in the church. It is both ambiguous and simplistic to say, as Jenson does regularly in his writing, that all communities have a spirit, and the church's is God's own.[148] To be sure, the Spirit indwells and empowers the church from within. But that is not to say either that the Spirit is limited to the church or that the Spirit's presence is as native or "at home" as Jenson's rhetoric implies.[149] Suppose the Spirit's presence in the church is that of an alien, One who does not belong, a troublemaker. What if God's Spirit is less akin to "my" spirit in me, and more akin to Jesus in Jerusalem—or, better, Jesus in the temple? Extending the analogy, Jerusalem and its temple were, unbeknownst to its leaders and inhabitants, "true" home for the Shekinah become flesh. And yet: "A prophet is not without honor, but in his hometown, and among his own kin, *and in his own house*" (Mark 6:4 KJV, my emphasis). The axiom applies by extension, and paradigmatically, in the life of the church. In this manner a principal work of the Spirit in the church is the turning-over of tables, the whip-like disturbance of God in person opposing truth to falsehood, faith to sin, justice to wickedness. Doubtless such a work does not exhaust description of the Spirit's life in the church. But perhaps it is an essential part of it. And

148. See, e.g., *Visible Words*, 53: "There is spirit wherever there is community. If a community has identity, if it is gathered around and as a specific body, then it has *a* spirit, an identifiable particular freedom that moves the community and moves those who encounter the community. . . . All Christianity's talk of the Spirit unpacks one simple but drastic experience and claim: the spirit of the Christian community and the personal spirit of Jesus of Nazareth are the same."

149. See Jenson's wide-ranging discussion of the Spirit in *Christian Dogmatics*, 2:105-85.

perhaps any account that suggests the Spirit is natural to the church, or leaves the church unperturbed, is an implicit denial of it.

The Church's (Spirit's) Book:
A Canon by and for a Magisterial Church

The Bible, for Jenson, is at once the Spirit's and the church's book, and each because of the other. It is the Spirit's book because the church is the Spirit-filled prophet of God and body of Christ, and therefore knew what to write and knows how to read its Scripture. The Bible is the church's book because the texts of Scripture have God's Spirit-inspired people as their author, collector, and publisher, and because they exist to no other purpose and in no other extant community than the ecclesial, whose founding mystery is the Word of God spoken and heard within it. The connections between the doctrinal loci of bibliology and ecclesiology are subtle but clear, with pneumatology and christology playing a distinctive role vis-à-vis both loci, though especially ecclesiology. The doctrine of the Trinity is thus to the fore (albeit in an atypical way) in Jenson's theological account of Scripture and church, having framed all three—God, God's Word, and God's people—with a particular understanding of narrative. God is a story, told by the metanarrative of Scripture, within which the church and its members are located.

Within Jenson's theology, however, the doctrine of Scripture does not have priority. Which is not to say that Scripture does not have *functional* priority, that is, material normativity in his arguments, theologoumena, and system as a whole. Constant reference to Scripture, through explicit citation, global narrative reference, and pericopetic exegesis, is a hallmark of Jenson's theology. But the doctrine of Scripture, though not quite *pro forma*, is treated (at least in the systematics) primarily in its role as an evangelical norm for theology—as an unmeasured measure of gospel-speech, of which theology is the hermeneutic—and only secondarily as a dogmatic locus unto itself.[150] The sheer givenness of Scripture, a material

---

150. This is in keeping with Jenson's retrieval and reappropriation of the Lutheran scholastic distinction between the (principal) sacramental or liturgical mode of Scripture's authority as the living word of God and its (secondary) doctrinal or statutory mode as norm for church teaching, practice, and belief. I expand on this distinction in East, *Doctrine of Scripture*, 125, 149–52.

feature of Jenson's dogmatic *proposal* for how the church should relate to Scripture in its daily life, is itself a formal feature of his discourse *about* it: it is just there; it is operative and normative by definition; gymnastics of the Protestant scholastic variety are tertiary or superfluous to secure this place and role. In the years following the publication of his systematics, Jenson devoted increasing attention to perennial questions in bibliology, up to and including the inspiration of Scripture. But the point remains: the doctrine of Scripture as such is neither systematically central nor materially foundational to Jenson's theology.[151]

What *is* central and foundational to Jenson's thought are the (for him) paired doctrines of Trinity and of church—the former including christology and pneumatology, apart from which no account of Jenson's ecclesiology would be complete. Both doctrines center on and derive from the person of Christ, particularly his incarnation (all abstraction from which, however traditional or well-motivated, is just that: abstraction); from here one spirals up and out into the other doctrines: to the Trinity (knowledge of which comes only through this One, the Israelite Messiah Jesus); to the Spirit (whose coming is paired, temporally and theologically, to Jesus's ascension, together delaying the kingdom's advent and thereby creating the time of *ekklēsia*); and to the church (instituted by Jesus's ministry, his resurrection into the sacramental body of believers, his ascension into heaven, and his pouring out the Spirit at Pentecost). In this way christology is the all-important doctrine, and so the core of Jenson's theology.[152] What is interesting, then, is that bibliology, though obviously related to christology in a number of ways, is not principally a function of christology, but for the most part only indirectly or secondarily connected to it. How so?

One way to put it is that, while Scripture for Jenson is materially christocentric, the theological warrant for such a claim, as well as further reflection on Scripture's nature and purpose, are located not in christology but in other dogmatic loci. Bibliology, in Jenson's thought, is first of all an ecclesio-missiological matter, just so a pneumatological matter, and

---

151. The location of his two discussions of Scripture in the systematic theology is instructive: on the one hand, in prolegomena, as a theological given prior to beginning the doctrine of God; on the other, in discussion of the works of God, in the section on ecclesiology, in the context of the sacraments (paired, in the same chapter, with iconology). What could be less Protestant?

152. This is but to say that Jenson, following Barth, is christocentric in his theology generally, though, unlike Barth, not in his theology of Scripture.

therefore a christological matter. Christology informs the doctrines of the Spirit and the church, and in that way influences, albeit at some distance, the doctrine of Scripture. Let me take up these claims in order.

Scripture as Materially Christocentric

The historical and theological judgment at the heart of Jenson's theology of Scripture is that "the purpose for which the church assembled this book in the first place" is that it would "be in its entirety and all its parts witness to Jesus' Resurrection and so to a particular God," the triune God of Israel.[153] "Thus the Christian Bible, Genesis to the Apocalypse, tells the one drama of Christ's coming."[154] The matter of the biblical story is the advent of Mary's son; chronologically prior moments in the story at once bear witness in advance to the risen Messiah of Israel and are themselves instances of his unveiling "ahead of schedule," as it were. So the "word" that comes to the prophets is not merely consonant with the later Logos that becomes flesh in Jesus; nor is it one and the same as the fleshless Word of God, the *logos asarkos*, "prior" to assuming flesh.[155] Rather, "the word that came to the prophets was in fact Christ acting in anticipation of his incarnate coming, and we might even gloss our clause ["The word of the Lord came to me"] as 'Christ came to me.'"[156] That is to say, "the Word in the Old Testament *is* the Word incarnate as Jesus."[157] As a rule for Christian reading, it follows that, "hearkening to the Word in the Old Testament, one should always be listening for the self-identification and for the intonations and rhetoric of the Gospels' protagonist."[158] Indeed, "we can . . . find out about the historical Jesus Christ from Isaiah or Zechariah or David," just because he came to them.[159] As a concrete example, in the

---

153. *Systematic Theology*, 1:58.

154. *Triune Story*, 160.

155. For there is no "prior" to the incarnation: "Time, as we see it framing biblical narrative, is neither linear nor cyclical but perhaps more like a helix, and what it spirals around is the risen Christ" (*Triune Story*, 118). He then asks, regarding John 1:14 and 8:58: "Which, then, comes first, the incarnation or Abraham? It depends entirely on which chapter of John you are in; that is, it depends on the discursive context."

156. *Ezekiel*, 27–28.

157. "Second Thought about Inspiration," 397 (emphasis mine); *Triune Story*, 125.

158. "Second Thought," in *Triune Story*, 125.

159. *Triune Story*, 119.

opening chapter of Ezekiel, the prophet sees a vision of a throne, above which is seated something or someone whose appearance is like a man (v. 26). Why, according to Jenson's christological hermeneutic, should this be? Because the second identity of the one God of Israel *is* a man, the human being Jesus. Premodern Christian readers of Ezekiel were therefore justified and well-formed exegetically to observe, with almost casual lack of flair, the name of the man seen by the prophet Ezekiel some centuries before the birth of Jesus.[160]

Christology, clearly, is central to Jenson's understanding of Scripture's substance (as a christological metanarrative), telos (bearing witness to Jesus's resurrection and the God thereby identified), authority (speaking the efficacious saving gospel address about Jesus), and proper interpretation (in light of the church's christological-trinitarian dogmatic faith). The Bible is misconstrued apart from Christ, the specific Christ of the Niceno-Constantinopolitan tradition. Christology, however, is not integral to Jenson's *bibliology*; that is, reflection on Christ is not at the core of his description of Scripture as a theological object in its own right. Questions about Scripture's provenance, purpose, attributes, and nature are all answered elsewhere, in other dogmatic loci. This non-christological systematic rooting entails that, when christology is brought back into the fold of bibliological discussion, its role is mediated by other loci. Moving from the architectonic level to the level of argument and proposal, it entails also (or simply reflects) an understanding of church and Scripture that gives a number of significant kinds of priority to the church over against Scripture.

Scripture as Ecclesiological

Jenson's bibliology is a two-sided affair, the church and the Spirit alike playing significant dogmatic roles. But the church is nevertheless first among equals in Jenson's theological description of Scripture. He never fails to begin discussion of Scripture with discussion of the church as its context, creator, collector, and canonizer. The specific book made up of the variety of texts that constitute the biblical canon owes its existence to

---

160. Jenson's example is St. Gregory the Great, who, in a homily on Ezekiel, "simply presumes that the one above the throne is the man Jesus and concerns himself rather to lay out this man's ontological status" (*Canon and Creed*, 84).

the covenant community: it has the pilgrim city of God as its (proximate) source and end. Holy Scripture is an ecclesial product, full stop. Inability to acknowledge this fact is, for Jenson, as theologically problematic as it is historically ignorant.

That last modifier is key: embedded within Jenson's bibliological argumentation regarding the church is a deeply held conviction about the theological force of history, of the irreversible nature of historical contingency as humanly definitional and providentially weighty. Jenson's argument does not run: Whatever may have happened with the canonizing process, the apostles *earlier* or the bishops *later* said such-and-such. Instead, Jenson's argument runs: Here is what the church did, across so many decades and centuries, and *that* event—howsoever complex and diachronic, only "an event" in retrospect—is constitutive of the Bible's nature, authority, purpose, and faithful reception. To be sure, such an event is contingent; it could have been otherwise. But, Jenson avers, it was not otherwise, and so there is nothing more to say.[161] As historical creatures, the past is determinative of who and what we are, which includes the texts and practices and institutions that our common life comprises. The church is not excepted from this dynamic. Moreover, the church has an additional reason to value the communally constitutive meaning of historically contingent events: namely divine providence, and specifically the Spirit's leading (and protection) of the church in time. It goes without saying that according such significance to historical process in conjunction with God's providence does not, for Jenson, sanctify whatever happens as straightforwardly good, irrevocable, fated, and/or pleasing to God. I elaborate this point in discussion of the Spirit below; for now, suffice it to say that Jenson places a premium on the timeful processes of the church's history, and that, with respect to Scripture, doing

161. Jenson's oft-rehearsed line about this is that, since God is God, things could have been otherwise, and God would still have been the triune God that God in fact "contingently" is, with us in our history, as Jesus with his Father in their Spirit. But about that "otherwise," he writes, we can say nothing—that is, there is nothing we can or should speculate about (no "there" there) regarding what God might have been apart from us. See, e.g., *Systematic Theology*, 1:65; *On Thinking*, 56. For a late shift, with respect to the propriety of even this kind of answer (here regarding his denial of a *logos asarkos*), see his "Once More the *Logos Asarkos*." For critique, see Crisp, "Robert Jenson"; Gathercole, "Pre-existence"; Molnar, *Divine Freedom*, 89–129. See Molnar's earlier review of vol. 1 of Jenson's systematics in *Scottish Journal of Theology* 52:1 (1999): 117–31, to which Jenson offered on the next page (132) an infamously terse reply exactly seven sentences long.

so gives argumentative as well as theological weight to the sheer facticity of what happened in the church's efforts to formalize, collect, authorize, and publish its sacred texts.

Finally, in terms of Jenson's dogmatic structure, the doctrine of Scripture is located in the doctrine of the church, thus reflecting accurately his normative claims about the two doctrines and their relationship to each other. Where Scripture is not prolegomenal, it is treated as a function of the church, situated after sacraments and before icons. Bibliology is an item of ecclesiology—which is not to reduce the Bible to an aspect of the church, nor to strip it of theological substance, nor still to uncouple it from theology proper. But the *way* in which it is theologically depicted, precisely in its relation to the triune persons (to God the Spirit and to Jesus the Son), is in the dogmatic locus of the church, its sacramental life and mission to the world. So before turning to the Spirit and the Son, it is worth pausing and considering this missiological component of Jenson's ecclesiological account of Scripture.

Scripture as Missiological

One of the most interesting features of Jenson's bibliology is his understanding of the different ways in which the Old and New Testaments are Scripture for the church. Here is his argument *in nuce*:

> The church . . . can very well be conceived apart from the existence of the New Testament. A church without a New Testament can be conceived because the church in fact lived and flourished in that state for slightly over a century, *and* because this fact is presumed by the New Testament itself. If the Lord had come for final judgment when he was first expected, the church would never have depended or been thought to depend on any other Scripture than Israel's. The church is thus not timelessly related to her New Testament; rather, her need for a New Testament was occasioned historically, and provision of that need was an event within her history.[162]

Jenson writes further that "the Old Testament is . . . the *Scripture* in the church's Scripture," whereas "the New Testament's textuality," its

---

162. *Inspiration*, 40; *Triune Story*, 205.

scripture-ness, "is instead a *substitute* for something other than text, for a *viva vox*, the voice of the living Apostles." Because the apostles died, texts were written, maintained, and gathered together lest the church lose its apostolic identity: "the New Testament is an *aide memoire*."[163]

So, on the one hand, the church is unthinkable apart from the Old Testament, "as a sheer object of necessary reference in the church's worship and proclamation and catechesis."[164] On the other hand, the church in its very being is itself the community of the Lord's delay, the people of the time opened for the gentiles to be welcomed into Israel. Accordingly the church is at once the postapostolic community and the missionary community: the latter because the former (since the church shares the dominical command to the apostles to *go*), the former because the latter (since the event-within-the-event of the gentiles entering Israel through the gospel outlived the apostles' mortality). Thus the New Testament is a missiological improvisation in response to an unforeseen situation: a continuing mission to the nations without the living evangelical guidance of the witnesses to the Lord's resurrection. This framework combines Jenson's understanding of the Spirit's role in historical contingency with missiology by identifying the necessity and sheer existence of one-half of the Christian canon as a function of the church's mission in an indefinite postapostolic period of time. If the church's mission is to speak the gospel, and the Bible is the book that rules gospel-speech (the Old Testament by grounding the gospel in Israel's history and life with the saving covenant God of Abraham and Moses; the New by displaying trustworthy instances of gospel-saying by the chosen witnesses of the living Jesus), then the Bible is, finally, a missionary document. It is there for enabling continued faithful testimony *on the mission field* to the God of the gospel of Jesus.

There are eschatological implications here. When the kingdom comes, the people of God will be translated into eternal glory, as all Israel, Jew and gentile alike, will be saved. The church, so to speak, has a future beyond its mission. So that church and mission, though coextensive given a restricted sense of *ekklēsia*, are not convertible, given a more theologically robust understanding of the church as gentile-including Israel, the whole city of God from Adam to the End.[165] The Bible, however, *is*

---

163. *Triune Story*, 121–22. Cf. *Systematic Theology*, 1:26–33.
164. *Triune Story*, 122. Contra, e.g., Bultmann, "Significance of the Old Testament."
165. In his commentary on the Apostles' Creed, St. Thomas Aquinas writes:

coterminous with the church's mission. It has no future beyond the apostolic task. When the kingdom comes, its purpose will have been fulfilled. When God is all in all, the body's head, Christ, will speak with fullness and immediacy, without need for past testimony (not to say that testimony will end, but the apostles will be alive in the glorified communion of saints, and so able to speak for themselves). In this way Jenson's missionary understanding of Scripture, his necessary reference to missiology within his ecclesiological grounding of bibliology, is simultaneously a specification of the high purpose and nature of Scripture and a temporal or economic qualification of it.

Scripture as Pneumatological

Pneumatology is the depth dimension of Jenson's historico-ecclesiological account of Scripture. As the other half of his bibliology, the doctrine of the Holy Spirit is what makes both his treatment of the Bible and his treatment of the church *theological*—and the one because the other. Picture Jenson's system as a web with lines running across and between different doctrinal loci. Within this dogmatic web, pneumatology "connects" to bibliology both directly and indirectly, through ecclesiology. The presence and gifts of the Spirit *in* the church are what warrant, in a more than purely historical sense, locating theology of Scripture in ecclesial context, for that context is already charged with the pneumatic, since the church is a pentecostal reality from beginning to end. Bibliology, then, is determined by pneumatology in these two ways: through primary speech about the Spirit's role in Scripture's production, formation, being, and purpose; and through secondary speech about the Spirit's role in the church, where the church is understood as Scripture's proximate source, earthly habitat, principal audience, and hermeneutical milieu. I will take up each in turn.

God's Spirit is the Spirit of prophecy, opening the mouths of women and men to speak the Lord's word—that is, to prophesy—inspiring them by the gift of the divine presence to give voice with their human voices

---

"There have been those who said that the Church was to last until a certain time, but this is false, since this Church began from the time of Abel and will endure to the end of the world . . . and after the end of the world it will continue in Heaven" (collected in *Aquinas Catechism*, 81).

to God's voice. This is the special way in which the Spirit brings about the reality of prophecy in general and the texts of Israel's Scripture in particular. The New Testament, as we have seen, is not "scripture" in the same way the Old Testament is; its inspiration is a function of the broader, more common role of the Spirit in guiding the church into truth and away from error. In both cases, though (albeit perhaps in a somewhat attenuated sense for the New Testament), the Spirit may simply be said to be the divine author of Scripture, an antecedent and "trumping" agent in the texts' origins, writing, editing, and fixed final form. It is this divine authorship, traditionally classed in a univocal way as "inspiration," that is the condition of the possibility, first, of Israel's sacred texts bearing prospective testimony to the person, work, and coming of Jesus the Christ; and, second, of the texts' meaning transcending the original historical contexts of their production, without being dissolved into the arbitrary play of inadjudicable interpretations. The Old Testament prophesies the *totus Christus*, the crucified and risen Lord of the apostles' proclamation together with his body, the church. The Holy Spirit's action is what makes this possible.

God's Spirit is the Spirit of God's people, and so the Spirit's action—to inspire prophecy, to author Scripture—is always ecclesial action, too. Just as "all Scripture is inspired by God" (2 Tim 3:16), so all Scripture is written by human beings, that is, by members of the covenant community, prophets of the Lord given words to speak and write that are, because granted by the Spirit, what God says. Moreover, the church, as the Lord's fulfillment of his promise to pour out his Spirit on his people, is a single communal prophet. Therefore what it says just is inspired speech, words spoken by the Spirit because its own collective spirit is the Lord's. Divine authorship of Scripture means ecclesial authorship of Scripture, and vice versa. It is not a slip for Jenson to gloss the Bible, on facing pages of his systematics, as "the Spirit's book" and "the church's book."[166] Nor are the phrases ornamental, lacking theological substance. It is the Spirit's book because the Spirit, directly and efficaciously, inspired the Bible's words and texts: (1) what Scripture says, the Spirit says. But it is also, equally and simultaneously, the church's book, because, on the one hand, the church wrote and collected the Bible's words and texts: (2) what Scripture says, the church says; and, on the other hand, because the church is the Spirit-filled prophet of God, and what either the Spirit or the church says

166. *Systematic Theology*, 2:276, 277n24.

is inseparable from the other, most of all in the Bible's words and texts: (3) what Scripture says, the church says, *because the Spirit says*. And that, finally, is why the church is uniquely and authoritatively situated to interpret Scripture aright: because Scripture is the (ecclesial) Spirit's book, "who may do with it what he will; and the church as his prophet knows what that is." The church, that is, as the pneumatic community, knows how to read its own book.[167]

Scripture as Christological

The Spirit does not act without the Word: divine authorship and inspiration are not exclusively pneumatological concepts, nor can ecclesiology be discussed in full apart from christology. But we arrive at christology, in the context of Jenson's bibliology, through the back door, as it were. Not only does christology impinge on bibliology only indirectly through talk of the church, but Jenson pairs it with pneumatology, which *does* inform bibliology in a direct way. By which I mean that pneumatology's prominence is only brought into further relief by the surprisingly—by comparison—minor role that christology plays in Jenson's theology of Scripture. Let me conclude by expanding a bit on this point.

The relevant details of Jenson's proposals are already before us. The church is a single corporate prophet because, first, the Spirit so fills and inspires the church as to make it thus and, second, the church is so united to Christ as his body that the communal prophet it is, with Christ as its head, *just is* the promised final prophet of God, Jesus the risen Messiah with his people—the *totus Christus*. The picture filled out, we see the ecclesiological explanation of the church's capacity (better, charism) at once to speak, write, recognize, and hear and read the true word of God, in the scriptures and in the sacraments. For the church is the body of Christ, indwelled by the Spirit. What it has to say is the gospel, and it will reliably persist in doing so because it is united, by the Spirit's grace, to the Word himself, the living Christ; so united, it cannot fail to speak God's word, or—as the case may be—to read and hear it in the texts of Scripture, thence to proclaim it to God, assembly, and world.

So christology enters into bibliological reflection, for Jenson, via ecclesiology; specifically, through his account of the *totus Christus*, which

167. *Systematic Theology*, 2:276.

locates the Word's role in the already-described Spirit-created prophet-hood of the church as a single community. To be sure, Jenson is happy to say that, like the Spirit, Christ is the author of Scripture, but the claim plays little substantive role in his bibliology. The role of christology in his theology of Scripture has to do, as I noted at the outset of this section, with Scripture's *matter*: its organizing logic, its inner dynamic, its final cause, its object of testimony. In the end, however, it is not the doctrine of Christ that determines Jenson's doctrine of Scripture, central as that topic is for his theology as a whole. It is ecclesiology (with a nod to missiology), and therewith pneumatology. These are the dogmatic loci within which bibliology is situated and discussed, and likewise they determine systematically what may and must be said about Scripture, according to the gospel.

Robert Jenson and John Webster have this in common, then, that theology of Scripture depends on and follows from ecclesiology. Given their differences on these matters, we can begin to see how opposing doctrines of the church inexorably generate divergent, if not always opposed, doctrines of Scripture. Though parts of Jenson's theological system are unique to him, the general presentation is catholic in character; he explicitly sides with Rome and Constantinople (and Canterbury?) over against Wittenberg and Geneva and Basel. But there is a third ecclesial type beyond the reformed and catholic approaches I have surveyed in these two chapters. That is the believers church, rooted in the radical reformation. To such an ecclesiology, the theology of Scripture it generates, and its representative in John Howard Yoder, we turn in chapter 6.

But before engaging Yoder's thought we must come to terms with his life—which is to say, with his sins, crimes, and hypocrisies. Next, then, is an excursus dedicated to that topic and to the questions it raises for whether and how to continue to read his published work.

Interpreting Yoder's Work in Light of His Abuse

Yoder's Sexual Abuse

Across his life and career John Howard Yoder engaged in consistent patterns of abusive sexual behavior toward women. Sometimes the behavior was "merely" inappropriate; sometimes it was illicit while superficially consensual; but much of the time it was coercive, constituting a disturbing, unjust, and outrageous abuse of power. The initial documented incidents come from the 1970s, while he taught at a Mennonite seminary,[1] but continued into the 1980s, while he taught at the University of Notre Dame.[2] Institutional awareness of Yoder's actions was piecemeal but, when it came, those who had the authority to discipline or fire him or to report him to the authorities neglected to do so. Institutional self-protection was one element of this negligence. Another was a desire to keep things "in house," without involving those outside denominational circles. A third was a culpable credulity and resulting ignorance regarding Yoder's behavior, which some saw as a kind of idiosyncratic but not per se immoral approach to Christian sexual ethics—an approach perhaps overly influenced by so-called sexual liberation (or, alternatively, by undiagnosed autism) but not an issue of formal wrongdoing and thus not a matter for public concern. The last element that helps to explain why Yoder continued for so long without being held to account is his own intransigence. Whether or not he was sincere in his declarations of innocence, he engaged in systematic schemes of adversarial noncooperation, rationalization, self-justification, stall tactics, passive aggressiveness, and the

---

1. Goossen, "'Defanging the Beast,'" 1–15, 21–39. See also Goossen, "Mennonite Bodies, Sexual Ethics."
2. Goossen, "'Defanging the Beast,'" 39–52.

like. Finally, in the 1990s, he reluctantly submitted himself to a denominational process of discipline. The results were ambivalent. On the one hand, his ministerial license was suspended; he withdrew from many speaking and writing opportunities; he appears not to have engaged in abusive behaviors in the final years of his life; and he was reconciled to his wife in their home church just two days before his passing. On the other hand, he consistently obstructed and protested the procedures of the disciplinary process; he was far from forthcoming in his personal admissions; his reticence to admit fault was persistent; his apologies were invariably manufactured, self-regarding, and unpersuasive; and worst of all, his victims went largely overlooked in the process—as if Yoder's behavior were primarily an issue for himself and his wife, not those he harmed. He died at the age of 70 in 1997.[3]

Beyond Mennonite circles and those who were close to Yoder, this information was not widely known for some time.[4] Rumors suggested something questionable in his sexual life; sometimes they implied behavior more akin to the caddish or the transgressive than the immoral or the criminal. Stanley Hauerwas, who popularized Yoder's work from the 1970s on, publicized parts of the story. For example, in an essay published in a 2000 book, Hauerwas referred to Yoder having "submitted to his church's discipline process regarding sexual misconduct."[5] A decade later, in his 2010 memoir, he expanded not only on his relationship to Yoder but on his knowledge of Yoder's behavior and his role in the disciplinary process. He wrote that "John was clearly misusing" women he had "seduced" by dint of how "intellectually overwhelming" he could be.[6] But details were scarce. Hauerwas did recount how he, Glen Stassen, and James McClendon persuaded Yoder via conference call to submit to the process.[7] Nevertheless, as Hauerwas later wrote in 2017, he did not realize—at the time or later, in the writing of his memoir—the extent, nature, or traumatic effects of Yoder's actions.[8]

3. Goossen, "'Defanging the Beast,'" 52–80. For further biographical information, see McClendon, "John Howard Yoder"; Nation, *John Howard Yoder*, 1–29. See also Steinfels, "John H. Yoder"; Oppenheimer, "Theologian's Influence."

4. See the five-part series in the local newspaper *The Elkhart Times*: "Theologian's Future Faces a 'Litmus Test.'" See also Krall, *God's Living Room*.

5. Hauerwas, *Better Hope*, 135–36.

6. Hauerwas, *Hannah's Child*, 242–47, esp. 244.

7. Hauerwas, *Hannah's Child*, 245. Cf. Goossen, "'Defanging the Beast,'" 59–60.

8. Hauerwas, "In Defense of 'Our Respectable Culture.'"

The prompt for Hauerwas's realization was the publication, in January 2015, of Rachel Waltner Goossen's "'Defanging the Beast': Mennonite Responses to John Howard Yoder's Sexual Abuse." Across seventy-four pages Goossen documents in painstaking detail the entire saga of what she terms Yoder's "experiment in human sexuality."[9] That ironic euphemism is not meant to disguise what she elsewhere names as sexual violence. It is meant, instead, to indict both Yoder and those who ignored or enabled his behavior for their attempts to obfuscate, discount, redescribe, or otherwise downplay the severity of his transgressions. Her article is the definitive account of Yoder's history of abuse. It functioned as the nail in the coffin for plausible deniability on the part of persons and institutions involved in Yoder's career as well as scholars, readers, and churches familiar with Yoder's work but not this dark, damning side to his life.

In the almost two decades that spanned Yoder's death to the publication of Goossen's article, secondary scholarship on Yoder flourished.[10] Not only works about Yoder's thought but edited volumes authored by Yoder himself appeared regularly; on average one such posthumous book was published every eighteen months or so.[11] Speaking for myself, I began reading Yoder in college in 2006, and apart from the essay and memoir by Hauerwas referenced above, I did not encounter mention of his abusive behavior until shortly before Goossen's article, and even then concrete information was hard to come by.[12] For those of us not associated with the Mennonite world, its institutions, or the extended Yoder family, the history remained opaque. It also appears to be the case, at least from afar, that those involved directly with Yoder's case did not

---

9. Goossen, "'Defanging the Beast,'" 7.

10. See, e.g., Hauerwas et al., *Wisdom of the Cross*; Carter, *Politics of the Cross*; Nation, *John Howard Yoder*; Sider, *To See History Doxologically*; Kerr, *Christ, History, and Apocalyptic*; Werntz, *Bodies of Peace*; Martens, *Heterodox Yoder*; Zimmerman, *Practicing the Politics of Jesus*; Parler, *Things Hold Together*; Doerksen, *Beyond Suspicion*; Nugent, *Politics of Yahweh*.

11. Across a little over seventeen years I count more than a dozen posthumous volumes. Put simply, Yoder's scholarly afterlife has stretched forward beyond his death for many years, as did, therefore, the reception of his work.

12. Beyond Hauerwas's limited comments, I recall reading and participating in conversations prompted by Barbra Graber, "John Howard Yoder." I suspect most academics and Christian readers outside of the Mennonite world learned about Yoder's abuse through some combination of Hauerwas's memoir, Graber's essay, and Goossen's article.

always agree about what constituted appropriate levels of disclosure or healthy transparency. This hesitation had in view simultaneously Yoder's victims, many of whom are still alive; Yoder's wife, Anne Marie, who outlived her husband by twenty-two years; and their many children and grandchildren. It is clear that Yoder's behavior should not have been tolerated from the outset and that, once it was recognized for what it was, information about it should have been made public immediately through the proper legal channels. One can understand, however, without affirming, the internal confusion and uncertainty regarding how best to move forward after his death.

Given the fog that obscured outsider knowledge of Yoder's actions in the 1980s and '90s and the general unclarity that followed, the question of what to do with Yoder's theological writing—that is, of whether and how to receive and interpret his work, now that we have a full, unvarnished, and unabridged account of his abusive behavior—is still relatively new. It is also of a piece with wider cultural movements, such as #MeToo, the Catholic Church sex abuse scandal, conversations about "separating the art from the artist," and collective memorialization of famous persons from the past who perpetrated or permitted evil deeds.[13] This excursus cannot address all the issues raised by these and

13. See, e.g., Kantor and Twohey, "Harvey Weinstein"; Farrow, "Aggressive Overtures." For a singularly thoughtful theological reflection on the preservation and destruction of public monuments, in conversation with Ryan Andrew Newson's *Cut in Stone*, see Hendreckson, "Monuments Can Be Destroyed"; cf. Schwartz, "Living Memory." For an example of the dialectic or dialogical process set off by questions regarding reception of past figures (including the loaded term "cancellation"), see the controversy over Flannery O'Connor in the summer of 2020: beginning with Angela Alaimo O'Donnell, *Radical Ambivalence*, and followed by Paul Elie, "How Racist Was Flannery O'Connor?" (Elie is the author of *The Life You Save May Be Your Own* as well as "What Flannery Knew"). Elie's essay is a review of O'Donnell's book; see also the review (written before the controversy) by Jessica Hooten Wilson, "O'Connor and Race." Wilson then responded to Elie with "How Flannery O'Connor Fought Racism." A few weeks later, when Loyola University Maryland announced that it would be renaming the Flannery O'Connor Residence Hall in light of the publication of O'Donnell's book and Elie's essay, Jennifer A. Frey wrote "Don't Cancel Flannery O'Connor." Once the renaming occurred, O'Donnell responded both to that and to Elie's essay in "The 'Canceling' of Flannery O'Connor?" Finally, Elie replied to O'Donnell in turn: "Confronting Flannery O'Connor's Racism." For an acerbic and less than helpful comment on the whole series of events, but worth reading as one more perspective in the conversation, see Allen, "Flannery O'Connor." For a response to Elie sympathetic to his criticisms but less caught up in the question of "cancellation" and

other recent events. By the end I will offer an account of how I think we ought to relate to artistic and discursive works whose creators or authors have acted in ways that we, as their interpreters, rightly judge abhorrent. That account underlies but does not determine my approach to Yoder in particular, however, not least since he was a Christian moral theologian. I will focus first, therefore, on Yoder himself, his actions, and the question of whether to continue reading him in light of what we now know—and if so, how.

Before going further, though, let me be clear. The first and overriding response to Yoder's abuse ought to be revulsion and repudiation. The problem with his actions is not that it makes reception of his work difficult. The problem is the pain he caused and the consequences for his victims. Discussion of offenders like Yoder is perennially curdled by forgetting this simple fact. Those harmed in this case are not his readers but those who were abused by him. Most of us are not in a position to know them personally or to help them directly. But we can certainly refuse to forget them.

Interpreting Yoder's Work

For some theological scholars, remembering Yoder's victims means letting go of his work. For example, Hilary Scarsella has written a powerful response to the 2017 essay in which Hauerwas tried to come to terms with Yoder's behavior. I encourage anyone who wants to reckon with Yoder or with the issues raised by his actions to read this essay. This is how she concludes it:

> The approach to theology represented by Yoder and Hauerwas has so far not been able to make much headway in resisting sexual violence, much less understanding it. As public knowledge of Yoder's sexually violent and predatory behavior settles in, what we need is to become willing to consider that this approach to theology is not currently equipped to help us understand sexual violence, hear the voices of survivors and resist this violence's systemic perpetuation. Hauerwas's repeated use of logics and rhetoric that perpetuate the harm of sex-

---

more focused on the moral questions raised by literature and its interpretation, see Griffith, "Flannery O'Connor Didn't Care."

ual violence suggests as much. Rather than investing our intellectual and spiritual energy in the goal of fixing a system of thought that has produced such harm, we would be wise instead to set our intention on cultivating theological space committed to thinking with and through the experiences of sexual violence survivors and the logics that empower survival and wellbeing in the face of sexual threat. Hauerwas is right to be anxious that the theological paradigm he holds dear may not survive the transition. It is shortsighted, however, not to realize that inviting the Yoderian thought-world to rest, lie quiet, listen and change is the only response to Yoder's violence that has the potential to avoid repeating Yoder's abuses.[14]

Though I do not ultimately agree with Scarsella's last recommendation, she may well be right. Hauerwas may be too invested in his reliance on Yoder to see the problems inherent in it, and I may be too. We are not yet twenty-five years removed from Yoder's passing, and Goossen's article was published only five years ago (as I write these words). Whether or not a consensus is reached in academic reception of Yoder's thought, Scarsella's proposal not only may be correct; it may win the day. Perhaps it ought to. My partial disagreement with her conclusion is provisional and tentative, subject to revision; even if what I suggest below is correct, or at least admissible, theological scholarship is certainly large enough for a divergence of views on this complicated question.

I think it is perfectly reasonable, in any case, to hold that Yoder's history of abuse places him beyond the pale for serious theological attention. Moreover, I do not think anyone—*anyone*—"ought" to read Yoder. Yoder is not *owed* a hearing. There are countless scholars, thinkers, and writers, living and dead, who repay study. Any practitioner in Christian theology or ethics who opts to bypass Yoder in her work is acting, it seems to me, well within her scholarly remit.

Why, then, have I included Yoder in this book? And how do I propose to interpret his thought?

The only honest initial answer is personal. Yoder's writing made a significant impact on my development as a Christian theologian, an impact that was at once spiritual, moral, intellectual, and vocational. It is difficult to unwind, unremember, or erase such an encounter. I had been

---

14. Scarsella, "Not Making Sense." For another critical response to Hauerwas's essay, see Hunter-Bowman, "Stanley Hauerwas's Response."

reading Yoder's work, using it in my writing, and publishing on it for almost a decade before I read Goossen's article. Once I did read it, apart from the bewildering horror at the thought of Yoder's victims and his contemptible avoidance of taking responsibility, my reflex was similar to Scarsella's: Yoder should be assigned and cited no longer; scholars and theologians should stop engaging his thought altogether. I no longer think that, but I cannot deny that, like Hauerwas, there is a measure of self-interest involved in including Yoder in this book. My reasons may amount to self-deception. Having spent so much time researching and writing on Yoder's thought—by the time this book is published, a full fifteen years—perhaps I simply need it to be true that there are grounds for doing so. Again, I do not think that is the case, but I admit that I am far from an unbiased party.

The primary substantive reason that Yoder is a part of this book is that I believe his work has something constructive to say to the church and to the theological academy. As I elaborate below regarding "the art and the artist," I am disinclined to think that an author of ideas is wedded to them in an indivisible way, that her character or even her intentions determine their meaning or reception, or that arguments and intellectual projects contain essential logics or generate inevitable consequences. That is why scholars are justified in continuing to read, for example, Plato, Aristotle, Smith, Kant, Jefferson, Marx, Nietzsche, Maurras, Schmitt, Heidegger, and Gandhi. Neither their deeds nor their bigotries nor the implementation of their ideas by others renders their work out of bounds for scholarly reception. Indeed, in many cases scholars read their works against themselves, that is, in ways of which they would not have approved.

Scarsella writes that Yoder's "system of thought . . . has produced . . . harm," and indicts an "approach to theology" common to Yoder, Hauerwas, and others for being unable "to make much headway in resisting sexual violence, much less understanding it." I want to interpret Scarsella carefully here, for her claim is complex and admits of more than one interpretation. Her aim, as I understand it, is to highlight or call attention to at least three things: (1) those academic discourses that focus on analyzing and undermining sexual violence;[15] (2) the ways in which Yoder

---

15. For recent writing at the intersection of theology and trauma, see Jones, *Trauma and Grace*; Rambo, *Spirit and Trauma*; Rambo, *Resurrecting Wounds*; Boynton and Capretto, *Trauma and Transcendence*; O'Donnell and Cross, *Feminist Trauma Theologies*;

used the written word to justify his abusive behavior, so that his public argumentation in scholarly venues remains inseparable from his private argumentation in memos, papers, and letters; (3) the enormous influence of Hauerwas on the American theological academy and of Yoder on Mennonite institutions and communities, an influence amounting to a kind of hegemony that in turn helped create the conditions for Yoder's actions to go unpunished.

If my interpretation is accurate, then there is little here from which I would want to dissent. The endeavor to "fix" Yoder's project is misbegotten, not to mention talk of redeeming or justifying it/him. And she is surely right to recommend the wisdom of "cultivating theological space committed to thinking with and through the experiences of sexual violence survivors."[16]

Scarsella likely means something more than this, though, and if so, it is worth stating clearly where and why we disagree. For instance, her language implies that there are "thought worlds," "rhetorics," and "logics" inoculated against violence and injustice. It also suggests an intrinsic relationship between particular modes of intellectual inquiry, on the one hand, and understanding and resisting sexual violence, on the other. If either of these interpretations is correct (and they may not be), then I want to say why I think they are mistaken.

To be sure, not every discourse is created equal, and there *are* ideas that are not only vicious but demand censure rather than engagement.[17]

Slee, *Fragments for Fractured Times*; Warner et al., *Tragedies and Christian Congregations*; Tushnet, *Christ's Body, Christ's Wounds*; Townes, *Troubling in My Soul*. For moral, pastoral, and theological writing on sexual violence in particular, see Adams and Fortune, *Violence against Women and Children*; Fortune, *Sexual Violence*; Crumpton, *Womanist Pastoral Theology*; Poling, *Understanding Male Violence*; West, *Wounds of the Spirit*; Cooper-White, "Intimate Violence." Scarsella's own co-authored article on these issues contains a useful and much larger bibliography: see Scarsella and Krehbiel, "Sexual Violence."

16. In, for example, online forums such as *Our Stories Untold* (http://www.our storiesuntold.com/) and its parent organization Into Account (https://intoaccount .org/), which are both run by Krehbiel and Scarsella, among others.

17. For example: Holocaust denial, phrenology, theories of racial supremacy. Though it is worth adding that sometimes the best response to even the most ludicrous or abhorrent views is systematic dismantling via dispassionate, comprehensive, unimpeachable argumentation. The most intellectually and morally impressive example of this that comes to my mind is Adolph Reed Jr.'s review of Richard J. Herrnstein and Charles Murray's *The Bell Curve* in *The Nation* (28 November 1994), now collected in Caldwell and Hitchens, *Left Hooks, Right Crosses*.

But in terms of disciplines, guilds, and modalities, there is, finally, no safe haven, no pure or innocent discursive technique. The hermeneutics of suspicion goes all the way down; "no one, not one" is just (cf. Rom 3:12). Nor is the purpose of most intellectual inquiry to avoid, resist, or understand sexual violence, or violence of any kind. The various academic disciplines (math, physics, astronomy, history, sociology, economics, literature, theology) certainly ought to have nothing to do with perpetrating or enabling sexual violence. But that is not their aim, their *raison d'être*. Rather, the presence or absence of violence in the lives of academics and intellectuals usually predates their writing, or rides on the back of it. Sometimes there is a substantive connection between them—as with, for example, the petition by certain continental philosophers in the late 1970s for age of consent laws in France to be abolished[18]—but just as often no such connection obtains.

In other words: methodology will not save us. Nor, even, will materially accurate or true judgments. Right-thinking people sometimes lead despicable lives, and wrong-thinking people sometimes lead admirable lives. The same goes for institutions, genres, and discursive modalities. This helps makes sense of the fact that there is no neat bifurcation on any of these questions between scholars of one sort or another. Theologians of all kinds—black and white, female and male, Catholic and Protestant, traditional and revisionist—differ on every significant topic under the sun, whether these be conceptually closer to or further from questions of personal identity, inequitable power, and those structures and practices found to reduce the likelihood of abuse or to increase protection of the vulnerable.

It therefore seems to me far preferable to judge particular arguments and ideas through close exegetical engagement than to suggest that whole authorial "thought worlds" will inexorably incite or license sexual violence. To follow the latter route is bound to be question-begging. Furthermore, it ends up reifying highly complex corpora into stable, essential objects no longer subject to disputation and interpretive adjudication. Or, if it is not the thought of the person that is problematic but the person himself, then the suggestion amounts to saying that the person has some-

---

18. Including, e.g., Sartre, Foucault, Derrida, Althusser, Barthes, de Beauvoir, Deleuze, and Lyotard. See "Lettre ouverte à la Commission de révision du code pénal pour la révision de certains textes régissant les rapports entre adultes et mineurs." Archive: http://www.dolto.fr/fd-code-penal-crp.html.

how placed himself in his words, or infected them by his moral pollution. His uncleanness renders the work unclean, and both lie under the ban.

Perhaps Yoder's theology is not weighty enough to warrant sustained attention and retrieval; that is a separate question. But at the general level, far too much would be lost to opt for this approach. And in any case, in lieu of "thought world" as a term of art for theology, let me suggest an alternative description. For if the subject matter of theology is the living divine reality revealed in the person and work of Jesus—together with the whole penumbra of witnesses and mediators, histories and texts, communities and practices that provide access to that revelation—then what theologians offer in their work is contemplative and hermeneutical *insights* into that reality. They glimpse some detail or truth, some connection or imperative, some implication or sublimity, and bring it to light for the rest of us. We their readers, for our part, sift the wheat from the chaff, testing their offerings not only for goodness, truth, and beauty, but also for usefulness, clarity, and edification. I submit that the theological writings Yoder left behind offer insights into the reality of Christ worth receiving, however critically, both now and into the future. I leave it to others to decide whether that judgment is accurate.

The secondary reason I have included Yoder in this book and believe his work is still worth engaging is that his influence hangs heavy over contemporary Christian theology. One response to that legacy, as we have seen, is to invite it "to rest, lie quiet, listen and change." That is a sensible approach; no one need do any more than that. But there are other options available. One is systematic critique, and a number of scholars have already published considered, closely argued treatments of Yoder's thought that bring knowledge of his abuse to bear on their interpretation of him: Isaac Samuel Villegas, Karen Guth, and Jamie Pitts, to name only a few.[19]

---

19. See Villegas, "Ecclesial Ethics"; Guth, "Doing Justice"; Pitts, "Anabaptist Re-Vision." See too, in direct or indirect response to Yoder, Koontz, "Seventy Times Seven"; Martens and Cramer, "By What Criteria"; Heggen, "Sexual Abuse"; Guth, "Moral Injury." There is also a collection of writings about Yoder from 2014 and 2015 in Bethel College's online archive of issues of *Mennonite Life*: https:// mla.bethelks.edu/ml-archive/2014/. One of the first theological responses to Yoder and the question of whether and how to interpret his work was Cramer et al., "Scandalizing John Howard Yoder." See, finally, Albrecht and Stephens, *Liberating the Politics of Jesus*. I learned of this volume in the final stages of preparing this manuscript and have yet to procure a copy, but it appears to be a critical, diagnostic, and constructive attempt to affirm the peace witness of baptist traditions while repudiating sexual vi-

Some tie Yoder's life more closely to his work than others; all are worth reading, and each offers insights worth attending to. As the next chapter will attest, I agree with some of these authors: there are in fact areas of Yoder's theology that either (at the time of writing) served to justify his behavior or (at some distance) propose an account of the church in which abuses akin to Yoder's would be likely to be held unaccountable. These critical approaches to Yoder's work serve an invaluable purpose, then.

Beyond rejection via disregard or critique, I will treat Yoder's writings as a viable source for constructive theological reflection in the present, and thus as continuing to make a modest but real contribution to Christian thought. In the chapters that follow I hope to model critical appropriation of a figure such as Yoder. Where his arguments, ideas, and readings are entangled with his record of abuse, I do my best to highlight and interrogate them. Where they are not, I consider his claims just as they stand on the page: interpreting or criticizing them as I would any other theologoumena.[20] As with the potential of Yoder's work to continue to speak to faith and theology today, readers will be the judge of the extent to which I succeed in my aims.

Cultural Artifacts, Original Sin, and the Church

For some, the foregoing will be sufficient as an explanation for my approach in this book. For others, more is called for. In the previous section I wanted to stay close to the details of this particular case prior to engaging

---

olence and offering hospitality to its victims; it contains essays by Scarsella, Guth, Sara Wenger Shenk, Linda Gehman Peachey, Nancy Bedford, and Karen Suderman.

20. Cf. Healy, *Hauerwas*, 14: "There is a difference between saying that our theological reflection is affected by our character, which is obviously true, and saying that our character needs to be known in order to understand our theological arguments. Martin Luther had his unique experiences, but we do not need to know them to understand and assess his theological arguments. It is useful for scholars of Luther to know his background and the pressing issues of his day, of course, in order to help them explain certain decisions he made in constructing those arguments. That Barth was a bourgeois Swiss male no doubt made some difference to his theology. But we can and should understand and critique their texts, insofar as they constitute a theological proposal, without knowing such things, or by ignoring them if we do. The construction of a theological argument may be influenced in various ways by one's character and history. *But in theology, as in the sciences, arguments should be assessed without any consideration of who constructed them*" (my emphasis).

in rather abstract reflection. In what follows, though, I want to offer a philosophical and theological rationale for both critical and constructive reception of cultural artifacts produced by human beings whose beliefs or actions call for moral condemnation. I will close by noting the ways in which this rationale is qualified or complicated by the Christian identity of the person in question.

To begin, it is my view that it is not only permissible but necessary, at least most of the time, to distinguish strongly between the product and the person(s) who produced it. Why? For at least four reasons.[21]

First, because of epistemic limitations. We know, and can know, next to nothing of the personal life or character of those responsible for most cultural artifacts. Most of the time, therefore, we are obliged as a matter of course, if usually implicitly, to make the distinction between what is made and the one(s) who made it.

Second, because human artifacts are in fact distinct from their sources. This is true in many respects. For example, artifacts outlive whoever makes them. Indeed, they often outlive the cultures of which they are a product. This is also literally true: a song, a portrait, a math equation, a book, a sculpture, a film—none of these is "bound" to its creator; each exists separate and apart from her. Most human encounters with such artifacts occur in almost total ignorance of the conditions of their production. Knowledge of such conditions might be useful or interesting for scholarly investigation, but if they were truly necessary, almost no one would ever be in a position to appreciate, understand, learn from, or enjoy works of human creativity. Finally, product and producer are distinct in the sense that creative or authorial intentions do not determine the meaning of what is made. Whether didactic or abstract, an object of any kind fashioned by human purpose outbids such purpose. Once it is in the world, others will make of it what they will, often contrary to the rationale of its maker.

Third, distinguishing the product from the producer is justified and even necessary because rarely is it the case that such a product owes its existence or qualities wholly to a single individual. More often than not, it is a group or even a community of persons who are responsible for a particular cultural artifact. In this way such artifacts may rightly be

---

21. For a classic meditation on some of the following issues, see Adams, "Saints." For recent comment on a situation similar to Yoder's, see Polet, "Problem of Eric Gill."

said to "belong" not to those who made them but to the social, religious, and cultural contexts that gave rise to them. In an incisive meditation on morality, art criticism, and Bill Cosby, Wesley Morris concludes in this way:

> The ["Cosby Show"] predicted the cultural climate we're in now—America as some fantasy of itself, yet also a place where black people were obviously black and more obviously people, a representation of life rather than imitation of it, comedy that made some of us us. It was pop entertainment, a parenting guide and an essential, unprecedented feat of folk art, and now the River Styx runs through the living room. But the show wasn't like one of those downed Confederate statues, a tribute erected and defended in cynicism and bad faith. It was called "The Cosby Show," but it was never really only his (there are lots of unpaid actors and crew members who can attest to that). Those 6,000 or so hours belong as much to the culture and country as they ever did to him. He canceled himself. He was never the show's legacy. That was always going to be us.[22]

Morris's claim suggests that a cultural product finally belongs not only to the people who made it possible but also to its history of reception, a history that is not abstract but local, subjective, and therefore beyond the organs of official or scholarly commentary.[23]

Fourth and last, the distinction I am proposing between producer and product is licit and sometimes requisite because of two interrelated truths: original sin, on the one hand, and the objectivity of the good, on the other. Beginning with the latter, the claim is metaphysical. It asserts that what are traditionally designated the transcendentals—truth, goodness, and beauty—obtain independently of our estimation or perception of them. Which is to say, they transcend us, at once preceding

22. Morris, "Morality Wars." Morris is critic-at-large for the *New York Times* and former film critic at *Grantland* and *The Boston Globe*. He has written extensively on these issues, including the particular case of Bill Cosby and African American reception of Cosby's comedy and television work in light of his crimes. See Morris, "Cliff Huxtable"; "How to Think about Bill Cosby"; Morris and Browne, "Bill Cosby Issue."

23. See further Robert Brandom's discussion of "Confession and Forgiveness, Recollection and Trust" in *Spirit of Trust*, 583–635. See also Hitz, *Lost in Thought*; Jacobs, *Breaking Bread*, esp. 1–58. I reflect at length on these latter two works in my essay "Befriending Books."

and grounding our existence and drawing us to themselves as to a final horizon or end. So that, if an inarguably wicked person were to make a scientific discovery, or compose a masterful symphony, or pronounce an indefeasible moral judgment, each of these would remain, respectively, true, beautiful, and good, regardless of the character of the human subject in question. The reason why this can be the case is that, at least according to Christian faith, "all have sinned and fall short of the glory of God" (Rom 3:23). That is, all human beings, without exception, are sinful, conceived and born as sinners from the start. Which means that *every* cultural artifact of human provenance has as its proximate origin a person who fails daily the simple test of virtue: to love God with one's whole being and to love one's neighbor as oneself. In short, whatever is good and lovely and true in any and every culture comes from blood-stained hands and greedy hearts; there are no others extant. That means we ought not to be surprised when artists, writers, thinkers, makers of every kind are broken and troubled souls who nonetheless produce moving and life-giving objects of genius and beauty.

Now: to say that we are all sinners, to affirm that we are all broken and troubled souls, does not flatten out moral evil, as if murder were on a par with a white lie. It does not leave undifferentiated our estimation of a genocidal dictator compared to one of his victims. Original sin does not render moral judgment moot.[24] What it does is force us to a bitter, though not tragic, realism about evil in the world, and our complicity in it. It further forbids us either the satisfying indulgence of self-righteousness or the principled withholding of mercy. So much of our culture's intractability and cyclical anger on these matters stems from recognizing the need for confession without having recourse to absolution, for truthful accusation without accompanying access to grace. Christians do not believe in cheap grace: forgiveness is not a "get out of jail free" card, a slap on the wrist and off one goes. Pardon in Christ is costly.[25] It demands the totality of one's being, body and soul, abased in self-renunciation, the mortification of the flesh, the dying of the old self, absolute repentance—and *only then* standing up, taking one's mat, and walking away

---

24. For two sensitive and theologically astute treatments of the doctrine of original sin with a view to these concerns, see McFarland, *In Adam's Fall*; McFadyen, *Bound to Sin*. Also relevant is the exegetical-theological proposal of Croasmun, *Emergence of Sin*.

25. See Bonhoeffer, *Discipleship*, 37–99.

healed (cf. Mark 2:1–12). Nor do we walk "away" from Christ but always toward him, behind him, with his voice lingering in our ears, "Go, and sin no more" (John 8:11 KJV).

It seems to me that this recognition—of the universal truth of original sin and the objectivity of the good—is the only viable means of making sense of how human works of cultural production can succeed in the first place, and of how cultures, institutions, and communities can endure without succumbing to entropy and despair. Far from leading to negligence or moral laxity, it ought to encourage vigilance, courage, and commitment to truth-telling while avoiding any propensity for self-loathing, the futile quest for an original innocence, or a perpetual redux in a revolutionary Year Zero.

That, in any case, is my understanding of cultural criticism and of why a strong distinction between human creators and their creative products is usually, perhaps always, a wise and justified practice. The question is more acute for Christian theology, however. Traditionally the church has had high moral standards for those ordained or called to lead or teach in the community.[26] Churches are right to enforce these standards and, when they are not met, to remand, rebuke, discipline, fire, defrock, or excommunicate those persons who fail them.[27] At least four factors, though, complicate Christian reception of the works and witness produced by problematic leaders and teachers in the church.

The first concerns anachronism. What are we to do with past figures whose behaviors were deemed acceptable at the time but are no longer considered so today? Where does interpretive generosity end and excuse-making begin? Think of St. Augustine's arguments for compelling the Donatists via imperial coercion, or St. John Chrysostom's virulently anti-Jewish rhetoric in his sermons.[28]

---

26. See, e.g., Volf and Croasmun, *For the Life of the World*, which argues throughout that the character of a theologian is an essential component of her thought—though there is an ambiguity in the text as to whether this is a prescriptive claim (i.e., theologians ought to live in accordance with their stated views and/or with the command of God) or whether it is a substantive precondition (i.e., those who fail to do so obviate the force of their arguments). I explore these ambiguities in "Must Theologians Be Faithful?"

27. Consider the case of Theodore McCarrick, the first cardinal ever defrocked for sexual abuse: see Dias, "Pope Defrocks Theodore McCarrick." See further the investigative reporting and commentary of Elizabeth Bruenig, "Catholics Face a Painful Question"; "He Wanted to Be a Priest"; "'Pray for Your Poor Uncle'"; "Everyone Knew about Theodore McCarrick"; "Catholic Sex Abuse Crisis."

28. See, e.g., Brown, "Religious Dissent"; Brown, "Religious Coercion"; Brown,

The second concerns influence. If a figure from the past or even from the present has already wielded enormous influence over others— whether in a church, a tradition, a region, a culture, or a whole civilization—then the time has passed for deciding *whether* to receive such influence. The question now is *how*. Think of Martin Luther, whose late writings against the Jews are a stain on his legacy but nevertheless deeply influenced his country;[29] or Karl Barth, who for the duration of his marriage maintained an adulterous relationship with his live-in research assistant, Charlotte von Kirschbaum.[30]

The third factor concerns the mixture of good with the bad. What of persons who did undeniably great things *and*, in some other area of their lives, did unquestionably bad things? Can we celebrate the one without providing cover for the other? Think of Martin Luther King Jr., who is worthy of lasting honor for his work in the Civil Rights Movement yet, during that time, used his fame, charisma, and power to seduce and sexually mistreat young women.[31] Or think of Jean Vanier, founder of L'Arche and international advocate for persons with intellectual disabilities, who, across his life, solicited sexual relationships with a number of women under his spiritual supervision.[32]

The fourth and last factor is the academy. Those who write and teach Christian theology today are no longer exclusively or principally ordained

"St. Augustine's Attitude." I owe knowledge of these articles to Ployd, *Augustine*, 14n36; see that extended footnote and the accompanying bibliography for further research on this topic. As for Chrysostom, see Wilken, *John Chrysostom and the Jews*.

29. See, e.g., Gritsch, *Martin Luther's Anti-Semitism*.

30. See now Tietz, "Karl Barth and Charlotte von Kirschbaum"; Tietz, *Karl Barth: A Life in Conflict*. See also Köbler, *In the Shadow of Karl Barth*; Selinger, *Charlotte von Kirschbaum*.

31. See Garrow, "Troubling Legacy of Martin Luther King"; cf. Ransby, "Black Feminist's Response."

32. See the "Summary Report" produced by L'Arche International, 22 February 2020, https://www.larche.org/documents/10181/2539004/Inquiry-Summary_Report -Final-2020_02_22-EN.pdf/6f25e92c-35fe-44e8-a80b-dd79ede4746b; see also the letter written by the leaders of L'Arche, Stephen Posner and Stacy Cates-Carney: https:// www.larche.org/documents/10181/2539004/Letter-Federation_International -Leaders_2020-02-22_EN.pdf/20d33d55-72e0-4c51-8703-8ab6foadb9b5. Catholic writer J. D. Flynn was deeply influenced by Vanier; he and his wife, Kate, adopted two children with Down syndrome and named one of them after Vanier. For his reflections in the aftermath of these revelations, see Flynn, "Daniel Vanier." For a similar situation that has just come to light as I write, see Silliman and Shellnutt, "Ravi Zacharias."

church leaders but rather academics whose institutional home is a university or, at most, a seminary. This book is itself a blending of the distinct but intertwined institutions of church and academy. Accordingly, the question before us concerns not so much the church's reception of church thinkers whose lives betrayed serious moral failure as it does Christian *academic* reception of Christian *academic* writing. Does that distinction make a difference? Should it?[33]

33. In a forceful statement that answers in the negative, see Griffiths, *Practice of Catholic Theology*. Having defined theology as any reasoned discourse about (the) god(s), and Christian theology as reasoned discourse about the triune Lord of the church's confession, Griffiths asks whether love for the Lord provides any cognitive advantages in the task of Christian theology. His answer is yes and no: it provides avenues of inquiry and insight unavailable to those lacking such love, even as it might close off other avenues available only to those lacking love for the Lord. What then of virtue? I quote his answer in full:

> Perhaps . . . moral goodness is necessary for . . . theologians, or at least useful for them. The moral virtues might permit theologians who have them to be conformed to Jesus more closely than those who lack them, and therefore to come to know him, and the triune Lord, better. Those virtues might even be necessary for good theology. Honesty, justice, courage, temperance, mercy—isn't a theologian with these better than one without them, and better not just as a person but also as a theologian? No. Certainly, these virtues are good to have, but they have nothing directly to do with the skills necessary for speaking and thinking well about the Lord. A man with only one leg lacks a good he'd be better off with, but that lack won't make him a worse (or better) theologian. Just so for a dishonest or cowardly theologian. There are and have been many good theologians whose moral character leaves much to be desired. Cyril of Alexandria, Jerome, Karl Barth, Paul Tillich, Martin Luther King, Jr.—these were, it seems likely, variously liars, plagiarists, adulterers, cholerically arrogant, and uncharitable. That didn't prevent them from thinking and writing well about the Lord; neither did it prevent them from writing and thinking better about the Lord than many theologians more morally virtuous than they.
>
> Perhaps their moral vices prevented them from thinking as well about the Lord as they might have, assuming that their development of moral virtue didn't call into question or degrade their intellectual virtues. Maybe their moral vices served as partial obstructions to the perspicuity and profundity of their theological thinking. Maybe. But this, even if true (and its truth cannot, in concrete cases, be known), is contingently true in something like the same sense that quadriplegics might be better theologians if they weren't paralyzed because they'd have easier access to books. The state of theologians' bodies has the same kind of relation to their capacity to speak and write good theology as the state of their morals. Which is to say, not much in the order of being and nothing at all in the

The question is a live one for Christian scholarship today. Lamentably, there are numerous instances of noxious and indefensible behavior not only in philosophy and theology but also in biblical studies.[34] The proper response of institutions and organizations should be clear enough: a policy of zero tolerance for abusive or coercive behavior of any kind. The response of scholars, in terms of their research and teaching, is less clear cut. I have laid out my own approach to these matters, but by no means do I think the answers are simple or obvious, or ought to be unanimous. Those who come to differing conclusions have my respect, as I hope I am able to earn theirs. Though to paraphrase St. Augustine: while I hope for generous readers, I want frank critics above all.[35] For humility is important, but truth is supreme. If the next chapter does not ultimately arise from and serve the truth, then better by far for it not to have been written at all.

---

order of knowing: no one can easily tell from reading a theologian's work what the state of his or her life was, and it's unseemly to try. The attempt makes reading tea-leaves or entrails seem perspicuous.

This too is a minority position within the tradition. Most [Christians] who've thought about the matter have approached, and sometimes affirmed, the position that a morally corrupt theologian is a contradiction in terms. This too is largely a lexical difference: "theology" is implicitly understood to label something good, and theologians are therefore thought to be of necessity good people. But it's hard to deny—and perhaps no one, when pressed, would—that bad people can think true things about the Lord, and once that's understood and instances of it produced (whether bad people can think true things about the Lord is best understood as an empirical question), the hard version of the majority position falls to the ground. (45-47)

34. See, e.g., the case of New Testament scholar Richard Pervo: Suzukamo, "E-mail Address"; or more recently, the case of Old Testament scholar Jan Joosten: Bland and Henley, "Oxford Professor." For a sharp rebuke to any suggestion that scholars might continue to use the work of these or any other academics (including figures like Yoder), see Young, "Love the Scholarship."

35. St. Augustine, *The Trinity* (*De Trinitate*), book 3, preface.2.

CHAPTER 5

John Howard Yoder

The Politics of Scripture in the Believers Church

Christian thought centers around events that really happened.[1]

The creation of "Scripture" is ... a critical event and not a conservative phenomenon.[2]

The Bible is the book of the congregation, the source of understanding and insight as the congregation seeks to be the interpreter of the divine purpose for humans in the congregation's own time and place with the assistance of the same Spirit under whose guidance the apostolic church produced these texts.[3]

The very existence of the church is its primary task.[4]

At its heart, the theological vision that unfolds across John Howard Yoder's writings is simple and consistent. It centers on Jesus of Nazareth, the human being attested in the apostolic writings as crucified Messiah and risen Lord, together with the community of disciples gathered around him, from Galilee up to the present, dedicated to following his way in a hostile and violent world.[5] Yoder's animating conviction is that Jesus, precisely as God incarnate, reveals what it means to be truly and fully human, and politically most of all: "Jesus is from beginning to end

---

1. *To Hear the Word*, 167. Citations in this chapter for works written by Yoder will not include authorial attribution.
2. *For the Nations*, 91.
3. *Revolutionary Christianity*, 20.
4. *Politics of Jesus*, 150.
5. Though see the revisionist interpretation of Paul Martens, *Heterodox Yoder*, 1–18.

homo politicus."[6] Salvation through Christ is therefore irreducibly social, moral, communal; life in Christ is inseparable from the community he established, the community of the new age, of Israel-with-the-gentiles. The life and teachings of Jesus, being the norm and ground of the *ekklē-sia*, are therefore a genuine option for human social life—principally for the church, through faith in Jesus and the power of his Spirit, but also, by derivation, for persons, peoples, and polities who do not know or follow Jesus.[7]

Jesus, in other words, is morally and politically *relevant*. Not because his way meets some universal, ostensibly "public" criterion of "responsibility," but because he is the New Man: the first instantiation of a whole revolution in human life; a person so wholly in union with God's will and character that he may be said to be the first truly human being. And so his humanity is not exceptional, but exemplary; not singular, but standard; not inimitable, but the one pattern worthy (and demanding) of imitation. Accordingly, the politics of the church as a community among communities must be that of its founder, head, and Lord. The church is therefore the herald and forerunner of the divine alternative to the world's lust for violence and death, an alternative announced by Jesus as the kingdom of God. The church is sent into the world to proclaim God's kingdom in speech and, most of all, to embody it in its common life. Insofar as the church incarnates the way of Jesus in the midst of the world, as a corporate witness to the coming advent of the Lord's peaceable reign of justice over the nations, it fulfills its mission.[8]

Here, at the intersection of christology, ecclesiology, missiology, eschatology, and social ethics, is the crux of Yoder's thought, and the site of all his theological proposals. It is where and why he articulates, for example, a mission-centered believers church ecclesiology (one, that is, that eschews sectarianism for ecumenism); a sympathetic engagement with Rabbinic Judaism as a "non-non-Christian" religion (and in its synagogal polity, often more faithful than magisterial churches); a constructive understanding of Christian pacifism and social action; a treatment of

---

6. *Revolutionary Christianity*, 65.

7. For works focused especially on these themes, see *Preface*; *Priestly Kingdom*; *Royal Priesthood*; *Christian Witness*; *Discipleship as Political Responsibility*.

8. See the important stand-alone essays "Meaning after Babble"; "Ethics and Eschatology"; "Ashamed of the Gospel"; and "Armaments and Eschatology." See also *Body Politics*; *When War Is Unjust*; *Christian Attitudes*; *Radical Christian Discipleship*; *Revolutionary Christian Citizenship*; *Real Christian Fellowship*.

universal ministry and the sacraments as political practices of the local congregation; an argument against capital punishment rooted in the forward movement of the biblical narrative; and, finally, an approach to theology that is rooted in close scriptural exegesis and an ecclesio-historical account of Scripture as a whole.[9]

That approach is vital for understanding Yoder's theology of Scripture. It is as much Yoder's *use* of the Bible in his theological argumentation as his formal reflection *on* the Bible as a theological object that constitutes his contribution to the field. Moreover, it typifies the very ecclesial logic for which Yoder is a representative: the baptist or believers church tradition, rooted (in his case) in the radical reformation. Though Yoder gives a good deal of direct attention to the canon of Scripture, he is wary of inflated theories that obtrude in the church's mundane practical uses of the text in its daily life. His response is to deflate them, and to find other means by which to affirm the church's historic trust in and reliance upon the Bible for its life, worship, mission, and teaching.

Those "other means" are inseparable from Yoder's account of the church. Put differently, his ecclesiology is ingredient in his deflationary approach to bibliology. That is just what this chapter sets out to explore. In the first section I discuss Yoder's theology of Scripture, which he describes as the sociopolitical charter of the Christian community, at once binding it historically to the community's founders (the apostles) and predecessors (the prophets) while norming its responses to challenges on the mission field and serving as a locus of unity for all the many divided branches of the one messianic tree. In the second section I turn to Yoder's theology of the church, which he depicts as the exemplary minority community of the new age in the midst of the old, sent by Christ as the "pulpit and paradigm" of God's will for humanity, the foretaste in miniature of life to come in God's kingdom. In the third section I examine the doctrinal moves that Yoder makes in his account of Scripture and church, drawing out in particular the ways in which he represents a distinctively radical-reformation (or "baptist") perspective in contrast to theologies

9. The publications here are voluminous. See the early *Anabaptism and Reformation* as well as the later essays "Primitivism in the Radical Reformation"; "On Christian Unity"; and "Ecumenical Movement." For further works that touch on the themes in this paragraph, see *Theology of Mission; Jewish-Christian Schism Revisited; Original Revolution; Nevertheless; He Came Preaching Peace; Nonviolence; War of the Lamb; Pacifist Way of Knowing*; "On Not Being in Charge"; *What Would You Do?; Fullness of Christ; End of Sacrifice.*

informed by either the magisterial reformation or the catholic tradition. It will remain an open question whether certain decisions by Yoder, for example to avoid high theories of Scripture's verbal inspiration, ought to be understood as characteristic of baptist thought more generally, or instead as unique to him. After all, such communities are often underrepresented in theological discourse; sometimes their theologians articulate what their communities take for granted, but sometimes, too, they trade on dogmatic indeterminacy in the service of eccentric or ingenious proposals. One of the challenges of interpreting Yoder, among many others, is distinguishing one from the other.

Bibliology: The Politics of Scripture

The Bible, for Yoder, is the pastoral-doxological document of the believing community, binding it historically to Israel and the apostles, norming its way of life (in action and in speech), and serving as a reliable touchstone for judgment and renewal as the church seeks to be faithful in its gospel mission across different times and places. Its significance lies in its practical function. Moreover, because it is a product of history, using it well requires historical understanding. These emphases sit somewhat at cross-grain with trends in bibliology and theological interpretation in recent decades. But Yoder is a historical critic through and through, having little but high praise for the method, and always employing it in his exegesis. Even apart from the specificities of method, however, his is a thoroughly *historical* biblical hermeneutic: the baseline of the text—not to say its exclusive significance—is the meaning it would have had in its original context. Yoder is fond of demolishing interpretive anachronisms by means of contemporary scholarship. Finally, his readings often, and by intention, challenge or repudiate traditional readings. Rarely is it the case that what the church has "always and everywhere said" regarding this or that text is trustworthy or true; the tradition is ordinarily a barrier, not a guide, to right reading.

Nevertheless, there is another side to Yoder's bibliology. Scripture is first and foremost the church's book, written and assembled for the purposes of this particular community; it must therefore be read in light of those purposes, in that community. Nor is historical criticism a distancing mechanism, as it so often becomes elsewhere. Its function is to concretize the Bible's stories and instruction, to put sociopolitical flesh and bones on them, in order to make them even more relevant to today's church than they have sometimes been thought to be. Furthermore, Yoder is not hermeneutically naïve. He knows readers bring presuppositions and beliefs to the text, and he believes the principal conviction that Christians should bring to the canonical text is christological: namely, that Christ is the telos, the content, and the measure of the diverse biblical witnesses. Perhaps most important of all, Yoder's theological method, if he has one, is nothing more elaborate than sustained topical or narrative biblical interpretation, governed by christological convictions and impelled by questions of social, moral, political, communal, and ecclesial import. Writing in a time when this sort of theological exegesis— uncluttered by theory, unburdened by prolegomena, unfussy in presentation—was sparse in the academy, Yoder repays study in his own right. The example of his work is also a reminder that established approaches to Scripture and its interpretation, whether in the ecclesial sense of magisterial traditions or in the disciplinary sense of institutional pedigree, are not the only ones on offer.

This section contains four parts, each focused on a feature of Yoder's bibliology. The first discusses Scripture as *historical*, that is, as a set of texts written and received in time and bound to particular contexts, chiefly that of Israel and the apostles, the latter being the first teachers of the church and the historical link between Jesus and all subsequent believers. The second explores Yoder's theology of Scripture as *deflationary*, that is, as intentionally non-theoretical and even, in a strong sense, non-doctrinal. The third considers Scripture's character as *communal*, that is, as a book of and for the local congregation, oriented to social and practical matters, thereby functioning as a critical norm centered on the politics of Jesus. Finally, I close the section with a critique of Yoder's *primitivism*, which is both cause and consequence of his skepticism of metaphysics and of genuine doctrinal development. Though Yoder affirms the theoretical possibility of organic growth in the church's life and faith, precisely in virtue of its historical character, in practice he repudiates it. The result, far from a historical community with a historical Bible at its center, is an immutable church with an originalist constitution. Though unintended, Yoder's biblicist suspicion of positive development superintended by the Holy Spirit is itself ahistorical; in the end it amounts to an a priori premise that cuts off the apostolic shape of the church's mission and of the canon meant to enable it.

Historical: Contingent Events, a Particular People,
and an Apostolic Canon

History is internal to the gospel, according to Yoder.[10] History—meaning (most broadly) the expanse of time in which human beings live their lives or (most simply) what happened in the past, as distinct from historiography, which attempts to *identify and understand* what happened in the past—is the theater of divine action and of its effects. In history we find the people Israel in all its consolidations and dispersions, the testimonies of prophets and apostles in speech and text to God's mighty acts, and most of all the man Jesus, a Jew born in Palestine under Roman rule who preached and ministered in Galilee and was executed outside Jerusalem by the imperial authorities. Times and places, culture and politics, language and cult: such particular, contextual, material matters are an ineradicable part of the gospel, because the good news that Christians tell concerns a human being who lived and died in a specific, locatable site in the world we inhabit, for a more or less measurable period of time, in our very own past. The gospel concerns *that* One at *that* time in *that* place, and therefore *not* some *other* person in some *other* time or place. The contingent features of Palestine in the early first century, the customs and practices and beliefs of its leaders and people, thus belong inescapably to what Christians have to say about Jesus, about their faith, and consequently about the Bible. For the Bible is itself a product of history—a product, that is, of a range of particular times and places, bound thereby to certain "wheres" and "whens" in this world, and therefore not an ahistorical item of some timeless non-place. These features informed what Christians in the first century thought they should say and believe about Jesus, Israel, and the church. Hence, though at some distance, they have gone on to inform what later Christians, up to the present, may know and say about the same.

From the importance of history, the importance of historiography follows. That is, because of the nature of the gospel, as a message about a historical figure who inhabited a time and place and culture other than our own, the *study* of history and the particularities of Jesus's sociocultural, political, and religious environs is necessary. To be sure, the relationship between history and historiography is a complex one, but, for

10. "Christian thought centers around events that really happened" (*To Hear the Word*, 167).

Yoder, the gospel of Jesus, and so the church's life and faith, are rooted in the former, and therefore call for the latter.[11]

Historiography is, furthermore, a fitting match to the source and authority for Christian faith—to, that is, the canon of Scripture. The texts that constitute the canon, like all texts but especially ancient texts, are artifacts of cultures and communities antecedent to and different from our own. They thus warrant study informed by the many branches and disciplines of "history": philology, text criticism, and archaeology, as well as every style of investigation into events, places, persons, institutions, conflicts, populations, demographics, culture, art, literature, music, travel, religion, sex, economics, and the rest. Such study has never been absent from Christian engagements with the Bible, though it has ebbed and flowed in its importance and sophistication. The Renaissance, Reformation, and Enlightenment brought the humanistic arts and in particular historiography and text criticism, precisely of the Bible, to the fore in Europe and eventually North America. Biblical interpretation, especially after the triumph of historical criticism in the nineteenth century, has never been the same; it is now taken for granted that such methods, tools, and approaches are an essential feature of intelligent biblical exegesis.[12] And with this judgment Yoder agrees wholeheartedly.

Historiography is called for, however, not only because of the nature of the texts and the events they report. Historiography also serves to bolster the Bible's independence in relation to its readers, in every time and place. The historical *differences* implied by the historical *distance* between "then and there" and "here and now"—whether the latter be the seventh, fourteenth, or twenty-first century—are one of the ways in which the biblical texts' *otherness* over against us may be expressed, recognized, and maintained. Not that such textual otherness can or will, of itself, encourage or ensure good reading, that is, reading that does not substitute the reader's views for what she might learn from the text. Rather, it is the recognition and ascetic preservation of this otherness that is the condition of the possibility for reading aright, for reading against oneself and

---

11. Cf. Barr, *Holy Scripture*, esp. 1–48: "Christianity as a faith is not directed in the first place towards a book, but towards the persons within and behind that book and the life of the ancient community which was their context and in which they made themselves known. Critical biblical study, in making known something more of that life and those persons, is thus—at the very least—contributing directly towards the understanding of the basis of authority that underlies the church" (48).

12. For an overview, see Reventlow, *History of Biblical Interpretation*, vols. 3–4.

one's presuppositions about what must be the case. "A text we know is most likely to speak to us tomorrow if it says something it did not say yesterday. So it is the interpreter's task to turn a suspicious eye to any well-established convention of interpretation, even the best-intentioned."[13] This is a form of hermeneutic suspicion, rooted in historical particularity and difference, whose object of suspicion is not limited to "tradition," that is, the whole interim sequence of interpretations from the text's first reader to its last. "The deep[est] reason" for Yoder's extensive attention to hermeneutical questions "is that I am committed to letting the text itself judge every prior use that anyone, including myself, has made of it," based on the commitment to "approaching a text with the assumption that it might have something to say, so that the form of suspicion that is most valuable is not doubting the text but doubting the adequacy of one's prior understanding of it."[14] To the language of "suspicion" Yoder prefers less negative characterization, such as "sitting loose to tradition" or "openness to alternative hypotheses." Such a posture entails that "I do not assume . . . that the majority tradition was always wrong, but neither do I give it the automatic benefit of the doubt."[15] The point is not to read as if one could be rid of presuppositions, but "rather that the presuppositions that are brought to a text can become, by virtue of sustained self-critical discipline, increasingly congruent with the intent of the text's author. Such self-critical discipline is not a given," furthermore, but "is a product of historical consciousness and of demanding post-scholastic study."[16] Indeed, the role of the theological teacher is precisely "to defend the historical objectivity of what the text said in the first place against the leverage of overly confident or 'relevant' applications"[17]—not because the latter are in principle problematic, but because they have a tendency to swamp biblical interpretation, effectively replacing the text, in all its historical particularity and otherness, with anachronistic opinions unrelated to the text. Which, finally, obviates the need to read the text at all.

So: the Bible is historical and ecclesial, and the best interpretive mode is one that respects and employs both aspects, with the hoped-for result that what *was* said, granted its historical distance and difference from

13. *To Hear the Word*, 26.
14. *To Hear the Word*, 52.
15. *To Hear the Word*, 57.
16. *To Hear the Word*, 74.
17. *To Hear the Word*, 83.

contemporary readers, might be read in such a way as to be not only interesting but relevant, even urgent, for the present.[18] But what, in greater detail, *is* the Bible? That is, how should Christians understand and describe their Scripture, according to Yoder? And to what extent should that understanding and description be *theological* in nature?

Yoder answers: "Scripture comes on the scene not as a receptacle of all possible inspired truths, but rather as witness to the historical baseline of the communities' origins and thereby as link to the historicity of their Lord's past presence."[19] Following Jesus's language in Matthew 13:52, "Scripture is the collective scribal memory" of God's people, "the store *par excellence* of treasures old and new."[20] In Yoder's view, Scripture may thus be described as (1) the corporate memory of (2) the believing community, which (3) binds believers to Jesus through (4) the witness of the apostles, and therefore serves as (5) a permanent touchstone for the community's core identity across time. As he elaborates:

> The label "Christ" as designating a revelatory authority is not simple but instead designates a semantic field. At the center there is the historic reality of Jesus. Surrounding that reality and mediating it to us, there is a circle of immediate interpretations by qualified witnesses who spoke about him in reliable Aramaic and Greek reports. Some of those reports were immediate testimonies about the life and work of Jesus. Others were less immediate in that they talked about the difference he made to them in terms of hope or atonement or initiation into community. The deposit of such testimonies is our New Testament.[21]

Notice that Yoder begins by observing that "Christ" is itself a complex term, insofar as it includes levels of mediated access to its referent, the man Jesus of Nazareth. Christians know Jesus only through the several witnesses, sometimes "closer" to him and sometimes "farther" from him, who first spoke orally about him, then fixed in writing their understanding of what he did, what he taught, what happened to him, and finally his identity and meaning in the light of God's raising him from the dead. The "Jesus of the story," as Yoder puts it, "is the Jesus of

---

18. See further Paddison, "Theological Exegesis."
19. *Priestly Kingdom*, 69.
20. *Priestly Kingdom*, 31.
21. *To Hear the Word*, 81.

history (i.e. what really happened) as mediated by real history (i.e., the traditioning process of the community)."[22] All this, further, happened in the context of the community of faith; inasmuch as mediation is apostolic, it is also ecclesial. Such mediation is unavoidably interpretive, but interpretation is not ancillary to knowledge of Jesus. It is essential. Christians should therefore "find some way to affirm that . . . [the] redaction process was not a betrayal, and that what it did to develop and define further the tradition should be recognized as also somehow right."[23] Broadly speaking, this involves a recognition at the general level that mediation and interpretation are inevitable features of any account of historical events. With respect to the Bible, though, it means reconceiving its function in relation to the church in a less extrinsic fashion. That is, the very process of interpretive traditioning evident in the texts of Scripture *is itself* part of Scripture's witness to the ongoing life of the community, insofar as believers here and now see how believers then and there worked out what it means to be faithful to the memory of Jesus in the face of new and unexpected communal challenges. It is true, then, that "trans-generational translation [in the first century] makes the message less literally 'historical' in the technical critical sense, but [it also] makes it more validly a part of the growing history of the community."[24] Thus Yoder concludes:

> If we read the canonical texts as guidance for the life of the Church and as reminders of the full meaning of Jesus, we may then affirm that this redactional process is theologically indispensable, not merely legitimate or excusable. High orthodox theology used the word "inspiration" for this legitimacy, but we need not take that systematic detour. Without it we can affirm that the authentic memory of the community, as preserved by that community's accredited elders, partakes of the normal authority of any human group's care for its path through

---

22. *To Hear the Word*, 106.

23. *To Hear the Word*, 102.

24. *To Hear the Word*, 103. The quote continues: "as long as the person doing the storytelling is a qualified witness and is recounting the story subject to the observation and possible correction of his or her peers. Thus it is not necessarily distortion when in Matthew's Gospel precision is added to Jesus's words about divorce. It may be organic extrapolation or clarification, by speaking with maximum fidelity to a more precisely defined case."

time.... [T]he memory *is* the reality it remembers; it cannot be known otherwise. In no other way can past reality exist than as remembered.[25]

In brief, "The real foundation ... for Christian witness is the historic objectivity of Jesus and the community he creates."[26] Faithful witness, then, has as its baseline the community's original witness to Jesus; this witness, written and gathered together as the texts of the Bible, is the community's shared memory of its own origins in Jesus and his apostles. Its historical component is then its function as the inseverable connection of all believers to the One in whom they believe, whereas its ecclesial component is the fact that this connection is apostolic and that the biblical texts are themselves church documents, written and read in and by concrete congregations of Christian faith.

Thus concludes Yoder's account of Scripture, specifically of the New Testament. But what of our second question: Is anything here theological? Or is what he has to say about the church and the Bible generically true of all human communities that have founders and leaders and governing texts?[27] The answer is complicated.

Deflationary: "Low" Church, High Theory, and the Bible Against Doctrine[28]

Yoder's "theology" of Scripture is deflationary by design. That is, it is meant as an antidote to what he sees as overly theological accounts of the Bible. Such accounts are not themselves "biblical," since they are by definition post-biblical. Yoder therefore self-consciously means to "bring back down to earth" Christian understandings of what Scripture is and is for. Theories of verbal inspiration, textual revelation, propositional

25. *To Hear the Word*, 103.
26. *To Hear the Word*, 88.
27. See *To Hear the Word*, 110–11; further discussion of this passage below.
28. In what follows the reader will note my equivocal usage of "high" and "low" predicated, variously, of a certain style of ecclesiology (hierarchical, sacramental, catholic) and a certain style of bibliology (scholastic, rarefied, magisterial) alongside, first, baptist accounts of the church that nonetheless center the local congregation (absent smells and bells) and, second, deflationary accounts of Scripture that nonetheless elevate the text to supreme authority (absent theories of verbal plenary inspiration). The equivocation is intentional, and not always ironic.

inerrancy, and the text's many senses are unnecessary, he argues; they function cumulatively as a kind of blockade between the church and the Bible. Congregations and readers cannot be required to sign on to such detailed proposals if the Bible is meant to be of practical use for them in all the quotidian routines of their lives. High bibliology tends, on this view, not to facilitate the faithful hearing of Scripture, but to enervate and obstruct it.[29]

Moreover, Yoder believes that specifically Protestant claims about Scripture are internally incoherent. For they elevate a post-biblical proposal about a postapostolic divine act to the status of a scriptural claim precisely in service of *sola scriptura*—a slogan that relativizes all extra-biblical proposals beneath the exclusive authority of the Bible, which was sealed with the death of the apostles. As he writes, "There is some kind of flaw in a doctrine that affirms that one specific act of Divine intervention in the life of the later Church"—namely, canonization—"can be located when there is no text, inspired or not, which says that, and when the use one wants to make of the rigid doctrine is to limit the teaching authority of the later Church."[30] In controversies over these issues "one sees at work a need that seems as much psychological as logical, namely the desire to have one's statement of the nature and power of Scripture be itself as sure and as safe as God."[31] Yoder would rather limit Christian claims about the Bible's status to the axiomatic and the functional, for to go beyond that, not least in terms of the Bible's nature and origin as a product of divine action, creates more problems than it solves.

This is not to say that Yoder's account of Scripture is non-theological. In at least three ways it goes beyond the merely descriptive or historico-communal and takes on theological weight. First, Yoder places a good deal of emphasis on the claim, to him self-evident, that the untidy historical processes of the canon's formation must be in accord with the divine will. Call it the providential correlative of Scripture's (and the gospel's) historicality. God deigned to become human, to enter into history as a particular man in a particular time and place, having before called and covenanted with a particular people, Israel. The indeterminacy and particularity of Scripture, as well as its being "handed over" to the believ-

29. See, e.g., *To Hear the Word*, 148: "scholasticism about 'Scripture' misrepresents the way the texts live in the Church."
30. *To Hear the Word*, 116.
31. *To Hear the Word*, 107.

ing community, is no different. God entrusts the message of the gospel about Jesus into the hands of the church, hands that are temporal, finite, imperfect, culturally formed, and fallen. But that just accords with who the God of Israel and Jesus *is*, and is exactly the kind of thing such a God would do. The particularity of the incarnation not only committed God to the one man Jesus; even more scandalously, it "committed God to the particularity *of an ongoing history*. God entrusted the incarnational disclosure not only to a first generation of witnesses of the man Jesus, but also to the necessarily ensuing chain of specific bodies of tradition-bearing, fallible people who through the centuries would unfold and distort the message. It is not a regrettable mistake of church strategy contrary to the divine plan" that the canon is neither self-enclosing nor self-interpreting. What Yoder calls "the unfinished quality of the definition of the Christian story" is of the essence of the gospel and the One it proclaims, not an adventitious or scurrilous feature needing to be explained away or resolved.[32]

Second, while Yoder does not locate the Holy Spirit's action at the site of Scripture's production—though he is willing, albeit with reservations, to call Scripture "revealed" or "the word of God"[33]—he does describe the church's *reception* of Scripture as guided and empowered by the Spirit. As he writes, "The free-church alternative to both [magisterial Protestantism and Roman Catholicism] recognizes the inadequacies of the text of Scripture standing alone uninterpreted, and appropriates the promise of the guidance of the Spirit throughout the ages, but locates the fulfillment of that promise in the assembly of those who gather around Scripture in the face of a given real moral challenge." This recognition is grounded in the affirmation "that the way God leads is that the Spirit gathers believers around Scripture. The Spirit, the gathering, and the Scripture are indispensable elements of the process."[34] These elements are in a way

32. *To Hear the Word*, 109 (emphasis mine). Yoder remarks later in the same essay that to accept the canon as a collection of "occasional historical documents" would place the church "in the continuing uncertainty of life within history, the arbitrariness and the particularity of all historical existence, and the arbitrariness and particularity of hermeneutics within history, which is precisely where we ought to be, since that is where God chose to be revealed in all the arbitrariness and particularity of Abraham and Sarah, Moses and Miriam, Jeremiah, Jesus and Pentecost, Luke and Paul, Peter and John" (111–12).

33. See the discussion in *Preface*, 330–59, esp. 334–35.

34. *Priestly Kingdom*, 117.

the formal marks of the church for Yoder. In that sense they capture the central business of a faithful church: discerning the will of God together in the context of contemporary challenges under the guidance and in the power of the Holy Spirit, the very Spirit of the One who promised to be present in his followers' gatherings, however small or unimposing (cf. Matt 18:20; 1 Cor 3:16; John 16:7–15). Thus, in one of Yoder's more wide-angle descriptions of this process, he writes:

> It is most lively and productive to think of one body of literature, the Bible, representing in any time and place the testimony of the narrative stretching from Abraham to the Apostles, which can be juxtaposed to any other age by its Psalms being sung again, its letters being read again, its stories and parables being retold. Then in the juxtaposition of those stories with our stories there leaps the spark of the Spirit, illuminating parallels and contrasts, to give us the grace to see our age in God's light and God's truth in our words. This picture of how it works is more representative of the experienced facts but also more rigorous than the classical scholastic vision of an unchanging body of timeless propositions needing to be twisted to fit a new age by the special skills of rationalistic linguists.[35]

"The Bible," in sum, "is the book of the congregation, the source of understanding and insight as the congregation seeks to be the interpreter of the divine purpose for humans in the congregation's own time and place with the assistance of the same Spirit under whose guidance the apostolic church produced these texts."[36] If, then, Scripture and Spirit are alike inseparable from the church, the church must itself be a crucial component of Yoder's bibliology, as indeed it is.

Accordingly, third, Yoder's primary move regarding Scripture, as we have already seen, is to locate it in the life of the believing, worshiping, and discerning missionary community of Christian discipleship. This in itself is a theological move, because the church is antecedently an object of thick theological description. Which is not to deny the deflationary force of Yoder's recourse to ecclesiology: it is usually, at least initially, a kind of empirical or commonsensical observation meant, like his other bibliological arguments, to unlearn so-called scholastic habits of Protes-

---

35. *To Hear the Word*, 86.
36. *Revolutionary Christianity*, 20. Cf. *Royal Priesthood*, 353.

208

tant orthodoxy. That is to say, in response to convoluted systems seeking to justify or explain the existence and authority of Scripture in the church, Yoder simply points to the social fact of this particular book's presence and centrality in the life of Christian communities, and says, *Let's start there*. Regarding, for example, the question of hermeneutical and theological prolegomena in approaching Scripture, Yoder writes, "The authentic prolegomenon is not the rational presupposition of another axiom that alone would permit us to say what we want to say. What needs to be said first is that we are already together in the believing community, praising God and supporting and admonishing one another."[37] *We are already together*: any account of the church or Scripture must avoid the temptation to think things "from scratch," as if that were possible. "In the church we already read the Bible, not only in the simple sense of opening the book and looking at the print but in the wider sense of gathering around the story that the Bible tells in the expectation that this story makes us who we are. *After* we start reading the Bible in the church, then we are, as a community, ready to ask later how we have been" thinking, interpreting, and embodying it.[38] Theology is critical reflection following and accompanying this time-taking process. But it does not and cannot start, actually or even hypothetically, prior to the simple experienced fact of the believing, reading community in its moral and liturgical life together. And that goes for theology of Scripture as much as for any other doctrinal topic.

The deflationary upshot also concerns bibliology as a stand-alone doctrinal locus, that is, treatment of Scripture *in se*, as a text and an object considered unto itself, divorced from its purpose (for the church), its social location (in the church), and its uses (by the church). Yoder argues that this theoretical isolation makes no sense, theological or otherwise:

> To speak of the Bible apart from persons reading it and apart from the specific questions which those persons reading it need to answer is to do violence to the very purpose for which we have been given the Holy Scripture. There is no such thing as an isolated word of the Bible carrying meaning in itself. It has meaning only when it is read by someone, and then only when that reader and the society in which

---

37. *To Hear the Word*, 89.
38. *Preface*, 400 (emphasis mine).

one lives can understand the issue to which it speaks. Thus, the most complete framework in which to affirm the authority of scripture is the context of its being read and applied by a believing congregation using its guidance to respond to concrete issues in the witness and obedience of this congregation.[39]

Granted these attempts to deflate Protestant scholastic orthodoxy in the doctrine of Scripture by recourse to ecclesiology, what then is the positive work being done by Yoder's turn to the church? I address details of his ecclesiology in the chapter's second section. In the next part of the present section, however, I take up the specific character of Yoder's grounding the Bible in the community—so that, simultaneously, the church is bibliocentric and the Bible ecclesiocentric. For up to this point we have been concerned with what Scripture is, but because Yoder's bibliology is an ecclesially functionalist account, we turn now to what Scripture is for.

Communal: A Political Paradigm for the Local Assembly

"The Bible is the book of the congregation." That is an aptly Yoderian riff on the title of this book, because while Yoder would not deny that the Bible is the *church's* book, his emphasis is more local and practical: it is the church's book because it is *this* or *that* church's book, at the center of a particular community's life, around which actual Christian believers are congregated. His account of the Bible is "functionalist," then, if by that term one means that the Bible is best understood in terms of what it is for, of its actual and potential uses; and the community for which it exists, the people who are the corporate agent of its usage, is the church. So the Bible is a function of the church, not in the sense that it is assimilated to the church or merely an instrument of its wielding, but rather in the sense that what it names is a practice, something done, by a living community. For the Bible has no other meaningful existence, nothing but a hypothetical life, apart from this ongoing corporate practice. Bibliology, in turn, is a function of ecclesiology, for what the Bible is and what it is for is answered only in consideration of the life of the congregation and its uses of and need for the Bible.

---

39. *Revolutionary Christianity*, 20. See again the nearly identical passage in *Royal Priesthood*, 353.

But is this community-centric account of the Bible extrinsic to what the Bible is, "in and of itself"? Not according to Yoder. For "the Bible itself is not what we could call theological in style. It speaks about God . . . in pastoral, ministerial, and argumentative contexts, not in systematic or historical or expository ways."[40] What distinguishes Christian faith, and by implication the Bible, is "the category of story and the claim of that story to be rooted in real people and places . . . . Th[e] faith is therefore documented not primarily in visions or in speculative theories about divine reality, but in narratives and pastoral letters"—indeed, a whole "multiplicity of literary forms that are mostly narrative in framework and doxological in tone"[41]—"that claim to be testimonies to the norming process within an ongoing community. That is how they claim to have been written and that is how we should best take them."[42] It is all too easy to lose sight of the fact "that what is recognized by the church as norming document is not a systematic text, not a catechism, and of course not a *Summa*, but a scattered series of documents emerging from the ongoing struggles of a community."[43]

It is true not only that members of the church wrote what we call the New Testament, that other members of the church received and distributed those texts, and that still others maintained and eventually gathered those same texts into a working collection of foundational authorities for the church in perpetuity. Yoder argues that the texts themselves, in their form and their content, show evidence of this ecclesial, communal purposiveness. Apostles (along with their networks of delegates and deputies) wrote the texts that make up what we call the New Testament, and every one of these texts was written for a congregation of believers as a witness to the gospel of Jesus so that the church might live, believe, and testify more faithfully to the gospel in the face of new challenges, questions, and contexts. The Old Testament is no different;[44] and together, Old and New alike are community-authoring documents that ground, norm, and shape the corporate identity, mission, and faith of the cov-

40. *To Hear the Word*, 87.
41. *To Hear the Word*, 88.
42. *To Hear the Word*, 105 (the whole sentence, before and after the parenthetic break).
43. *To Hear the Word*, 105.
44. Or rather, its differences do not affect the commonality: both Testaments are intended to shape and govern the community's daily life and were written and edited in the context of and/or with a view to life in dispersion.

enant people of God. That is what the Bible does, and therefore that is what the Bible is—not because the church takes it to be so, but because in itself the Bible's shape and substance show it to be so.

What does this look like in practice? In order to describe the relationship between the church, its tradition, and the role of Scripture therein Yoder uses the metaphor of a vine. He writes,

> the wholesome growth of a tradition is like a vine: a story of constant interruption of organic growth in favor of pruning and a new chance for the roots. This renewed appeal to origins is not primitivism, nor an effort to recapture some pristine purity. It is rather a "looping back," a glance over the shoulder to enable a midcourse correction, a rediscovery of something from the past whose pertinence was not seen before, because only a new question or challenge enables us to see it speaking to us. . . . *Ecclesia reformata semper reformanda* is not really a statement about the church. It is a statement about the earlier tradition's permanent accessibility, as witnessed to and normed by Scripture at its nucleus, but always including more dimensions than the Bible itself contains, functioning as an instance of appeal as we call for renewed faithfulness and denounce renewed apostasy. The most important operational meaning of the Bible . . . is not that we do just what it says in some way that we can derive deductively. It is rather that we are able, thanks to the combined gifts of teachers and prophets, to become aware that we do not do what it says, and that the dissonance we thereby create enables our renewal.[45]

As he elaborates, "What is at stake is not whether there can be change but whether there is such a thing as unfaithfulness. Is there a difference between compatible extrapolation and incompatible deviation?"[46] Sometimes there is "reversal" and not "an organic development." Granted this possibility, "the reason the reformers challenge some usage or idea is not that it is not in the Scriptures, but that it is counter to the Scriptures; not that it is an ancient idea insufficiently validated by ancient texts, but that it is a later introduction invalidated by its contradicting the ancient

---

45. *Priestly Kingdom*, 69–70. For Yoder's remarks on primitivism, see "Primitivism in the Radical Reformation." See also the encapsulating comments in "Historiography," which was written and published in the final months of Yoder's life.
46. *Priestly Kingdom*, 67.

message.... What we need is tools to identify and denounce error, while welcoming variety and celebrating complementarity."[47]

In one respect Yoder can go so far as to affirm "ongoing" or "continuing revelation."[48] The Holy Spirit will lead the church into new truths in the face of new challenges and questions it faces on its mission. But this process is necessarily a canonical movement, in which the community submits its proposed developments to the bar of Scripture. In that respect, then, "the creation of 'Scripture' is . . . a critical event and not a conservative phenomenon."[49] That is to say, Scripture-as-norm exists not to encase in amber a pure original from which all change is suspect and corrupt, but rather to approve of change that is faithful, and to sit in judgment on change that is not. The canon of Scripture is the means by which faithfulness is determined. The challenge of determining faithfulness is itself the impetus for the canon's formation in the first place. "The church is not built upon a canon. Scripture comes into being with status as 'canon' in midstream, as a believing community needs to illuminate and adjudicate choices among alternative futures in order to be true to the common past."[50] It is true that "the Church does . . . create the canon," as no one should deny. But the force of this action "was *not* to give authority to those texts, as a revelatory magisterial act, but to *recognize* that those texts already were exercising authority. The churches did that as a way of submitting to the texts, not ruling over them or creating them."[51] In

47. *Priestly Kingdom*, 76 (I have corrected the last word's errant spelling in the original).

48. *Priestly Kingdom*, 72. Cf. *Preface*, 379–80. In the words of Puritan leader John Robinson, from his farewell address to the Pilgrims bound from Holland for the new world in 1620: "the Lord hath yet more Light and Truth to break forth from His Holy Word." This is one of Yoder's most quoted lines. See *Body Politics*, 59; *Jewish-Christian Schism Revisited*, 138; *Priestly Kingdom*, 133; *To Hear the Word*, 4, 86, 92, 124, 137; *Karl Barth and the Problem of War*, 172. One of his principal examples is the biblical theme of liberation: "The Bible was always a liberation storybook: now we are ready to read it that way" (*Priestly Kingdom*, 71). Liberation theology therefore entails "an affirmation and not, as many conservative evangelicals have reflexively assumed, a questioning of biblical authority" (*To Hear the Word*, 92). See further Yoder's reflections on liberation theology: "Exodus and Exile"; "Biblical Roots of Liberation Theology"; "Wider Setting of 'Liberation Theology'"; review of Gustavo Gutiérrez and Richard Shaull, *Liberation and Change*.

49. *For the Nations*, 91.

50. *For the Nations*, 90. Like Barth, Yoder affirms an open canon (116–19).

51. *To Hear the Word*, 149. See further 104; cf. 116. See also the later comment: "The real function of the notion of canon then is that it enables a norming process

sum, *the canon is the condition of the possibility for Christian faithfulness, because it is the condition of the possibility for ecclesial reform.* "The clash is not tradition versus Scripture but faithful tradition versus irresponsible tradition. Only if we can with Jesus and Paul . . . denounce *wrong* traditioning, can we validly affirm the rest."[52] Indeed, resort to the scriptures as the final authority on Jesus is how the church knows whether reform is called for in specific situations at all.[53]

The church both creates and submits to the canon, for the canon mediates the story and authority of Jesus. Yoder therefore affirms that "the story of Jesus is the canon within the canon."[54] First, formally: as a matter of objective literary and historical investigation, it is patent that Jesus's person and story are the unifying center of the Bible generally and the New Testament especially. The nature of the apostolic documents, as we have seen, is evidence of this judgment:

> The story begins with Jesus, so important that we have four texts about him. Then it moves on in direct continuity into a very selective account of some strands of the life of the early communities, and then letters are gathered that represent candid snapshots out of the community's life. They all record that the way the leaders of this community sought to foster its faithfulness was by continually reminding one another of their past story, of which Jesus and the Hebrew scriptures were the primary orientation.[55]

But Scripture is also christocentric in its content. In one respect this is simply another way of stating the formal point: *because* Jesus is the center of concern for the apostles and their writings, his story, his person, his teachings, his actions and sufferings are inescapably the center of

---

within diversity, rather than assuming (with modernism) that pluralism is the end of all norms, or (with 'orthodoxy') that norms are the end of pluralism" (119). See too Cullmann, "Tradition."

52. *Priestly Kingdom*, 68. Cf. *Royal Priesthood*, 238.

53. See *To Hear the Word*, 90.

54. *To Hear the Word*, 115; cf. 85: "The ultimate canon within the canon must in the end, however, be the person of Jesus and, in a broader sense, the narration of the saving acts of God." But see *Preface*, 372–73, for a denial of a canon within the canon, although his account there is effectively the same as in *To Hear the Word*; what he is denying, in other words, is not what he affirms elsewhere.

55. *To Hear the Word*, 115.

concern for all Christian believers after them, most of all in their reading of Scripture. In another respect, however, Jesus is the center of the Bible—the whole Bible, not just the New Testament. And this material claim raises two issues at once: the status of the Old Testament, and how to read it in relation to the New.

Yoder is no Marcionite.[56] The God and Father of Jesus the Messiah is the Lord of Israel revealed at exodus and Sinai. He affirms the Old Testament as canonical Scripture no less than the New.[57] The question is how to order and interpret them. His proposal is what he calls a "directional" reading of the Bible. This approach construes the canon as a movement, at any point in the story, *forward to Christ* or, if after him in time, then *on from him as primal touchstone.*[58] Call it a fulfillment hermeneutic or a literary gloss on Scripture's figural unity; Yoder's point, however, runs somewhat aslant to the concerns that animate those historic proposals. What he wants to avoid is a timeless Bible containing a timeless revelation for a timeless people. The Bible's own internal movement simultaneously testifies to the historical, ever-unfolding character of God's word and work in the world and serves as a kind of impulse for the church's own life in mission. How does the church discern God's living will in the world today? Yoder's answer outlines the implications of his directional hermeneutic, and thereby expands on the canonical, pneumatological, and missiological issues raised above:

> Faithful reading of Scripture will not simply repeat what was said a century ago, but will always involve shifts in meaning. New challenges will come at the church.... Therefore our faithfulness in reading Scripture will have to be measured not by the stability of our interpretation but by its integrity, flexibility, and the ability to speak to every new question from the same documentary base. The integrity of the believing community consists precisely in its historical movement. A faithful church is not a solid social body but a pilgrim people making choices as they move along. The question, "Where are we going?" is a deeper question than, "What did we say?" ... We test our conformity

56. For discussion, see Nugent, *Politics of Yahweh*, 145–48.
57. See his comments in, e.g., *Theology of Mission*, 61.
58. This recalls Barth's formulation of the Old and New Testaments as, respectively, the times (or texts) of "expectation" and "recollection"; see Barth, *Church Dogmatics* I/2, 70–121.

to Scripture therefore not by asking whether we keep saying the same thing without change, but rather by asking a more difficult question: Is the way we keep moving in conformity with the way God's people were led to move in formative times?[59]

Ecclesial faithfulness is not only a matter of discerning the Spirit's leading in the reading of Scripture in face of new challenges in the world. It is also a reflection and an extension of the forward movement of God's work in the world, as told by the scriptural narrative and embodied by its form; it is the same narrative, the same mode of working, continued in the life of the believing community in the power of the Holy Spirit. The church, in this way, is faithful insofar as it conforms to Scripture's directional character, to its forward thrust of promise and fulfillment, and so to its center and climax in the story of Jesus—to whom all history leads, in whom all hopes cohere, by whom all history is governed, from whom all else derives or departs.

And so we come to politics. For the centrality of Jesus includes preeminently his political exemplarity; Jesus is the key and core not only of Scripture and church, of history and salvation, but also and especially of human life together: ethics, society, community, economy. This is because, as the Word incarnate, as God become a human being, Jesus is doubly revelatory: of true divinity and of true humanity, that is, of the character and will of the living God and of the form and mode of human life most fully aligned with God's character and will.[60] The root conviction of Christian ethics, according to Yoder, is "that the life of Jesus is our pattern," because "Christian obedience [is] rooted in the character of God as manifested in the life of Jesus."[61] If, then, "the life of Jesus is a revelation of true humanity . . . and a revelation of what it means to do God's will in this world";[62] and if not just human life in general but Jesus's life in particular are constituted by and interwoven with political matters,

59. *Preface*, 372–73; cf. *Priestly Kingdom*, 7–12.
60. So, for example, Christian willingness to imitate the cruciform pattern of Jesus "is founded . . . in confession of the nature of the God who has revealed himself in Jesus Christ. It is founded doctrinally . . . in the confession that he who as truly God gave his life at our hands was at one and the same time truly human, the revelation of that true humanity which is God's instrument in the world" (*Revolutionary Christianity*, 83; cf. 65).
61. *Revolutionary Christianity*, 38–39.
62. *Revolutionary Christianity*, 39.

then Jesus is politically paradigmatic: "Jesus is from beginning to end *homo politicus.*"[63] There is no abstracting the sociopolitical element from Jesus's humanity and life. If he is God's Word in the flesh, then he is what God has to say about politics in this world—full stop.

The character of Scripture and its role in the church fall into place accordingly. Scripture is the story that tells of God's mighty acts of liberation in the world, with Jesus as the story's central protagonist and inner rationale. But more, Scripture is the Christian community's *memory* of God's life with the world, his relation to the community, and his saving acts. It is therefore the community-*forming* charter, baseline, and source for ongoing faithfulness to the normative way of Jesus. Finally, because Jesus is the God-man, the authoritative and final vision of *vere deus* and *vere homo* and thus the sociopolitical revelation of human life in the world, Scripture is a political document, *the* political text bar none. The Bible, in a word, is the christological politics of the church.

In a syllogism: the church's politics must be Jesus's own; but the politics of Jesus is found nowhere else than in Scripture; therefore the politics of Scripture is determinative for the politics of the church—they are one and the same. Which is to say, the function of the book we call the Bible is political, for it is the book that norms the political community we call the church. The canon of Old and New Testament is thus meant, on the one hand, to be read "toward" Jesus as the twofold revelation of who God is and how humanity should live; and, on the other hand, to function as the social and moral norm for that community which professes faith in Jesus as the Messiah of Israel. When and where that happens, Scripture is at work in the way that it ought to be.[64]

As we will see below, Yoder believes the heart of Jesus's political exemplarity is his relationship to and exercise of power, namely, his refusal of violence and his willingness to suffer and be killed on the cross. By implication, this "center of the center" is also Scripture's center—that to which it leads, as its fulfillment and encapsulation—and the church's

---

63. *Revolutionary Christianity*, 65. If Aristotle is right about the nature of the human creature, then for Jesus to be *vere homo* he too must be a political animal.

64. In other words, that is what Scripture is there for, *by way of contrast* to views that would see Scripture's role as primarily a source for doctrine, a timeless repository of divine truths, an instigation to metaphysical speculation, a first draft to be revised and rewritten over time, an inerrant record of what happened historically, etc. Subordinating or denying these bibliological claims is the force of calling Scripture the politically normative book of the church.

center too. Scripture is a *pacifist* political charter. Therefore, the hallmark of a church faithful to Jesus is nonviolence.[65] Scripture norms politically when its witness is read as rejecting violence and its readers realize this rejection in their lives. If we were to want a Yoderian test for ecclesial fidelity to the politics of Scripture, that would be it.[66]

Immutable: Metaphysics, Primitivism, and the Development of Tradition

Yoder's bibliology is functionalist: the Bible is defined and constituted by its role or function in the community of faith. This is not to say that it is reducible to that function. The Bible is conceived, rather, not as something of importance in itself, but as a tool or instrument with a task to fulfill. Positively, its charge is to norm the Christian community over time in faithful continuity with the story of Jesus. Negatively, this involves checking the community's tendency to turn to the right or to the left of Jesus's way by judging deviations, correcting unfaithful innovations, and calling the church to renewal, reform, or restitution, as the case may be. This understanding of Scripture's function in the church is a traditional one, especially for Protestants, and most of all for heirs to the radical reformation. What distinguishes Yoder's treatment is his emphasis on Scripture as a primal touchstone or baseline for the community, and therefore as a potential locus of unity for the divided traditions of Christendom. To this emphasis Yoder joins an affirmation that development and innovation are both possible and inevitable; Scripture's role is to judge the fidelity of change, not predetermine its infidelity tout court.

Yoder succeeds at holding these claims together at the theoretical level, as a doctrinal claim about Scripture and the church, but he fails at the level of application. For the principle ought to operate as a means of resolving actual disputed questions regarding how to read Scripture in light of developments since the apostles.[67] But for all his protests, Yoder remains, at heart, a primitivist. Outside of just war and pacifism,

---

65. Cf. Hauerwas, *Peaceable Kingdom*, xvi: "nonviolence [is] the hallmark of the Christian moral life."

66. It goes without saying that this is a test Yoder failed, tragically but culpably, in his own life.

67. The classic account is St. Newman, *Development of Christian Doctrine*. See also Pelikan, *Christian Tradition*, vols. 1–5; Rowan Williams, *Why Study the Past?*

it is unclear what warrants his confidence that so many developments in the Christian tradition—trinitarian doctrine, transubstantiation, the priesthood, the cult of the saints, monepiscopacy, mariology, even civil establishment of the church in a particular society—are unquestionably deviations from the canonical witness, which is to say, developments that are "inorganic" or discontinuous with it. His posture of presumptive suspicion of the tradition appears to be rooted in another principle.

One such principle, or at least disposition, is his allergy to metaphysics.[68] In Yoder's hands theology is a form of practical reasoning; it is not a speculative or theoretical science. It is not, for example, the rational contemplation of God and all things relative to God under the twofold end of God's infinite glory and ever-greater creaturely knowledge of God in himself. The theologian's proper task, rather, is to keep vigilant watch over the community's language, in order to make sure, so far as possible, that it remains faithful to its object and message; theology is "working with words in the light of faith."[69] The end of this work is the holiness of a people, that is, the faithful life, witness, and worship of the church of Christ, set apart from the world.

Yoder is therefore deeply skeptical of every variety of "philosophizing," "Platonizing," "Hellenizing," or "speculative" theology that would claim to be Christian. At least sometimes this bogeyman is pitched, as it once was in biblical scholarship, as a contest between "Greek" and "Hebraic" forms of thought.[70] Whereas the former is supposedly concerned with abstract, timeless, and immaterial ideas and concepts, the latter is said to be earth-bound, focusing on the whole panoply of human life: people, places, time, history, actions, particularity, embodiment. Even where this is used only as a heuristic or framing device, Yoder is confident that the Bible, the church's faith, and Christian theology are plainly, and therefore ought to be normatively, "Hebraic" in orientation and content. When and where they are marked

---

68. Though it is worth noting that this allergy is conspicuously absent when Yoder turns to christology. Perhaps the most charitable interpretation is that, even when Yoder is willing to make metaphysical claims about Christ, or claims about Christ with profound metaphysical implications, he is uninterested in exploring the nature of those claims from a philosophical, ontological, or conceptual vantage point.

69. *Preface*, 41.

70. For detailed treatment and definitive rejection of what he calls "the Theory of Theology's Fall into Hellenistic Philosophy," see Gavrilyuk, *Suffering of the Impassible God*, esp. 1–46, 176–79.

by "Greek" patterns of thought, this is nothing short of capitulation.[71] Such a view is mutually reinforcing with an overall negative judgment on the Nicene and especially post-Nicene church fathers on into the early Middle Ages. Yoder thinks it a mistake on the part of the magisterial reformers that they dated the fall of the church to the medieval rather than the patristic period, isolating the fathers' theology from the political revolutions of the fourth century. For Yoder thinks these to be of a piece: Nicaea is inseparable from the Milvian Bridge and the Edict of Milan, and is logically and historically subsequent to them. The site of the second ecumenical council, which promulgated the revised statement of faith we call the Nicene Creed, was *Constantin*ople, after all. Or take St. Augustine, the post-Nicene church father par excellence. Prima facie, Yoder argues, the bishop of Hippo should not be an authority for the church, for his thought is the first mature instance of a theology that had fully internalized the logic of the Constantinian shift. This shift, for Yoder, is indistinguishable from the shift in what it meant to be the church and to be a Christian, and therefore what it meant to practice theology. To think about the meaning and import of the faith for believers now entailed doing so as and for imperial citizens, baptized at birth. "It is true," Yoder writes, "that Augustine . . . organize[d] his historic vision around two cities, one of them celestial: but that was because he was a Neo-Platonist, not because he was Christian. The earthly city which Augustine was concerned at the time to relativize and to be on good pastoral terms with was not Jerusalem but Rome, not a holy city but an empire."[72] Once Constantine and all that he represents became a given, not only the church, but theology with it, was forever transformed, with ruinous consequence for the gospel of Jesus and his mission in the world.

Given Yoder's training and his arguments for the importance of historiography for Christian faith and theology, it is regrettable how tendentious this account is. Nor is it limited to stray asides: It is foundational to his project. In the next section I say more about the role it plays in his ecclesiology. For now let me conclude this section with a brief reflection

---

71. See, e.g., *Radical Christian Discipleship*, 48–52; *To Hear the Word*, 167–71; *Preface*, passim.

72. *Jewish-Christian Schism Revisited*, 160. It is breathtaking how unfair and inaccurate this claim is. For recent instances of political theology that use Augustinian thought as a point of departure, see Gregory, *Politics*; Mathewes, *Theology of Public Life*; O'Donovan, *Desire of the Nations*; Markus, *Saeculum*.

on the ways in which this imbalanced, uncharitable, and exaggerated account of the church's failures from Constantine to Luther informs Yoder's doctrine of Scripture.

First, because Yoder eschews ontological or metaphysical reflection, he has little to nothing to say about God's relationship to Scripture apart from its reception in and by the church. He provides no account of why the canon is worthy of believers' trust—the sort of trust that would justify a willingness to die for the contents contained within it. What Yoder overlooks in his avoidance of anything approximating scholastic schemes of verbal inerrancy is their pastoral function. The doctrine of inspiration is a *theoretical* (or metaphysical) answer to a *practical* (or pastoral) question. For it is the inspiration of Scripture that warrants the ordinary Christian's living faith in the Bible as a source of truth and guidance for how to act in the world as a follower of Jesus and member of the church. To respond instead with answers in a historical or social register misses the point and ultimately leaves the baptized bereft of confidence that the living God stands behind the text.

Likewise, the combination of Yoder's metaphysical allergy together with his declension narrative of church history produces a posture toward the theological tradition marked by suspicion, hostility, and critique. From St. Augustine to Luther—perhaps from Origen to Reimarus—the church's exegesis is irredeemably spiritual, detached from the hard soil of the letter and carried to heights of fancy in the spirit. Eventually the Bible becomes a kind of theological textbook, available for brief excerpts as proof-texts in abstract and irrelevant speculative arguments entirely divorced from either the purpose of the Bible in the church or the daily concerns of regular believers in the community. Thus the *Hellēnes* subjugate the *ekklēsia*, the faith goes imperial, and Rome sanctions the gospel: a new cult just like the old cult. Priests perform sacrifices (however bloodless) in temples and become experts in reading the scriptures in a way no ordinary person would. Thereby the canon is kept out of the unwashed hands and untrained eyes of the laity, lest they upend the good order established by God, his servant the emperor, and *his* servants the bishops.

Yoder's description is not always this hyperbolic, but the overall picture is representative. It not only trades on caricature and generalization. It fails to understand either the nature of spiritual interpretation or the development of historicist methods. The former is an exercise in imitation: following the exegetical paths charted by the apostles in the New

Testament.[73] The proper object of Yoder's obloquy, as shown by more consistent critics than he, is not medieval monks or church fathers. It is the Hellenism of Hebrews. It is St. Paul, St. Peter, St. John the Seer, and the Evangelists. But if not them, then not their successors either. Furthermore, the latter—that is, the hermeneutical shifts in the Reformation and the Enlightenment—are not discoveries, or re-discoveries, of "the" or "the best" way of reading the Bible. Such a view fails to grasp what these shifts really amount to. For they are not the results of excavation or awakened memory, akin to Josiah finding the book of the Law. They are best described, instead, as the *creation* of a whole new way of reading the Bible.[74] One may stipulate that they are excellent interpretive strategies, even that they should be privileged among Christians' approaches to exegesis. Yet it remains a strange thing to fault predecessors in the faith, inhabitants of particular times and places with certain given ways of knowing, thinking, and reading, for not having invented something prior to its time. St. Bernard is no more guilty of never having practiced historical criticism than he is of never having driven a car. Technologies of knowledge come and go, and are as contingent as any other feature of human life. There are very few things that qualify for anachronistic judgment on the past, and they are usually of a high moral order. Allegorical exegesis does not belong on the list.

The result, for Yoder, is a comprehensively but nevertheless superficially skeptical relationship to the church's tradition, both its doctrine and its biblical interpretation. This is intolerable at the ecclesial level: How can one belong to a transnational community stretching back millennia if one's judgment of its life and teaching, with only the barest of exceptions, is condemnation? Even at the exegetical level, the upshot is that the intervening centuries between the apostles and the present are in effect a hurdle to be jumped over rather than a possible avenue for perceiving the sense of the text.[75] For example, clarity in reading the Gospels has *only* come, in Yoder's words, "as successive generations of students have read the New Testament text more and more independently of tra-

73. For only a few examples from the New Testament, see 1 Cor 10; Gal 3–4; Heb 1; Acts 2; etc.

74. See, e.g., Preus, *Spinoza*; Sheehan, *Enlightenment Bible*; Legaspi, *Death of Scripture*.

75. The point is only strengthened when one realizes the truth of Gerhard Ebeling's claim, captured so poignantly in the title of his essay: "Church History is the History of the Exposition of Scripture," in *Word of God*, 11–31.

ditional dogma," having "been so brainwashed by theological tradition that we cannot (most of us) read" it as if for the first time, with eyes to see what is "really" there, without the blinders of the tradition obstructing our vision.[76]

The irony for this radical "baptist" position is that it lacks the resources to justify its commitment to *sola scriptura*. The catholic tradition appeals to the church's authority to recognize and seal the canon, while the reformed tradition grounds the Scripture principle in thick claims regarding sovereign divine action and the veridical sufficiency of the text. Yoder elevates the church *as an institution* to a status equivalent to the catholic approach while wanting the Bible to function over against the church *as a community* in the reformed manner. It is far from clear that this mixed account works. Practically speaking, Yoder's church ought to be capable of issuing dogma, yet he rejects the impulse. He is insistent, for example, that the Trinity is not "revealed," because it is not "in" the Bible. It may have been a culturally appropriate reading of the Bible, or one expression of necessary questions raised by the Bible, but the answer itself is not a revealed truth. It is thus secondary to what is revealed, which is found in the plain meaning of the texts of Scripture.[77]

Such a view trades on an underdeveloped doctrine of revelation, usually unstated and unargued for.[78] More to the point, if the doctrine of the Trinity is an interpretation of Scripture's witness, why could not the church, akin to the Jerusalem Council in Acts 15, offer a definitive

---

76. *Revolutionary Christianity*, 60. Cf. *To Hear the Word* 152, 180; *For the Nations*, 81–82: "the reading of the Bible was freed by [the E]nlightenment's methodical doubt from the assumed orthodox identity between what it says and what we believe. . . . [The] Enlightenment [thus] enhances the objectivity of the Bible over against our previous appropriation of it." Although it is evident what Yoder means, there remains the unavoidable problem that Yoder, like all Christians, *does* think that what he believes is what the Bible says, and vice versa. He simply thinks that he has good reasons to suppose that what he believes follows from careful interpretation of the Bible. Again, one grasps his point—I and the Bible are two, not one—but it has to be more subtly articulated in order to gain the kind of critical purchase he wants it to have.

77. See *Preface*, 204: "As a matter of fact, [the doctrine of the Trinity] was not given us by revelation. . . . It is something the Cappadocians figured out in the fourth century. . . . It is not itself a revealed truth. . . ." For a nuanced account, see the extensive discussion in Sanders, *Triune God*.

78. Cf. *Preface*, 328–76, for Yoder's most sustained reflection on revelation. Note well that the lectures gathered in that book were published posthumously.

reading of another question similarly vital to its mission?[79] Ultimately, Yoder's biblicism trades on a kind of preferential option for primitivism: development is suspect, and what the many churches need to do is work backward to the apostolic church, model themselves after it, and thereby become more similar by eliminating the differences that have arisen in the interim.[80] And if it is not meant to be primitivist (and Yoder insists that it is not, though it functions that way in his thought), his account neglects to offer either principles or examples of acceptable change by which to make informed judgments about disputed developments, *including approval of some*. It is not unreasonable to ask for examples of faithful development, and it is not unfair to reject his proposal when no positive examples are forthcoming. In the end, Yoder is either an overt or a covert primitivist in his treatment of both Scripture and the church. And as he is quick to acknowledge, primitivism is not a viable option for Christian theology.[81]

Ecclesiology: The Politics of Jesus's Community

Of the many topics addressed in Yoder's work, the three primary foci are christology, ecclesiology, and ethics—with bibliology as a kind of ricochet of these, being so tied to each of them (and to his method of approaching them) that, in the aggregate, it becomes a fourth focus of his thought. Having looked at his bibliology and, to an extent, his christology and ethics, it should be evident why ecclesiology is so important. The Bible is the congregation's book, which bears to it and within it the story of Jesus, for the sake of its life and speech. All three topics are grounded in and centered on the community of faith. In this way Yoder's theology may be said to be "ecclesiocentric." Christian faith and ethics, the story and politics of Jesus, the witness and import of Scripture: these are inseparable from the church, indeed unintelligible apart from it. To attempt to understand any of them divorced from the concrete life and history of the church—an attempt regularly made in theology after the Enlightenment—is profoundly to misapprehend these

79. For further discussion, see Weaver, "Missionary Christology."

80. Another example, perhaps more practical than trinitarian doctrine, is polity. See Yoder's polemic against the historic episcopate and general practice of ordination in *Fullness of Christ*; cf. his brief "Could There Be a Baptist Bishop?"

81. This theme is ubiquitous in his work; development is real, the only question is whether it is faithful development. See, e.g., "Historical Development."

elements of the Christian life and the role of the church in the Christian gospel. Non-ecclesial moral theology, christology, or bibliology is a surd. To put it in non-Yoderian terms: The church is a necessary object of theological intelligence, particularly if one's aim is to be catholic and evangelical.

Yoder's account of the church is arguably the feature of his thought that has received the most attention in the secondary literature, a fact reflective of its prominence in his work. I will not, therefore, be offering a comprehensive treatment of Yoder's ecclesiology.[82] Rather I seek to highlight and comment on those features of his ecclesiology that are most relevant to understanding his bibliology, whether these be in direct relationship to Scripture or necessary context for understanding his theological vision as a whole.

My engagement with Yoder's theology of the church proceeds in three parts. The first discusses the church's character as the "pulpit and paradigm" of the good news of Christ, that is, the announcement (in speech) and embodiment (in practice) of the essentially visible form of life made possible by the cross and resurrection of Jesus. The second expands on this form of life as embodied in a violent world by a necessarily peaceful church. The third goes on to explore issues of "defectibility and renewal," that is, the live possibility that the church may fall into error, even fall away from the gospel, and the avenues of renewal, reform, and restitution open to it, not least through the reading of Scripture. This opens into a critique of Yoder's ecclesiology as overly optimistic in its expectations of obedience, resulting in a low doctrine of sin alongside a high doctrine of the church community (a "high" ecclesiology, that is, for a "low church" tradition). Yoder envisions a community centered on a canon whose social and political norms are described as "radical," "deviant," and utterly set off from the world of sin and violence. This constellation of features is at best imbalanced and at worst a recipe for disaster.

The Visibility of Christ's Body

In the foregoing I have offered a number of condensed summaries of Yoder's ecclesiology. They have all focused on Yoder's two-pronged ac-

---

82. For discussion, see Sider, *To See History*; Kerr, *Christ, History, and Apocalyptic*; Park, *Missional Ecclesiologies*; Schmidt, *Church and World*; Nigel Goring Wright, *Disavowing Constantine*; Ens, *Boundaries Thick and Permeable*. See also East, "Undefensive Presence."

count of the origins of the church, first in the ministry and message of Jesus, then in the development of that initial work by the apostles (in, Yoder avers, deep continuity with Jesus's own actions and intentions). His account, then, is rooted in (1) the announcement and inauguration of the reign of God by Jesus, himself the *autobasileia*; (2) the formation of a community of committed followers around the person of Jesus; (3) the new form of life to which this community is called in obedience to Jesus's teachings and example; (4) the way in which this new community is both fulfillment of and judgment upon the hopes, beliefs, and practices of Israel and its leaders; (5) the climactic events of cross and resurrection as determinative of both Jesus's and his community's identities; (6) the sending of Jesus's apostles and followers into the world to bear witness to the good news of his resurrection, lordship, and reconciling love; and (7) the outpouring of the Holy Spirit upon his disciples. Pentecost completes the formation of the church, empowering it for its mission and granting it a share in the life and power of the new age, which dawned in Jesus's rising and will be consummated by his eventual return. Yoder's ecclesiology, in short, is centered on the incarnate, crucified, and risen Jesus; the community he founded; its Spirit-filled life; its mission to the nations; and its inhabitation of the time between the times—which is to say, its eschatological existence in the power of Christ's Spirit.

These features come to a head in a single term: *visibility*. The church, for Yoder, is irreducibly visible.[83] And this visibility arises for bedrock theological reasons. On the one hand, it is a function of the incarnation. The Word really did become flesh; Jesus was truly and without qualification the Son of God, the Lord in person living a fully human life. How much more the community that claims to worship and follow him in the world! Christians are no more disembodied than Nazareth's itinerant artisan. Docetism in ecclesiology is, Yoder believes, as perilous as it is in christology; to reject it in the latter requires rejecting it in the former. In the words of William Cavanaugh, "If the church is the body of Christ, then all ecclesiology must be Christology."[84] On the other hand, aside from its continuity with Jesus's own lived example, the church's life, purpose, and mission require visibility and embodiment, lest it contradict its own message. The church is to bear witness to the new way of Jesus in and

---

83. See Sider, *To See History*, esp. 1–16, 97–132.
84. See Cavanaugh, *Migrations of the Holy*, 154.

to the world, not only in speech but also in action, in its life together. How could it do so if its testimony were inaudible, its example invisible?

The evangel incarnated in community: that is the church for Yoder. Not simple parity with other polities, but eschatological visibility. What is seen is the good news of Jesus lived and spoken by the people of Pentecost in the dispersion—a diaspora that, unlike the plight of the Jews in Babylon, is neither accidental nor disastrous but rather part of the positive plan of God for the reconciliation of the world.[85] One of Yoder's most-cited passages is St. Paul's programmatic announcement in 2 Corinthians 5:17–20 of believers' ambassadorship of the message of reconciliation. Combine this with one of his other oft-quoted passages, the appeal of Jeremiah to the exiles in Babylon to "seek the peace of the city" (Jer 29:7 KJV), and we have the rudiments of Yoder's entire theology of mission, which in many respects just is his theology of the church.

Eschatological visibility means suffering, so long as the life of the new age encounters the obstinacy of the defeated powers as they persevere in the old age, just as Jesus did in paradoxical triumph through the cross.[86] Thus: "The cross of the church is a prolongation of the cross of Christ, as the church is his continuing life in his body."[87] The church—which is to say, the community of Christ's disciples beginning with the Twelve and expanding and extending up to the present time—is the cruciform community that continues to embody the way of Jesus after him. Moreover, the church's cross isn't suffering or trial in general. It has concrete meaning: "The believer's cross is [not] any and every kind of suffering, sickness, or tension, the bearing of which is demanded. The believer's cross is, like that of Jesus, the price of social nonconformity. It is not, like sickness or catastrophe, an inexplicable, unpredictable suffering; it is the end of a path freely chosen after counting the cost. It is not . . . an inward wrestling of the sensitive soul with self and sin; it is the social reality of representing in an unwilling world the Order to come." When Jesus, in John 15:20, promises his followers the same persecution that followed him, "it is a normative statement about the relation of our social obedi-

---

85. Now the same may be said of the exile and lingering dispersion; but the point here is that the Great Commission, far from being a calamity governed by the terrible but ultimately wise providence of God, is the joyful sending of the church into the world, a positive mark of its life and purpose, not one to be lamented or suffered as punishment.

86. See further Berkhof, *Christ and the Powers.*

87. *Revolutionary Christianity,* 68.

ence to the messianity of Jesus."[88] To embody Jesus's way in the world, in the old age that is passing away, is to provoke the only response the world knows: ostracization, violence, death.

To suffer in this way is part and parcel of the church's cruciform life, centered on Christ and its apostolic mission, sent by Christ to the nations as his witness: "the very existence of the church is its primary task. It is in itself a proclamation of the lordship of Christ to the powers from whose dominion the church has begun to be liberated. The church does not attack the powers; this Christ has done. The church concentrates upon not being seduced by them. By existing the church demonstrates that their rebellion has been vanquished."[89] Thus "the primary social structure through which the gospel works to change other structures is that of the Christian community."[90] The work of Jesus the crucified Messiah and that of the community that worships, follows, and proclaims him are bound together at this crucial point.

For Yoder, therefore, the church is intrinsic to the gospel; part of the announcement itself, not merely the result of it. That is, the good news is not limited to talk of Jesus, precisely because Jesus may not be abstracted from the particular details of the Gospel narratives. The good news includes talk also of the ministry of Jesus, and constitutive of that ministry was the formation of a new community centered on his example and teachings. To belong to that community meant being committed to living his way as a citizen of God's kingdom in advance of its full advent. Jesus was no lone figure, beating the air but losing ground; "Jesus' strategy for change began and ended with the creation of a covenant community," which was "a revolutionary power" because "the Christian community, in all its weakness, is a demonstration of the reality of a kind of life in reconciliation, already sustained and beginning to be changed by faith, hope, and love." From which follows the claim "that the most fundamental social revolution of all time was that of Pentecost,"[91] which Yoder elsewhere calls "the original revolution[:] the creation of a distinct community with its own deviant set of values and its coherent

---

88. *Politics of Jesus*, 96.
89. *Politics of Jesus*, 150.
90. *Politics of Jesus*, 154.
91. *Revolutionary Christianity*, 158. Cf. 161: "The self-emptying of God . . . is the most revolutionary event . . . in the history of the race." The two claims' proximity (in print) and similarity (in substance) only reinforce how intertwined christology and ecclesiology are for Yoder.

way of incarnating them."[92] The church is the creation of Jesus and his Spirit. It is the means through which God works in the world for change. It is the divine instrument of contesting and challenging the demonic powers' claims to rule. And, just so, it is the announcement to the world of the good news of Jesus, a message inseparable from the church's own existence and the actuality, not only the possibility, of the way of life it offers to others. Christ's body belongs to Christ's gospel; the good news is incomplete without mention of the church.

Yoder's default scriptural resource here is the first two chapters of Ephesians, on which he comments: "This creation of the one new humanity is itself the purpose that God had in all ages, is itself the 'mystery,' the gospel now to be proclaimed."[93] He writes further, with clarity about the implications: "This new Christian community . . . is not only a vehicle of the gospel or only a fruit of the gospel; *it is the good news.* It is not merely the agent of mission or the constituency of a mission agency. This is the mission,"[94] namely, belonging to and building up the life of this particular community, the *ekklēsia* of Jesus Christ.

Accordingly, it is proper to the church to have some measure of inward focus. Its task, put simply, is to be itself: "The most urgent and ultimately the most effective task for the church in our day . . . is to be the church."[95] We have already seen the reason why: The sheer presence of this community, with its unique practices and beliefs, is at once a permanent black eye in the face of the powers that be and the principal medium of *God's* power at work in the world. This claim is a confession of faith; it is not evident to natural perception. But it is consistent with the gospel of a crucified Messiah, namely, that almighty God deigns to work not first of all in the hallways of human power and parliamentary proceedings and political elites' jostling, but in the unremarkable, unappealing little band of ordinary people huddled together in an out-of-the-way neighborhood sharing goods, forgiving debts, welcoming the stranger, feeding the hungry, refusing the false peace of the sword. Contrary to common sense, typical expectations, and enlightened reason, *this* is the locus of divine action and change in the world; *this* is where and how the living

---

92. *Original Revolution*, 28.
93. *Royal Priesthood*, 74. Cf. *Revolutionary Christianity*, 8: "the meaning of the gospel [is] summed up in the creation of a new kind of community."
94. *Royal Priesthood*, 91.
95. *Revolutionary Christianity*, 158.

God pitches a tent and works to overcome human violence, greed, and deceit. "The ultimate meaning of history is to be found in the work of the church."[96] But no common life of this kind is possible without nurture, reflection, and sustained attention devoted to its development, maintenance, and faithfulness in the face of unexpected challenges. "Therefore, in all of the challenges posed to the church, the key to its success in witness and faithfulness will be maintaining its own identity."[97] In this way, the rallying cry "let the church be the church" is directed also to perennial temptations: to see God "really" at work elsewhere than in the church; to desire more immediate or effective results; to transfer allegiance or energy to "responsible" efforts of the state; to lose faith in the little way of Jesus and the path that ends in crucifixion, which to the world looks like little more than futility and unfulfilled hopes. But this is unbelief, not faith in the Crucified. For "the relationship between the obedience of God's people and the triumph of God's cause is not a relationship of cause and effect but one of cross and resurrection."[98] Good Friday and Easter Sunday are the only orienting coordinates for the church's life in the world. Nothing else will suffice.

A Peaceful Church in a Violent World

Where critics might see withdrawal or irresponsibility in the account so far outlined, Yoder counters with the fundamental peaceableness of the way of Jesus, which must be the church's way too. Magisterial Christianity embraces what Yoder calls "the fundamental axiom that it is the obligation of the Christian to direct the course of history so that it attains the goals he chooses," or more succinctly, the commandment that "Thou shalt make history come out right."[99] But this is the antithesis of Christ crucified. Jesus's cross is normative for the church, and at Gethsemane Jesus once for all rejected the temptation of "responsible" use of the sword in service of "just ends."[100] The crucifixion does not involve tak-

96. *Original Revolution*, 61.
97. *Revolutionary Christianity*, 136.
98. *Politics of Jesus*, 232.
99. *Original Revolution*, 132-33.
100. See *Politics of Jesus*, 45-48, 144-58, 193-210. In the famous line from Tertullian, in disarming St. Peter, Jesus disarmed all would-be soldiers who would seek to follow him. For critique, see Biggar, *In Defense of War*, esp. 16-60.

ing history by the reins—yet nowhere else did the life and ministry of the church's Lord terminate than Golgotha. Just so, the "common sense" of using the "necessary" means to ensure history "turns out right" is, for Yoder, the church's primary enduring temptation. For it is the first step down an ineluctable path to justifying coercion—a piece of jargon that veils, in its abstraction, the killing of human beings for whom Christ died.

To refuse to kill is to refuse the bribe of so-called public responsibility. The church need not accept the terms of the offer, as though its public witness were dependent on the willingness to kill. It is not. The question, then, is not whether the church will engage the world in legible, relevant, or effective ways, but how.[101] In other words, who or what is the subject of Christian ethics, and by what criteria is faithfulness measured? Answer: The criterion is Christ, and the subject is Christ's disciple, who has considered discipleship's cost and freely chosen to sign up.[102] It is not the disciple alone, however. It is the community of disciples that collectively incarnates—or seeks to incarnate—the kingdom announced and perfectly incarnated in Jesus. "The believing community is the new world on the way,"[103] for "the people of God is called to be today what the world is called to be ultimately."[104]

To make this distinction, between church and world and the relevant moral possibilities available to each of them, is not to carve up the globe into a righteous few and a wicked many; nor is it to isolate them, as though they may neither communicate nor interact with each other,

---

101. See *War of the Lamb*, 180: "The renunciation of violence is not right because it 'works' (sometimes); it works (sometimes) because it is right. If and when, in a given frame of time or place, it did not work, it is still right." For analysis and critique of Yoder's shifting appeals to political relevance as part of a larger program of reducing doctrine to ethics, see Martens, *Heterodox Yoder*, esp. 54–86, 116–47.

102. See *Royal Priesthood*, 265: "membership in the church includes moral accountability for the individual and, therefore, enables moral solidarity for the group.... [A]dult celebration of baptism [is predicated] ... upon the candidate's readiness to enter wittingly and willingly into a covenant of mutual accountability.... [This] enables the local congregation to have solidarity without legalism and pastoral responsibility without clericalism."

103. *For the Nations*, 50.

104. *Body Politics*, ix. Not to say that living faithfully will *install* or *bring about* the kingdom: "We are not marching to Zion because we think that by our own momentum we can get there.... We are marching to Zion because, when God lets down from heaven the new Jerusalem prepared for us, we want to be the kind of persons and the kind of community that will not feel strange there" (*Original Revolution*, 159).

much less be transformed by the encounter. Distinguishing them does, however, order them, giving a twofold priority to the church. "The church precedes the world epistemologically[:] We know more fully from Jesus Christ and in the context of the confessed faith than we know in other ways. . . . The church precedes the world as well axiologically, in that the lordship of Christ is the center which must guide critical value choices, so that we may be called to subordinate or even to reject those values which contradict Jesus."[105] But this ordered priority between the two is precisely the condition for relationship, for interaction and speech, since dialogue requires two parties. Indeed, the church not only can speak to and change the world, it has already done so in history. But it has done so most faithfully, most effectively, and most lastingly, not through top-down imposition of power, but through bottom-up, noncoercive influence. "The alternative community discharges a modeling mission. . . . The church is . . . not chaplain or priest to the powers running the world: she is called to be a microcosm of the wider society, not only as an idea, but also in her function."[106] "The challenge to the faith community," therefore, "should not be to dilute or filter or translate its witness, so that the 'public' community can handle it without believing, but so to purify and clarify and exemplify it that the world can perceive it to be good news without having to learn a foreign language."[107] It is good news in that people will and should want to join the church and begin to live in this liberative new way. But it is also good news inasmuch as "the order of the faith community constitutes a public offer to the entire society."[108] The church's life and message are not only a form of direct evangelization but also a kind of sociocultural leavening: it democratizes leadership, prioritizes dialogue, resolves conflict, shares goods, and overcomes division, and presents practices and principles to the wider watching world that are available for approximation and analogy.[109]

To bring matters full circle: Without ecclesial visibility, there is no new world on the way; no site of "already" amid the "not yet"; no living, systemic challenge to the powers and principalities; no concrete offer to a fallen and wayward world; no corporate analogue to Jesus's exemplary

---

105. *Priestly Kingdom*, 11.

106. *Priestly Kingdom*, 92. See further Parler, *Things Hold Together*. Cf. Hunter, *To Change the World*, esp. 48–78, 150–66.

107. *For the Nations*, 24.

108. *For the Nations*, 27 (emphasis removed).

109. *Royal Priesthood*, 364. See the larger discussion in *Body Politics*.

life, no body to his head, no continuation of the community he founded around himself. This positive, theologically grounded emphasis on the church's visibility is paired, negatively, with the traditional concept of the church's "invisibility." Yoder judges this concept a grievous error, for the church and for the gospel.[110] He reads it as perhaps *the* fundamental underlying shift that occurred during and after the fourth century, a shift that, according to him, obliterated the distinction between (visible) world and (visible) church. "Before Constantine,[111] one knew as a fact of everyday experience that there was a believing Christian community but one had to 'take it on faith' that God was governing history. After Constantine, one had to believe without seeing that there was a community of believers, within the larger nominally Christian mass, but one knew for a fact that God was in control of history."[112] For "with the age of Constantine, Providence no longer needed to be an object of faith, for God's governance of history had become empirically evident in the person of the Christian ruler of the world."[113] Apart from the many other problems that result from this change, the erasure of the all-too-visible and obvious difference between church and world eliminates, in one fell swoop, the church's very *raison d'être*. How can the church be a challenge to the powers, the herald of the kingdom, the body of the Messiah, the proclamation of the gospel, the firstfruits of the new creation—how can the church be all this without a world, distinct from the church, to be the audience and theater of this witness?[114] How can the church be faithful in the execution of this mission if the world is folded into the church, thereby attenuating or even nullifying the expectation of obedience? In order to understand Yoder's theology of the church, it is vital to see that the problem with Constantine is not some absolutist concern about whether or not it is ever in principle permissible for Christians to govern or to kill. The problem

110. For discussion, see *Revolutionary Christianity*, 109–19; *For the Nations*, 113–15; *Priestly Kingdom*, 135–47; *Royal Priesthood*, 73–75.

111. The role and meaning of the figure of Constantine in Yoder's thought is complex and disputed; see further Leithart, *Defending Constantine*; Roth, *Constantine Revisited*; Sider, *To See History*, 57–132; Nigel Goring Wright, *Disavowing Constantine*, 57–104; Schmidt, *Church and World*, 97–147.

112. *Priestly Kingdom*, 137. For an alternative to Yoder's critique of so-called Constantinian Christianity, see Daniélou, *Prayer as a Political Problem*.

113. *Priestly Kingdom*, 136.

114. For Calvin, the world is the theater of God's glory. For Yoder, the world is the theater of the church's witness.

with Constantine is that he represents the abolition of the conditions necessary for the church—the first-fruits and vehicle of God's glad tidings for the world in Jesus—to fulfill its mission, to discharge its task, indeed, to exist at all. Constantine renders the *ekklēsia* null and void; its reason for being vanishes by imperial fiat. The result, in Yoder's judgment, is nothing short of ruin.

A charged and epochal theological term has attached itself, not without Yoder's approval, to the historical changes wrought by and after Constantine: the fall. As in "the Constantinian fall of the church." But fallenness presumes the possibility of falling, which raises the question of defectibility. Yoder addresses this question head-on, and his answer will round out both our discussion of his ecclesiology and my critique of it.

The Possibility of Obedience, the Judgment of Scripture, and the Wages of Sin

For Yoder, genuine ecclesial obedience to God's will is a real possibility. As such it should define our expectations. The presumption of failure is itself a failure to understand the nature of the life made possible by Christ's Spirit. If the gospel is true, then followers of Jesus must be able to follow him. If that is a fiction, then so is the gospel. Yoder does not thereby mean to discount the possibility of disobedience. Rather, disobedience is meaningful, it is worthy of blame, only if it can be avoided. Apostasy is a live threat only if faithfulness is a live option. The church's defectibility is a necessary condition for there to be real stakes about right faith and right action. The heirs of St. Augustine thus have it the wrong way around. As Yoder sees it, the Augustinian tradition's high hamartiology obviates actual lived obedience, even as it is underwritten by the church's absolute indefectibility. He argues to the contrary that sin does not render faithfulness a surd, but exactly because the church may stay on the narrow path, it likewise may depart from it, in which case the church is defectible.[115]

The church, therefore, can keep faith, but the church also can fall.[116] Fallenness does not mean imperfection, however, much less isolable er-

---

115. For discussion, see *Jewish-Christian Schism Revisited*, 121–43.
116. For why obedience is possible, and why this claim is not Pelagian, see *Jewish-Christian Schism Revisited*, 123.

rors. To such symptoms "mere" reform might be the cure. Fallenness is fatal: no remedies can bring the patient back to life. A new start must be made. The Bible is the source of that new start, as it is of every reform and call to renewal prior to reaching that final threshold. *Sola scriptura* is thus an encapsulating axiom of believers church ecclesiology. It teaches, first, that the church is subject to judgment, because it has a Lord, the risen Jesus who rules by the Spirit through the canon of Scripture. Second, that the church may truly be faithful to its Lord by fidelity to this book. Third, that the church may truly be unfaithful to its Lord by infidelity to this book. Fourth and finally, that the church has a future and this book will be the means and measure of its perseverance.

"The true church," in sum, "is the free church,"[117] and one of the marks of the free or believers church is the centrality, independence, and authority of the Bible in, from, and over the church. Other marks include the sacraments, which Yoder terms "body politics," that is, the constitutive practices of the body politic that is the church. At the end of the last section I drew attention to Yoder's anti-metaphysical understanding of theology as a practical science. One upshot of this approach is his tendency to reduce theology to ethics, or to immanentize supra-mundane claims by making them "really" about the church community.[118] Nowhere is this more evident than in his treatment of the sacraments. Though he readily affirms that God works in, with, and under the practices in question, his depiction of them, while rooted in biblical exegesis, is largely non-theological. By the end of his career they become, in effect, socially edifying and politically exemplary corporate habits adoptable in principle by any community that desires to overcome ethnic, gender, and class division, hierarchy, and inequality.[119]

---

117. *Revolutionary Christianity*, 118.

118. See again Martens, *Heterodox Yoder*, 142: "Yoder seems to leave us with a Jesus who has become merely an ethico-political paradigm that opens the door for a supersessive secular ethic. . . . To the extent that Yoder seeks to discipline and bend theological terms and categories systematically toward an ethical end . . . I take him to fit within the modern trajectory of theologians—including but not limited to Kant, Hegel, Harnack, Ritschl, and Rauschenbusch—with formally similar agendas." Cf. Healy, *Hauerwas*. To be sure, this is not what Yoder understands himself to be doing, nor is it even what the explicit claims and arguments of his text formally commit him to. Nonetheless it is a persuasive reading of the overarching trajectory of Yoder's work, however unintended.

119. See further (sometimes directly, sometimes less so) *Body Politics*; *Fullness of Christ*; *Royal Priesthood*, esp. 323-73; *Revolutionary Christianity*, esp. 3-44; *War of*

If the sacraments are reduced to social ethics, it is with the latter topic that we will close this section. I have already raised issues with aspects of Yoder's ecclesiology, such as its primitivism and its inability to articulate a workable account of doctrinal development in the church's history. I want now to discuss a different set of problems that beset his understanding of the church, problems that bear also on his depiction of Scripture's role in the church.

We may categorize these problems as following from either too *low* of a hamartiology or too *high* of an ecclesiology. Yoder largely relegates the power and presence of sin to the world of unbelief outside the church, renounced and repented of at one's baptismal initiation into the church. The obverse of this relegation, whether as motivation or consequence, is his attribution to the church of the capacity to live as God would have it, to be obedient to the way of Jesus, to live in a comprehensively faithful manner. Where Yoder does allow for continuing sin in the community, he is at his least convincing, for his solution is an undifferentiated and universal application of "binding and loosing."[120] Otherwise, the picture of the church that Yoder offers is overwhelmingly optimistic in its expectation of the church's success in obedience.[121]

This tenuous reckoning with sin within the church is a problem in multiple ways. For our purposes I will focus on its connection to the Bible. To start, it is a problem because it severely underplays Christians' temp-

---

the Lamb, esp. 125–63; *For the Nations*, esp. 1–93; *Priestly Kingdom*, esp. 80–122; *Real Christian Fellowship*, 74–140. For sacramentology that unites the spiritual and the social together, see, e.g., Schmemann, *Of Water and the Spirit*; Schmemann, *Eucharist*; Davison, *Why Sacraments?*; Cavanaugh, "Politics and Reconciliation," esp. 207.

120. As, for example, when the one sinned against has significantly less power—whether speaking socially, legally, institutionally, or physically—relative to the one she would confront. Cf. *Body Politics*, 1–13; *Royal Priesthood*, 323–58. See further Villegas, "Ecclesial Ethics."

121. See the similar critique in Reimer, "Theological Orthodoxy," 434: "It has always seemed to me that Yoder did not allow adequately for the human fallibility of individual Christians as well as the Christian community." Cf. Yoder's unpublished essay from the late 1960s, posthumously collected in *Real Christian Fellowship*, 109–19, as "Repenting from Sin." It is eerie to read this early essay in light of the decades that followed. Much of the essay is dedicated to diagnosing "counterfeit forms of repentance" (116) by which guilty persons "avoid taking full responsibility for their past sin" through recourse to "excuses, substitutes, and loopholes" (115). By contrast, the true discipline of actual repentance "entails confessing, accepting responsibility for past wrongs, declaring what must not happen again, and beginning to behave immediately in such a way that the transgression is unlikely to happen again" (119).

tation, even propensity, to sin in their use and reading of the text. On one side, this is a corporate and external problem: the church as a whole justifying evil (its own or its society's) by means of Scripture, whether that be chattel slavery, the torture of heretics, or the expansion of empire. On the other side, this is an individual and internal problem. If the church in view is the kind proposed by Yoder, it will be marked by strong boundaries, visibly and sometimes geographically distinct from its host society and from neighboring communities. It will further be a numerical minority in society (Yoder thinks this inevitable and therefore a measure of commitment to discipleship) as well as congregationalist in polity; though it will be egalitarian to some degree, it will also have leaders who guide and teach it. What Yoder fails to address is how such a community is to prevent its leaders from misusing the biblical text to hurt church members under their care. In effect he provides a theoretical structure in which such abuse could—not necessarily would, but could—flourish due to the meager built-in accountability for leaders who perpetrate it. In an alternative minority community that sets its own standards, accords little to no epistemic or moral value to standards outside it, and is both voluntary and self-policing, it is difficult to see by what measures, strong and reliable, leaders might be held accountable and restrained from actions that abuse their power.[122]

The wicked and tragic events of Yoder's life show forth in just these shortcomings; in that way they are a sort of negative apocalypse: "Nothing is covered up that will not be revealed, or hidden that will not be known. Therefore whatever you have said in the dark shall be heard in the light, and what you have whispered in private rooms shall be proclaimed upon the housetops" (Luke 12:2-3 RSV).[123] But regardless of the

122. Though it is worth being clear on this point: no matter the guardrails on interpretation, no matter the accuracy of Christian exegesis, evil can always find a way, and self-justification is infinitely malleable. In a word, the correctness of one's reading of the Bible is neither necessary nor sufficient to avoid injustice.

123. In my view, it was not a breakdown in the system as it was constructed that failed to stop Yoder or to hold him accountable. There plainly was no recourse. That seems to me to be true of the ecclesiology that Yoder articulates. Indeed, combine that ecclesio-social context with the solitary genius who defends his actions by "brilliant," "innovative," "radical," even "transgressive" exegesis of the Bible, all while engaging in behavior considered "deviant" by the mores of the culture but reinterpreted as "experimental" and "cutting edge" on the grounds of consonance with the ministry of Jesus—one sees the problem. It is not a stretch, *at this particular point*, to see the connections between, on the one hand, Yoder's abusive actions, self-justifications,

nature and extent of the connection between Yoder's thought and life in this respect, the critique of his ecclesiology stands. Any Christian doctrine of the church and of the Bible within it must assume that sin will be operative in the life of the first and the reading of the second, and that wholesale obedience, though not impossible under God, will be the exception rather than the rule. Intrinsic to such doctrines, and their relation one to the other, must be an account of disobedience—of the unceasing need for the forgiveness of sins; of how to check one's own and others' temptation to sin in reading and teaching the Bible; of how to be modest and humble in exegesis for that very reason; of how to avoid a situation in which the lone radical or solitary genius is categorically invincible in reasoning and held to be wrong only in the event that he is convinced of his error. The Bible is the book of the congregation, without question. But the congregation is, without exception, composed of sinners. The Bible must therefore first of all be the book—which is to say, the sword (Eph 6:17)—of the Spirit, for it is the Spirit who abides in the community (1 Cor 3:16) while convicting its members of sin (John 16:8–11).[124] Perhaps a high ecclesiology with a deflationary bibliology is possible in principle. But to lack a thick account of hermeneutical sin and the Spirit's checks against it, as Yoder does, is fatal to the endeavor.

"High" Church, "Low" Scripture: The Community of Christ and the Community's Book

Theology, for Yoder, is principally a form of practical reasoning, the communal context and subject of that reasoning is the church, and the lived shape of such reasoning, the concrete actuality of theology, is the contestation of readings of the Bible. The congregation gathered together in prayerful discernment over what to do, say, or think in response to a given practical challenge, united in common study of the prophets and apostles: that, in a nutshell, is a faithful church for Yoder, and what "theology" names as a practice embodied in the everyday.

---

and private self-understanding, and on the other the presentation of the church, the Bible, and the office of theologian offered in his published, scholarly work.

124. John 16:8–9 speaks of the Spirit convicting the *world* of sin, but recall that elsewhere in Johannine discourse *kosmos* does not exclude believers: "For God so loved the world . . ." (3:16).

This section takes up the two poles of this picture of theology, the doctrinal loci of the Bible and the church, and seeks to tease out the relationship between them. In what follows I analyze the dogmatic architecture of Yoder's thought on these two topics: the influence of each on the other, the relative priorities assigned to them and to other doctrines, and the particular ways in which Yoder coordinates them in a single whole. Doing so should give us critical purchase as well as perspective on Yoder's unique approach to these theological topics as well as the ways in which his approach represents the baptist tradition.

Yoder is a most unsystematic thinker, insofar as his writings are nearly always occasional and topical. He never produced a "big book" that tied everything together; nor is the matter helped by the fact that, at this point, a third of his books have been published posthumously, and so lack the kind of revisions, polish, and organization that characterize the rest of his work. Yoder's lack of systematicity is not accidental: he distrusted a *Dogmatik* or a *Summa* at the formal level, as perhaps well-intended but nonetheless unfitting attempts to schematize and systematize, and therefore to improve upon, an original that does not need improvement precisely in its situational, ramshackle diversity. The Bible is not a *Summa*, and it is better for that. Why force a square peg into a round hole?

Yoder is unsystematic, then, at least at the level of methodology. But in other ways he is quite systematic, in that the whole of his thought is interconnected, intertwined, each part inseparable from every other. Nearly all his essays concern a specific topic (say, christology), but alongside that topic the reader will find a dozen others lying near to hand, not least ecclesiology, missiology, bibliology, eschatology, social ethics, pacifism, and more. If he deals with one, he invariably deals with the others. In that respect Yoder's theology meets the definition of a system, if by that one means simply that there *is* a whole, that it is coherent, that the parts make a kind of ordered sense, and that, in isolation, each part is patient of analysis without being sufficient unto itself, since the sense it makes is in conjunction with the rest. Yoder's enmity to "systems" has less to do with these features than with a difference of temperament and style, underwritten by a sense of fittingness between the mode of knowing and the object known. Theology should fit together the way Genesis, the Psalms, the Synoptics, and Romans fit together: less a set of equations, more a unity in diversity that is self-involving in the recognition and the construction of it.

So we may expect, in approaching Yoder's thought in the singular, both that it will be coherent, even systematic, and that, whatever system-like features we find, they will not be on the surface, but embedded within and distributed across the many writings his corpus comprises. Lacking a table of contents for his *loci communes*, we must make our way on our own. How to proceed, then? What to say about Yoder's theology of Scripture and the church?

By way of orientation, I will designate Yoder's approach to Scripture a "low" bibliology. The term is descriptive, not pejorative or evaluative; Yoder's Anabaptist tradition, for example, is "low church," which characterizes its polity and liturgy, not its sense of the importance or centrality of the church—far from it! Yoder's bibliology is "low," then, in that the primary claims he makes for the Bible are neither theological nor theologically funded. To high Protestant scholasticism, Yoder opposes "an historical modulation of the sociology of knowledge," phrased in the form of a question: "What would we come up with if we were to ask what it means for any human movement, deriving its identity from a limited set of foundational events, to seek to be faithful to the meaning of those events within the flux of historical (i.e., changing) existence?"[125] In an important sense, Yoder's theology of the Bible is no theology at all; it is a particular application of the general way in which communities maintain self-identity across time through accountability to founding texts (texts, that is, that faithfully mediate founding events). I have called this approach a deflationary account of Scripture. Yoder presents it as a corrective to overly ambitious and metaphysically technical bibliologies that are themselves, in his view, patently non-biblical, abstracted from the vagaries of history. Bloated and weighed down by sheer mass, they are doomed to fail in their appointed task: to indicate the reality and purpose of the scriptural canon while aiding the church in its practical recourse to the text.

Yoder's corrective, a kind of anti-bibliology, is not devoid of all theological content, however. What it lacks theologically lies in its consideration of the Bible "in and of itself"; what makes it a theological account in spite of that lack is what it receives from outside itself, as it were, from other doctrinal loci. That is to say, Yoder's bibliology is buttressed, or bookended, by christology, on one side, and ecclesiology, on the other. What makes his account of Scripture more than an application of "the sociology of knowledge" to the religious community of the *ekklēsia* is the material content derived from his twofold depiction of Christ and

125. *To Hear the Word*, 110-11.

the community that bears his name—each of which, in his presentation, is robustly theological.

Jesus is the Bible's hinge, its summit, and (for the New Testament) its subject matter. The people Israel and the Old Testament alike find the consummation of their faith, hope, and moral vision in the Messiah born in Bethlehem and crucified outside Jerusalem. Everything turns on his coming, death, resurrection, and ascension. The New Testament is his followers' written testimony to him and to the whole scope of his interpreted person and work. Together, these books are formally and materially christocentric, internally ordered to Jesus Christ and his kingdom. A mere historian could go along some ways here, since this is in part a description of the Christian construction of the canon. But Yoder means more. Since it is *true* that the man Jesus of Nazareth taught in Galilee, preached God's reign, and exorcised demons, was crucified under Pontius Pilate, rose from the dead on the third day, and ascended into heaven to rule over history as the viceroy of Israel's God, it thereby follows that the Bible *is* ordered to him, forward and backward. If it is to be read well, therefore, it must be read in accordance with this ordering. What the Bible is and how it should be read follow from who Jesus is and what he did. Bibliology follows christology.

The same can be said regarding the church. The church—the one people of God from Abraham to Apollos and beyond, Israel according to the flesh *and* Israel according to the Spirit—is the context, source, and audience of the biblical texts, their home, their steward, and (like Jesus) their subject matter. Humanly speaking, these texts were written by members of this particular community, constituted by its history, beliefs, and practices in light of its experiences and convictions accumulated over time about where it had come from, where it was going, and how, in the meantime, to continue living together in the world in obedience to God. Theologically speaking, the community in question is the elect people of God, called by divine grace and created by divine deliverance, given the Law and the promises by the one true and only living God. These texts, then, are sites of the community working out in real time how to *be* this people, given God's mighty acts, commands, and promises, culminating in the death and resurrection of the Messiah, Jesus. After Pentecost, this elect people is made up of Jew and gentile alike, filled and directed by the very Spirit of the risen Jesus. The church therefore confesses that the texts of the Bible, and those of the New Testament in particular, were (1) written by the power of the Holy Spirit, and thus (2) bear true witness to Jesus while (3) offering trustworthy apostolic guidance to (4) the church's ongoing mission to the nations. How so? By showing how the church at the outset discerned and processed faithfulness to the gospel in the midst of conflicts and unforeseen challenges encountered along the way, and accordingly how the church in the present may do the same.

The character as well as the sequence of these claims are important for understanding Yoder's argument. The church does not trust Scripture because it is "inspired." The church trusts Scripture because it trusts the Spirit of Jesus in its midst, at work today and in the past. Which means that, in a sense, the church trusts Scripture because it trusts itself—that is, it trusts that it is in fact the church, the community of Christ enlivened by his Spirit; that this is no illusion, but the truth of the matter; and that this was true of forebears in the faith, of the church in prior generations, all the way to the first apostles and their own predecessors in Israel. What the Bible is and what should be said of it follow from what the church is and what it has said and done in the past. Bibliology follows ecclesiology.

Note the subordinate elements in this account, as well as the major ones missing. Of the latter, the biggest is the doctrine of God: there is no filled-out theology of the Trinity (or of God *simpliciter*) behind or above Yoder's treatment of Scripture, church, and Jesus. This in turn accounts for the relative lack of another significant doctrine, an absence particularly notable in a late twentieth-century theologian who studied under Barth: namely, that of revelation. This is not to say that Yoder does not discuss God or revelation, only that neither plays a substantive role in his theology of Scripture, or in that of the related loci of Christ and the church.

As for the subordinate elements that are present, there are at least three. The first, pneumatology, is ambiguous. It seems to me that, for the most part in Yoder's theology, the Spirit functions as an extension of Christ; the Spirit is thus the locus of Christ's rule and presence in the church, governing it as head of the body during the time of his session at the Father's right hand. The force of this reading would be that the Spirit is effectively sidelined in Yoder's thought, less a distinct hypostasis and more a function or feature of the person and work of the risen Jesus, who does receive comprehensive theological description. Now, this account is to some degree in continuity with broad strands of pneumatology in Western theology, not least Barth himself;[126] moreover, it is arguably

126. For critique, e.g., of Barth on this score, see Jenson, "Where the Spirit Went";

consonant with the picture of the Spirit found in parts of the New Testament.[127] So while it is fair to say that pneumatology plays a minimal substantive role in Yoder's bibliology proper, one may withhold judgment regarding the extent to which this is due to a defective pneumatology—depreciated in value, as it were, due to disproportionate magnification of christology. Either way, it is evident that the Spirit plays little direct role in Yoder's treatment of Scripture in itself.

Via ecclesiology, however, there is a bit more influence, given the Spirit's abiding presence in the community and the Bible's status as the community's book. In the power of the Spirit the church both acts and deliberates how to act, while the Spirit guides the deliberative process and enables it to be faithful in its mode and its terminus (here a right end does not justify a wrong means). Call it a proceduralism of the Spirit. The church prayerfully deliberates, discerns, and tests the spirits in a twofold manner through open conversation and through study of Scripture, each under the Spirit, each mutually reinforcing the other.[128] Invocation of the Spirit and trust that the Spirit will lead the congregation into truth—into God's will, into action corresponding to the example of Christ, into faith in accordance with the gospel—is the governing conviction that carries the process to its conclusion. Internal to this conviction is trust that the Spirit now leading the fellowship of believers is one and the same as the Spirit who led the prophets and apostles long ago in their own conflictual processes of discernment and witness, and in their eventual inscription in texts of their experiences of this living movement of faith in community. In this way, albeit at some remove, pneumatology bears on Yoder's bibliology, for the Holy Spirit's action establishes both the trustworthiness of the texts consulted for guidance and the possibility of success in coming to corporate agreement about what their guidance means for today. The Bible is one-half of the promise that fidelity to Jesus is possible: keep faith with these texts. The presence of the Spirit in the church

---

Rowan Williams, "Barth on the Triune God"; Rosato, *Spirit as Lord*; Rogers, *After the Spirit*, 19–23. Cf. Hunsinger, "Mediator of Communion."

127. See esp. 1 Cor 15:35–58 and 2 Cor 3:1–18.

128. See *For the Nations*, 187: "the Christian community is a decision-making body, a place where prophetic discernment is tested and confirmed, the organ for updating and applying the understanding of the revealed law of God, the context for the promised further guidance of the Spirit. . . . [T]he Christian community provides both a place from which to say to the world something critically new and a place to keep testing and exercising the understanding of that critical message."

is the other half: Jesus will enable faithfulness to himself through these texts by his own Spirit, who has brooded over them from their inception to the present. Together, the Bible in the church and in the Spirit makes possible the unity, obedience, and perseverance promised the church in the New Testament.

In sum, pneumatology's import for the doctrine of Scripture is indirect, via ecclesiology, as well as downstream from an account of Scripture's production. Yoder is explicit, as we have seen, in his rejection of thick accounts of the Spirit's authorship or inspiration of Scripture "at the source." Why? Because they over-promise and under-deliver; because they stake too much on an isolated verse or two; and because they dehistoricize, in an idealist and abstracting vein, the untidy particularities of the scriptural texts' actual generation and relation to one another. Yoder believes this untidiness is integral to the very character of Scripture— to its subject matter, how it is read, and the community that reads it. The move to reject here is not only negative, then; Yoder has a substitute for the old doctrines of inspiration.

That substitute is history, and it is the second subordinate element in Yoder's bibliology. The Bible is historical in a number of theologically resonant ways. The most significant in Yoder's thought is the way in which the Bible displays *divine vulnerability* in relation to history's messiness. God condescends to act through the insignificant people Israel, the disregarded figure of Jesus, and the outnumbered nobodies of the church; through texts and reports that invite disconfirmation or doubt; through witnesses whose credibility might be questioned or whose lives might be inadequate; through local communities across time that are free to discredit the message with which they have been entrusted, indeed, to fall so far from faithfulness that they repudiate the faith altogether. This picture encapsulates at once the timefulness of God's work in the world, the love God has for lost creatures in respecting their freedom and their fallibility, and the noncoercive character of God's power and his manner of exercising it in relation to human beings. Jesus embodies this nonviolent vulnerability that marks the ways and works of Israel's God more broadly: he lets himself be taken by the evildoer, abandoned by his followers, crucified outside the holy city, all out of a refusal to demean or violate the integrity of the beloved other, made in the image of God.[129]

---

129. There is a surprising degree of overlap here with the metaphysically rich work

This christological vulnerability, rooted in the essentially histori-cal character of God's chosen means of working in the world through God's people, is a property also of the Bible, and it is not accidental to it. The Bible shares this historicality with Jesus and the church, be-cause like them it is of a seamless whole with God's unfailing com-mitment to and action in the world. Its authors were fallible, fallen human beings like the rest of us, members and teachers of God's peo-ple, attesting God in their historical moment—each testimony but one contribution to the total deposit of faith that is the inheritance of the church in via. That they were enmeshed in their culture, time, and context is not a problem to be solved. That there is no huskless kernel, no timeless message separable from the medium of its delivery, is it-self a testament to the God of Israel, the Living One who raised up Je-sus from the grave and a band of slaves out of Egypt. Such constitutive historicality is therefore a *theological* feature of the Bible, Christianly understood. A theology of history is a necessary component of the theology of Scripture.

One upshot of this claim is hermeneutical. And here is where Yoder's protest of the tradition and his embrace of historical-critical methods are theologically relevant. Modes of ahistorical interpretation of the Bible are not just unfitting to the texts considered as historical docu-ments. They are unfitting as a Christian theological engagement with them. For part of their essential character *is* their historicality, and to ignore that is to ignore God's ordination of history to be the medium in which God works, acts, speaks, and reveals himself. Texts can be ignored, misread, abused: Scripture is thus of a piece with the "fool-ishness" of God's desire to work historically. Interpretation of Scripture informed by the methods and norms of historiography thus becomes not only a way of obeying and respecting God's inviolable decision to work in this way in and through history, but also a kind of exeget-ical mode of nonviolent hospitality to the neighbor. For it refuses, for example, to make St. Paul say what he did not and would never say, and seeks instead to understand what he in fact did and sought to say. Historical-critical exegesis enacts interpretive respect for the text and its human author as a mode of love for God and neighbor.[130] History,

---

of Rowan Williams, *Christ the Heart of Creation*. In a different vein, see Wiebe, "Frac-turing Evangelical Recognitions of Christ."

130. Cf. Vanhoozer, *Is There a Meaning in This Text?*

therefore, is a theological category for Yoder, and one crucial to an adequate bibliology.

Bookended, then, by christology and ecclesiology, basically lacking a doctrine of God or of revelation but informed indirectly by pneumatology and more strongly by a theology of history, Yoder's bibliology contains a final subordinate element: missiology. The church is a missionary people. It is constituted by its mission, such that its being is identical with its given task and its task just is, in part, itself. "Mission" names *this* people, on the move, scattered in exile among the nations, sent by God to proclaim and embody the good news of Jesus. But "mission" names also the sheer existence of this people, whose flourishing life of peace, joy, faith, hope, and love in the midst of pagans and polities ruled by power, violence, greed, and lust announces God's holy alternative, being itself the offer of this alternative. "Repent and believe the good news" and "Come and join the life of this community" are one and the same message; that is why baptism is simultaneously the washing away of sin and the rite of initiation into the church. To be joined to Christ is to be joined to his body.

No reader of Yoder's work could suppose that all that matters is the church's existence as a formal matter, absent the specification of the content of the church's life and message. The measure of that content is faithfulness: to the apostles, to the gospel they proclaimed, to Jesus the subject of the good news, to the God he called Father. How, though, is the church to be faithful to the apostles, faithful precisely in the mission they commenced, in the face of ever-changing contexts that present perennial challenges to the church's fidelity? Yoder answers:

> If the locus of our given unity is Jesus Christ, it would seem that the only feasible solution to the problem of authority would be to declare inadmissible the attribution of authoritative character to any particular historical development and to recognize as the only legitimate judge Christ himself *as he is made known through Scripture to the congregation of those who seek to know him and his will.* This would not necessarily mean that all evolution would ipso facto be condemned, nor would it commit us to an infantile literalism in the use of Scripture; but there would have to be the mutual abandon of any attempt to have recourse to any particular evolution as a canon of interpretation. [No contingent cultural or ecclesial time period or document or commitment] would

have the right to stand above, or beside, or even authoritatively under Christ and Scripture.[131]

Faithfulness to the successive mediating links that bind believers to God in Christ means faithfulness, finally, to the church's canon of Scripture. Furthermore, the way in which the canon functions as the church's sole authority is not merely in accurate reporting about Jesus or binding commands that follow for disciples, though each of these has its place. It is in modeling the missionary move *from* faith in Jesus *to* encounter with some concrete feature (person, value, claim) of the world of unbelief. Yoder describes the formal aspects of this move as maintaining fidelity to the gospel while articulating it in a new language. Commenting on examples from the New Testament (e.g., John 1:1–18; Phil 2:5–11; Col 1:15–20; Heb 1–2; Rev 4–5), Yoder extrapolates the exemplary model offered to the missional church:

> A handful of messianic Jews, moving beyond the defenses of their somewhat separate society to attack the intellectual bastions of majority culture, refused to contextualize their message by clothing it in the categories the world held ready. Instead, they seized the categories, hammered them into other shapes, and turned the cosmology on its head, with Jesus both at the bottom, crucified as a common criminal, and at the top, preexistent Son and creator, and the church his instrument in today's battle. It is not the world, culture, civilization, which is the definitional category, which the church comes along to join up with, approve, and embellish with some correctives and complements. The Rule of God is the basic category. The rebellious but already (in principle) defeated cosmos is being brought to its knees by the Lamb. The development of a high Christology is the natural cultural ricochet of a missionary ecclesiology when it collides as it must with whatever cosmology explains and governs the world it invades.[132]

The challenge for the church in mission today, then, is "not to translate [the apostles'] results but to emulate their exercise," that is, "to renew

---

131. *Royal Priesthood*, 225 (emphasis mine; emphasis removed from "Christ himself").

132. *Priestly Kingdom*, 54.

in the language of pluralism/relativism an analogue to what those first transcultural [read: *missionary*] reconceptualizers did."[133]

So the Bible, on this view, is at once (1) a missionary document, written in contexts of missionary encounter and the challenges that arose therein; (2) a missionary handbook, republished as a set of trustworthy models for processing new challenges the church will face in the future; and (3) a missionary touchstone, a shared origin and norm to which to return, in order to judge whether the proposed innovations of this or that community are consonant with and an organic outgrowth of the apostolic testimony to the story of Jesus. Here is where the double precedence of the Bible, aletheic and axiological, has its place: in the context of the church's mission, the questions that arise as a result of it, and the "first recourse" the church has to the Bible as "sole" authority.[134] Missionally contextualized, the Bible's truth for faith and morals assumes a different shape than in Protestant scholastic accounts, which in Yoder's view construe it in flat-footed ways as timeless, universal, and absolute, rather than historical, particular, and relative. To opt for the latter eliminates, for Yoder, many of the self-created problems endemic to "high" doctrines of Scripture that treat the Bible like a kind of divinely authored spiritual textbook, where errors, contradictions, and context-specific beliefs and injunctions—in other words, anything recognizably "human"—would have no place. But if the Bible is, in essence and in function, a book for the mission of God, then that purpose qualifies and reorients how to understand the "facts" and "values" of the texts. Further, it clarifies how such time-bound writings relate to their more primary normative character, that is, as exemplary models for how to undertake the mission in faithfulness to the gospel. Missiology, in this way, is one of the supporting elements of Yoder's bibliology. And it is no accident that, once again, a doctrinal locus that belongs properly to ecclesiology is brought to bear on how to understand and describe the Bible theologically.

This chapter brings Part II of this book to a close. Across three chapters we have engaged the simultaneously idiosyncratic and representative theologies of John Webster, Robert Jenson, and John Howard Yoder. We now move, in Part III, from individual exposition and critique to synthetic analysis and constructive proposals.

---

133. *Priestly Kingdom*, 56.

134. In Yoder's articulation, it is the church that has precedence (to the world). But as we see here, the material precedence redounds finally to the church's canon of authoritative scriptures.

Holy Scripture

The Church's Book in Mission,
Tradition, and Doctrine

CHAPTER 6

The Word of God

Theology of Scripture in Ecclesial Context

The apostolic community means concretely the community which hears the apostolic witness of the New Testament, which implies that of the Old, and recognizes and puts this witness into effect as the source and norm of its existence. The apostolic Church is the Church which accepts and reads the Scriptures in their specific character as the direct attestation of Jesus Christ alive yesterday and today, respecting them as the canon and following their direction.... The Church is apostolic and therefore catholic when it exists on the basis of Scripture and in conformity with it, i.e., in the orientation which it accepts when it looks only in the direction indicated by the witness which speaks to it in Scripture, with no glances aside in any other direction. The Bible itself cannot do this merely as a sacred but closed book.... What counts is that the Bible speaks and is heard.... [The Bible] is not a prescript either for doctrine or for life. It is a witness, and as such it demands attention, respect and obedience. What it wants from the Church, what it impels the Church towards—and it is the Holy Spirit moving in it who does this—is agreement with the direction in which it looks itself. And the direction in which it looks is to the living Jesus Christ. As Scripture stirs up and invites and summons and impels the Church to look in this same direction there takes place the work of the Spirit of Scripture who is the Holy Spirit. Scripture then works in the service of its Lord, and the Church becomes and is apostolic and therefore the true Church.

—Karl Barth[1]

1. Barth, *Church Dogmatics* IV/1, 722–23.

251

The previous parts of this book consist of relatively self-contained excavation, tracing a line from Barth to the present, then exegeting the texts and ideas of our three primary theologians. My aim, in Part II, was for each thinker to stand on his own, in the integrity of his unique voice, idiom, emphases, and arguments. Though I analyzed and criticized, I did not want outright comparison to intrude on understanding each project in its own right. This decision serves a number of ends. First, it shows the diverse trajectories in which theologies of Scripture can be taken, even theologies that share a common intellectual heritage and similar academic and cultural contexts. Second, it exhibits the distinctive ecclesiological logic (as well as other governing theological commitments) undergirding each bibliology, and therefore the way in which a certain ecclesiology funds every bibliology. Webster's church is not Jenson's is not Yoder's, either in theory or in practice. The ways in which these differences ground and animate differences regarding Scripture are significant, and are more easily seen within each figure's thought prior to comparison with other perspectives. Third, presenting the logical and theological interwovenness of each thinker's bibliology and ecclesiology is advantageous for recommending their material claims with the greatest force. Since one goal of this book is to mine these theologians for their insights regarding how best to understand and approach Scripture theologically, and further to synthesize those insights in a constructive proposal, I thought it important to lay out their respective visions separately, with maximum persuasive power.

Now, however, it is time to bring them together. First, though, I offer a brief retrospect on Barth's influence on these theologians, now that we have their positions before us. Second, I set those positions side by side for comparison. This section is not mere description; rather, I extend my critical evaluations in the previous chapters by suggesting ways in which each theologian's system supplements the shortcomings of the others. Third, I offer a sketch of further constructive work to be done on the basis of Webster, Jenson, and Yoder's proposals regarding Scripture. The next and final chapter takes up what I have called the dogmatic architecture of their work; it explores how the foregoing analysis of the relationship between the doctrinal loci of Scripture and church might shed some light on the field of theological interpretation today.

Barthian Retrospect

The three theologians on whom this book has focused are united by, among other things, their connection to Karl Barth. That all three were in one way or another taught by Barth and communicated aspects of his legacy to American theological audiences does not, however, specify the nature of his influence on their actual thought. Now more than half a century since Barth's passing, with the fields of biblical studies, biblical theology, systematic theology, and theological interpretation all, to varying degrees, bearing Barth's imprint—or actively refusing it—it is worth asking in what ways Webster, Jenson, and Yoder also show his influence. And not merely in general, but in the substance of their accounts of Scripture and church.

At the end of chapter 2, following my exposition of Barth's treatment of these matters, I set forth ten issues raised by his work. Beyond summarizing the main features of his theology of the church's book, the list aimed to lift up those aspects of his doctrine of Scripture that are specifically and starkly *Barthian*; emphases and arguments that then set the table for others after him. Whether a theologian ignores, assumes, contests, or repurposes them tells one a great deal about where, if at all, she stands in relation to Barth. The issues, by way of reminder, were (1) the centrality of Christ, (2) the priority of divine revelation, (3) "witness" as a governing category applied to the Bible, (4) the practice of theology beyond modernity's presuppositions, (5) exegesis as the method and purpose of dogmatics, (6) the church as hermeneutically definitive for the canon, (7) the restricted utility of historical criticism, (8) narrative as the overarching genre for Holy Scripture, (9) the importance of Israel and its sacred texts, and (10) the value of premodern theology and interpretation. We are now in a position to ask: On the other side of engaging our primary figures, do these topics play a prominent role in their work? How do their approaches to the loci of Scripture and church compare to Barth's?

After reviewing this list in light of the particular theological systems of Webster, Jenson, and Yoder, what is immediately striking is that Barth's influence is simultaneously everywhere and nowhere. That is to say, at the formal level, Barth really does set the table: the questions he asks, the categories in which he writes, the devices by which he frames the discussion, the encapsulating theses and programmatic propositions—

these are ubiquitous, even taken for granted, not just in the work of our theologians but in that of others as well.[2] Barth's importance *to the field of theology as it is practiced* cannot be overstated: "the most important Protestant theologian since Schleiermacher," his work's significance "in his chosen sphere is comparable to that of, say, Wittgenstein, Heidegger, Freud, Weber or Saussure in theirs, in that he decisively reorganized an entire discipline."[3] Compare theology today to a century ago, whether in German- or in English-speaking contexts, and the truth of the claim is borne out. We need not assign sole responsibility to Barth to recognize the central role he played.

So Barth's fingerprints are everywhere: in contemporary theology, in the areas of Scripture and church, and in the work of our theologians. All the more noteworthy, then, is the absence of Barth's direct *material* influence on their thought, at least with regard to bibliology and ecclesiology.[4] With the partial exception of Webster—whose earlier writings on Scripture expand and extend Barth's particular program but whose later writings look to other sources and approaches—none of their proposals on these loci could be described as "Barthian." Whatever they share with Barth they do so in a manner that does not rely on or appropriate his substantive claims (that is, in these loci). To root Scripture in the church, to find Christ at Scripture's center, to reject modern epistemic presuppositions, to relativize historical criticism, to retrieve premodern

2. For a small selection of diverse samples of Barth's imprint—leaving aside our primary figures and actual secondary literature on Barth—see Van Harvey, *Historian and the Believer*; Frei, *Eclipse of Biblical Narrative*; Lindbeck, *Nature of Doctrine*; Kelsey, *Proving Doctrine*; Watson, *Text, Church, and World*; Hector, *Theology without Metaphysics*; Christian Smith, *Bible Made Impossible*; Work, *Living and Active*; Hays, *Moral Vision of the New Testament*; Jeanrond, *Theological Hermeneutics*; Wolterstorff, *Divine Discourse*; Abraham, *Canon and Criterion*; Tanner, *Jesus, Humanity, and the Trinity*; Sonderegger, *Doctrine of God*; Rogers, *Sexuality and the Christian Body*. Perhaps the text that bears Barth's most lasting (if modest) influence is *Dei Verbum*, the Dogmatic Constitution on Divine Revelation promulgated in 1965 by Pope Paul VI during Vatican II. Cf. Gallagher, "Obedience of Faith."

3. Webster, *Barth*, 1. Cf. Jenson's comment, writing in the late 1960s: "the story of our theological situation is still very largely the story of Karl Barth and his reception, despite rumors of his antiquation recurring annually since 1923" (*God after God*, ix).

4. For example, more than once in Jenson's systematics (see, e.g., *Systematic Theology*, 2:73) he simply states Barth's position on a matter and registers his assent—though never regarding either of these two loci. Webster likewise continues to be influenced by Barth elsewhere in his thought, perhaps above all in his doctrine of revelation. I am less certain about Yoder.

figures, to read the canon as a narrative: none of these moves is unique to Barth, many of them predate Barth, and all of them can be undertaken in ways that Barth would have disapproved of or, in his lifetime, explicitly disclaimed.[5] What makes Barth such an epochal figure is the fact that he contained all these within himself, and more besides, and that he asserted them so tirelessly and with such concentration, prolixity, and courage, in a time when they were unfashionable in the extreme. In the doctrine of Scripture, at least for Yoder, Jenson, and the mature Webster, it must be said that Barth's actual theologoumena make little impression. But in wider scope, with only a touch of hyperbole, his theology of Scripture is the condition of the possibility for theirs.

Moreover, Barth was fully aware of the relationship between the dogmatic loci of Scripture and church, and that understanding informed both his methods and his views. Recall again the quote adduced more than once in earlier chapters: Barth writes that he is "conscious that," in offering a theological account of Scripture, "what we pursue is Evangelical and Reformation exegesis of the reality of the Church."[6] In compressed form, Barth's insight is an axiom of this book: *bibliology just is ecclesiology in the outworking of its implications for Scripture.*[7] That is, theological understanding of the church's source, being, and mission generates and is determinative of theological understanding of Scripture's nature, authority, and end. A church defined by reformed understanding of the Pauline *evangel* will necessarily have a different account of the Bible—we might say a different Bible altogether—than a church defined otherwise.[8]

---

5. For all his polemics against both Protestant liberalism and historical criticism, for example, Barth nonetheless remained indebted and even in a certain way devoted to them across his career. Put differently, many of Barth's ostensible heirs today would have no business with a Schleiermacher or a Harnack, but Barth took for granted that they were crucial interlocutors for serious Christian dogmatics (and not just because of their renown). If Barth was a prophet to modernity, that is because he was himself a child of modernity, and he did not finally achieve, or desire, emancipation. Whereas many today abjure the modern, through either renewal of the premodern or pursuit of the postmodern.

6. Barth, *Church Dogmatics* I/1, 100.

7. Recall the quotation from William Cavanaugh in the previous chapter: "If the church is the body of Christ, then all ecclesiology must be Christology" (*Migrations of the Holy*, 154). It is true for Barth, Webster, Jenson, and Yoder alike that their ecclesiology follows from their christology, and their bibliology from their ecclesiology. Whether christology is the source of the doctrine of the Trinity, or vice versa, is where they part ways.

8. This is true at the conceptual level, regarding how the Bible functions and is

Barth is by no means the first to recognize this truth. But the clarity of his approach together with his influence on the discipline is a spur to renewing this insight and making it operative in our own understanding of and arguments over Holy Scripture.

There is far more to Barth's thought than volume I of the *Church Dogmatics*; far more to his legacy than our three theologians. But it is helpful to see that Daniel Treier was precise in his observation that "advocacy for theological interpretation involves a series of loosely 'postmodern' riffs on Barth-inspired themes."[9] What Barth provides for theological interpretation and, more broadly, theology of Scripture today is *thematic*. His example is a goad to similarly fearless and unapologetic dogmatic labor. His proposals are not prefabricated answers to recite, regurgitate, or even revise so much as a template for the theological task, a set of perennial questions for contemplation and disputation. Perhaps in this respect Barth is less an Origen or St. Thomas than a St. Irenaeus or St. John Damascene: a genius and a doctor of the church, to be sure, but not the founder of a school. Centuries hence, will there be Barthians? Whatever the answer, that is not the measure of a theologian's contribution. Sometimes, instead, a theologian is called to put an end to so much nonsense in the church, to recapitulate the faith in intelligible and compelling positive form, and to hand on the restored but unfinished task to the next generation. If that is Barth's legacy, it is quite a legacy indeed.[10]

Theologians in Conversation

The decision to focus on these particular figures and not others assumes not only that they are relevant in a historical trajectory or illustrative of

---

interpreted, but it is also true in the most literal sense: there is a different Bible in reformed pews compared to catholic pews. "The word of the Lord from the Wisdom of Solomon" is not a phrase one is likely to hear in Protestant liturgy.

9. Treier, "What Is Theological Interpretation?," 152.

10. T. F. Torrance wrote on the centenary of Barth's birth "that the far-reaching significance of Karl Barth for the universal Church in the twentieth century may best be indicated by relating it to that of St. Athanasius in the fourth century." Whether the bishop of Alexandria is more like Origen or more like the Damascene, in my proposed comparative scheme, I leave to others to decide. See Torrance, "Legacy of Karl Barth," 289. He goes on to call Barth "the most outstanding and consistently evangelical theologian that the world has seen in modern times" (308), so that "if anyone in our day is to be honored as *Doctor Ecclesiae Universalis*, it must surely be Karl Barth" (292).

dogmatic argumentation but also that they have something to offer in and of themselves, on their own terms. Set side by side, moreover, the virtues of one help to ameliorate the vices of another. We saw in the preceding chapters the many ways in which our theologians both succeed and fail in their theologies of Scripture. How might they relate to one another in a useful way?

Start with what they share, particularly as background commitments that ground and orient their respective approaches. For all of them, the Bible (1) is the proper primary source for Christian faith and knowledge; (2) is a legitimate object of theological reflection; (3) is the book of the gospel of Jesus Christ; (4) has its being in and for the church of Jesus Christ; (5) consists of a unity of Old and New Testament, each of which is canonical Scripture for the church; (6) is, as an authority, subject to and encompassed within the divine authority of the living Christ. As for hermeneutics: (7) the canon warrants historiographic inquiry into itself and its originating contexts; (8) such inquiry is not separate from but, like ethics, is an integral aspect of dogmatics; (9) exegesis, therefore, is the principal mode of theological inquiry; (10) in and through Scripture's reading, the risen Messiah speaks by his Spirit; (11) in and through its hearing, the saving good news of Jesus is communicated and received; (12) in and through its interpretation by the community, the will of God is discerned for life and action; (13) such interpretation (hearing, reading, exegesis) is not a matter of simple transparency, but requires at once the sophisticated rigors of hermeneutics and the daily spiritual disciplines of the baptized.

Webster, Jenson, and Yoder are at odds about a number of things, but about these thirteen commitments they are of one mind.

What divides them? The question concerns both actual disagreement and differences of emphasis. The latter, though, can amount to a disagreement if one figure takes something to be of central importance and another gives it only sparing attention. Moreover, our theologians disagree about many things beyond the purview of this study.[11] Two questions guide the discussion that follows, then. First, what do Webster, Jenson, and Yoder disagree about with respect to the doctrines of Scripture and church? Second, granted my earlier evaluation of their proposals, what are the ways in which the merits of one complement or correct the flaws of another? I will proceed with each theologian in turn, circling round by the end.

---

11. For example, both the normative status and the material content of the doctrine of the Trinity.

John Webster

Webster's account, as we saw, is marked by a thoroughly theo- and christocentric character, robustly dogmatic and unapologetically metaphysical, and quite in keeping with its scholastic and reformed influences. Scripture is neither identical to nor separated from the eternal divine Word, but serves faithfully in its ordained capacity as sanctified witness to the gospel of Christ and the whole economy of salvation. Though not *merely* an item in the social culture of the religious community of the church, Scripture is irreducibly ecclesial, as the means by which Christ, by the Spirit, rules his people, judging and forgiving their sins, putting them to death and making them alive again. In this role Scripture plays a fundamentally critical function, standing over against the community as a norm beyond, behind, or around which the church has neither the ability nor the authority to go.

We saw, however, what weaknesses attend this account as well. One relates to Webster's highly theoretical dogmatic mode, which tends toward abstraction from the texture and obtrusive details of the text (for example, leaving Israel out of condensed summaries of the biblical story, or describing the incarnate Son's work with little to no reference to the narrative density of the Gospels' depiction of Jesus in his earthly ministry). The other weaknesses concern ecclesiology, particularly the relation between divine and human action. Webster is so concerned to counterbalance recent decades' emphasis on the human aspect of Scripture and church that he consistently downplays creaturely action relative to God's, resulting in a picture that suggests the two are in competition (the more of one, the less of the other). This is most evident in his treatment of Scripture's canonization, the church's reading strategies, individual biblical interpretation, and the political nature of scriptural texts and their exegesis. Finally, though of less import for bibliology, Webster's missiology is lacking to the point of sheer absence, the implication being that the church is less sent than merely dispersed. This lacuna may go some ways to explain, or at least provide context for, his reticence regarding the church's action.

How do Jenson and Yoder help here? Perhaps surprisingly, they help in similar ways, though from different vantage points. First, Yoder's distaste for abstraction pushes against any approach to Scripture that does not dwell in the human and historical details; no account of salvation history, however succinct, is complete without reference to Sinai and Babylon,

Tabor and Gethsemane. Second, such abstraction is an ecclesiological problem, because it fails to understand the role of Israel's calling in the divine plan, apart from which one cannot grasp either the church's mission in the world or the work of Christ to unite Jew and gentile in his one body, which is nothing less than the mystery of the gospel (see Eph 1–2). Third, textual and historical abstraction and an attenuated theology of Israel and the church's mission enable, or are enabled by, a christology without ethics. That is, Webster's Jesus is apolitical—one lacks any sense, for example, that Jesus lived his life under imperial occupation or died a slave's death reserved for bandits, revolutionaries, and men condemned for sedition—and so his christology turns out to be amoral. Christ is *archēgos*, at most, as the firstborn of God's many sons and daughters, but not as archetype of a life lived in accordance with God's will, exemplifying the proper shape of faithful human life before God. In contrast, Yoder's counterproposal points, on the one hand, to the Jesus of the Gospels, whose life and ministry are politically and morally normative from the figural death of his baptism to the literal death of his crucifixion, and, on the other hand, to the witness of the New Testament as a whole, for which obedience to God consists in conformity to Christ: "For I have set you an example, that you also should do as I have done to you" (John 13:15).[12] Yoder rightly sees that a morally and politically normative Christ presupposes a preexistent, divine, sovereign Christ: moral christology presumes and supports high orthodox christology.[13] In this way Webster need not give up his christocentric commitments. On the contrary, Webster's proposals on this score affirm too little, not the wrong things. At the formal level, his proclivity for idealist abstraction from Scripture's concrete details calls for amendment. At the material level, he needs an account of Israel that makes its calling and history integral rather than

12. "Therefore be imitators of God, as beloved children. And walk in love, as Christ loved us and gave himself up for us, a fragrant offering and sacrifice to God" (Eph 5:1–2 RSV); "But if you endure when you do right and suffer for it, you have God's approval. For to this you have been called, because Christ also suffered for you, leaving you an example, so that you should follow in his steps" (1 Pet 2:20–21).

13. This is perhaps too strong as a strictly summary statement of Yoder's views. But he says something like it at times in his work and, in my judgment, the logic of his position requires it as a premise, even if he would phrase it less forcefully or in less dogmatic language. For some of his most metaphysically unguarded moments, see Yoder, *Priestly Kingdom*, 46–62; *For the Nations*, 199–218; *Royal Priesthood*, 127–40; *Original Revolution*, 52–84.

accidental to the economy of grace and salvation history. Thus we might think of Yoder's correctives as more supplemental than subtractive.

Jenson's counterproposals, by contrast, are more directly critical. Jenson concurs with Yoder regarding the irreducible particularity of Jew and gentile, Israel and church, and the crucial importance of getting those identities and their relationship right, with the Old Testament playing a prominent role in the process. Jenson even thinks of the Old Testament as primary in a certain sense over against the New Testament, a truly "scriptural" Scripture compared to an apostolic witness fixed in writing out of necessity, since the apostles' living voices are no longer with us. Beyond those specific details, the foundational insight is that the Bible is a differentiated unity consisting of two equally important parts, and that this fact ought to make itself felt in one's doctrine of Scripture. But where Jenson's bibliology really cuts against Webster's is in ecclesiology. And it mostly comes down to simple counter-assertions: No, churchly action does not deny or replace divine action. No, reflection on diverse hermeneutical strategies for scriptural interpretation is not a bypassing of God's active speech in and through Scripture. No, focus on the timeful habituation of practices of reading is not a presumptuous seizure of God's promise or presence. Finally, yes, it was indeed the people of God—in the persons of the prophets and apostles (as well as editors, redactors, tradents, and other anonymous souls)—who authored Scripture's texts and eventually—in the persons of the bishops—formalized it as a canon. Was Scripture's authorship and canonization ultimately a matter of the divine work and will? Without question. Does such an affirmation in any way attenuate or denude the previous affirmation regarding human agency in writing and canonizing? No. To be sure, it qualifies it in such a way that it requires redescription: the Spirit so working in the community across time as its members wrote, amended, kept, used, gathered, and finally definitively collected these and just these texts as the community's authoritative Scripture, and in such a way that those involved did so as the persons they were, freely and willingly, with their given capacities, talents, skills, and knowledge. Hence: though preeminently and preveniently divine, Scripture remains human and fully human nonetheless. And if so, then Jenson presses the issue to Webster further. If it was human beings—the church at certain times and places—that issued the final (human) decision regarding what constitutes the canon, and if Scripture, as the church's premier authority, does not itself supply an authoritative answer on the question (for its own status and constitution is what is at issue), then some measure of authority, even dogmatic authority, must be accorded the church, at least in this instance. But if in this instance, then why not in others? And to the charge that this invests the church with authority over against Scripture or, worse, over against God, Jenson replies that this authority is far from unlimited (and, in any case, that it is instituted by God).[14] Yet it remains necessary, since Scripture must be interpreted. Furthermore, the promise of the guiding presence of the Holy Spirit in the church is not only a promise of judgment but a promise to be led ever further into knowledge of the truth (cf. John 16:13). Put differently, the Spirit's presence does elicit judgment—on heresy—but just thereby it illuminates in a positive manner—via dogma.[15] Thus Jenson's correctives to Webster's problems are not merely supplemental, as with Yoder, but take issue with substantive features of Webster's ecclesiology, which bear directly, and problematically, on his bibliology.

Robert Jenson

But what of Jenson's own account? In chapter 4 we saw the many virtues of Jenson's theology of Scripture: its creative theological hermeneutics, centered on Christ's advent and framed by the one story of the triune God with God's people; its combination of dogmatic description of Scripture's being and ends with a settled ease regarding its muddled historical origins; its open-ended and practical approach to the formative power of Scripture on everyday Christians and the exercise of its authority over them; its insistence that at every step in the process of Scripture's formation, preservation, reception, and ongoing use it is the church that is the creaturely communal agent at work. For the church is the graced instrument of the divine Spirit who abides within the church and impels its

14. See, e.g., Jenson and Gritsch, *Lutheranism*, 2-7; Jenson, *Systematic Theology*, 1:23-41; 2:47-103; Jenson, *Canon and Creed*, 53-76.

15. As Stanley Hauerwas remarks, "we are never quite sure what we believe until someone gets it wrong. That is why those we call *heretics* are so blessed because without them we would not know what we believe" (see "Begotten, Not Made"). Cf. St. Newman, *Development of Christian Doctrine*, 151: "No doctrine is defined till it is violated." St. Augustine anticipates both comments: "The rejection of heretics brings into relief what your Church holds and what sound doctrine maintains. 'It was necessary for heresies to occur so that the approved may be made manifest' among the weak" (*Confessions* 7.19.25).

actions both upon and beneath Scripture. Just so, the church is Scripture's privileged interpreter inasmuch as it is its principal audience, to which Scripture is directed as the voice of the Word whose authority it bears.

What shortcomings attend this account? Primarily the oversanguine ecclesiology that underwrites it. Jenson has supreme confidence in the church's ability to read Scripture aright, rooted in a pneumatological conviction that the church's corporate spirit is God's own Spirit and, as the Lord's inspired prophet, the church as a matter of course knows what Scripture means. The church goes wrong, and often, but according to Jenson that is a kind of surd. The church's defection might even be described as an impossible possibility: lacking adequate explanation, we ought to rely instead on the promise of Christ that the gates of hell shall never defeat the church. But how, on this account, is Scripture a critical element in and over the church's life? How does it resist ideologization, that is, subsumption into the self-contained, impregnable culture of the church as but one more native item immanent to its life? In what manner and by what means can Scripture exercise *judgment* on the church, or better, be an instrument of *God's* acts of judgment and rule? By what criterion is the church to determine the abiding versus the passing force of moral directives in Scripture? Finally, are there viable alternatives to Jenson's hyper-Cyrillian ecclesiology that nonetheless retain the Spirit's presence in the church to empower its scriptural interpretation in the service of dogmatic confession?

To this last question, Yoder and Webster answer in the affirmative. Yes, the Spirit is promised to lead the church into knowledge of the truth, and Scripture is one of the means by which this is to happen. But that does not eliminate the power of Spirit or Scripture to judge, condemn, and convict of sin—first of all in the church. As Yoder affirms, Scripture's power for renewal is predicated upon its critical, not conservative, force; as the word of the Lord, it speaks ever anew the inaugural announcement of Jesus: "repent and believe..." (Mark 1:15 ESV). Both words are imperatives, each remains operative following baptism, and the second follows the first, even as the judgment of the first is incomplete without—because encompassed within—the grace of the second. Furthermore, Yoder is right to argue for Scripture's independence or externality. This claim entails neither denial of Scripture's human craftsmanship and ecclesial habitat (which Yoder acknowledges), nor reference to its antiquity and alien cultural origins (which Yoder does at times fall prey to), but rather recognition of its inassimilable character as other than and prior[16] to the church. It is therefore not a plastic cultural entity in the hands of a church at liberty to assume that whatever it does is the Spirit's own doing. Whether or not, in Lindbeck's words, the text absorbs the world,[17] the church must not absorb the text, however interwoven and deeply embedded the text may and ought to be in the church's devotional and liturgical life. The church, Yoder concurs with Jenson, may surely be bold and confident in its discernment of the Spirit's will through the apostolic testimony. But such confident boldness ought to be accompanied by correlative spiritual and interpretive virtues: humility, openness to correction, repentance of sin, recognition of fallibility, provisionality in proposals (where appropriate), and eagerness to spy the ever-adaptable mutations of self-deception.[18]

With these suggestions, Webster is in wholesale agreement. What more might he add? Most forcefully, he would maintain from a variety of angles a single crucial point, in the absence of which any doctrine of Scripture—indeed, any Christian doctrine at all—falls short: the perfection of the one God in sovereign beatitude *a se* and in absolute distinction from creation.[19] Such a claim spins out numberless implications for Christian theology. Christ is and remains Lord and head of his body, the church. Webster is therefore correct, when discussing Jenson's description of church reform as "the risen Christ's self-discipline in the Spirit,"[20] to declare it "an emergency measure," possible only in a theology in which "the attribute of perfection had ceased to bear any real weight."[21] The Spirit, further, though present in power to the church, is present in the power of sovereign divine *freedom*, and so is equally free to judge,

16. Primarily in the sense of *having* priority (i.e., authority, precedence), but also, in part, chronological priority. Israel and its Scriptures (i.e., the Old Testament) precede Pentecost absolutely, and the apostles and their writings (i.e., the New Testament) precede the rest of the church for the most part. But note that neither chronological priority nor cultural alienness is a necessary condition for true otherness or authority. The present pope is other than me, but contemporaneous and perhaps culturally familiar. Those latter two features do not ipso facto nullify his (potential and potentially infallible) authority over me.

17. See Lindbeck, *Nature of Doctrine*, 118.

18. A recommendation betrayed by Yoder's own life. For further reflection on the character of the Christian reader, see Sarisky, *Scriptural Interpretation*; Winner, *Dangers of Christian Practice*.

19. See, e.g., Webster, *God without Measure*, 1:13–28, 115–26.

20. Jenson, *Systematic Theology*, 2:213.

21. Webster, *God without Measure*, 1:186.

rebuke, and whip the moneychangers in God's house as he is to heal, inspire, and unite in peace. In both instances the union Jenson rightly depicts between God and church, filled and animated by Christ's Spirit, becomes a kind of divine self-limitation via self-attachment (Jenson does not rely conceptually on *kenosis*, though something like it is not far off). Christ is risen into the church with its sacraments, and so, in his very objectivity, he is at the church's whim; the Spirit—since he is the church's own spirit, filling as he must Christ's body—ensures that the church's whim will be in accord with the Father's. But what happens when Christ, handed over to the church on the altar, no longer remains a bloodless sacrifice, but becomes all too bloody, in acts of wickedness perpetrated by God's people in God's name? What happens when Scripture is brought in for justification?[22] Does the church—Christ's own body filled with his Spirit—know, with the confidence of a prophet, the meaning of Scripture? With what resources, theologically speaking, may the church be censured, called to repentance, set back on the path of righteousness? This is the point Webster wants to press most stringently against Jenson's ecclesio-bibliology. For, though not in his explicit proposals, Jenson functionally blurs the distinction between Creator and creature, Christ and church, Spirit and community. The consequence for bibliology is an overweening but under-theorized optimism in the church's interpretive capacity and a concomitantly impoverished account of Scripture's status as in some sense the church's *adversary*. Scripture speaks the good and loving saving address of God, and effects divine consolation for aggrieved and desperate sinners suffering in a world of evil. But at times it also speaks as its hearers' nemesis, indicting their sloth and rebellion, shining a light on their pettinesses and secret evils, reproving their self-satisfactions and apathy toward justice, convicting them of their sin before God and neighbor. Jenson's account makes space for this role in individual believers' lives, before and after conversion.[23] And though he would surely admit it in the church's communal life, too—Jenson being

22. See, e.g., the catalogue of crimes and errors—rarely far from the biblical text, its translation, reception, and application—analyzed and interpreted in Jennings, *Christian Imagination*. See further Smith, *Awaiting the King*, 165–208, for analysis of what Smith calls "the Godfather problem."

23. See, e.g., his remarks in Jenson, *Christian Dogmatics*, 2:367–89; *Large Catechism*, 37–46. See also his brief comments on the sacrament of penance in *Systematic Theology*, 2:262–64.

no stranger to the church's many failures over the centuries[24]—the actual substance of his account can make little sense of it, which is why he ultimately throws up his hands in response to the issue.[25]

John Howard Yoder

We turn at last to Yoder. In chapter 5 we explored the unique features of Yoder's bibliology, not least of which is that it is by intention a deflationary account. By removing the air from the most inflated metaphysical claims that Christians, and especially Protestant scholastics, have made about the Bible over the centuries, Yoder seeks not to naturalize but to de-controversialize the status and authority of the Bible in the church. That is, the Bible, whatever "more" it may be, is not *less* than a product of the community of faith, kept and repurposed and passed on for the well-being, good order, and faithful life of the community with and before God, wherever it may find itself. It is, as a book, as portable as the exilic-cum-missionary community whose book it is, for it was authored and collected with the exigencies of that mission in mind.

Multiple strengths mark Yoder's bibliology, each related to the earthbound character of this vision: the centrality of Jesus of Nazareth; the social and political contours of the canon, rooted in the message it mediates; and the historicality not only of the canon's many stories and characters but also of the canon as such. In this respect Yoder's proposal is an important pushback against the tendency, magnified of late, to sideline the role of historiography in the church's reading of Scripture—a tendency to which Jenson and Webster, and I myself, are not immune.[26]

---

24. Longtime readers of Jenson will recall his fondness for the term "disaster" as a sort of term of art for episodes in church history that he deems to be historical, moral, or doctrinal debacles of one kind or another.

25. See Jenson, *On the Inspiration of Scripture*, 43–47; *Triune Story*, 207–9.

26. For critique, see Davies, *Whose Bible Is It Anyway?*; Barton, *Biblical Criticism*, esp. 31–68; Watson, "Does Historical Criticism Exist?" For programmatic dispute, see Louth, *Discerning the Mystery*, esp. 73–131; Rae, *History and Hermeneutics*; Morrow, *Pretensions of Objectivity*; East, "Hermeneutics of Theological Interpretation," 30–52. For measured reflection on the boundaries and overlap of the disciplines, see Bockmuehl, *Seeing the Word*; Moberly, *Bible, Theology, and Faith*; Sarisky, *Reading the Bible Theologically*, esp. 151–87, 239–83; Schneiders, *Revelatory Text*, esp. 97–131.

Yoder's position is not without weaknesses for all that. The greatest and most encompassing of these is of a piece with its deflationary character, namely its anti-metaphysical bent. While some measure of deflation is understandable, given the outsize claims made on Scripture's behalf in the post-Reformation period, the scholastics and their heirs were right to take seriously the questions that arose in the wake of the break with Rome, questions that go to the heart of the matter: What is God's relationship to Scripture? In what way does it come from God? When and how is God involved with it, and is God's activity in relation to Scripture finished or ongoing? Yoder's rejection or avoidance of these questions—supported, he argues, by the Bible's purported lack of interest in them, as though that settled it—is bound up with other problems. For in deflating traditional bibliology Yoder also diminishes the strength of the reasons supporting a strong commitment to *sola scriptura*, which for the reformers requires a thick account of God and of his sovereign self-communicating and saving action in and through the media of the scriptural texts. In addition, Yoder comes close to rejecting the church's reading practices prior to the advent of modern historical-critical methods, beset as they supposedly are by anti-biblical exegetical strategies that systematically distort Scripture's meaning. In a parallel move, Yoder comes equally close to reducing theology to ethics through nearly exclusive emphasis on Scripture's practical import. Finally, although so dissimilar to Jenson regarding Scripture's essentially critical nature, Yoder is like Jenson in his over-confidence in the church's ability to live faithfully and therefore to read successfully.[27] He thus discounts the abiding effects of sin in Christian interpretation and therewith the propensity to abuse the power exercised over the community in the interpretive task. The Bible, however, is for sinners: they are its only audience, its sole readership. An adequate theology of Scripture is therefore incomplete without a hermeneutics of sin or (let us call it) hamartiology of exegesis. Like so many others, Yoder has little in the way of one.

27. At first glance this similarity is hard to square with my use of Yoder to critique Jenson, whose understanding of Scripture's function is what Yoder would pejoratively term conservative rather than critical. One way to make sense of the discrepancy is to distinguish between Yoder's understanding of Scripture's nature and purpose and his own interpretive confidence with respect to Scripture—confidence transferred, implicitly, to Mennonite communities and to the idealized church of his theological vision.

How might the proposals of Jenson and Webster respond to, and so correct for, these problems? They certainly make common cause against the anti-metaphysical and primitivist shape of Yoder's theology of Scripture and church. In particular, Jenson offers four correctives to Yoder. First, Jenson offers a non-declensionary ecclesiology, which is to say that he does not view the church and its history as living forever in the ruins of a single great fall (whether that be the last apostle's death, the conversion of Constantine, or the theology of Scotus) or in the ever-new wakes of perennial, smaller, but no less calamitous falls (being the inner logic of ever-multiplying and ever-dividing radical Protestant sects: there is always a pure origin spurned and reclaimed). Rather, in the words of William Cavanaugh, church history is penitential history, the unbroken but deeply wounded and all too visible story of a people being redeemed from their sins in real time. Such history should not be moralistic, judging or rejecting our forebears. Instead, it should be pedagogical, as we in our own time, as fellow imperfect sojourners, learn from their mistakes with charity and forgiveness conditioning our being instructed by them.[28] Second, such an ecclesiology is capacious enough to view the tradition with both the critical eye and the generosity that hindsight affords, discerning where the church—in this case, its reading of Scripture—went off track but also where it stayed the course or charted a new path. Perhaps the possibility may be admitted in principle that some whole epoch or generation of the church (in some local particular region?) erred, apostatized, and fell away.[29] Though doubtful—for example, Scotus and Ockham, whipping boys of contemporary theology, had Dante for a contemporary and Julian of Norwich for a successor—are we in a position to make such a judgment? Does it befit the sort of posture Christians ought to have to forerunners in the faith?[30] Jenson would answer no, and his own work on the tradition would bear it out. For just one example, as committed as he is to the authority of dogma and the truth of the councils, his long-held position is that, historically considered, Chalcedon was a disaster; its Definition required reinterpretation by later figures like St. Maximus

---

28. See Cavanaugh, *Field Hospital*, 157-74.

29. Even Calvin does not "deny . . . to the papists those vestiges of a church which the Lord has allowed to remain among them amid the dissipation." Indeed, "while we are unwilling simply to concede the name of church to the papists, we do not deny that there are churches among them." See Calvin, *Institutes*, 4.2.11-12.

30. As Barth says, our posture to previous generations in the faith, not least theologians, stands under the Fifth Commandment. See *Credo*, 179-83.

to keep it from doing lasting damage to the doctrine of Christ.[31] Such a view assumes and accepts the tradition as it was and is, yet not uncritically, and without rancor or presumption, but marked above all by a view to the Spirit's providential hand.

Third, the Spirit's work in the penitent church's one history is found, according to Jenson, in its teaching office. Which is not to deny that it is found also and even primarily elsewhere: in the lives of the poor and the saints; in liturgy and prayer; in acts and movements for justice and social welfare; in individuals' reflection and action across their daily lives, whether or not their thoughts and deeds are recorded for posterity. Nor need we specify, with Jenson, the precise nature of the teaching office as the magisterium of the Roman Catholic Church.[32] The point is simpler than that. Local congregations and the church as a whole, in order to lead lives of faith, hope, and love, do not require the expertise of the scholar, the innovations of the radical, or the genius of the virtuoso. In communion with the universal church not only across space but across time, reaching backward to those trusted teachers of the faith now handed on to them by teachers in the present, members of the local body have resources sufficient to endure, even to thrive. That goes for the reading of Scripture as much as anything else. To say this is not to say that "any reading goes." But a potentially infinite variety of readings *do*, and the way their proponents may know their creativity has not strayed from the truth is by recourse to the symbols of the faith: creed, dogma, worship, common prayer. The church as a teacher instructs its members what to believe and how to live, in modesty and humility. As regards Scripture, it sets loose bounds and only intervenes (or should intervene) when matters essential to the faith are in question. My parenthetical remark should make clear: this view does not presuppose flawless exercise of this office; it too is a part of the church's history, that is, of the ongoing public confession and forgiveness of the church's manifold sins.[33] It is rather a normative view of how the church ought to operate, buoyed by trust that the Spirit will not abandon the church in its times of need.[34] And it is a corrective to Yoder, because it presumes neither the occasionalism of the

---

31. See the discussion in Jenson, *Systematic Theology*, 1:125-45, esp. 127-38.

32. See now Cary, *Free Churches*. Cary writes out of the Stone-Campbellite tradition; with Jenson and Rowan Williams as interlocutors, he argues for the necessity of something like a formal teaching office of the church.

33. See here McBride, *Church for the World*.

34. Though see Radner, *End of the Church*, esp. 1-56, 335-54.

innovator nor the elitism of the expert, and instead locates the Spirit's ceaseless work in the muddle of the church's less than radiant tradition, in every time and place, however meek or mild.

Fourth and finally, Jenson affirms the value of non-literal or spiritual interpretation of Scripture. Yoder and, to some extent, Webster limit their exegesis to the so-called literal sense, meaning, at least for Yoder, what the text could or would have meant at the time of its writing or first (intended audience's) hearing. There are many reasons to be dissatisfied with this approach, some of which I have presented in previous chapters. The simplest reason is that the New Testament texts as well as all premodern Christian interpreters of the Bible engage in reading practices that do not conform to the standards of what counts as "good" reading in academic scholarship, especially scholarship normed by the methods of historical criticism. Unless we are willing to disregard and reject these many and varied reading practices of the apostles, fathers, medievals, and reformers,[35] then we will have to make space for interpretive strategies that do not enjoy cultural, intellectual, or hermeneutical prestige today. Jenson does this very thing, fashioning a "roomy" hermeneutic that welcomes premodern procedures alongside modern and postmodern approaches. In doing so he makes clear that this does not entail the refusal or dismissal of historiography, but rather its proper qualification relative to communities, practitioners, and their interpretive ends. The rediscovery and redeployment of ancient methods of spiritual interpretation in today's theology continues to be a lovely and emboldening sight, and Jenson's work has been in the vanguard.

Having begun this section with Webster, let me close with him now. What in particular from his bibliology works to supplement the shortcomings of Yoder's? Two features stand out. First, his richly drawn dogmatic description of Scripture is a model instance of *theological* reflection, that is, an account of its subject matter that relates it primarily and fundamentally to God. So that the doctrine of Scripture becomes, as Webster puts it, a function of the doctrine of the Holy Trinity, for no doctrinal locus has content independent of its source, namely theology

---

35. Attempting to split the difference, by allowing our benighted forebears their poor habits of reading while repudiating those habits for all Christian readers today, is not a viable option. Such habits are not limited to some cultural epoch other than our own: if they were, we would not feel compelled to repudiate them. Contra, e.g., Longenecker, *Biblical Exegesis*, xiii–xli, 185–98.

proper.[36] Scripture and the doctrine thereof are subordinate to, derivative of, and conditioned by the will and work of the eternal and living Holy One. Scripture has its source, being, and ends in this One and this One alone, whatever else may be said of it as a medium manufactured by and for rational creatures. On such grounds and within such an account Webster has much to say about the divine provenance and purposes of Scripture, about divine action in, on, and through Scripture, about the role of God in Scripture's reading and hearing. As I have argued, theology must talk about these matters, in service of the church's questions and beliefs regarding the Bible. Yoder is right to be worried about floating into the speculative ether. But Webster is equally right in his judgment that to let all the air out collapses a doctrine that needs to do some heavy lifting. Whatever the proper balance, Yoder's deflation goes too far.

Second, Webster comes the closest of any of our theologians to what I called above a hermeneutics of sin. Particularly in his earlier writings on Scripture, his relentlessly negative treatment, though problematic in one way (for Scripture is not *only* critical in its force), takes for granted that Scripture's audience consists of sinners prone to self-aggrandizement, self-justification, and abuse of others by whatever means at hand.[37] Now, because Scripture is the instrument of divine revelation, the sanctified witness to the living voice of God, which slays and makes alive, Webster draws a different lesson than others do. Far from diminishing Scripture's authority in response to the pervasive threat of sin, he heightens it. Our sin must be checked by Christ himself as he strikes us with the rod of Scripture. And our comportment toward Scripture ought therefore to be marked by docility, humility, and submission, rather than haughtiness, self-assurance, or self-satisfaction. Scripture is a means of our being judged, wounded at the hip, cut to the marrow; it is not an inert object at our disposal, to be used at our pleasure or to the detriment of others. Its holiness includes and demands its separateness from us—we who would be holy (and by its help) but persist in sin—and thus to presume against it, to set ourselves up over against it, to enter its presence clad with shoes and trembling not, is to incur on us the same judgment that

---

36. See Webster, *Holy Scripture*, 43; *God without Measure*, 1:159.

37. "If the canon is a function of God's communicative fellowship with an unruly church, if it is part of the history of judgment and mercy, then it cannot simply be a stabilizing factor, a legitimating authority. Rather, as the place where divine speech may be heard, it is—or ought to be—a knife at the church's heart" (Webster, *Word and Church*, 46).

smote Uzzah, Hophni and Phinehas, and any foolhardy trespasser in the holy of holies.[38]

Thus Webster on Scripture's relation to sinful readers. Does he go far enough? Probably not, though in fairness to him, he does not take up the question directly. The task remains for others.[39] The point here is that Yoder's account is not neutral or benignly silent, but actively obstructive in its positive features and thus in its implications for Christians' abuse of Scripture. Webster starts us on our way, even if he does not finish the journey.

Toward a Constructive Theology of Scripture

In this section I want to draw together the theological projects so far canvassed in service of a synthetic, constructive proposal. This proposal is meant as more than the mere sum of the component parts of Webster, Jenson, and Yoder. It should stand on its own two feet, as it were. It takes their achievements as a point of departure and their deficiencies as warnings to avoid, weaving and interleaving as best I can. What follows is meant as a down payment for further work elsewhere, and thus can only amount to a gesture. What it gestures at, though, is one possible productive path for Christian theology of Holy Scripture.[40]

Like all Christian doctrines, the doctrine of Scripture comprises a set of balancing acts. The major features that constitute a theological account of Scripture lie between poles, each of which exerts a great deal of pull (or pressure), tending in one way or another to upend or tip over the particular issue in question, thereby distorting the overall presentation. The dogmatic challenge, therefore, is more complicated than simply holding complex or seemingly contrary claims together, albeit in tension with each other; some poles are extreme, exuding a kind of irresistible magnetism, drawing all else to them or in their service. Theo-

---

38. See 2 Sam 6:1–8; 1 Sam 2:12–36; 4:1–22.

39. See, e.g., Radner, *Hope among the Fragments*. From a different angle, see Jacobs, *Theology of Reading*. See also Trible, *Texts of Terror*; Schüssler Fiorenza, *Bread Not Stone*; Smith, *I Found God in Me*.

40. I have pursued this at greater length in East, *Doctrine of Scripture*. As it happens, that book was drafted following this one, though it was published some months before this book's release. Each is best read in light of the other; they are companion volumes.

logians never quite manage to achieve perfect balance. For us, there is only the trying.

In what follows I proceed according to a schema that focuses on those areas in which Webster, Jenson, and Yoder are most useful to a constructive theology of Scripture. This schema consists of a set of five relationships: that between (1) divine and human action; (2) the theological and the historical; (3) the metaphysical and the moral; (4) scriptural and ecclesial authority; and (5) determinate and open-ended meaning. By way of advance summary: A systematic theology of Holy Scripture informed by the thought of our three theologians will affirm, on the one hand, the antecedent, preeminent, prevenient, and pervasive will and work of God in, on, and through the Bible, exercising the living divine authority through it and investing it with the trustworthiness necessary for the church to rely on it as the word of the Lord. It will equally and unreservedly affirm, on the other hand, the Bible's unqualified human character; the particular, contextual, and therefore limited nature of its authors and texts; the unavoidable necessity of definitive ecclesial judgments regarding Scripture's teaching; and maximal creative freedom permitted to believing exegesis. Such exegesis presupposes a multiplicity, indeed an infinite variety, of valid interpretive possibilities for the word of the Lord communicated in and through the canon without thereby negating Scripture's authority or making of it a wax nose in the arbitrary hands of its readers.

How to hold these claims together? How do our theologians help us do so? Let us see.

Divine and Human Action

In the past few centuries in the West there has been a general drift away from thick theological claims about Scripture and toward ever greater recognition of it as artifice, a product of human making. This has arisen both as a ricochet from an explosion of new knowledges and methods of inquiry into the Bible and as a reaction to high doctrines of Scripture. Such doctrines seemed to many to be either (1) detached from the text and its inarguably human character or (2) disproportionately weighed down by matters better distributed across the dogmatic spectrum; tasked with too much lifting, they seemed likely to collapse in the process. Emphasizing the human, the thinking went, was an attractive solution—one rooted in historical reason, founded on scholarly knowledge, and planted in the soil of the empirical—that could keep readers from drifting off into the clouds of speculation. For such speculation often generated interminable argument about fine scholastic details undecidable in principle by any recourse to acknowledged authority and known only to an elite few. The humanness of Scripture, by contrast, admits universal exposure and analysis, and so invites both greater agreement about the questions at hand and greater unity in answers offered to them.[41]

As productive as such a focus has proven to be, no such consensus or unanimity has been forthcoming. On the contrary, granting the many gains afforded by it, the field is more divided, fractured, and splintered than ever. Does that mean Scripture's human character should be relegated, put back in its place, in order to talk largely or exclusively about its divine character? By no means. What has been lacking, instead, and what would prove most useful in today's discussion, is a classical theological understanding of the relationship between divine and human action applied to bibliology. Among our theologians it is Webster who has most subtly and forcefully addressed this theme, arguing that divine and human action are not mutually exclusive (even if, as we saw, this emphasis led to an imbalance in his own work).[42] They do not compete with each other for space or actuality. One need not decrease for the other to increase; neither must make space for the other to be present or operative. A single event, individual action, or complex process may simultaneously and wholly be the product of God and of human beings. For God is not a creature. Unlike our fellow creatures, he does not act in a way that is commensurate with human action. An effect rightly assigned to my causal activity is not thereby excepted from God's: to attribute the effect to both of us, equally and fully though in the modes appropriate to our natures, is not only possible but necessary. Consider, as special examples that illuminate the general, the speech of the prophet, the apostle's miracle of healing, the consecration of the elements, or the

---

41. One can begin the story before or after Spinoza, but it is useful to mark the start of something remarkably new (barely a century after Calvin's death) with his *Theological-Political Treatise*; cf. Preus, *Spinoza*; Legaspi, *Death of Scripture*; Sheehan, *Enlightenment Bible*. For a substantive contemporary proposal, see Barton, *Biblical Criticism*. For critique of the methodological naturalism of both Spinoza and Barton, along with counterproposal, see Sarisky, *Reading the Bible Theologically*, esp. 346–65.

42. See, e.g., Webster, "Inspiration of Holy Scripture"; "Dignity of Creatures." See also, programmatically, Tanner, *God and Creation*.

entirety of the life of Jesus (whose every deed was at once creaturely and the Creator's).[43]

The same goes for Holy Scripture. It must be affirmed as completely (not to say exhaustively) and without diminishment the work of human hands—written, rewritten, edited, redacted, organized, collected, interpreted, canonized, and republished by particular men and women across many centuries, in a variety of places, cultures, and societies. At one and the same time, these very texts are the work of the triune God, who so inwardly moved the aforesaid men and women, and so conduced the vagaries of historical process in all its irreducible complexity, to produce the single collection of writings that the Christian church confesses to be Holy Scripture. Its readers and hearers are therefore right to acclaim it as the word of the Lord. These two truths are equiprimordial, coextensive, and coterminous with each other. Except in the ontological sense that divine action precedes and activates creaturely action, neither of these descriptions of Scripture's origins and formation is truer, or more real, than the other. Neither was added to the other after the fact. Both were true at all times and remain true at all times. The liturgical introduction "The word of the Lord from St. Paul's Epistle to the Romans" has it just right, alerting the gathering of believers that what they are about to hear is for them the living speech of God as written by the man Paul of Tarsus long ago to another community in another time and place. This is possible because God is capable of—indeed, delights in—using human persons as the instrument of God's work and word (whether they know it or not), and this, in turn, because it is the ordinary way of things. For God lives not in contrast to creatures, but as their very condition of existence at every moment and in every way, nearer and more inward to them than they are to themselves; yet not identified with them, but transcending them in absolute distinction and perfect plenitude of being.[44]

In sum, following Webster, while we should be mindful of the dangers of overemphasizing divine action to the detriment of the human, we may

43. For recent work in christology presupposing and extending this theological commitment, see Tanner, *Christ the Key*; White, *Incarnate Lord*; Williams, *Christ the Heart of Creation*; McFarland, *Word Made Flesh*.

44. See the classic statement in St. Augustine, *Confessions* 3.6.11: "you were more inward than my most inward part and higher than the highest element within me." For demurral, or at least complication, with respect to "divine authorship" and the doctrine of inspiration, see Rahner, *Inspiration in the Bible*, 10–39. See further Farkas-falvy, *Theology of the Christian Bible*, 29–62.

say that a healthy doctrine of Scripture calls for a metaphysically robust doctrine of God's agency as Creator, of human beings' agency as creatures, and of the relationship between the two.

The Theological and the Historical

The Bible is an artifact. It is a made thing, the result of an extended, complex historical process. Expanding on the description above, it follows that the discrete activities and events that constituted this process, the individuals and groups who participated in it, and the contexts of their involvement are all wholly human and creaturely—the kinds of things that happen in any and every human community and that human beings do as a matter of course. Therefore they warrant historiographic study. Christian theology of Scripture has nothing to lose and everything to gain from such study of the texts of Scripture, and for that reason it has no objection to it. That is why the centuries-long development of historical-critical methods is in large part a Christian story; and where it is not, the Christian and the non-Christian are interwoven to the point of inseparability. Whether one begins as early as Origen and St. Jerome or later with the Renaissance-inflected humanist work of Erasmus, Luther, and Calvin, the line from them through the rise, evolution, expansion, and settlement of modern historical criticism is populated by Christian scholars animated by a deep love for Scripture and a conviction that historiographic inquiry into the canon is both an expression of that love and a form of faith seeking understanding.[45] The line is not straight, nor its participants uniform: some Christians opposed this methodological shift, others saw it as the site of a battle over Christian truth. Not all of its methods and claims are cogent or compelling, and some of those who played crucial roles in its development would not describe themselves as believing, orthodox Christians. But the point remains: for Christian theology to affirm the use of historical reason in exegesis of the Bible is not to engage in revisionist history. This affirmation is consistent with

45. To be clear, I am not denying modernizing, secularizing, anti-doctrinal, and indeed anti-Christian figures and motivations in the development of historical-critical methods vis-à-vis the Bible. The point, rather, is that to make these the only—even the predominant—elements in the story is disingenuous and incomplete, not least because in many cases the forces and persons in question understood their task in explicitly Christian terms.

long-standing Christian claims about and approaches to the Bible, and is at the root of a good many developments in the practice itself.

Having said that, two problems present themselves. The first is that the study of history is not innocent. The second is the false opposition and hierarchy long presupposed between the historical and the theological considered as modes of knowledge. These problems are related. Where theology is understood to be sectarian and therefore private (assuming it is acknowledged as more than a kind of socially acceptable superstition on a par with alchemy), historical reason is put forth as neutral, universal, and therefore public.[46] Put differently, whereas the "public" of theology is the particularistic tradition of Christian faith and its accompanying idioms, habits, and beliefs, the "public" of historiography is unrestricted, unbound to any particular community, and thus not a function or item of an exclusive tradition. The binary here tracks liberal distinctions between fact and value, or between the hard sciences and the humanities. That helps to explain the perduring prestige of academic historiography and even of historical-critical biblical scholarship to this day.

As a good deal of scholarship, not all of it Christian or religious in nature, has shown in recent decades, this account is little more than a just-so story used to justify the hegemony of a certain style of historiographic study.[47] That style is the product of a particular history no less than Christian theology, and it belongs to a particular community defined by a particular set of commitments, presuppositions, and practices. The latter are neither neutral nor universal. Their supremacy over and repudiation of theological norms and ways of knowing are not the result of an irrefutable methodology, much less the conclusion of a rational demon-

---

46. At the outset of his Gifford lectures, for example, N. T. Wright explores and delineates multiple subtly distinct definitions of "history." By the end, however, "history" assumes a kind of cross-disciplinary magisterial status; what it is capable of delivering is simply extraordinary, and one is therefore either its opponent or its partisan. See Wright, *History and Eschatology*, 73-127, 155-214.

47. See, e.g., Adam, *New Testament Theology*; Moore and Sherwood, *Invention of the Biblical Scholar*. For a representative though far from comprehensive sample of historic views, see Adolf von Harnack, *What Is Christianity?*; Kähler, *So-Called Historical Jesus*; Troeltsch, *Absoluteness of Christianity*; Schweitzer, *Quest of the Historical Jesus*; Bultmann, *New Testament*; Morgan with Barton, *Biblical Interpretation*; Collins, *Encounters with Biblical Theology*; Morgan, "*Sachkritik* in Reception History"; Johnson, *Real Jesus*. See also the detailed discussion of, among others, de Wette, Strauss, Baur, Holtzmann, Wellhausen, Gunkel, Bousset, and Weiss in Reventlow, *History of Biblical Interpretation*, 4:231-377.

stration. They are merely the contingent and therefore contestable premises of one among many ways of studying history.[48] The upshot is twofold. First, Christian faith and theology need not kowtow to or be threatened by the historical-critical regime of the last two centuries. Second, to refuse these postures need not entail rejecting disciplined investigation into the originating conditions and historical character of the church and its sacred texts. It involves instead wise discernment, sifting the wheat from the chaff, as well as creative rethinking about what it means for Christians to undertake and learn from historiographic research that (1) does not bracket the truth of the gospel but (2) may raise questions about long-held beliefs *bound up with* the gospel.[49]

48. See, e.g., Capetz, "Historical-Critical Study." Here Capetz delineates with crystal clarity the view I am opposing here. As he writes in the conclusion,

By insisting upon the insights of historical study as constitutive of any normative interpretation of Christian faith today, I do not imply any disrespect for the classical tradition and its ways of reading the Bible, nor do I thereby disqualify premodern Christians from membership in the church. Nevertheless, I do not see how we can in good conscience rehabilitate premodern ways of reading the Bible after two centuries of historical-critical labor. In showing the Bible to be fully explicable as a human product of the history of religion, historical criticism has made it very difficult for post-Enlightenment persons to continue to regard the Bible as the repository or criterion of all religious and moral truth. Hermann Gunkel made the point well when articulating the basic premise of all historical-critical investigation: "the Bible is in the first instance a book produced by human means in human ways. . . . Research has brought it down from heaven and set it up in the midst of earth." On this view, claims for the Bible's divine character or authority are nothing short of idolatrous. (487)

Apart from sleights of hand like "post-Enlightenment persons" and "all religious and moral truth," this summary is a consistent application of Troeltschian historicism to Christian faith, theology, and biblical interpretation (see, e.g., Troeltsch, "Historical and Dogmatic Method"). What it reveals most poignantly is the unstated, unargued, and presumably often unwitting presumption of incompatibilism, that is to say, a doctrine of divine action necessarily contrasted with human action. Nothing could better illustrate the implicitly theological character of historical criticism.

49. For diverse reflections, see again the texts cited above by Rae, Harvey, Louth, Barton, Bockmuehl, Sarisky, Schneiders, Moberly, and Watson. See also Ebeling, *Problem of Historicity*; Clark, *History, Theory, Text*; Sommer, *Revelation and Authority*; Levenson, *Hebrew Bible*; Anderson, *Christian Doctrine*; Radner, *Time and the Word*; Collins, *Bible after Babel*; Moberly, *Bible in a Disenchanted Age*; Green, *Practicing Theological Interpretation*; Levering, *Participatory Biblical Exegesis*. For classic treatment, see Fischer, *Historians' Fallacies*.

Yoder and Jenson chart a useful path here, one I can only outline. Let me lift up five points. First, the historical and the theological are not in principle opposed. Though distinct and independent—for they are, and should be recognized as, different forms of reason and of knowing—they may be complementary to each other, mutually supportive and inform-ing.[50] Second, in certain respects historiography may indeed influence, and sometimes call for changes in, theological understanding. Think of philological analysis of *metanoia*, text-critical work on the dating of Isaiah 40–66, disputes over the Pastoral Epistles,[51] or questions regarding the historicity of the exodus from Egypt or conquest of Canaan.[52] Theology must not avoid the challenges posed by such work, and ideally it should emerge from the encounter strengthened in maturity and depth.

Nevertheless, theology should respect, but need not entrust itself to the judgments of, historical-critical scholarship. This is the third point, namely, that the theologian retains the prerogative to make judgments *about* the judgments the historian makes.[53] In real time, historiographic proposals ought to be treated as provisional at best; the stronger or more radical the claim, the warier and more suspicious theology ought to be. Moreover, fourth, the study of history is not merely a matter of under-determined judgments of varying probability. It is also a reliable vehicle of ideology and anti-theological malice.[54] The ostensible suspension of be-liefs about God or references to faith is not an impartial absence, a benign leveling of the methodological playing field. It is a positive disciplinary norm that shapes one's questions and judgments. Whether witting or un-witting, it is thus a normative conviction that informs the inquiry.[55] That is

50. Which is not to affirm that they are non-overlapping: contra Gould, *Rocks of Ages*. Cf. Harrison, *Rise of Natural Science*; Harrison, *Territories of Science and Religion*.

51. See the excellent treatment in Johnson, *Constructing Paul*, esp. 1–122.

52. For example, even stout defense of the historicity of the exodus takes for granted that what it is plausible to conclude as having happened is something far less than what the canonical text narrates; see now Friedman, *Exodus*.

53. In many ways *The Politics of Jesus* is Yoder's exercise in this theological liberty to sift, discriminate, and use the results of historiography in service of Christian moral-theological ends. See also the principled but ad hoc use of historical-critical biblical scholarship in Jenson, *Ezekiel*.

54. For further along this line, see East, "Hermeneutics of Theological Interpre-tation," esp. 45–52.

55. One such norming conviction is that Christian beliefs will corrupt the inter-pretive procedure. See, e.g., Barton, *Biblical Criticism*, esp. 69–116, 137–86. As Barton writes: "To try to discover what the biblical text *actually* means, rather than to *impose*

no denial that worthwhile historiographic work on the Bible can be done in the absence of Christian theological convictions.[56] What it means is that historians' and critics' *claims* about Scripture and its history are not eo ipso incontestable. Theology has other norms and sources of knowledge. Even if, by its own circumscribed criteria, historiography cautiously but justifiably issues a judgment about the Bible, theology is not limited to those criteria for its own judgments about the same matter.[57] That the typical historian may not recognize the rationality of theology, its sources and norms, or its character as knowledge makes no difference to the point.

Fifth and finally, there is a material priority between the two disciplines. The work of historians is an essentially ascetic task, restricted in its purview and limited in both the scope and the kinds of judgments it permits itself to make, according to standards of evidence and warrant that intentionally exclude a variety of forms of reasoning, arguing, and judging common to other intellectual practices. By contrast, as Webster so stubbornly reminds his readers at the outset of each essay, theology is comprehensive in scope.[58] Its subject matter is God and all things in God. Its principal source and standard is Holy Scripture, but by no means

---

on it our own theological categories, is to honor the text as part of the givenness of a world we did not make. . . . Biblical criticism is the necessary precondition of the Bible's coming alive in [a relevant] way. . . . Criticism is not the enemy of a contemporary religious appropriation of the biblical text but its necessary precondition" (182, 184, emphases mine).

56. Though it does mean that, even apart from the question of the truth of the canonical texts, what one takes them to mean in the first place will invariably be shaped by methodological presuppositions both about the nature of the text (is it, or is it not, a collection of signs commissioned by the risen Christ in order to facilitate communion with the Holy Trinity?) and about the relevant contexts within which the text should be read in order truly to understand it (its linguistic, authorial, communal, cultural, and/or political origins of production; the total witness of the divinely inspired canonical scriptures; the liturgical life of Christ's body; the sacred tradition of the catholic church).

57. The great hermeneutical virtue of the church, therefore, is patience. It is not lethargy or sloth that animates the church's lumbering and sometimes generationally delayed response to the intellectual *Zeitgeist*, certainly not in the realm of history and biblical exegesis. It is wisdom. It is a feature of the church's teaching office, not a bug.

58. "Theology is . . . at once a most particular and a most comprehensive science: intelligence devoted to the study of the one from whom all things derive and on whom all things depend" (*God without Measure*, 2:159). Cf. Jenson's comment: "theology, with whatever sophistication or lack thereof, claims to know the one God of all and so to know the one decisive fact about all things, so that theology must be either a universal and founding discipline or a delusion" (*Systematic Theology*, 2:20).

does that exhaust its sources, standards, means, or methods of knowing. Theology treats the study of history as one among many possible and possibly useful sources of knowledge and conversation partners in its rational contemplation of God and all else in God. In this case, when theology turns to the Bible, it considers it, in its manifold diversity and complexity, first of all relative to God, and then relative to certain other dogmatic topics: the missions of Son and Spirit, salvation history, the election of Israel, soteriology, ecclesiology, revelation, and more. Other non-theological disciplines inform this consideration, including but not limited to hermeneutics, philosophy, sociology, and cosmology. Historiography takes its place among these. Theologians and historians may therefore proceed on friendly terms. Their respective disciplines are by no means at loggerheads or mutually exclusive practices; they have integrity and independence as distinct intellectual disciplines. In the relationship between them, however, theology has priority, and is the more encompassing of the two. Much goes amiss, and has gone amiss, in ignoring or reversing this character of their relationship.

The Metaphysical and the Moral

Whether theology is a speculative or a practical science is a disputed question in the church's history. Though it does not line up neatly with the Catholic-Protestant divide—such a debate was already brewing among the Dominicans and Franciscans prior to the Reformation—the question is often correlated with it, not least by participants in the dispute. Among Protestants, Baptists, Pietists, and liberals have each rooted theology's character in their understanding of Scripture and the gospel as essentially practical. For them, theology's forays into speculation thus constituted a departure from Scripture's proper concern: namely, the conduct, virtue, and/or inward disposition of individual believers. Such an account dovetails nicely with a declension story of the church and the development (or degeneration) of doctrine, not to mention an understanding of postapostolic ideas as foreign contaminants that infect and corrupt the host body of the once pure gospel. In this story, the good news of Jesus for the ordinary believer in every facet of her life—social, moral, political—is slowly transformed under the aegis of a parasitic speculative system, turning its attention away from such mundane realities toward the unseen, the timeless, the infinite. Allegorical exegesis, so the argument goes, is but one manifestation of this larger disease.

Though incomplete, the allegation is not without merit. Consequently, any affirmation of the speculative—more specifically, approval of the possibility and positive good of knowledge of God in himself, of rational discourse progressing in it, of contemplation of the invisible and the eternal, of rapt adoration of the infinite holy and triune One—must neither imply nor involve demotion or repudiation of the practical.[59] For the two are intertwined and equally necessary in Christian faith and theology, and thus in a full treatment of Holy Scripture. Jenson and Webster both argue persuasively: The texts of Scripture, in the manner appropriate to their genres, make claims of considerable ontological and metaphysical force.[60] It took centuries to absorb the implications of that force for the church's articulation of its faith, a process that continues into the present.[61] Assertions to the contrary, that Scripture "lacks interest" in such matters, are both too bold (just how does one determine a text's lack of interest in something?) and too reticent (why would seeing the assumptions or implications of a claim be "outside" the proper scope of the text's true focus?). Consider simple examples from the canon. That God is one; that God rules as sovereign over the nations; that God raised Jesus from the dead; that God calls into being things that are not; that God is the Father of Jesus; that Jesus and the Father are one; that God is Spirit and the Spirit Lord; that at the coming of Christ God will be all in all—such claims are reality-defining, and if true they both exclude a number of alternative reality claims and engender further hermeneutical activity that seeks to make explicit what is implicit in them.[62]

Such "theoretical" inquiry is not at odds with a practical focus, nor does it bear negatively in any way on an engagement with Scripture that assumes its moral and sociopolitical normativity. Just as the Bible trades in declarations of what is the case—of, in one register, the indicative—so

---

59. See the laudable treatment of these themes in Duby, *God in Himself,* esp. 1-10, 293-95.

60. Consider just one: "[God] raised us up with [Christ] and seated us with him in the heavenly places in Christ Jesus" (Eph 2:6). What could it mean to bracket metaphysics in interpreting this verse?

61. See the classic study in Kelly, *Early Christian Doctrines,* as well as the five volumes of Pelikan, *Christian Tradition.*

62. See, e.g., the excellent discussion in Hector, *Theology without Metaphysics,* 103-47.

it also, *passim*, issues in exhortation of what ought to be the case—of, that is, the imperative. Nor is this limited to the grammatical, as if directly stated commands exhausted the moral force of Scripture. Exemplarity and imitation are at the heart of the scriptural witness. Depiction and understanding of the person and work of Jesus is illustrative here. So-called "high" versus "low" christology is a false dichotomy. Both the New Testament and subsequent dogmatic reflection are simultaneously "high" and "low," not only because they affirm the heavenly origin and divine identity of Jesus alongside his fully human and earthly existence, but also because the former conditions and enables the latter, just as the latter requires and confirms the former.[63] Moreover, creedal confession of the full divinity of the person of the Son entails the perfect and unrestricted union of the divine and the human in Jesus. This in turn functions as an affirmation and sanctification of concrete human life, and of Jesus's life in particular as exemplary in every respect. *Omnis Christi actio nostra est instructio*, as one notable speculative Dominican has it: All of Christ's action is our instruction.[64] Although deflationary at the doctrinal level, Yoder's christological exegesis is most incisive at this point: That Jesus was and is God incarnate and Lord of the cosmos and risen in glory is the reason *why* his life and teaching are normative for human life, morally and politically most of all. Here is what life looks like when lived by life's Author; here is the human creature as the Creator would have it; here is the shape of obedience to the divine rule as performed by the Ruler himself. As God has acted in Christ, summed up in his passion and death, so are Christ's followers to act in accord with his example. And this, because he is God from God, light from light, true God from true God, begotten not made, consubstantial with the Father—and not otherwise.

Christology, in short, illustrates in miniature the more general truth: Scripture, like theology, is at once practical and speculative, and the one because of, not in spite of, the other. A constructive theology of Scripture will therefore not pit the moral against the metaphysical, but affirm and hold together both, particularly through emphasis on Scripture's political authority (rooted in the career and crucifixion of Jesus) and on hermeneutical strategies that are spiritual in nature. Success depends on demonstrating the ability of the two to coexist in peace.[65]

63. See McFarland, *Word Made Flesh*, 71–155.
64. Aquinas, *Summa Theologica*, III, q. 40, a. 1 ad 3.
65. None of our theologians, in fact very few theologians at all, achieve clear suc-

Scriptural and Ecclesial Authority[66]

The church stands beneath the authority of Scripture. Yet Scripture must be interpreted in faithful and trustworthy ways. The church's members are not tasked with this job individually. The church has leaders, past and present, who are appointed to the service of sacred doctrine, that is, to the ministry of instruction through the exposition, explanation, and application of Holy Scripture. This is the church's teaching office, which may but need not refer to a specific institutional formalization thereof.[67] Such an office is necessary in some form, however. And as the time of the church increases, its teaching will expand accordingly. It follows that a body of teaching—teaching, let us not forget, regarding what *Scripture* teaches—will develop as the church makes its way in its mission to the nations, across time and space.[68] And so it has. Such teaching includes but is not limited to the church's liturgical and devotional practices; revered theologians and theological texts; local and celebrated confessions and creeds; ecumenical agreements; widely received and approved documents produced by consultations, synods, and councils; officially authoritative statements of faith; and finally promulgations of dogma. In every respect the teaching embodied, recommended, and received in these forms of church doctrine ought to be, or to seek to be, biblical exegesis of an edifying, clarifying, and/or necessary character.[69] What authority such church teaching bears is an extension and application of Scripture's own authority, and in that way it is the living exercise of that authority in and through the authority proper to the church that stands beneath it.

Two factors underwrite this account of the matter (beyond its circularity, from which there is no escape), an account that Webster and Yoder affirm in their own partial ways, but which draws principally on Jenson.

The first is the priority the church has vis-à-vis Scripture. The Protestant principle of *sola scriptura*, for example, is prone to mischaracterizing this priority, given the (rightful) primacy it accords Scripture via the (mislead-

---

cess at this task. But it remains a task, indeed a necessary and unavoidable one, if theology, ethics, and exegesis would perform their common labor faithfully. For an exception to the rule, see Williams, *Christ on Trial*.

66. I adapted portions of the following for a section of my article "What Are the Standards of Excellence."

67. See the discussion in Jenson, *Systematic Theology*, 1:3–41.

68. See St. Newman, *Development of Christian Doctrine*, esp. 207–445.

69. See Levering, *Participatory Biblical Exegesis*, esp. 107–40.

ing) solitariness or self-sufficiency it unavoidably implies.[70] For Scripture is a passing, not a lasting, reality. It is literally provisional, a provision to God's people for the time between the times. It is not permanent.[71] God's living and eternal Word is permanent, and Scripture serves and speaks the saving word of that Word in and to the faithful: hence its authority over against them. But it is a servant, not the Master; a means, not the End; an instrument, not the Person wielding it.[72] Whereas the church, as the people of God in via, *is* lasting. Not of its own power or virtue, but by God's grace, the church is destined for eternal glory: for participation in God, for life in a city not made by human hands, for resurrected life in the new creation under God's unending reign of peace, justice, joy, and love. The Father did not send the Son to sanctify a book for himself, but a people. The Son did not pour out the Spirit on a set of texts, but on all flesh. To be sure, Christ does set apart a book for his service, and the Spirit inspires that book for that purpose.[73] But these are proximate ends, and in truth means to greater ends, all with a view to the beloved community, Christ's own body and bride. Like Jesus's teaching about the Sabbath, Scripture is for the church, not the church for Scripture (cf. Mark 2:23-28). God's people, the Israel of gentile and Jew bound together in unity, is the object and aim of God's work in Christ and the Spirit. Scripture has a role to play in that work, but its existence and purpose are directed entirely to the *bene esse* of the church: its calling, upbuilding, sending, and consummation.[74] When the End comes, Scripture's own role will be complete, and the *signa* will fade before the *res*, the medium before the speaker, the herald before the king.[75]

---

70. For a defense of all the Protestant "*solas,*" see Vanhoozer, *Biblical Authority.* For a brief rejoinder, see Jenson, *Triune Story*, 183-86.

71. See Griffiths, *Practice of Catholic Theology*, 57: "Scripture is . . . not a necessary condition for the existence of either Christians or Jews. Both have existed without it, and will again: it is part of the grammar of Christian orthodoxy to say that scripture belongs to the devastation only; it had no place in paradise and will have none in heaven."

72. For a possible dissent from this account, see Radner, *Time and the Word*, esp. 83-110.

73. It is telling, though, that within the Bible itself, by far the greater emphasis is on the people of God and its (far clearer and more powerfully described) reception of the Holy Spirit than on Scripture's inspiration or holiness.

74. For judicious application of this distinction, between the being and upbuilding of the church, to baptist ecclesiology in conversation with Ratzinger and Zizioulas, see Volf, *After Our Likeness*, esp. 127-58.

75. Thus turning the cessationist reading of 1 Cor 13:8-13 on its head: far from

High doctrines of Scripture, funded by overweening emphasis on Scripture's authority, have a tendency to obscure this fact. Yoder is right to worry here: at times Scripture appears to assume attributes approximating God's, which are unlike creaturely attributes in that they are perfections. But Scripture is not perfect, and never will be. Whereas the church, by Christ's efficacious word (cf. Matt 5:48; 1 Pet 1:16), is both destined to become, and called to be, *teleios*. That is to say, while Scripture's holiness is temporary, the church's is proleptic: an indelible seal and deposit in the present, to be completed at the end of all things. However little the church now evidences its election to the holiness and perfection of God's own life, the reality and the promise should clarify, definitively, the relative priority between the church and Scripture. To recognize this is to confirm the church's necessary interpretive authority with respect to Scripture without for a moment weakening Scripture's ordained authority over the church.[76]

The second factor is related to the first, and here Jenson and Yoder are at one. The Bible is a missionary document, a book intended (by God) and collected (by the church) for a particular purpose: to assist the community of Christ as it fulfills Christ's commission to make disciples from all nations. In this respect the canon is fundamentally apostolic in character in at least four ways. First, Holy Scripture is a sent and sending collection of texts. Second, its principal segment—that is, the Old Testament—was taken for granted by the actual apostles, who were the original followers of Jesus and his appointed representatives

---

Scripture's completion as a canon being "the perfect" (RSV), it is in its essential nature *not* that which is "the perfect." Rather, it is precisely when the economy of salvation terminates in the epiphany of the Lord from heaven—when the end for which God created the world and elected the seed of Abraham is manifested for all to see—that the canon, that wonderful but provisional medium of the Lord's word to his people, passes away. "For now we see in a mirror, dimly, but then we will see face to face. Now I know in part; then I will know fully, even as I have been fully known" (v. 12).

76. Perhaps the task here is to show that the church can indeed interpret, authoritatively, the indictment of Scripture against the church itself. If, following Jenson, the church's members are alike "prophets" filled with the Spirit, then surely this can be the case, both because some of the church's members can remind others of their sin or ignorance and because there are members who will not flinch from reading against themselves, and so in turn against the whole community. It is a pressing challenge to develop and inculcate the kinds of reading practices that foster this contra-church interpretation as well as institutional avenues for its public vocalization and reception. See, briefly, Levering, *Participatory Biblical Exegesis*, 214n64.

and first teachers of the church. What they taught was the gospel; what they taught out of was Israel's scriptures. Third, the canon comes appended with texts bearing the apostles' names and authority, whose teaching is here preserved as a permanently binding and trustworthy source, both for Christian faith and for the church's reading of the Law, the Prophets, and the Psalms. And fourth, the New Testament contains model exercises in missional discernment, lived and inscribed examples in real time of the kinds of judgments—moral, pastoral, exegetical, theological—necessary for the church to make on the mission field, at the congregational and the wider (catholic) level.[77] This fourth sense is most pertinent to our purposes, namely the question of the church's authority in relation to Scripture's authority. The apostles and their texts, exemplified by St. Paul, are a microcosm and exemplification of the nature and manner of Scripture's authority for a people on the move. It is not merely that texts require interpretation, that their meaning or import is not self-evident without the labor of exegesis. It is also, and more significantly, that the missionary character of both the community and its texts means that they should not be read literalistically, that is, as if they were meant to elicit one-for-one correspondence between what they say and their enactment in the present. Faithful interpretation will be missional interpretation, and therefore interpretation marked by virtues and skills of improvisation.[78] The sequence begins with this or that apostle having said X in order to speak the gospel in his context; after him, the saints and trusted teachers of the church read him to mean Y, and in turn said Z in their own times and places.[79] The question for us, then, is: What shall we now say (or do) in order to speak (and live) the gospel? That is the specifically missionary authority of Scripture at work in the specifically missionary life of the church. And hence, per Jenson, the need for the church to have (which is to say, for theology to recognize that God has invested the church with) the authority to discern in the present—based on contemporary context, historic doctrine, and the Spirit's active guidance— the teaching and meaning of Scripture.

Which brings us to the final area of discussion.

---

77. See Yoder, *To Hear the Word*, esp. 77–119.

78. See Vanhoozer, *Drama of Doctrine*; Wells, *Improvisation*; Young, *Art of Performance*.

79. This second step is the one present in Jenson and mostly lacking in Yoder.

Determinate and Open-Ended Meaning

Does each biblical text contain many meanings or only one? For most of its history, the church has affirmed multiplicity within bounds: there are things the texts—in general and considered discretely—do *not* mean, and such meanings should be scrupulously identified and rejected; but within the (quite large) frame thus created, extraordinary freedom is permitted the sacred interpreter, not merely for a variety of readings but in principle for an infinite number of them.[80] The task of reading Scripture is therefore urgent, in the face of the community's business, and joyful, unburdened by the need to excavate "the" "right" meaning of the text and instead compelled in gladness and delight to descend ever deeper into the inexhaustible depths of God's word. Repurposing St. Augustine's remark about love, we might sum up the church's premodern hermeneutics as: Believe, and read as you please.[81]

But what about Scripture's doctrinal authority? What about its power to command assent, to clarify confusion, to teach with precision, to communicate truth? Must not there be *content*, of a fixed and determinate sort, for Scripture to function in this way? If there is a potentially infinite multiplicity of meanings, are we not relying on the subjective whims of merely human readers? And what of the original authors? Are they nothing but lifeless mannequins on whose face we twist the wax nose of their writings? And what of the liberal and humanistic arts? If Scripture means whatever we take it to mean, do these tools and skills of the critical mind simply go unused, being irrelevant to the exegetical task?

Such questions are not answerable in only a few paragraphs. The point I want to make here, however, following Jenson quite closely, is that Christian theology of Scripture ought to affirm and validate the concerns that animate these questions without withdrawing the claims of classical theological hermeneutics regarding Scripture's multiplicity of meanings. One way in which this has already been happening in recent scholarship is by closing the loop of premodern and postmodern hermeneutics, that is, showing that while the concerns typical of modernity for fixed mean-

80. See, e.g., St. Augustine's exegetical reflections in the closing portion of the *Confessions* (books 11–13).

81. The original remark is "Love, and do as you will" (*dilige et quod vis fac*), from his seventh homily on 1 John. The principle that underlies the command is: "let the root of love be within, of this root can nothing spring but what is good." See Augustine, *Homilies on the First Epistle of John* 7.8.

ing and historical accuracy are valid and worth retaining, they go astray when used to underwrite theories of texts and their interpretation that allow for but a single meaning to any one text, and the original meaning of the author's intention at that. Such theories are demonstrably false, unworkable in practice, and theologically ruinous for the needs and ends of scriptural interpretation.

Premodern and modern interpreters alike agree that Scripture teaches, that its teaching is substantive and legible, and that faith in the gospel is dependent on such teaching being accessible in principle and in actuality. What they disagree about are the implications for theological hermeneutics and whether the full range of the text's sense should be taken as determinate or open-ended. The principal thing we have learned from our theologians, broadly speaking, is that this question requires clarity regarding the ecclesiology grounding and informing one's bibliology (more on this in the next chapter). But at the more granular level, we have seen that, within a well-ordered account of the church's interpretive authority, maximal creative freedom with Scripture fits hand in glove. It is not that "anything goes." Rather, what goes is what accords with—or, even, does not oppose—evangelical faith and catholic truth. "Anything goes" that goes with *that*. Moreover, such a claim, far from obviating the aletheic significance of the text, supports and is supported by it. Scripture teaches clearly, plainly, and authoritatively that, for example, the one God of Israel created all that is not God, called and chose Israel to be God's people, delivered the Law and spoke through the prophets, sent and commissioned Jesus of Nazareth and raised him from the dead, poured out the Holy Spirit at Pentecost, desires Jew and gentile alike to be reconciled through Christ's cross in his one body, the church, and so on. That is at once the synthetic and the plain sense of Scripture as a whole and in all its parts. No reading "goes" that disagrees with such basic elements of Christian confession of the gospel. Which is not to say that unanimity in what constitutes the gospel is self-evident from Scripture. But as St. Thomas says, following St. Augustine, the spiritual sense is rooted in the literal sense—the figural is a function of the historical—and furthermore, the plain sense holds pride of place for sacred doctrine.[82]

82. See Aquinas, *Summa Theologica*, I, q. 1, a. 10 ad 1. This raises interesting questions for what one might call outlier dogma, such as Mary's bodily assumption, which is not an interpretation of a disputed Marian biblical text but an explicitly post-biblical item of church teaching meant to secure other Mariological teaching, which latter teaching *is* scriptural, or at least a consequence of scripturally informed christology.

288

The central point is clear enough: Premodern theological hermeneutics presupposes and upholds the positive identifiable content of Scripture, such that true and definite meaning must be possible to read therein, and trustworthily so, or Scripture and faith together fall to the ground. But the premodern will say further, along with the postmodern— in this case, our guide Jenson—that from that affirmation a commitment to a fixed original meaning does not follow.[83] Nor need this claim imply disrespect for the original human authors and editors, a negligence of modern critical methods, or a "making familiar" of what ought to be and to remain strange: God's word written and delivered through the embassy of his apostles and prophets. The human historicity of the texts remains unqualified. To list only a few examples: the history and environment of the ancient Near East is of crucial importance to making sense of the Old Testament; knowledge of the beliefs and practices of Jesus's opponents holds remarkable potential for understanding the Gospels;[84] study of Greco-Roman culture and politics is a gift of lasting value to exegesis of St. Paul. These and other benefits of contemporary scholarship are of enduring relevance to the church's interpretation of Scripture. The question is whether they settle, or have the power to settle, "the" meaning of any one text in the Bible. To which the answer is a simple but forceful *No*. Nor, certainly, do they disqualify the great and lovely polyphony of readings the church catholic has undertaken and continues to engage in today, however unscientific or anachronistic or eisegetical such readings may ostensibly be. Through them believers hear God's word and witness

---

See the discussion in Levering, *Mary's Bodily Assumption*, 83–129. The role of figural or typological reading in theological argument also calls for further exploration in light of the Augustinian-Thomistic rule regarding the spiritual sense, given the centrality of such reading in the formulation of christological and trinitarian doctrine. See further Young, *Biblical Exegesis*; Dawson, *Christian Figural Reading*; Ayres, *Nicaea and Its Legacy*; Anatolios, *Retrieving Nicaea*; Behr, *John the Theologian*.

83. For example, consider an analogy to infinite sets. The set of numbers between 2 and 3 is infinite, but there is also an infinite set of numbers *not* found between 2 and 3. An unfaithful reading of Scripture would be analogous to suggesting that 4 lies between 2 and 3. But faithful readings would include 2.1, 2.11, 2.111, and so on. The mistaken hermeneutical argument would be to claim that, because 2.1 is not identical to 2.11, it fails to discern the one true fixed meaning of the text. I owe this observation to Mitch East. For stimulating reflection on pure mathematics and theology, see Kilby, *Limits of Theology*, 139–154.

84. I almost said "can only illuminate the Gospels," but that is false, as any familiarity with historical Jesus scholarship will show.

its power: to convict, to convert, to send, to heal. Through them members of Christ's body have seen him where one might have supposed he was least likely to be found, both in the text and in the world. For the reading of Scripture is a spiritual act, and the Spirit blows where he wills. The Spirit's freedom is bound neither by past piety nor by present theory. The letter is at the service of the Spirit, not vice versa. And where the Spirit is found, there are sure to be signs and wonders.

CHAPTER 7

The People of God

Dogmatics, Divisions, and Hermeneutics

Where the Scriptures are read in the fellowship of faith, under the guidance of the living voice of the church, her creeds, and her sacraments, [their] *perspicuitas*, [their] transparency to Christ, is a work of the Holy Spirit through them.

—Christopher Bryan[1]

The Holy Scriptures . . . are essentially the church's book; they are recognizable as sacred only through her, they are given to her, only she can interpret them and thus bring their inner nature to actualization. The concrete, fully realized essence of the church includes the Scriptures; they are a constitutive element of her.

—Karl Rahner[2]

The Holy Spirit, who gives life to the church, enables us to interpret the Scriptures authoritatively. The Bible is the church's book, and its essential place in the church's life gives rise to its genuine interpretation. . . . The Bible was written by the people of God for the people of God, under the inspiration of the Holy Spirit. Only in this communion with the people of God can we truly enter as a "we" into the heart of the truth that God himself wishes to convey to us. . . . [T]he ecclesial dimension of biblical interpretation is not a requirement imposed from without: the

1. Bryan, *Listening to the Bible*, 128-29. For stylistic consistency, in this and the next two epigraphs I have rendered in lowercase multiple words that are capitalized in the original: *church, creeds, sacraments, book, catholic, people*, etc.
2. Rahner, *Inspiration in the Bible*, 50.

291

book is the very voice of the pilgrim people of God, and only within the faith of this people are we, so to speak, attuned to understand sacred Scripture. An authentic interpretation of the Bible must always be in harmony with the faith of the catholic church.

—Pope Benedict XVI[3]

The previous chapter focused on the material proposals of our primary theologians: their connection to Barth, their relation to one another, and the ways in which they might be synthesized for constructive theological reflection on Scripture today. This final chapter focuses less on the substance and more on the form of their proposals: not so much the *what* as the *how* and *why*. Throughout the book I have maintained a two-track system, as it were, engaging claims and arguments in the doctrine of Scripture while periodically stepping back to observe their location and rationale within the larger dogmatic whole. The result is not only an exposition and commendation of Webster, Jenson, and Yoder's ideas, but also an analysis of the role the doctrine of the church plays in the doctrine of Scripture, and the ways in which that relationship reflects the power of ecclesial tradition to inform and even determine how the Bible is understood. Seemingly inadjudicable arguments in theological hermeneutics are often rooted in disagreements in bibliology, which in turn have their source in divergent ecclesiologies. Recognition of this fact, wedded to awareness of the ecclesiological logics that underwrite particular approaches to Scripture, both in one's own work and in the work of others, offers a way forward for conversations that face an impasse. At the very least, one route is to recognize the issues *as* intractable, not because of an inability to agree on hermeneutics but because of opposed commitments regarding the nature and authority of the church. Intelligible disagreement is to be preferred by far to puzzled consternation.

In what follows I hope to mitigate such consternation. In the first section I review and extend my previous analysis of the dogmatic logics coordinating our theologians' respective doctrines of Scripture and church by setting them alongside one another and noting the discrepancies, above all in their methods and ecclesiological commitments. In the second section I offer a threefold typology of the church and its sacred book rooted

---

3. Benedict XVI, *Verbum Domini*, 1.29–30.

in the catholic, reformed, and baptist traditions represented by Jenson, Webster, and Yoder. The images and analogies deployed in this section are meant as a heuristic to sharpen what may still be a vague outline. As I noted in the last chapter, there is a real sense in which different accounts of the church produce not just a different idea of the Bible, but a different Bible altogether. Here I delineate how divided Christian traditions reflect not just different ways of being church, but different churches entirely. In the third section I note areas in contemporary discussion of Scripture and its interpretation that are tied closely to, or follow from, judgments in ecclesiology. I make suggestions for how to avoid overlooking these connections without simply annexing one doctrine to the other. I close with concrete examples of leading figures in the field whose contrasting positions both reveal the nature of the discursive gridlock in view and exemplify the deeper source of scriptural and hermeneutical convictions in the doctrine of the church.

Bibliology and Ecclesiology

The subject of this section is the doctrine of Scripture considered as a discourse in itself and in relation to ecclesiology. I chose the examples of Webster, Jenson, and Yoder for this book in part because they hold potential for substantive contributions *to* the field, but also because they model different ways of engaging in the practice *of* bibliology, and in particular of coordinating doctrinal loci in clear and methodologically explicit ways. I want now to summarize and expand on the results of my earlier analyses of the logical structure of their proposals. I will again explore the way in which each of them orders the relevant loci—not just the two major loci in view, but others involved in the doctrine of Scripture as well. In the process I will both review and compare the distinct strategies and paths that each thinker takes in theologizing the Bible.

We began with Webster because his account is the most formally clear as well as the most direct and classical in its approach to the doctrine. Whereas Jenson and Yoder are revisionist in certain ways, Webster is self-consciously scholastic, both in method and style and in actual appreciation for and engagement with scholastic theology of Scripture. Moreover, part of his critique of modern bibliology concerns its lack of a well-ordered and proportional dogmatic approach to the topic; not only is discussion dominated by sociology and hermeneutics, the subject matter is dogmatically misplaced. Instead of being located in the doctrine of revelation and, more broadly, in the doctrine of the Trinity, it is located instead in ecclesiology. Such a location inevitably distorts the matter, Webster argues, because Scripture, while essentially related to the church, is not a function or auxiliary of the church; so understood, it either becomes naturalized or is made merely one among many aspects of ecclesial tradition, thereby severing its transcendent origin, nature, and end. Relocated to its proper place in the dogmatic corpus, Scripture is rightly understood as a function of God's self-communicative presence, that is, of God's saving will and action to speak as the living One in our midst. Scripture is thus the servant of divine revelation. This formulation both elevates Scripture (the servant of *divine revelation*) and relativizes it (the *servant* of divine revelation). God remains sovereign, active, and all-encompassing, while Scripture assumes a role at once crucial and de-limited, commanding but diaconal.

But as we saw in our analysis, while this description works at one level—as a proposal for how a dogmatics of Scripture ought to function, both formally and materially—it fails, or at least is incomplete, when viewed from a different angle, as a description of Webster's own theo-logical argumentation. That is, the logic of Webster's argument consists of more than a simple one- or two-pronged movement, beginning with the doctrine of God and moving "through" revelation "to" Scripture, with the possible addition of a parallel movement "from" God "to" the church, which stands in relation to Scripture. For the real pressure on Webster's bibliology comes from his ecclesiology, compelling him to ask: *What must Scripture be, given what the church is?* This move, common to every doctrine of Scripture, is not a denial of the theocentric character of his account of Scripture, but rather its explanation and motive. For Webster, the reality of the church in light of the gospel—which proclaims the grace of God for undeserving sinners in and through Christ alone—illuminates and clarifies the reality of Scripture. And given Webster's reformed com-mitments, the church's reality is simultaneously glorious, consisting in spiritual fellowship with God in Christ, and qualified, being subordinate to the sovereign majesty of God, living and omnipotent. The church re-mains populated by depraved sinners awaiting the fulfillment of their election to glory. Ordered by divine law and set within definite bounds, the church ought therefore to avoid transgressing that line by one inch. To do so is to reenact Adam's overreach, an act not only of pride and disobe-dience, but one that seeks to blur the absolute distinction between Creator and creature. As in the Garden, so in the church (where Adam's fall is undone, for God became the new man that the old man might become God's adopted child through the obedience of the Son): the unrestricted prerogative, authority, power, and action of God must never be confused with that of the creature. Hence the conflict with Rome, which, so Calvin and his comrades argued, arrogated to itself what only God can do. God alone is God; Christ alone saves; salvation comes by grace alone; saving grace comes through faith alone; faith comes through the gospel alone. The community conjured by these affirmations is the reformed church. And here enters the sixth and final maxim: the gospel of saving grace through faith in Christ alone is found—truly, clearly, and efficaciously—in Scripture alone. Given what the church is, what the gospel is, and who God is, it follows that merely human thought about God or the gospel, merely human authority, is inadequate. Accordingly, Scripture's authority in and over the church must be supreme and exclusive. How else could the church and its God be what the gospel says they are—sinful, lowly creatures on the one hand, and the holy and almighty Creator on the other—while bound together in communicative, obedient fellowship?

In short, a theological description of the church is funded by a theological understanding of God and the gospel (the work of God in Christ and the Spirit, the nature of salvation, the kind of community it generates), and together these—the former directly, the latter indirectly—inform a theological account of Scripture. In particular, they entail that Scripture, in dogmatic depiction, must be uncoupled in certain ways *from* the church, lest it be one more item of merely human tradition, and in turn be connected *to* God in the tightest manner possible, strengthening its status as an object of the divine will and action. Now such a result might seem to undermine the argumentative pathway that led to it. But this formal structure is the ordinary pattern for all theological argument more complex than simple repetition of kerygmatic or creedal assertions. *What must Scripture be, given what the church is?* is formally identical to the question *What must Jesus be, given that he saves?* (answer: God) or *What must God be, given who Jesus is?* (answer: triune). The point here is the order of the argument and the pressure exerted by one locus on the other: it is not a theological account of Scripture that comes first, which then generates and fills out a theological account of the church; the order and movement come from the other direction. How, that is to say, can a church without magisterium or pope or trustworthy tradition—a church that cannot absolve sins or mediate the real presence of Christ—nonetheless rely on its faith in God? Answer: Through recourse to and dependence on Holy Scripture, and nothing else, as the site and source of the saving word of the saving grace of the only living Savior, who alone represents and communicates himself, the Lord.

Thus Webster, confirming Barth's axiom about Protestant bibliology being but an unfolding of Protestant ecclesiology. What of Jenson, our representative of the catholic tradition?

Unlike Webster, Jenson is not concerned to maintain the boundary line between Scripture and church as a kind of analogy to the distinction between Creator and creature, or the two natures of Christ. Indeed, Jenson pushes in the other direction: just as Christ is a single protagonist or character, as a union "out of" (ex) the two natures, and just as Christ and the church form the *totus Christus*, the one corporate person of Christ together with his body, so Scripture's divine and human qualities are blurred, neither easily distinguished nor disentangled. (An unremarked application of the Lutheran *communicatio idiomatum* to Scripture?)[4] For Scripture is at once the church's and the Spirit's book, the church's as its author and audience, the Spirit's through his inspiration and illumination of its production and reception in and by the people of God. Bibliology is therefore properly located in ecclesiology, according to Jenson, partly for the same reason as Webster: it is simply unavoidable, given the relationship between Scripture and church and the church's theological priority. But the more determinative reason, within Jenson's thought, is that ecclesiology is itself very nearly annexed to the doctrine of God, and thereby also nearly annexed to the doctrines of Trinity, Christ, and the Spirit (no dogmatic move could more fully realize Webster's worries about modern theology's elevation of the church to quasi-divine status!). *Though it is not so annexed*, these doctrines run the other way and directly inform the nature, identity, and authority of the church, and in that respect—funneled through ecclesiology—they indirectly inform the doctrine of Scripture.

The contrast with Webster is a clarifying one. The pressure and sequence of Webster's argumentation runs, as we saw, from the bedrock axioms of the magisterial reformation (God, Christ, salvation, faith, gospel) to ecclesiology and only thence to bibliology. But the result is that Webster's material theological proposals about Scripture render it *less*

---

4. See Jenson, *Systematic Theology*, 1:129-30, 144-45, 203-4; Jenson, "Christ in the Trinity"; Jenson and Gritsch, *Lutheranism*, 91-109. Cf. Holmes, "Radicalizing the *Communicatio*."

centered on and defined by the church and *more* governed by and ordered to God, revelation, and the gospel of grace. With Webster, in other words, one must look past the arguments' claims in order to see the logic of the arguments themselves. In doing so one can see how his proposals regarding the relationship between Scripture and church do not correspond *structurally* to the dogmatic warrants and patterns underlying them. At the formal level the priority, sequence, and relationship between the *doctrines* of Scripture and church may be—and, in this case, are—quite different. This observation is not an exposé, as if Webster did not know what he was doing, much less a critique that the difference between the two levels reveals an inconsistency or undermines the arguments. On the contrary, the warrants motivating the theological description of the church, which in turn motivates the theological description of Scripture, not only may be justified but may result in exactly the goals desired by Webster. These goals include diminishing the elevated role of the church vis-à-vis Scripture, defining Scripture principally by means of reference to God's will and action, and maintaining the crucial distinction between divine and human speech and authority. In short, Webster's *doctrine* of the church, informed by his *doctrine* of God, motivates a *doctrine* of Scripture that proposes, at the first-order level, a magnification of the role of the *actual* Bible in the *actual* church alongside a minimization of the church's agential role in producing the Bible. Priority at the second-order level does not map onto priority at the first-order level. The relationship between Bible and church does not correspond to the relationship between bibliology and ecclesiology. For just that reason, both relationships—that between the entities and that between the doctrines thereof—must be understood and related to each other *as* relationships even as they are kept distinct.

As for Jenson, there is less discrepancy between his proposals and the logic of his argumentation. That should not surprise us, since accounts like Jenson's—with both an expansive ecclesiology and a community-constituted Scripture—are the object of Webster's explicit critique and counterproposal. Thus, for Jenson, the relationship between Scripture and church, on the one hand, and the relationship between the *doctrines* of each, on the other, are quite similar. Whatever Scripture is, even and especially before God, it is so by the hand of the church. It is only consistent, then, for Jenson's dogmatic structure and argumentation to reflect this—and so it does. The doctrine of Scripture, as we saw, is located in the section of his systematics devoted to the church, paired in the same chapter with his treatment of icons.[5] Whereas Webster's argumentation moves from God through church to Scripture, resulting in a theological account of Scripture primarily determined by God apart from the church, Jenson's proposals mirror the movement of his argumentation quite closely. What makes his account of Scripture theological—that is, more than a hermeneutical or sociological treatment of an important text in the life of a community, defining it instead by reference to God—is the way in which the church is itself "already" theologically "charged." In other words, just in virtue of setting this particular book in the context of the church as a constituent part of its life, it receives secondary or indirect theological description as a matter of course. Tying the church so closely to the life of the triune God, Scripture receives theological description derivatively, by reference to what the church is in relation to the Spirit and Son of God.

Per Jenson, the church is the missionary people of God, sent by the risen Christ and empowered with his Spirit to speak the gospel to and among all nations until the End. The church, further, is Christ's body in the world, filled and animated by his Spirit, who acts in and through the church in history both to lead it ever further into the truth and to protect it from irreparable defection. The primary doctrines that inform his bibliology via ecclesiology are missiology and pneumatology, with christology contributing only at a distance, as it were, through them. Missiology clarifies what kind of book Scripture is (one assembled for a community on the move, across time as well as space), its purpose (fidelity in gospel speech, continuity with old Israel), its provisional status (existing in and for, and only in and for, the time between the times), and the priority of the Old Testament relative to the New (the latter being but an *aide-mémoire* for apostolic speech, in the contingent event of the apostles' deaths). Pneumatology does the heavy lifting, informing a depiction of the community as a Spirit-indwelled body whose mouth, individually and corporately, the Spirit opens for prophecy, that is, to speak the word of God. The prophets of Israel and the eventual literary executors of Israel's scriptures exercised this gift, filled and impelled by God's liveliness to communicate the Lord's word to their time and place and to put it down in writing for future generations of the Lord's people. Pentecost is the universalization within God's people of the gift of the Spirit's prophecy-generating presence. The church, therefore, as the body of the living Christ, is the one

---

5. See Jenson, "The Word and the Icons," in *Systematic Theology*, 2:270-88.

communal prophet of the Lord, speaking his word as it speaks the gospel. Having inspired the texts' production and transmission the Spirit continues, through the church's enduring pentecostal inspiration, to act in and on Scripture: to produce the apostolic writings, to collect and maintain them, to append them to Israel's scriptures, to canonize them dogmatically, and to interpret them authoritatively for the whole people of God in face of error, heresy, and apostasy. This last point is crucial, for it is the logical endpoint of Jenson's pneumato-bibliology. The Spirit's indwelling presence and work of inspiration and guidance never cease in the church's history; as the condition of its life and of its union with Christ as its head, they are permanent and abiding. Indeed, the promise of that abiding presence and work in the church is one and the same as the promise that the gates of hell shall not prevail against it.

In sum, the dogmatic substructure of Jenson's bibliology is a pneumatologically dense doctrine of the church as the missionary people of God and the body of Christ in the world. The source, nature, properties, purpose, and interpretation of Scripture are understood in light of the community convoked at Pentecost, forever animated and never abandoned by the abiding, guiding presence of the Holy Spirit. The lines of influence and pressure run, for Jenson, from ecclesiology, funded by pneumatology (along with missiology and christology), to bibliology. The result, at the level of normative recommendation for how Christians ought to understand Scripture, is a corresponding trajectory, emphasizing the centrality of the church for the location and determination of Scripture. In Jenson's system, all created reality is most truly itself in anticipation of the End, which is to say, baptized. Baptism is an action of the church that incorporates the baptizand into Christ's body and bestows on her the gift of the Spirit. Let our concluding image for Jenson's doctrine of Scripture be, therefore, that of the Bible sanctified by the church's sacramental action in the Spirit. Holy Scripture is the book of the baptized; the church's book alone is baptized by the Holy Spirit.

Turning to Yoder, perhaps the most interesting thing to note about his theology of Scripture and church is by way of comparison with Jenson. On the one hand, Yoder tracks with Jenson on a number of formal points: a lack of interest in high scholastic doctrines of Scripture; little investment in the notion of biblical inspiration (at least until Jenson's late tract on the topic); beginning with the incontestable givenness of Scripture always already within the church; working backward to Scripture's authority from the community's present rather than forward from infallibly inspired "original autographs"; situating, describing, and defining Scripture by reference to the living, missionary church of the apostles. On the other hand, Jenson views the church—conceived as the one people of God from Abraham to the Eschaton—as a medium of the Spirit's action. Which is to say, ecclesiology, as the larger locus of which bibliology is a part, is also the means by which pneumatological claims come to bear on theological description of Scripture. Further, Jenson then uses the temporal expansiveness of pneumatology and ecclesiology to offer a description of the canon's long history antecedent to canonization, and of the Spirit's work within it. In contrast to Jenson, Yoder's "low" bibliology is largely lacking in pneumatological description and receives content from the two other most important loci in his thought: christology and ecclesiology. So while christology does little work in Jenson's account of Scripture, it does a great deal in Yoder's. Moreover, the sort of work his ecclesiology does is different than its function in Jenson's perspective, with the exception that both of them understand Scripture as constitutively missionary in character, in accordance with the church's identity.

Yoder's bibliology is christocentric, but not because (with Webster) the Bible is the medium of Christ's self-communicative presence, or because (with Jenson) the Bible is the one word always spoken by the prophets, namely the incarnate Son. It is materially christocentric, to be sure, but not in the sense that the Old Testament authors, inspired or not, "wrote of his coming." Rather, christology's bearing on bibliology for Yoder has more to do with a reality claim about the identity of Christ and the impact of his work. Given that Jesus is who he is and did what he did, it follows that the Old Testament may, after the fact, be read as leading to him— because in fact it did lead to him. Jesus interprets Scripture in the same way that he interprets all of life, being the key to existence itself, the One in whom all things hold together. Moreover, the Bible's principal purpose is the witness it bears to Israel's Messiah, neither term of which is intelligible apart from the other: he himself is the *fulfillment* of Israel's calling and history, but the calling and history of which he is the fulfillment is *Israel's*. Finally, Jesus is alive and reigns over the cosmos, vindicating the church's confession that he embodies the form or inner logic of creaturely flourishing, knowledge of which and obedience to which are found in the testimony of the prophets and apostles. It is there (Luke 24:44–47) that he directs his people to look (John 5:39) as they seek his face (Ps 105:4), that is, his kingdom and his justice (Matt 6:33; Ps 89:14). In Scripture believers find Christ's will for their lives, read through the lens of his own life, which is itself a living exegesis of the Law, the Prophets, and the Psalms.

So christology partially determines bibliology for Yoder. Ecclesiology provides the rest—although contained within it, as we saw, are subordinate commitments that indirectly bear on his account of Scripture, such as pneumatology, missiology, and a theology of history. Leaving aside full rehearsal of these claims, Yoder's overall presentation goes something like this. The church is a fully human, fully historical community like any other, generated and maintained by founding events in accordance with which it seeks to continue to live in ever-changing contexts, as it pursues its mission to bear witness to Jesus among all nations. The character of this community matches the character of Jesus, who himself, as God incarnate, embodies and reveals the character of God by forbearing from coercion and submitting to the disarray and painful vulnerability of creaturely life in a fallen world. Just so, the character of Scripture corresponds to this consistent historical character. In itself Scripture reveals its own historicality, its unfinished and in-process nature, consisting in snapshots of different moments in the imperfect life of God's people. Of these, the apostolic snapshots are authoritative most of all, for they offer different models to the ongoing, time-bound church for negotiating the unforeseen challenges of new cultures and contexts. Scripture itself is therefore both historical and missional in its very being. Its authority consists in its context-specific missionary exemplarity for future generations; it unites, or ought to unite, the dispersed church by linkage to this historical moment in time, checking its past and present life by this singular point of common reference. History is change, mission requires change. Scripture is the means and criterion of faithful change for the community sent by Christ as much "into history" as into the gentile nations.

In this way Yoder is like Webster, for he begins with a thick theological understanding of the gospel—namely, the person and work of Jesus—and, combining it with an equally thick theological understanding of the church—namely, the community called and sent by Jesus—constructs a theological understanding of the Bible on these twin bases. Yet unlike Webster, for whom much more theological content is included in an account of the gospel (such as the doctrines of Trinity, salvation, grace, and faith), for Yoder the gospel is single-minded in its focus on Jesus, though not to say it is simple-minded as a result. For Webster, moreover, the movement of the argument results in an account of Scripture somewhat detached from the church, and thus bound more tightly (from inception to reception) to the will and action of God, whereas for Yoder the importance of ecclesiology in informing bibliology remains at the level of coordinating the two entities in reality. That is, there is no separation of Scripture from the church, no reconnection to a God who sovereignly authors or illuminates Scripture prior to and apart from the church. Instead, the fittingness of the double character of the church as historical and missionary corresponds exactly to the double character of Scripture, syncing them together in a way that fittingly bears witness to the nature and will of the God revealed in Jesus. It is notable, in this respect, that Webster's bibliology is thinnest on these points, lacking much of substance to say about the historical processes of Scripture's production, its character as historical, or almost anything at all about the church's mission or Scripture's role within it. If Jenson's temptation in his ecclesiology, and so to some extent in his bibliology, is to lean toward a hyper-Cyrillean emphasis on the divine—a sort of monophysitism of the church, or at least of its scriptural interpretation in the Spirit—Webster's temptation is to relegate the human entirely to the church and the divine entirely to Scripture.[6] In contrast, Yoder's response is the reverse, humanizing Scripture and divinizing the church—or, if not divinizing, then eschatologically idealizing it. In his own idiom, it is the church that is the new world on the way, the presence of the new age in the midst of the old, the sign of the kingdom athwart the defeated principalities and powers, the pulpit and paradigm of the new humanity made possible by the risen Lord. Scripture has its being in furthering *that*—in a word, the apocalypse of God's reign in and through Christ's cruciform body—and theological description of Scripture follows from the new reality the church is, a reality created, miraculously, by Christ. And recall that the good news, for Yoder, consists in telling of Christ and the life he makes possible *in and through the public life of the community that bears his name*. So a theology of the gospel really does bear crucially on Yoder's theology of Scripture. In that sense we might term it a genuinely evangelical bibliology.

Doubtless much more could be said about each of our theologians on these issues. By comparing and contrasting their positions with one another, my aim has been to show the architecture of their arguments and of the different logics embedded in each of them. The details matter, because in them consist the decisions and judgments that ripple outward

---

6. Indeed, Webster's move is so to divinize the canon and its ratification as Holy Scripture that God, as it were, takes the process out of the church's hands.

along the surface, manifesting in differences that can appear incommensurate, insuperable, irreconcilable. Similar procedures are necessary for analysis of any significant theological disagreement, not least with respect to the dogmatic topics in this book's purview.

True, these are only three individuals. In my reading of them, however, they speak not only for themselves but for their communities, which represent the three major traditions of global Christendom, divided as it is. In the next section I suggest ways in which we might extrapolate the inner rationales or theological logics on display in Jenson, Webster, and Yoder. Using focal images to organize each view, I propose a threefold typology for construing the nature of the church vis-à-vis the proper role that Scripture has to play therein.

Deputy, Beneficiary, Vanguard:
A Typology of the Church's Relationship to Scripture

This section is an exercise in redescription. Presupposing the divisions between catholic, reformed, and baptist traditions, I offer analogies for each tradition's peculiar way of understanding the identity and purpose of the Christian community and of the sacred scriptures at its heart. The result should be not only a measure of clarity but a sharpening of the boundaries between each tradition's type. The heuristic value of this typology lies in its power to elucidate the inner logic of the traditions' respective accounts—both lived and taught—of the relationship between Scripture and the church. One benefit of the images I propose is that they show that churchly division is not a function of whether one has a "high" view of Scripture, for they all do. Nor is the fundamental question whether or not the church's doctrinal tradition may play a role in Scripture's interpretation: it may and must. Nor still is the issue primarily a hermeneutical one, since one's exegetical procedures are always already constituted by ecclesiological commitments. Because the context of exegesis lies in *this* particular community of readers, its nature and ends invariably, if only partially, determine what counts as good reading. In other words, arguments about these and related matters turn on theological judgments about the church. In the absence of that recognition, such arguments will prove interminable, not to mention unintelligible.

In any case, the following typology is not meant as a set of global construals of the church as such (as in, e.g., Dulles's models of the church).[7] Rather, it concerns the church *as* the Bible-bearing, Bible-reading, Bible-obeying community. How does each theological tradition embody and transmit its unique approach to the nature of this relationship?

The Catholic Church as Deputy

The catholic logic of the church's relationship to Scripture is that of a deputy. Scripture is the directive or missive from a royal ruler sent with or to his official representative; this directive comprises instructions for the representative either to perform herself, or to relay to another in an official capacity, or to communicate to subordinates in her care or under her supervision. Such a representative is deputized by the ruler, that is, appointed to serve, act, and speak in the ruler's stead and invested with the authority to do so. The deputizer entrusts the status and purposes of his office to the deputized; what the deputized says and does, she does as an expression or extension of the deputizer. Her words are his words, because they "stand in" for them, and thus stand "for" them. The deputizer is responsible, accountable, for the words and deeds of the deputized. Her authority is not her own, but it is genuine authority nonetheless. Those who hear her are to treat her as if she were herself the one who deputized her; she is due respect and honor, if not quite matching that of the one she represents, then something approximating it. Most crucially for our purposes, she does not act without direction or by her own spontaneity. She is directed from without, with a commission either coextensive with her sending or subsequent thereto, received in the field. Such direction the deputy is then to implement as best she can; her will is to enact the will of the sovereign. And yet, she is deputized for the very reason that the task requires more than mere passivity: it calls for ingenuity, creativity, presence of mind, wisdom, insight, the capacity to interpret both the sovereign's communiqué and the context to which it comes, and thus to realize the directive's instructions in a manner fitting to the circumstances. For though she bears authority, that authority is not her own and she must proceed with care, balancing humility with confidence as the royal representative: not the king himself, but his vicar, on whose judgment both the king and the people rely.

7. See Dulles, *Models of the Church.*

The church, by catholic logic, is the deputy—the ambassador or representative—of God, the sovereign, and the Bible is the Lord's royal instructions for her specific commission. This picture elucidates a number of important features of the catholic construal of the church vis-à-vis Scripture. It captures the character of the church as at once an authoritative, a hermeneutical, and a subordinate community. The church has its source and being in God, who is its Creator, commissioner, and companion. No treatment of catholic ecclesiology succeeds that elides this point: God remains God, while the church, though endowed with any number of gifts and privileges, remains a servant and representative entity whose life lies beyond itself. At the same time, the servant is tasked with a great charge, invested with extraordinary authority ("If you forgive the sins of any, they are forgiven them; if you retain the sins of any, they are retained"; John 20:23), and though this authority is a gift, it is not merely potentially but actually received as such. The church's authority is deputized authority, that is, authority bestowed by the word of a superior for the execution of a purpose in the fulfillment of a mission, standing in the superior's stead. "Jesus said to them again, 'Peace be with you. As the Father has sent me, so I send you.' When he had said this, he breathed on them and said to them, 'Receive the Holy Spirit'" (20:21-22). The Holy Spirit is the invisible presence of the sovereign Lord, the sign and seal, the effective token of the church's deputized status, the One who enables and empowers the exercise of divine authority on the part of a creaturely community. Finally, this corporate deputy does not simply know as a matter of course what it should be or do; it must be told and directed by the Lord who sent and authorized it in his name. There falls to it, that is, the enduring hermeneutical task. Scripture constitutes the set of instructions the community must—with authority and submission in equal parts—interpret and never cease to interpret in its ongoing life. Scripture just is the will of the sovereign, in written form. But, though materially sufficient, it lacks formal sufficiency; it must be read, must be construed and made sense of and implemented in concrete situations. And so the church-as-deputy *receives* its directive as the authoritative word of its Lord, *reads* it with docility and reverence, and *decides* what its message entails for itself and for others. In this way the church acts in the capacity of the Levites when Ezra read the Law to the assembly of Israel: they "helped the people to understand the law, while the people remained in their places. So they read from the book, from the law of God, with interpretation. They gave the sense, so that the people understood the reading" (Neh 8:7–8). The church gives the sense, because the church's book must be interpreted.[8]

Those familiar with the argument of Nicholas Wolterstorff in his book *Divine Discourse* will have seen the similarity between my account and his. But the difference between them is important. Wolterstorff uses the concept of deputization in order to explain the notion that God speaks in and through human speech. He thus suggests that we ought to understand prophecy as deputized speech, and the Bible as a whole as such.[9] My claim here is that we should understand the catholic logic of construing the church's relationship to the Bible as itself one of a deputy receiving (and reading and implementing) a directive from the sending sovereign; that is, represented by its ordained leaders in apostolic succession, the living church is deputized by God, and not merely the original authors of the biblical texts. This serves to clarify what separates a catholic from a reformed account of the church. For while there are no more apostles, the apostolic *office* continues in the church, thereby extending the apostles' deputized status forward into the future. This extension invests the church in general and its teaching office in particular with an authority derived from the apostles themselves.[10]

8. "Now as God revealed his Word and spoke, or preached, by the mouth of the fathers and Prophets, and at last by his own Son, then by the Apostles and evangelists, whose tongues were but as the pens of scribes writing rapidly, God thus employing men to speak to men; so to propose, apply, and declare this his Word, he employs his visible spouse as his mouthpiece and the interpreter of his intentions. It is God then who rules over Christian belief, but with two instruments, in a double way: (1) by his Word as by a formal rule and (2) by his Church as by the hand of the measurer and rule-user. Let us put it thus: God is the painter, our faith the picture, the colors are the Word of God, the brush is the Church. Here then are two ordinary and infallible rules of our belief: the Word of God, which is the fundamental and formal rule; the Church of God, which is the rule of application and explanation." St. Francis de Sales, *Catholic Controversy*, part 2, introduction.

9. See Wolterstorff, *Divine Discourse*, esp. 37–129.

10. "In the office of the apostles there is one aspect that cannot be transmitted: to be the chosen witnesses of the Lord's Resurrection and so the foundation stones of the Church. But their office also has a permanent aspect," namely the divine mission of witness and teaching; their successors in leading the church in this task are the bishops. What is permanent, then, is "the office, which the apostles received, of shepherding the Church. . . . Hence the Church teaches that 'the bishops have by divine institution taken the place of the apostles as pastors of the Church'" (quoting *Lumen Gentium* 3.20). The college of bishops constitutes and transmits across time the teaching office of the church. "It is this Magisterium's task to preserve God's people

Moreover, there is an ambiguity in the tripartite image of the deputy, the sovereign, and the directive. Is the deputy already on the ground, distant from the sovereign, when she receives the directive? Or does she receive the directive in the presence of the sovereign, who gives it to her when he deputizes her—perhaps even fashioning it in her presence or with her collaboration? It seems to me that the ambiguity between these two possibilities is a fruitful one. It allows for the deputy both to have had a hand in the writing of the directive and to receive it from beyond herself, just as Scripture is simultaneously written by human beings (inspired or, in Wolterstorff's proposal, deputized by God) and received by them as the will and word of the Lord. It further captures the generational or temporal aspect of the church's authoritative hermeneutical task. The apostles (those originally deputized in the presence of the sovereign: i.e., in the upper room, on the mountain, and at Pentecost)[11] are indeed sent and commissioned by the Lord himself, and write part of the directive that the deputized community receives as being from the Lord. But as the community goes on, though it retains its status as deputy and the authority that follows therefrom, it no longer includes the directive's co-authors, and so receives its instructions as originating wholly externally to itself (as though, already in the field, the sovereign sent the missive afresh). The postapostolic church, in other words, no longer reads the Bible with the knowledge that comes from being its coauthor; its authority consists elsewhere, namely in the divine investiture produced by the presence of the Holy Spirit. What further "authoring" it has to do—committing its interpretations, the sense it finds in Scripture, to writing, so that each generation is able to rely on past teaching, rather than having to begin anew—it does so as a function of its hermeneutical charge. However authoritative, this charge is the exercise of its magisterial, priestly role (à la Ezra's Levites); it sanctions neither the writing of new scriptures nor the creation of an authority superior to that of the canon. What the catholic church teaches with authority, it does so on the basis of and as a logical extension of what Scripture's dispatch teaches. The authority with which it teaches what Scripture teaches is thus the authority of an ambassador,

---

from deviations and defections and to guarantee them the objective possibility of professing the true faith without error. . . . To fulfill this service, Christ endowed the Church's shepherds with the charism of infallibility in matters of faith and morals." See *Catechism of the Catholic Church*, 248, 249, 256 (860, 862, 890).

11. John 20:19–23; Matt 28:16–20; Acts 1:1–11; 2:1–4.

which is to say, an authority at once necessary, substantial, and derived from a superior.[12] And on the day of the royal visitation, the need for either representation or interpretation will fall away, as will the written instructions themselves. For the deputy will meet the sovereign face to face, and he will make his will known plainly.

The Reformed Church as Beneficiary

The reformed logic of the church's relationship to Scripture is that of a beneficiary. Scripture is the last will and testament of the divine testator, of whom the church is the legal heir. Its contents contain the entire will of the one who initiates, completes, and imparts it to his beneficiary upon his departure. It provides for the beneficiary's care. It communicates the testator's wishes for her life and imparts his life's blessings, both known and unknown, to this recipient, whose receipt of whatever gifts come her way is wholly a matter of the giver's generosity and based in no part on something she has done. The words of this testament are legally binding and efficacious—they do what they say, carrying the weight of law (a judge does not author but executes what it says). A will often surprises, showing partiality to the youngest and not to the eldest, say, or to one outside the bloodlines of the family, or to one unbeloved by the world, for reasons of status or appearance, but treasured by the testator, for reasons inscrutable. What the will enacts is definitive: there is no court of appeal, properly speaking, because it is a *final* will and testament; its author has spoken once for all and is no longer available for comment. The executor may get involved on matters of fine interpretation, but the substance of the will is clear enough, to others and to the beneficiary. All the beneficiary has to do is be present, listen, and receive with thanksgiving. It may be that on this day her whole life will change.

The church, by reformed logic, is the beneficiary—the legal heir and addressee—of God, the testator, and the Bible is the Lord's last will and testament left for the welfare of the elect upon his departure. What are the virtues of this picture for our understanding of the specifically reformed construal of the church vis-à-vis Scripture? To begin, it accurately captures

---

12. For an Eastern Orthodox articulation of the relationship between God, Scripture, tradition, and church, see *The Longer Catechism of St. Philaret of Moscow* in Schooping, *Holy Standards*, 107–297, esp. 114–27.

reformed theology's depiction of the relationship between God, text, and community. Here the church bears no authority, but is entirely passive and dependent on the person and will of the testator, God, embodied and communicated in the form of a last will and testament, Scripture. The distinguishing feature of a legal will is its *fixity*. It may not be amended. It is final, complete: *tetelestai*. There is no gainsaying this testament; it is what it is, and it unquestionably expresses the will of the one on whose behalf it speaks. The church may here be figured by Israel at Sinai: "Moses came and told the people all the words of the Lord and all the ordinances; and all the people answered with one voice, and said, 'All the words that the Lord has spoken we will do.' And Moses wrote down all the words of the Lord" (Exod 24:3-4). Then later, east of the Jordan: "When Moses had finished reciting all these words to all Israel, he said to them, 'Take to heart all the words that I am giving in witness against you today; give them as a command to your children, so that they may diligently observe all the words of this law. This is no trifling matter for you, but rather your very life; through it you may live long in the land that you are crossing over the Jordan to possess'" (Deut 32:45-47). The Law binds the people together in covenant; in fact, a covenant is a kind of will and testament. As Paul writes, "once a person's will [or covenant: *diathēkē*] has been ratified, no one adds to it or annuls it" (Gal 3:15). Indeed, following Hebrews, we might even use the image of Scripture as a testator's will in relation to Christ's death: "Where a *diathēkē* is involved, the death of the one who made it must be established. For a *diathēkē* takes effect only at death, since it is not in force as long as the one who made it is alive" (9:16-17). This relieves the picture of some of its inconsonance, for Scripture is the last wishes not of a dead person, but of the living God; yet, in a different and no less literal sense, it *is* the will of a dead person—the crucified Christ—whose death on Good Friday certifies and effects its contents. Raised by the Father, Christ deputes his Spirit to serve as his executor in the church, which in turn stands as the beneficiary of the kindness of his unbreakable will. Further still, through the Spirit the church stands with Christ as co-heir, adopted in him as child of the Father, and thereby gratuitously given the rights and privileges of sonship, including the fullness of the divine inheritance (cf. John 1:12-13; Rom 8:14-17; Gal 3:15-4:7). Scripture is the word of this binding decree, as merciful as it is unconditioned.[13]

---

13. For discussion, see Barclay, *Paul and the Gift*, esp. 66-78, 562-74. See also Barclay, *Paul and the Power of Grace*.

The church, then, is a beneficiary in several ways. It is, strictly speaking, the recipient of benefits: through the biblical announcement of the good news, depraved sinners without merit are given fellowship with God, adoption as children, the promise of eternal life. Word and sacrament distribute these divine benefits in the life of the church.

Second, the church is beneficiary in the sense explored above: by adoption through grace, a child and heir of God the Father, through the faithfulness of God's Son.

Third, the church is ontologically wholly recipient: it is not the author of its salvation, and only in the most attenuated manner of speaking is it the author of Scripture. For Scripture's author is the Spirit, who used the instrumentality of a few chosen human beings long ago to serve as amanuenses for the divine speech. The church, in relation to God and therefore in relation to Scripture, is nothing but its receiver, auditor, and addressee. What it has, it has been given by God, and thus excludes all pride and boasting. For "what do you have that you did not receive? And if you received it, why do you boast as if it were not a gift?" (1 Cor 4:7).

Fourth and finally, in its relationship to the Bible, the church's posture is marked by all the features of one summoned to the execution of a will (accomplished by the execution of the Messiah) and thence to its commencement (in the resurrection and ascension of Christ and the Spirit's outpouring and eventual closure of the canon). By reformed logic, the double departure of Christ—his ratifying crucifixion, his absconding ascension—combined with the Spirit's advent and subsequent confection of Scripture, entails relating to the canon as to a fixed, finalized, and future-altering document of abiding relevance. Christ rules in the heart by his Spirit and in the church by his word. Obedience to his will means nothing else than obedience to Scripture. Its interpretation is all-important, then, because everything hangs on understanding his wishes. But interpretation is equally called into question, for what a last will and testament requires—as the definitive, perspicuous, effective, and coherent statement of the testator's desires—is not parsing but realization, not disputation but implementation, not contestation but compliance. The problem, on this account, is presumption, not incomprehension. The challenge, appearances to the contrary, is not hermeneutical in nature. It is the obstinate will of the fallen heart, which bucks at the bridle of Scripture, the yoke of Jesus. The difficulty, in short, is not that of understanding Scripture but of obeying it:

receive with meekness the implanted word, which is able to save your souls. But be ye doers of the word, and not hearers only, deceiving yourselves. For if anyone is a hearer of the word and not a doer, he is like a man observing his natural face in a mirror; for he observes himself, goes away, and immediately forgets what kind of man he was. But he who looks into the perfect law of liberty and continues in it, and is not a forgetful hearer but a doer of the work, this one will be blessed in what he does. (Jas 1:21–25 NKJV)[14]

The reformed church is a dutiful child before the canon, seeking with undivided heart to hear and obey the will and word of her Father, astonished at the liberality afforded her in a wholly unforeseen manner, and resolved, in undying gratitude, to live in accordance with his wishes all the days of her life.

The Believers Church as Vanguard

The baptist logic of the church's relationship to Scripture is that of a vanguard. Scripture is the set of orders from the commander for those elite units tasked with leading the charge, spreading out, and infiltrating enemy territory. This imagery for the church militant is, paradoxically, the most martial for that tradition of Christendom most known for peaceableness. But it is apt, given the baptist tradition's self-understanding and particularly its relation to Scripture. A vanguard is the highly disciplined and well-trained forefront of an attack. It is marked by self-sufficiency, independence, and situational judgment. It is strenuous, rigorous, courageous, dangerous. Its risks are great, its odds of success low. Its existence by definition assumes a kind of self-chosen exile, surrounded by the enemy, immersed in hostile terrain. It cannot assume a warm welcome or friendly reception. Rather, it assumes enmity, rejection, violence, suffering, death. But it believes in the right of its cause and fights, despite the threats and the odds, in the bravery of belief and the bond of its band of brothers, however small. Its mission, on the one hand, is constituted by the orders with which it was initially deployed: these orders are its *raison d'être*; obedience to them is its only criterion of success. On the

---

14. I have reinserted "ye" to this translation, which the NKJV removed in its revision of the KJV.

other hand, the situation on the ground is fluid and unpredictable, and the company must make decisions about how best to follow orders in the face of unforeseen challenges. Moreover, the vanguard is small but distributed across a variety of settings; the lay of the land determines how to obey the same orders in one place versus another. Each subunit of the unitary vanguard must therefore come to its own judgments about the meaning and import of its orders based on evaluation of the situation. Orders are orders, though, and however much leeway lieutenants have to direct the company in this way or that, the orders remain the same; nor may one lieutenant overrule another, for each group is autonomous and self-directing, empowered by the commander to make decisions in the moment, rather than relying on new and different orders. If one group wants to follow the lead of another, it may do so by its own resolve, but not out of pressure or coercion. The unity of the whole depends not on the identical execution of common orders but on sharing one and the same commander and being directed to one and the same goal by one and the same set of orders. All else is adiaphora.

The church, by baptist logic, is the vanguard—the front line or beach-head—of God's kingdom in the world, and the Bible is the Lord's orders for the mission entrusted to it. How does this picture help us grasp the distinct aspects that constitute the baptist construal of the church vis-à-vis Scripture? I might have chosen others: colony, outpost, priest, herald, stage director, assistant.[15] None of these, however, quite achieves the right combination of elite discipline and democratization as that of a vanguard, nor the dynamism and activity of the non-metaphorical component of being sent on a mission. For the radical reformation elevates by leveling, that is, it sweeps away the hierarchies of centralization and just thereby flattens out the locus of authority while universalizing expectations for obedience. Consequently the priesthood of all believers means less that everyone is a priest and more that, because no one is a priest, everyone is a disciple.[16] The New Testament describes believers

---

15. See, e.g., Vanhoozer, *Drama of Doctrine*; Yoder, *Royal Priesthood*; Hauerwas and Willimon, *Resident Aliens*.

16. See McClendon, *Doctrine*, who writes that the absence in the New Testament of any clear priestly class in the church "speaks of deliverance from the world of sacral authorities into the world of the good news" (368). This involves not so much the abolition of priests as the abolition of laity (368-69). "Every member is called to discipleship; baptism . . . is commissioning for this ministry; thus it occupies the place ordination must in churches that celebrate a 'clergy'" (369). This helps to explain the

as soldiers for a reason—and notably it does not excuse anyone from the appellation (cf. Phlm 2; 2 Tim 2:3-4; Phil 2:25; Rev 14:1-5). The call of discipleship to Jesus is thus patterned, for the peace-loving but martial baptists, according to Jesus's namesake, the commander of Israel's army and the leader of the conquest.[17] Let Jesus's own words and the opening charge of Joshua mutually interpret each other; together, they form a representative battle cry for baptist Bible-reading militancy.

Jesus says, "Follow me, and I will make you fishers of men. . . . Go therefore and make disciples of all nations, baptizing them in the name of the Father and of the Son and of the Holy Spirit, and teaching them to obey everything that I have commanded you. And remember, I am with you always, to the end of the age. . . . As you go, proclaim the good news, 'The kingdom of heaven is at hand.' . . . See, I am sending you out like sheep into the midst of wolves; so be wise as serpents and innocent as doves" (Matt 4:19; 28:19-20; 10:7, 16).[18] Prefiguring and filling out this charge, the book of Joshua opens with the Lord's words to Moses's successor, here altered as if addressed by God to the baptist rank and file:

No one shall be able to stand against you all the days of your life. As I was with [Jesus], so I will be with you; I will not fail you or forsake you. . . . Only be strong and very courageous, being careful to act in accordance with all the [words] that [Scripture] command[s] you; do not turn from it to the right hand or to the left, so that you may be successful wherever you go. This book . . . shall not depart out of your mouth; you shall meditate on it day and night, so that you may be careful to act in accordance with all that is written in it. For then you shall make your way prosperous, and then you shall be successful. I hereby command you: Be strong and courageous; do not be frightened or dismayed, for the Lord your God is with you wherever you go. (Josh 1:5, 7-9)

The new and better Joshua—in truth the very same speaker as in the passage just quoted, Israel's Lord in the flesh—concludes his commissioning speech for his once and future disciples thus:

---

short shrift McClendon gives to priesthood and sacrifice in his narrative depiction of atonement vis-à-vis both Israel's past and the church's future (235).

17. Along these lines, see the creative revisionist history of the Mennonite scholar Lind, *Yahweh Is a Warrior*.

18. The first verse (4:19) is from the ESV; the rest is from the NRSV.

You will be hated by all because of my name. But the one who endures to the end will be saved. When they persecute you in one town, flee to the next; for truly I tell you, you will not have gone through all the towns of [the world] before the Son of Man comes. A disciple is not above the teacher, nor a slave above the master; it is enough for the disciple to be like the teacher, and the slave like the master. So have no fear of them. . . . Do not fear those who kill the body but cannot kill the soul; rather fear him who can destroy both soul and body in hell. Are not two sparrows sold for a penny? Yet not one of them will fall to the ground apart from your Father. And even the hairs of your head are all counted. So do not be afraid; you are of more value than many sparrows. Everyone therefore who acknowledges me before others, I also will acknowledge before my Father in heaven; but whoever denies me before others, I also will deny before my Father in heaven. Do not think that I have come to bring peace to the earth; I have not come to bring peace, but a sword. . . . Whoever loves father or mother more than me is not worthy of me; and whoever loves son or daughter more than me is not worthy of me; and whoever does not take up the cross and follow me is not worthy of me. Those who find their life will lose it, and those who lose their life for my sake will find it. (Matt 10:22–26, 28–34, 37–39)

Nothing could better encapsulate the vision and drive of the baptist church. Hence the fittingness of the image of a vanguard.

But how does it characterize the baptist church's relationship to Scripture? In the following five ways. First, Scripture is ordered to a particular end and has its power and authority in its capacity to direct to that end. That end is the prior and encompassing mission of God, begun in Israel and Jesus and taken to the ends of the earth by the Spirit through the trans-national church. Scripture, in other words, has its being in furthering, enabling, and completing this one all-important mission.

Second, Scripture's orders are issued by the divine commander, Christ Jesus. Like Israel with the Law after the death of Moses, Christians are to treasure the words of Scripture like precious stones; like a spring gushing up with life-giving water. Jesus addresses the church through Scripture like Moses before Israel, saying, "I call heaven and earth to witness against you . . . that I have set before you life and death, blessings and curses. Choose life so that you and your descendants may live, loving the Lord your God, obeying him, and holding fast to him; for that means life to you and length of days" (Deut 30:19–20). The baptist church responds, as much to Scripture as to Christ, as St. Peter did: "Lord, to whom can we go? You have the words of eternal life. We have come to believe and know that you are the Holy One of God" (John 6:68–69).

Third, however, there is ambiguity in the tradition on this point, for "baptist" encompasses many tribes and sects. Sometimes it doubles down on the high scholasticism of the reformed, as in American fundamentalism. But sometimes, perhaps often, it finds the schoolmen's formulations too clever by half, instead taking for granted Scripture's authority but functionalizing it, making it an intimate part of the church and the Christian's life—*familiar* in the etymological sense. This lack of interest in specifying metaphysics of authorship might be transposed in our image as a kind of agnosticism about the precise origin of the company's orders: Did the lieutenant receive them directly from the commander, in person? Secondhand, through another? Pieced together from garbled messages? So long as all share in the confidence that they are the commander's orders and that they serve the same mission, arguing over the answer will not accomplish anything.

Relatedly, fourth, the understanding and application of Scripture's orders are indeed democratized, distributed, diversely realized. The baptist logic of the church vis-à-vis Scripture assumes a variety of in themselves unimportant (because accidental) modes of reception and obedience to Scripture's orders. Each believer (or soldier) is charged with self-governing response, just as is each local congregation (or company). It is the non-uniform character of the dispersed movement—many communities visibly marked by unity-in-diversity—that both reveals its deep consistency and expresses the strategic, open-ended, empowered autonomy proper to each instantiation of it. (Recall here the ubiquitous language in baptist, especially evangelical, statements of faith: confession of the universal church's *spiritual* unity, bound by nothing more or less than shared trust in Jesus for salvation.) Geography, culture, language, locality determine in large part the shape of the baptist church as vanguard of the kingdom. Scripture's flexibility and the congregational task of fitting it to time and circumstance—the organic missionary adaptability of both text and people—are part and parcel of the gospel's tactics against the enemy.

Fifth and finally, the church is the bridgehead of another country planting its flag in alien soil. Christ defeated the principalities and powers; though they linger on, their final defeat is assured. The analogy has often been made to D-Day in the finale of World War II: the storming of Normandy was the beginning of the end for the Axis powers, though they did not know it at the time. Or, strengthening the point's force, the analogy takes Christ's death and resurrection as the actual defeat and surrender of the Axis leaders, but before word got out to the still-fighting soldiers dispersed across the continent and globe: the latter kept the conflict alive, not knowing it was finished. In either example, the end has come. Scripture, on this construal, consists not only of orders for the completion of the mission, but also of instructions for living as victors, and for announcing victory, in the midst of forces still fighting as though the war were yet undecided. "If the world hates you, know that it has hated me before it hated you. If you were of the world, the world would love its own; but because you are not of the world, but I chose you out of the world, therefore the world hates you" (John 15:18-19 RSV). The Bible, by baptist logic, amounts to marching orders for life in enemy territory, when hatred and hostility are the norm. But the mission continues, because the baptist church knows the fate of its Lord: crucifixion, followed by resurrection. "In the world you face persecution. But take courage; I have conquered the world!" (16:33). Citizens of heaven therefore read heaven's book for guidance in the interim time before the city of man is finally conquered by the city of God. Until then it keeps faith with Jesus, and continues the campaign with the courage of Joshua.

*   *   *

By way of conclusion: These types elaborate the specific construal of the church qua Scripture-community, and so leave aside other aspects of those ecclesial identities that make up the full picture. This only partial correlation means that the consequent "mapping" is bound to be inexact, and for good reason: not every individual member, much less theologian, of a particular ecclesial tradition embodies her tradition's commitments in every respect; all the more so for commitments regarding Scripture. In that sense a Roman Catholic's bibliology may come closer to approximating the vanguard than the deputy type; or a Protestant mainliner with ambiguous ecclesial commitments may evince, in comments about Scripture, a clear assumption of the deputy type instead of the reformed; and so on. The point is not to impose an artificial schema onto diverse theologians, but to use the typology as a means of making sense of otherwise confusing disagreements, whether to clarify or to resolve what is at issue. In any case, we turn now to the contemporary field, for diagnosis and application.

Theological Hermeneutics in a Divided Church

I began this book with the hypothesis, floated by Stephen Fowl, that confessional or ecclesial commitments stand behind fractures in the erstwhile united front of theological interpretation.[19] I have shown the different ways in which this is true for specific figures; more, how even the least ecclesiocentric bibliology is nonetheless governed by ecclesiological commitments. I have shown as well the varieties of relationships that obtain between diverse claims about the church and those about Scripture, and the different logics undergirding alternative accounts of the Bible. There are many issues in the field this analysis might illuminate. Recall, though, that to argue that bibliology is (sometimes; in part) a function of ecclesiology is not to *functionalize* the Bible in the manner that, some argue, has become a trend in recent theological reflection. It is, rather, to note the *role* that ecclesiology has in the task of bibliology—informing, though not necessarily predetermining, one's proposals regarding the Bible in its relation to the church, as well as to the other elements of the dogmatic corpus. For, as we have seen, material consequences follow from different ecclesiological positions; particular commitments in the doctrine of the church create (allow, enable, require) concrete possibilities in the doctrine of Scripture, while other commitments remove (discourage, disallow, deny) other possibilities.

In what follows, in other words, my aim is not to reduce bibliology to ecclesiology. I am not suggesting that we relocate the conversation entirely from questions about the nature of Scripture and its interpretation to questions about the nature of the church and its mission. What I want to do, instead, is identify perennial topics in Christian theology of Scripture that are most intimately, inseparably, and reciprocally bound to fundamental judgments in Christian theology of the church. Thus identified, these may serve as useful—though far from exclusive—foci for further discussion and disputation in theological interpretation of Scripture.

All four topics turn, in one way or another, on the matter of ecclesial action.[20] That is to say: What is the nature and authority of the church's

---

19. Fowl, *Theological Interpretation of Scripture*, 73–75.
20. As Daniel Treier writes, "many disagreements among advocates of theological interpretation of Scripture concern how ... churchly reception of divine grace works,"

historic and corporate activity, either in the teachings of its ordained leaders or in its sacramental practices, or both?[21]

The first topic is canonization. The Bible is what it is in the economy of grace, but that economy extends beyond the biblical narrative and thus requires both theological and historical description.[22] Such description varies across different ecclesial traditions, but all of them agree that Scripture cannot be *an* item in the economy of salvation unless and until it is understood as, and thus made to be, a single entity, a unified object, one book.[23] Jenson and other catholic theologians press this point home from the vantage of ecclesiology: the canon is a dogmatic decision of the church, with canonization ratifying the unity and authority of Holy Scripture while, by that very act, asserting the authority of the church to do so. Barthians and other reformed theologians protest this point, given the lack of such (definitive) authority in their doctrine of the church. The canon, they argue, imposes itself on the church; the church does not make but receives the canon. The canon's contents are basically agreed upon, and to insist on the question is to exaggerate the level of disagreement.[24] The matter of whether the canon is closed is the rub,

---

that is, the role and agency of the church in not only receiving but mediating God's gifts to the faithful. See Treier, *Theological Interpretation*, 20.

21. As I noted at the end of chapter 1, a distinctively baptist perspective begins to drop out in what follows. Why is that? There are multiple plausible explanations: because the differences between reformed and baptist logics are most pronounced in concrete church life rather than at the level of theory regarding Scripture; because reformed scholarship has a longer history and greater prestige than baptist scholarship; because reformed traditions care much more about formal theology than baptist traditions; because with respect to *sola scriptura* both traditions are united against the catholic tradition as a common enemy; because of my own insufficient attentiveness to the nuances between the two; and more. As I said at the book's outset, I leave it to others to pursue this question further.

22. For a recent comprehensive treatment of these issues, interweaving theology and history, see Gordon, *Divine Scripture*.

23. This raises questions about predicating "necessity" as an attribute of Scripture. Discussion of this matter in reformed theology is quite nuanced. See, e.g., Bavinck, *Reformed Dogmatics*, 1:465–74. Bavinck allows without qualification that the church in a certain sense preexists the canon of Scripture and, under God, could have existed without it. "The necessity of Scripture," therefore, "is not absolute but 'based on the premise of the good pleasure of God'" (470).

24. See again Vanhoozer, *Drama of Doctrine*; cf. *Biblical Authority*, esp. 109–46. See also Kruger, *Question of Canon*; and by contrast: Allert, *High View of Scripture?* At the broadest level, see McDonald, *Biblical Canon*.

though, for Protestants generally want to insist that it is, even as Barth demurs. Yet he sees the catch-22: if it isn't closed, if the texts are negotiable, what holds the Bible together, and what adjudicates rival claims to canonicity? At the same time, if it is closed, on whose authority was it closed, and on what basis?

Like Roman Catholic Luke Timothy Johnson, for example, evangelical Kevin Vanhoozer sees the need for a closed canon, but unlike Johnson he lacks the ecclesiological resources to specify sufficiently how it can be done.[25] The catholic or the baptist route appears more consistent; the latter, at least, is more realist in its deflated approach to the texts' status in the community. For most of the participants in this discussion want to avoid the position represented by Gerhard Ebeling, wherein each and every successive generation of the church judges each and every particular text of a permanently open canon for the validity of its canonical inclusion. In doing so, he argues, it discerns the text's testimony to Jesus, which is judged according to criteria derived from the canon as a whole.[26] Ebeling's *Sachkritik* may be an outlier, in the tradition and at present, but it is not on the fringe.[27] It is one logical endpoint of a certain kind of Protestant doctrine of the church, namely, one marked by a *sola scriptura* understanding of tradition *applied to Scripture itself*.[28] The self-critique begun with the church terminates, with an assist from biblical criticism, in critique of Scripture on the basis of Scripture: Scripture alone, one might say, but not all of it. (The logic is easy to see: Jesus is the one unimpeachable criterion for judgment—until, that is, the question of the

---

25. See Vanhoozer, *Drama of Doctrine*, 113–237, esp. 231–37; cf. Johnson, *Writings of the New Testament*, 525–46.

26. See Ebeling, *Problem of Historicity*, esp. 37–80. Ebeling claims, for example, that "canon" and "Scripture" are not coterminous (63), for the former denotes an act of the church and is thus an item of fallible tradition, while the latter identifies texts inspired by God's Spirit to bear faithful witness to Jesus Christ. Only texts of the second class are truly Scripture and therefore aptly described as the word of God.

27. See the excellent account in Morgan, "*Sachkritik* in Reception History," with attention to Barth, Bultmann, and Käsemann (Ebeling's contemporary).

28. This brand of hyper-Protestant European scholarship is little more than speculative kerygmatic reductionism (*sola scriptura* become *sola kerygma*). The singular criterion is the gospel announcement, albeit in a historically conditioned, culturally clothed, and textually transmitted form. Hence the need for husking the shell for the kernel inside, a never-ending task of dubious epistemic range (notwithstanding the confidence of its practitioners). Such a program is something of a full-employment bill for enterprising scholars, since no one but they are adequate to the task.

historical Jesus takes the reformed critique to faith's previously impregnable heart. At that point, the center can no longer hold.)[29]
The thing to see here is that ecclesiology is a primary determinant of
one's judgments about Scripture's place in the economy of grace. Does
the church have the authority to identify and canonize Scripture? Is there
an absolute or a relative break between apostolic and non-apostolic texts,
between Scripture and tradition?[30] Under what circumstances and on
what basis could the church add to or subtract from canonical Scripture?
Answers to such questions about the church are the soil and seed of their
fruition in claims about the Bible.

29. Thus, e.g., confident revisionist reconstruction of Jesus's life and teachings
by scholars who want somehow thereby to preserve it as worthy of faith, or at least
retrieval. For the classic account, see Schweitzer, *Quest of the Historical Jesus*; for a
contemporary example, see the conversation recorded in Borg and Wright, *Meaning
of Jesus*; for critique, see Johnson, *Real Jesus*. This method has additional uses worth
mentioning. Turned not against Jesus but against the scriptures that Jesus and his
apostles presupposed and interpreted, the method is deployed in the service of ostensibly non-Marcionite rejection of whole swaths of the Old Testament. See, e.g.,
Boyd, *Crucifixion of the Warrior God*. By way of response, see the insightful review by
Cornell, "Greg Boyd."

30. Past theologians, especially of a reformed bent, are much more confident in
their assertions regarding the self-evident distinction between canonical and non-
canonical (or apostolic and postapostolic) writings. See, e.g., the remark of B. B.
Warfield: "There is no other such gulf in the history of human thought as that which
is cleft between the apostolic and the immediately succeeding ages. To pass from
the latest apostolic writings to the earliest compositions of uninspired Christian
pens is to fall through such a giddy height that it is no wonder if we rise dazed and
almost unable to determine our whereabouts. Here is the great fault—as the geol-
ogists would say—in the history of Christian doctrine. There is every evidence of
continuity—but, oh, at how much lower a level! The rich vein of evangelical religion
has run well-nigh out; and, though there are masses of apostolic origin lying everywhere, they are but fragments, and are evidently only the talus which has fallen
from the cliffs above and scattered itself over the lowered surface" (*Significance
of the Westminster Standards*, 4; cited in Allen and Swain, *Reformed Catholicity*, 1).
Or consider the comments of Calvin: "Scripture bears upon the face of it as clear
evidence of its truth, as white and black do of their color, sweet and bitter of their
taste"; "in elegance and beauty, no, splendor, the style of some of the prophets
is not surpassed by the eloquence of heathen writers. . . . [I]n regard to the holy
Scriptures, however petulant men may attempt to carp at them, they are replete
with sentiments which it is clear that man never could have conceived. Let each of
the prophets be examined, and not one will be found who does not rise far higher
than human reach. Those who feel their works insipid must be absolutely devoid
of taste" (*Institutes*, 1.7.2; 1.8.2).

The second topic is authorship. More to the point, the Bible's divine *and ecclesial* authorship. There is a way of narrating the canon's formation that renders the church utterly passive: disparate communities found themselves using and relying on these texts; those communities communicated and shared their texts with one another; eventually most of these communities discovered that they were in substantial agreement about which texts should be treated as authoritative, which as edifying, which as questionable, and which as untrustworthy. Regardless of the virtues or vices of this way of telling the story, no one can deny that the texts eventually canonized did not write themselves; human beings did. These human beings were members, in one way or another, at one time or another, of the covenant community. In that respect, God's word was written by God's people, the church's book by the church itself—that is, by some untold number among them. Yet if the church is not to be in dialogue with itself, if the Bible truly is a word from God to God's people, then there must be more (though not less) than a creaturely cause behind its production, more than one *kind* of author, granted the plurality of human authors behind its diverse texts.

More or less everyone working formally in the doctrine of Scripture affirms both sides of Scripture's origin. There is, however, a not inconsiderable cohort of those in theological scholarship who effectively treat the biblical texts as wholly human-authored. Inspiration, if it bears any force, assumes the classical role of illumination, resulting in the texts' authority and power becoming a function of God's *present use* of them in the community of faith.[31] Multiple factors inform this view. The two factors of interest to us are ecclesiological. On the one hand, this perspective depicts the church as the ongoing context of God's living (redemptive) reappropriation of ancient (sometimes problematic) texts. On the other hand, it sees the church as that corporate agent whose experience and discernment rightly determine the evangelical quality of discrete texts, that is, the extent to which they speak good news, and how to reinterpret them if they do not. The locus and energy of Scripture's power lies not in itself or in its origins but in the community of which it is a part, in which it is read, and to which

---

31. In what follows I have in mind methodologically critical and liberative approaches to the Bible, but one might also include postliberal examples such as Lindbeck, "Scripture, Consensus, and Community"; "The Story-Shaped Church"; "Postcritical Canonical Interpretation." Cf. Tanner, "Theology and the Plain Sense"; "Scripture as Popular Text."

it speaks—the community of the living Spirit of Christ, who will aid the community to read ever anew by the light of the gospel. Though Scripture may continue to exert a critical force, on this view, it is the *community* that exercises a critical suspicion as it reads the text; not to excise the offending parts, but to use them—to be transparent to the Spirit's use of them—in new, creative, life-giving ways, in accordance with the emancipating power of Christ. Different forms of radical Christian biblical criticism understand Scripture in these broad terms, such as feminist, womanist, and queer theologies, as well as a significant slice of liberal and liberation theology.[32] It is important to see, first, that these critical approaches remain theologically inflected, even as the site and instrument of divine work has shifted from the text as such to the community of readers; and, second, that ecclesiology remains crucial for theological depiction of Scripture, especially where Scripture is uncoupled from divine causation or authorship.[33] Ecclesiology must absorb at least some of the dogmatic work once done by bibliology; in this case, inspiration migrates from one doctrine to the other, for the logical reason that the work it performs must be retained in some other manner. The upshot is that, in order to engage such an account, much less to contest it, it is no use to reiterate arguments for the divine origins of Scripture. For the changes in the doctrine of Scripture are an outgrowth of prior revisions to other dogmatic loci. Those revisions are not limited to ecclesiology, but many of them begin there or settle there. Participants, in short, will avoid talking past one another if they go to the root cause, rather than its effects.[34]

32. See, e.g., Williams, *Sisters in the Wilderness*, esp. 143–77; Newsom and Ringe, *Women's Bible Commentary*, esp. Ringe's contribution to the volume, "When Women Interpret the Bible," 1–9; Cone, *Black Theology*, esp. 22–41; Cone, *God of the Oppressed*, esp. ix–xviii, 56–76; Tonstad, *Queer Theology*; Fulkerson, *Places of Redemption*, esp. 159–92; Trible, *Texts of Terror*; Johnson, *She Who Is*, esp. 61–120; Schüssler Fiorenza, *In Memory of Her*.

33. For a constructive proposal that touches at once on the doctrine of inspiration, the status of the canon as the church's book, and feminist interpretation, see Schneiders, *Revelatory Text*, esp. 27–93. See, e.g., her claim that "the question of mode of inspiration shifts our focus from that which is perceived in and through the biblical text to the actual human experience with the text that mediates revelation under the influence of the Spirit of God. To ask how inspiration takes place is not to ask for a description of the divine operations but for a phenomenology of the human experience of divine revelation mediated by the revelatory text of scripture" (53).

34. In other words, what might be presupposed in another discursive context must be argued for in this one.

As for those who affirm Scripture's dual origins, the primary cleavage is between those who emphasize the divine to the near exclusion of the human-ecclesial and those who hold both affirmations together. The two groups are not neatly divided by communion with an ancient see, however. Catholics and Orthodox as much as Protestants may overlook or elide the significance of the biblical texts' human origins, treating them for all intents and purposes as if they fell from heaven. And Protestants, whether with magisterial roots in Renaissance humanism or under contemporary influence from biblical criticism, readily engage the texts as historical documents produced by human hands. Catholic ecclesiology has proved a double-edged sword in this regard, for while it offers conceptual resources for unqualified affirmation of Scripture's created and uncreated causes, magisterial teaching resisted modern biblical criticism for some time, seeing in it the seeds of the Bible's unraveling (a not unjustified anxiety!).[35] But in the decades since Pope Pius XII's promulgation of *Divino Afflante Spiritu* in 1943, and its recapitulation and extension twenty-two years later in *Dei Verbum* at Vatican II, Roman Catholic ecclesiology and bibliology have been, at the ecclesiastical and the scholarly level, relatively consistent in emphasizing the divine and human voices of Holy Scripture.[36]

In any case, we have seen how ecclesiology informs the issue of Scripture's twofold cause. Older Protestant scholastic accounts, for example, describe the role of the human author as the amanuensis to the Holy Spirit's dictation. Of the prophets and apostles, Gerhard writes:

> we correctly call them the amanuenses of God, the hands of Christ, the scribes or notaries of the Holy Spirit. They neither spoke nor wrote by human or their own will; rather, they were moved, driven, led, impelled by the Holy Spirit and controlled by him. They did not write as men but as "holy men of God," that is, they wrote as God's servants and as the unique instruments of the Holy Spirit. Therefore when we

35. For productive dialogue, see Johnson and Kurz, *Future of Catholic Biblical Scholarship*.

36. To be clear, I am not speaking to *hermeneutical success* in the concrete task of interpreting the biblical text in a way that honors its historicity within and alongside its appointment by the Spirit to be God's word for the church. Not only is such a task harder in practice than in theory; it does not always follow neatly or directly from "correct" theoretical or theological commitments. See further Ayres and Fowl, "(Mis)reading the Face of God." Cf. Levering, "Scriptures and Their Interpretation."

call some canonical book a "book of Moses," "the Psalter of David," "an epistle of Paul," we are doing this merely by reason of their ministry, not by reason of its principal cause.[37]

Some of this language is easily mishandled and caricatured; some of it, though, lends itself to a mechanical or literalistic picture, as portrayed in paintings of the Holy Spirit whispering in the scribe's ear.[38] In any case, it is worth asking what motivates this picture. Partly the answer is a theology of sin. But the details of that hamartiology follow from a specific Pauline and Augustinian soteriology, which in turn informs the doctrine of the church. The nature of salvation in Christ and the depravity of sinful humanity entail that the church may be neither mediator nor source of salvation or saving truth; only the word of God may be trusted for that, and God's word is found in Holy Scripture. But fallen humans, members of God's sinful people, authored Scripture. Therefore they must have been little more than conduits, nothing in themselves but impure instruments manipulated by God for an in itself pure and untainted end. (Inspiration bordering on possession.)[39] Thus, the unexceptionable historical claim that the church is the author of Scripture is evacuated of content, and thereby denuded of any real import for understanding Scripture theologically. This move has consequences for the topic discussed above, Scripture's role in the economy of grace. For if Scripture can be properly understood without any significance accorded its human and historical character, then it can be received in the church absent those features as well. The result is a divine tome absolutely antecedent to the community, bearing precedence at once in authority, in derivation, and in time.

As I said already, catholic ecclesiology has fewer problems conceptually, though more problems historically, with accounting for Scripture's human authorship. For an understanding of the church as the mediator of

---

37. Gerhard, *On the Nature of Theology and Scripture*, 1.18.2.

38. For detailed discussion, see Preus, *Inspiration of Scripture*.

39. This is an exaggeration of a tendency found more at the popular level than articulated and defended by the best of the reformed tradition. See, e.g., B. B. Warfield's critique of "a quite mechanical and magical process of inspiration," according to which certain of Paul's statements would be "wholly disconnected with his own fundamental thought, . . . [as] spoken through him by an overmastering spiritual influence; as a phenomenon, in a word, similar to the oracles of heathen shrines, and without analogy in Scripture except perhaps in such cases as that of Balaam" (*Inspiration and Authority*, 201).

divine action—the instrumental agent of an action that is also, originally and ultimately, God's—is ingredient in catholic theology of the church.[40] More subtly stated, Protestant thought draws a bright red line between the apostles and their successors: they *were* and their texts *are* mediators of divine action and speech, but such mediation, at least in such strong form, no longer obtains after their passing.[41] It is concentrated instead in the canon.[42] Yet catholic ease regarding past and present ecclesial mediation of divine action and authority raises questions as well, similar in kind to the ones with which we concluded the previous discussion. What sets Scripture apart from tradition? Are there different kinds of ecclesial mediation? Is mediation, which suggests sacramental action, the right conceptual framework for Scripture's production?[43] Divergent answers to these questions are not resolvable by reference to consideration of Scripture alone. For this discussion is downstream of where the real conflict lies: the nature and authority of the church.

The third topic is Scripture's attributes, in particular clarity and sufficiency. For these cut to the heart of the ecclesiological divide in the doctrine of Scripture. Indeed, they are predicates of Scripture necessary for a church without authoritative liturgy, tradition, or teaching office.[44] If I cannot rely on the church's (historic and contemporary) interpretation of Scripture, then I must be able to rely on my own interpretation of it—not because I myself am reliable, but because Scripture is. It is reliable, first, because it is clear: any person who reads or hears it may understand its essential message. For God is a God of light, not darkness, of understanding, not confusion, and God so determined the writing of God's word that it communicates intelligibly and effectively, without distortion or opacity. "Perspicuity teaches, not obscurity."[45] This is not to deny the effort involved in the act of understanding on the part of fallen creatures,

40. For discussion, see Burtchaell, *Catholic Theories of Biblical Inspiration*.

41. A kind of cessationism of ecclesial authority, or an ecclesial cessationism of prophetic speech.

42. And sometimes in the sacraments.

43. See now Boersma, *Scripture as Real Presence*.

44. "Authority" is also an attribute of Scripture, but it will become clear that this is both a precondition and a corollary of the other attributes. Put differently: how Scripture's authority is understood is a function of claims regarding the relationship between church and canon. The issue then is not whether Scripture is authoritative—here all agree—but rather its nature and scope and its relationship to other authorities, both within the church and without.

45. Gerhard, *On Sacred Scripture*, 1.5.82.

or the benefits of studiousness. Nor does Scripture's clarity obviate the need for the Holy Spirit's illumination. Consider a metaphor: The Bible is clear water. That light, not darkness, is required to see it and to see through it does not refute but confirms its clarity. It is true that a blind person cannot see it, nor can one who refuses to open her eyes or, opening them, to look away from the sky and land into the water. But none of these objections bears on the water's clarity, only on the observer or the obstacles, extrinsic or intrinsic, that keep her from seeing it. Reformed advocates argue the same regarding Scripture's clarity. The nature of the canon depends not on its readers' capacities or desires but on God, who makes it what it is.

The second and related attribute is sufficiency. Catholics and Protestants agree about Scripture's material sufficiency: it contains all that is necessary for saving faith in Christ. Their disagreement concerns formal sufficiency. Are Scripture's contents self-constituting, that is to say, self-authenticating?[46] Is the integrity and substance of its message internal to itself, or does it require readers to put it together—or, better yet, teachers (like St. Philip) to provide the key to puzzled readers (like the Ethiopian eunuch)? Granted the sufficiency of its contents, does the canon need supplementation in the construction of the whole and the potentially diverse shapes its matter might take? If in itself it *is* complete, or perfect, apart from such supplementation, by what means and by what criteria is its form to be discerned? If it is *not*, who is in a position to judge its form with authority? As one Protestant divine puts it, "The perfection of Scripture . . . does not exclude either the ecclesiastical ministry . . . or the internal power of the Holy Spirit necessary for conversion. It only excludes the necessity of another rule for external direction added to the Scriptures to make them perfect. A rule is not therefore imperfect because it requires the hand of the architect for its application."[47]

The attributes of sufficiency and clarity derive from a particular ecclesiology. That ecclesiology is itself derivative, most of all from the doctrines of God, Christ, salvation, and sin. But having underwritten an account of the church, they in turn generate an account of Scripture. My own view is that formal sufficiency is neither necessary nor true, and that clarity requires so many qualifications that the claim becomes devoid of content, thereby ceasing to do the work that it was originally fashioned

46. Cf. *Westminster Confession of Faith*, 1.4–5.
47. Turretin, *Institutes of Elenctic Theology*, 1:141.

to do.[48] But my judgment of the normative question is immaterial to the present point. There are eminent theologians on both sides of the debate.[49] The point, rather, is that to decide for these two attributes is at once to decide for one account of the church over another. Better still, to decide for these two attributes is *already to have decided* for one account of the church over another. They follow, because something like them must follow, if one rejects the authority of the church as a definitive and trustworthy interpreter of Scripture. In contrast, catholic bibliology, following catholic ecclesiology, confesses the authority of the church as the Lord's deputy. This status is contingent, since the church's authority is not native to itself but granted from without by God's good pleasure. But it is also necessary, because texts are not self-interpreting, and history's multifarious schisms and heresies and Scripture's infinite potential for varying interpretations demand it. Had God not provided a canon of texts as the medium of his ruling and saving word among and for his people, perhaps a living teaching office would not have been called for. But he did. So it was.

Discussion of these two attributes can perhaps proceed some way on their own terms, within the locus of the doctrine of Scripture: reformed arguments seeking to demonstrate clarity and sufficiency by recourse to the text, catholic arguments seeking to deny them by similar recourse. But this procedure, especially the positive one (for how does one show the self-attestation of a collection of texts independent of the one doing the showing?), dead-ends rather quickly. For the quarrel concerns the church. What kind of community is the church, precisely as a community founded by a message and centered on a book, both of which must be interpreted? Is the church invested with binding authority by God to interpret Scripture or not? May the church, in short, promulgate dogma? These are the questions at issue.

Having asked what the Bible is, let us turn finally to the question of what it is for. The fourth topic, accordingly, is the purpose or end of Scripture. Beyond broadly shared answers—Scripture's appointment to communicate the gospel, to build up the church in faith and love, and so on—a theologian's understanding of the canon's telos is deeply revealing of her ecclesial commitments. Consider, in closing, two pairs of

---

48. See further East, *Doctrine of Scripture*, 73–81.
49. See, e.g., the sensitive and wide-ranging discussion in Thompson, "Generous Gift."

contemporary theological interpreters who illustrate the point; both of them home in on scriptural teleology, in particular the Bible's power to speak continually to the church. What is the shape of that power? What is it fundamentally aimed at? Is it essentially corrective, a strange and intrusive word that constantly unsettles past readings and doctrines? Or is it something else?

The first pair is Paul Griffiths and N. T. Wright. Griffiths is a Roman Catholic philosophical theologian of an idiosyncratic but nonetheless traditional bent, whereas Wright is an evangelical Anglican scholar of the New Testament interested in the historical origins of the Christian movement.[50] Both are theological readers of the sacred page; both are eager to interpret the text in ways that are sensitive to pressing intellectual questions and challenges of the day; both know their languages and their academic scholarship; both are churchmen who believe the canon of Holy Scripture to be the word of the Lord to the covenant people of Christ in the present tense.[51] Yet their hermeneutical procedures could not be more different. When Griffiths approaches the Bible, he seeks to read not only for the plain sense but also for the infinitely fecund figural signification contained in the Bible's depths. Such signification is lavishly anachronistic, delighting in the illumination of the text offered by the church's dogmatic tradition. Griffiths's commentary on the Song of Songs, for example, relishes discovering in every jot and tittle types and tokens of the incarnate Lord, his passion, his presence in the Eucharist, and his mother Mary. Griffiths is not merely having fun. His readings stake a claim to participating in an unbroken line of similar readings of

---

50. See Griffiths, *Song of Songs*; *Religious Reading*; "Words of Scripture"; *Practice of Catholic Theology*; *Decreation*; *Christian Flesh*; "On Radner's *Time and the Word*." From N. T. Wright's voluminous oeuvre, see the first four volumes of his ongoing series, *Christian Origins and the Question of God*, as well as the newly published three-volume *Collected Essays* on Jesus, Paul, and Scripture. See also Wright, *Scripture and the Authority of God*; *Surprised by Scripture*; and the series of responses Wright offers to essays engaging his work in Perrin and Hays, *Jesus, Paul, and the People of God*. Wright lays out his exegetical and theological methodology most clearly in *The New Testament and the People of God*, 3–144; cf. Wright, *History and Eschatology*. I have written at length about the latter book in East, "Jesus of History."

51. For instance, Wright and Griffiths have both written biblical commentaries as well as entries in dictionaries on theological interpretation. See, e.g., their respective contributions to the *Dictionary for Theological Interpretation of the Bible*. Wright has himself written a brief commentary, intended for popular audiences, on every book of the New Testament; see his *New Testament for Everyone*.

the Song stretching backward through the centuries, with countless doctors of the church as exemplars, all the way to the apostolic fathers and even the apostles themselves.[52] What makes such a line possible is not merely a *doctrine* of the church but rather the church's whole sacramental, commentarial, and magisterial life: one that models, encourages, and theologically grounds figural and spiritual reading, gives it a home and makes good sense of it. That postmodern hermeneutics adds a theoretical nod of approval is a complementary but far from necessary feature of this practice.

Wright's exegesis is not quite a repudiation of Griffiths's approach, but only just so. He believes that any responsible interpretation of the Bible worthy of the name will be informed, of necessity and from start to finish, by the study of history. "History" as the designation of a formal academic discipline has a kind of totemic status in Wright's work. At issue is not so much matters of philology and text criticism, though they are important, but instead the three-dimensional character of the human persons and events narrated by the Bible, who like us lived in space and time, culture and context, all of which are crucial for comprehending who they were and what they might mean in the unfolding story of God's purposes. Anachronism, therefore, is anathema for Wright. This is an intellectual and hermeneutical commitment unto itself, but it is important to see the way in which it is also an ecclesiological commitment, in its origins and in its contemporary deployment. For if, per Protestant teaching, the Bible is the supreme arbiter of Christian faith and life; if it alone plays this role, apart from human or ecclesial interpretive authority; and if it is therefore perspicuous and sufficient in and of itself—then it follows that Scripture's content must be both determinate and identifiable. Determinate, because to be amorphous would suggest either formal inadequacy or fluidity of meaning, thereby rendering it unable to fulfill its role. Identifiable, because "ought" implies "can": the command to hear God's word in Scripture must in principle be obeyable, lest God be a liar or the church be left alone in its mission. Yet how to secure the necessarily determinate and identifiable content of Scripture? The specifically Protestant answer, ever since the Renaissance, the Reformation, and especially the Enlightenment, is *history*—or rather, those modes of inquiry that take "history" for their object. Historiography becomes the means by which biblical interpretation may be confident in its results.

---

52. See further East, "Reading the Trinity."

For the study of history affords a kind of independent witness regarding one's reading. Did David really do such-and-such? Could Paul really have said so-and-so? These questions, once thought unfalsifiable, now become subject to verification. As matters of human *scientia*, they are no longer condemned to the infinite deferral of perpetual undecidability. Of what use is a magisterium to adjudicate opposed readings? Now the church has historians.

One can thus see the way in which recourse to historiography as the instrument of surety in biblical interpretation is, in part, a product of an account of the church that requires Scripture's content to be both fixed and intelligible. This requirement, recall, is but the obverse of the rejection of the church conceived as arbiter of diverse and equally plausible interpretations of a formally underdetermined Scripture. That is why anachronism is such a bugbear, because *not* to read anachronistically is just to read correctly for Scripture's single true and abiding meaning. Whether or not Scripture admits of a multiplicity of non-anachronistic meanings, at the very least identifying anachronism is the easiest and strongest way to eliminate false interpretive possibilities.[53] Doing so in turn shores up the stability and transparency of Scripture as sole authority for the church, an authority not only final over against the community, but independent thereof.[54]

53. This approach typically generates a strong doctrine of inspiration wedded to a strict hermeneutic of original human authorial intention, so that whatever the human author intended, and only what the human author intended—as that intention is accessible to scholarly exegetical labor—is synonymous with the authorial intention of the Holy Spirit. See, e.g., Schreiner, *Interpreting the Pauline Epistles*, 20: "The meaning of Scripture cannot be separated from the intention of the author as that intention is expressed in the words of the text. . . . It is . . . incorrect to say that our goal is to discover *God's* intention in the biblical text rather than the intention of the human author. We aim to discover God's meaning, but such a meaning cannot be known apart from the intention of the human author. God has so designed it that his meaning is known when the meaning of the human author is known. If we claim that God's intention in the text is not the same as that of the human author, how can we substantiate or demonstrate God's intention in the text?"

54. Lest the picture here appear imbalanced, the issue is not historiography *versus* figuralism. No less than the Pope Emeritus, Benedict XVI, has for the entirety of his career been a staunch advocate of engagement with and deployment of historical-critical research in Catholic biblical interpretation. See, e.g., the earlier pieces collected in Ratzinger, *God's Word*. The essay on biblical interpretation in that volume (91–126) is a lecture Ratzinger delivered numerous times in the 1980s, in both English and German, including as the Erasmus lecture gathered in Neuhaus, *Biblical Inter-*

Much of this book has already adjudicated these questions at the material level; I do not mean to relitigate them here. I mean only to show how different accounts of the church produce different interpretive postures—in this case, toward anachronism. The causality may run in either direction (that is, the hermeneutic might precede or parallel its rooting in a particular tradition, either historically or personally), but nevertheless the foundation is *there* for Griffiths's spiritual interpretation in a way that it simply is not for Wright, and the foundation is ecclesial. Change the foundation, and the condition of the possibility for the hermeneutic changes with it. Or, to switch metaphors, peek under the hood of the exegesis, however theological, and the engine on which it runs is ecclesiological.

Let me conclude with a second pair, Richard Hays and Matthew Levering, who articulate a disagreement that touches more directly on Scripture's critical role in the church's life. Hays, a Protestant New Testament scholar, represents a view common to post-Reformation bibliology: namely, that one of Scripture's purposes is to judge the church, to correct its course when it goes astray, to remedy mistaken claims or beliefs by new or renewed readings of the selfsame Scripture. This view presumes more than a fallibilist ecclesiology. It takes for granted that the church will (always? perpetually?) err in the most profound ways, and that Scripture—unchanged and unchanging, the non-normed norm of the church's life—is the means of the church's rectification. Already we see how scriptural teleology follows from a particular account of the church. What Scripture is for is a function, in part, of the nature of the church. Together, moreover, these form an argument, for Hays, against the concept of dogma.[55] For dogma's irrevocability not only assumes the church has the authority to settle the matter; it also contradicts the principle of the church's propensity for error (1) in any and every matter and (2) in perpetuity. Dogma presumes an alternative ecclesiology: that in certain matters the church may arrive at the truth *for good*, that is, infallibly, for-

pretation in Crisis; cf. Ratzinger, *Schriftauslegung im Widerstreit*. See also the post-synodal apostolic exhortation *Verbum Domini* promulgated during his pontificate; for the Latin, see *Acta Apostolicae Sedis* 102.11 (2010): 681–787. Finally, see his trilogy on the life of Christ, titled *Jesus of Nazareth*. Two recent volumes feature Protestant responses to Ratzinger's thought: in *Joseph Ratzinger and the Healing of the Reformation-Era Divisions*, see Sweeney, "Ratzinger on Scripture"; in *The Theology of Benedict XVI: A Protestant Appreciation*, see Vanhoozer, "Expounding the Word."

55. Cf. the discussion in O'Donovan, "Moral Authority of Scripture."

ever. Dogma would then be cordoned off from Scripture's function as a critical corrective, in Hays's view, owing to a different understanding of the church's relationship to Scripture.[56]

But there is an alternative, positive way to frame the view that Hays opposes. Let Levering, a Roman Catholic systematic theologian, speak for this view.[57] Perhaps, he writes, what Scripture is for is *not* to sit in continuous judgment on an ever errant church. Perhaps, instead, Scripture exists, by the Spirit's unfailing power, to guide the church into ever deeper knowledge of God, ever closer fellowship with Christ, ever richer understanding of the truth. Recognition of error and rejection of heresy—that is, of engagements with Scripture that are not expressions of this Spirit-led movement—are part and parcel of the process. But that negative component remains subordinate to the larger, more comprehensive positive purpose. Moreover, contestation and dialogue are the means of this long-term guidance by the Spirit. And dogma enters in at exactly this point: not to quench the Spirit or stifle God's freedom, but to reiterate the truth of Scripture's teaching—to say, once and for all, that those who say or teach otherwise stand outside the scripturally mediated knowledge of and fellowship with God. Dogma, in other words, is the *exercise* of Scripture's critical authority.[58] To deny the divinity of Christ or the triunity of God becomes, by conciliar dogmatic judgment, a denial of Scripture's witness, Scripture's truth. Thus and not otherwise does Scripture func-

---

56. See Hays, "Future of *Christian* Biblical Scholarship." Hays is hardly an opponent of Christian exegesis being assisted or led by sacred tradition, however; there is a good deal of evolution in Hays's writings on this point across his career. Cf. Hays, *Moral Vision of the New Testament*, alongside his newly published collection, *Reading with the Grain*, esp. 9–86.

57. See Levering, *Participatory Biblical Exegesis*, esp. 107–40. As he writes later: "will not a robust account of the Church's participation in and mediation of the Word of God result in the Church's controlling and eventually muting Christ, in a profound distortion of what should be? [By way of response:] Catholics, recognizing the sinfulness of human beings, nonetheless trust in faith that Christ, through the gift of the Holy Spirit, will sustain his Bride in faithfully witnessing, though not with eschatological fullness, to his cruciform image by mediating sacramentally and doctrinally his deifying wisdom and love to the world. This confidence in Christ, which fuels rather than mitigates the call for constant renewal of the Church in holiness, partakes in Christian 'foolishness'" (214n64).

58. For a less determinate but possibly complementary approach, see Williams, *On Christian Theology*, esp. 79–180. See also Williams, *Why Study the Past?* For appreciative partial dissent, see Jenson's review of *On Christian Theology* published in 2002.

tion to correct errors once for all, rather than piecemeal and perennially. Just thereby the Holy Spirit, one and the same as he who inspired the scriptures, leads the church into the truth of God—in this case, to lasting, definitive confession of Jesus as himself one of the Holy Trinity.

But only a certain kind of church—Levering's Catholicism, not Hays's Methodism—can affirm such an account of Scripture. What Scripture is for depends on and follows from what the church is. The disagreement between Hays and Levering consists in opposed claims, not so much about the nature and purpose of the Bible, as about the nature and purpose of the church. Relocate the discussion there, and the argument gains traction.

To gain traction, after all, is no small thing. It is the altogether small ambition of the foregoing analysis to aid in such gains. In a real sense I have spent an entire book laboring to point out a very obvious truth: *what we think about the church matters for what we think about the Bible.* The detail comes in observing the patterns and logics that emerge as a result and the habit of overlooking these in arguing over symptoms rather than causes. It comes too in attending to concrete cases and representatives of enormously complex and irreducible traditions of Christian faith, practice, and biblical interpretation. Beyond the other goals of this work (the genealogical, tracking Barth's legacy in some of his heirs; the expository, commenting on and in certain places recommending the thought of Webster, Jenson, and Yoder; and the constructive, synthesizing and proposing paths forward in the doctrine of Scripture), I hope my exploration of the relationship between bibliology and ecclesiology might function in two ways. On the one hand, as a reminder of what we already know but at times neglect in practice; on the other hand, as a scalpel, one potentially useful in the dissection of disagreements, their bases, and their warrants. No doctrine of Scripture is fully successful, but no attempt at the doctrine will even get off the ground if it fails to reckon with the canon's dual identity as the Lord's word and the church's book. That, in brief, is the mystery of Holy Scripture. If theology would serve the church, it would do well not to forget it.

Bibliography

Abraham, William J. *Canon and Criterion in Christian Theology: From the Fathers to Feminism.* New York: Oxford University Press, 1998.

———. *The Divine Inspiration of Holy Scripture.* New York: Oxford University Press, 1981.

Adam, A. K. M. *Making Sense of New Testament Theology: "Modern" Problems and Prospects.* Macon, GA: Mercer University Press, 1995.

Adam, A. K. M., Stephen E. Fowl, Kevin J. Vanhoozer, and Francis Watson. *Reading Scripture with the Church: Toward a Hermeneutic for Theological Interpretation.* Grand Rapids: Baker Academic, 2006.

Adams, Carol J., and Marie M. Fortune, eds. *Violence against Women and Children: A Christian Theological Sourcebook.* New York: Continuum, 1995.

Adams, Robert Merrihew. "Saints." *The Journal of Philosophy* 81:7 (1984): 392–401.

Allen, Charlotte. "Flannery O'Connor and the Ideological War on Literature." *Quillette,* 17 August 2020. Online at https://quillette.com/2020/08/17/flannery-oconnor-and-the-ideological-war-on-literature/.

Allen, Michael. "Reading John Webster: An Introduction." In *T&T Clark Reader in John Webster,* edited by Michael Allen, 1–19. New York: T&T Clark, 2020.

———. "Theological Theology." *First Things,* November 2020, 19–23.

———. "Toward Theological Anthropology: Tracing the Anthropological Principles of John Webster." *International Journal of Systematic Theology* 19:1 (2017): 6–29.

———. "Toward Theological Theology: Tracing the Methodological Principles of John Webster." *Themelios* 41 (2016): 217–37.

Allen, Michael, ed. *Theological Commentary: Evangelical Perspectives.* New York: T&T Clark, 2011.

Allen, Michael, and R. David Nelson, eds. *A Companion to the Theology of John Webster.* Grand Rapids: Eerdmans, 2021.

Allen, Michael, and Scott R. Swain. *Reformed Catholicity: The Promise of Retrieval for Theology and Biblical Interpretation*. Grand Rapids: Baker Academic, 2015.

Allert, Craig D. *A High View of Scripture? The Authority of the Bible and the Formation of the New Testament Canon*. Grand Rapids: Baker Academic, 2007.

Anatolios, Khaled. *Retrieving Nicaea: The Development and Meaning of Trinitarian Doctrine*. Grand Rapids: Baker Academic, 2011.

Anderson, Gary A. *Christian Doctrine and the Old Testament: Theology in the Service of Biblical Exegesis*. Grand Rapids: Baker Academic, 2017.

Augustine, St. *Confessions*. Translated by Henry Chadwick. New York: Oxford University Press, 1991.

———. "Homilies on the First Epistle of John." Translated by H. Browne and Joseph H. Myers. In vol. 7 of *The Nicene and Post-Nicene Fathers*. Series 1. Edited by Philip Schaff. 1888. Reprint, Peabody, MA: Hendrickson, 2012.

———. *Teaching Christianity (De Doctrina Christiana)*. Translated by Edmund Hill, OP. Vol. 11 of *The Works of Saint Augustine: A Translation for the 21st Century. Part 1: Books*. Hyde Park, NY: New City, 1996.

———. "Tractates on the Gospel According to St. John." Translated by John Gibb and James Innes. In vol. 7 of *Nicene and Post-Nicene Fathers*. Series 1. Edited by Philip Schaff. 1888. Reprint, Peabody, MA: Hendrickson, 2012.

———. *The Trinity (De Trinitate)*. Translated by Edmund Hill. Edited by John E. Rotelle. Vol. 5 of *The Works of Saint Augustine: A Translation for the 21st Century. Part 1: Books*. Hyde Park, NY: New City, 1991.

Ayres, Lewis. *Nicaea and Its Legacy: An Approach to Fourth-Century Trinitarian Theology*. New York: Oxford University Press, 2004.

———. "'There's Fire in That Rain': On Reading the Letter and Reading Allegorically." *Modern Theology* 28 (2012): 616–34.

Ayres, Lewis, and Stephen E. Fowl. "(Mis)reading the Face of God: The Interpretation of the Bible in the Church." *Theological Studies* 60 (1999): 513–28.

Balthasar, Hans Urs von. *Mysterium Paschale: The Mystery of Easter*. Translated by Aidan Nichols. San Francisco: T&T Clark, 1990.

———. *The Theology of Karl Barth*. Translated by Edward T. Oakes. San Francisco: Ignatius, 1992.

———. *The Word Made Flesh: Explorations in Theology I*. Translated by A. V. Littledale and Alexander Dru. San Francisco: Ignatius, 1989.

Barclay, John M. G. *Paul and the Gift*. Grand Rapids: Eerdmans, 2015.

———. *Paul and the Power of Grace.* Grand Rapids: Eerdmans, 2020.

Barr, James. *Holy Scripture: Canon, Authority, Criticism.* Philadelphia: Westminster, 1983.

Barth, Karl. *Church Dogmatics, I/1: The Doctrine of the Word of God.* Translated by G. W. Bromiley. 1975. Reprint, Peabody, MA: Hendrickson, 2010.

———. *Church Dogmatics, I/2: The Doctrine of the Word of God.* Translated by G. T. Thomson and Harold Knight. 1956. Reprint, Peabody, MA: Hendrickson, 2010.

———. *Church Dogmatics, II/2: The Doctrine of God.* Translated by G. W. Bromiley et al. 1957. Reprint, Peabody, MA: Hendrickson, 2010.

———. *Church Dogmatics, IV/1: The Doctrine of Reconciliation.* Translated by G. W. Bromiley. 1956. Reprint, Peabody, MA: Hendrickson, 2010.

———. *Church Dogmatics, IV/3.1: The Doctrine of Reconciliation.* Translated by G. W. Bromiley. 1961. Reprint, Peabody, MA: Hendrickson, 2010.

———. *Credo: A Presentation of the Chief Problems of Dogmatics with Reference to the Apostles' Creed.* Translated by J. Strathearn McNab. London: Hodder & Stoughton, 1936.

———. *Dogmatics in Outline.* Translated by G. T. Thomson. New York: Harper & Row, 1959.

———. *The Epistle to the Romans.* 6th ed. Translated by Edwyn C. Hoskyns. New York: Oxford University Press, 1933.

———. *Witness to the Word: A Commentary on John 1.* Edited by Walther Fürst. Translated by Geoffrey W. Bromiley. Grand Rapids: Eerdmans, 1986.

Barth, Karl, and Eduard Thurneysen. *Come, Holy Spirit: Sermons.* Translated by George W. Richards, Elmer G. Homrighausen, and Karl J. Ernst. 1933. Reprint, Eugene, OR: Wipf & Stock, 2009.

Bartholomew, Craig G. "Biblical Theology." In *Dictionary for Theological Interpretation of the Bible*, edited by Kevin J. Vanhoozer with Craig G. Bartholomew, Daniel J. Treier, and N. T. Wright, 84–90. Grand Rapids: Baker Academic, 2005.

Bartholomew, Craig G., and Heath A. Thomas, eds. *A Manifesto for Theological Interpretation.* Grand Rapids: Baker Academic, 2016.

Barton, John. *The Nature of Biblical Criticism.* Louisville: Westminster John Knox, 2007.

Battle, Michael. *The Black Church in America: African American Christian Spirituality.* Malden, MA: Blackwell, 2006.

Bavinck, Herman. *Prolegomena.* Vol. 1 of *Reformed Dogmatics.* Translated by John Vriend. Edited by John Bolt. Grand Rapids: Baker Academic, 2003.

Behr, John. *John the Theologian and His Paschal Gospel: A Prologue to Theology.* New York: Oxford University Press, 2019.

———. *The Mystery of Christ: Life in Death.* Crestwood, NY: St. Vladimir's Seminary Press, 2006.

Bender, Kimlyn J. *Confessing Christ for Church and World: Studies in Modern Theology.* Downers Grove, IL: IVP, 2014.

Berkhof, Hendrik. *Christ and the Powers.* Translated by John Howard Yoder. Scottdale, PA: Herald, 1977.

Bernard of Clairvaux. *Song of Songs I.* Vol. 2 of *The Works of Bernard of Clairvaux.* Translated by Kilian Walsh. Collegeville, MN: Cistercian, 2008.

Biggar, Nigel. *In Defense of War.* New York: Oxford University Press, 2013.

———, ed. *Reckoning with Barth: Essays in Commemoration of the Centenary of Karl Barth's Birth.* Oxford: Mowbray, 1988.

Billings, J. Todd. *The Word of God for the People of God: An Entryway to the Theological Interpretation of Scripture.* Grand Rapids: Eerdmans, 2010.

Bland, Archie, and Jon Henley. "Oxford Professor Sentenced to Jail in France over Child Abuse Images." *The Guardian,* 22 June 2020. Online at https://www.theguardian.com/world/2020/jun/22/oxford-university -professor-jan-joosten-jailed-france-child-abuse-images.

Bockmuehl, Markus. *Seeing the Word: Refocusing New Testament Study.* Grand Rapids: Baker Academic, 2006.

Boersma, Hans. *Scripture as Real Presence: Sacramental Exegesis in the Early Church.* Grand Rapids: Baker Academic, 2017.

Bonhoeffer, Dietrich. *Discipleship.* Translated by Barbara Green and Reinhard Krauss. Edited by Geffrey B. Kelly and John D. Godsey. Vol. 4 of *Dietrich Bonhoeffer Works.* Minneapolis: Fortress, 2001.

Borg, Marcus J., and N. T. Wright. *The Meaning of Jesus: Two Visions.* New York: HarperOne, 1999.

Bowald, Mark Alan. *Rendering the Word in Theological Hermeneutics: Mapping Divine and Human Agency.* Studies in Historical and Systematic Theology. Bellingham, WA: Lexham, 2015.

Boyd, Gregory A. *Crucifixion of the Warrior God: Interpreting the Old Testament's Violent Portraits of God in Light of the Cross.* 2 vols. Minneapolis: Fortress, 2017.

Boynton, Eric, and Peter Capretto, eds. *Trauma and Transcendence: Suffering and the Limits of Theory.* New York: Fordham University Press, 2018.

Braaten, Carl E. "A Personal Tribute to Robert William Jenson (1930–2017)." *Pro Ecclesia* 27:3 (2018): 255–58.

———. "Robert William Jenson—A Personal Memoir." In *Trinity, Time, and*

Church: A Response to the Theology of Robert W. Jenson, edited by Colin Gunton, 1–9. Grand Rapids: Eerdmans, 2000.

Braaten, Carl E., and Robert W. Jenson, eds. *Jews and Christians: People of God*. Grand Rapids: Eerdmans, 2003.

Brandom, Robert. *A Spirit of Trust: A Reading of Hegel's "Phenomenology."* Cambridge: Belknap, 2019.

Branson, Mark Lau, and Juan F. Martínez. *Churches, Cultures, and Leadership: A Practical Theology of Congregations and Ethnicities*. Downers Grove, IL: IVP Academic, 2011.

Brittain, Christopher Craig. "Why Ecclesiology Cannot Live by Doctrine Alone: A Reply to John Webster's 'In the Society of God.'" *Ecclesial Practices* 1 (2014): 5–30.

Brown, Peter. "St. Augustine's Attitude to Religious Coercion." *Journal of Roman Studies* 54 (1964): 107–16.

——. "Religious Coercion in the Later Roman Empire: The Case of North Africa." *History* 48 (1963): 285–305.

——. "Religious Dissent in the Later Roman Empire: The Case of North Africa." *History* 46 (1961): 83–101.

Bruenig, Elizabeth. "Catholics Face a Painful Question: Is It True?" *Washington Post*, 29 August 2018. Online at https://www.washingtonpost.com/opinions/catholics-face-a-painful-question-is-it-true/2018/08/29/25601210-abbd-11e8-b1da-ff7faa680710_story.html.

——. "The Catholic Sex Abuse Crisis Is Far from Over." *New York Times*, 10 November 2020. Online at https://www.nytimes.com/2020/11/10/opinion/McCarrick-Catholic-sex-abuse.html.

——. "Everyone Knew about Theodore McCarrick." *New York Times*, 10 November 2020. Online at https://www.nytimes.com/2020/11/10/opinion/theodore-mccarrick-investigation.html.

——. "He Wanted to Be a Priest. He Says Archbishop Mccarrick Used That to Abuse Him." *Washington Post*, 12 September 2018. Online at https://www.washingtonpost.com/opinions/he-wanted-to-be-a-priest-he-says-archbishop-mccarrick-used-that-to-abuse-him/2018/09/12/eff6e726-b606-11e8-94eb-3bd52dfe917b_story.html.

——. "'Pray for Your Poor Uncle,' a Predatory Priest Told His Victims." *New York Times*, 15 July 2020. Online at https://www.nytimes.com/2020/07/15/opinion/sunday/theodore-mccarrick-catholic-abuse.html.

Brunner, Emil. *Revelation and Reason: The Christian Doctrine of Faith and Knowledge*. Translated by Olive Wyon. Philadelphia: Westminster, 1946.

Bryan, Christopher. *Listening to the Bible: The Art of Faithful Biblical Interpretation*. New York: Oxford University Press, 2014.

Bultmann, Rudolf. *New Testament and Mythology and Other Basic Writings.* Translated by Schubert M. Ogden. Philadelphia: Fortress, 1984.

———. *Theology of the New Testament.* Translated by Kendrick Grobel. Waco: Baylor University Press, 2007.

———. "The Significance of the Old Testament for the Christian Faith." In *The Old Testament and the Christian Faith,* edited by Bernhard W. Anderson, 8–35. New York: Harper & Row, 1963.

Burnett, Richard E. *Karl Barth's Theological Exegesis: The Hermeneutical Principles of the Römerbrief Period.* Grand Rapids: Eerdmans, 2004.

Burtchaell, James Tunstead. *Catholic Theories of Biblical Inspiration Since 1810: A Review and Critique.* New York: Cambridge University Press, 1969.

Busch, Eberhard. *Karl Barth: His Life from Letters and Autobiographical Texts.* Translated by John Bowden. Grand Rapids: Eerdmans, 1976. Repr. Eugene, OR: Wipf & Stock, 2005.

Byassee, Jason. *Praise Seeking Understanding: Reading the Psalms with Augustine.* Grand Rapids: Eerdmans, 2007.

Calvin, John. *Institutes of the Christian Religion.* Translated by Henry Beveridge. Peabody, MA: Hendrickson, 2008.

Capetz, Paul E. "Theology and the Historical-Critical Study of the Bible." *Harvard Theological Review* 104:4 (2011): 459–88.

Carson, D. A. "Three More Books on the Bible: A Critical Review." *Trinity Journal* 27 (2006): 1–62.

Carter, Craig A. *The Politics of the Cross: The Theology and Social Ethics of John Howard Yoder.* Grand Rapids: Brazos, 2001.

Cary, Jeffrey W. *Free Churches and the Body of Christ: Authority, Unity, and Truthfulness.* Eugene, OR: Wipf & Stock, 2012.

Castelo, Daniel, and Robert W. Wall. *The Marks of Scripture: Rethinking the Nature of the Bible.* Grand Rapids: Baker Academic, 2019.

Catechism of the Catholic Church. 2nd ed. New York: Doubleday, 1995.

Cavanaugh, William T. *Field Hospital: The Church's Engagement with a Wounded World.* Grand Rapids: Eerdmans, 2016.

———. *Migrations of the Holy: God, State, and the Political Meaning of the Church.* Grand Rapids: Eerdmans, 2011.

———. "Politics and Reconciliation." In *The Blackwell Companion to Christian Ethics,* edited by Stanley Hauerwas and Samuel Wells, 196–208. Malden, MA: Blackwell, 2006.

———. *Torture and Eucharist: Theology, Politics, and the Body of Christ.* Malden, MA: Blackwell, 1998.

Chapman, Stephen B. *1 Samuel as Christian Scripture: A Theological Commentary*. Grand Rapids: Eerdmans, 2016.

Charry, Ellen. *By the Renewing of Your Minds: The Pastoral Function of Christian Doctrine*. New York: Oxford University Press, 1999.

Childs, Brevard S. *Biblical Theology in Crisis*. Philadelphia: Westminster, 1970.

——. *Biblical Theology of the Old and New Testaments: Theological Reflection on the Christian Bible*. Minneapolis: Fortress, 1992.

——. *The Church's Guide for Reading Paul: The Canonical Shaping of the Pauline Corpus*. Grand Rapids: Eerdmans, 2008.

——. *Introduction to the Old Testament as Scripture*. Minneapolis: Fortress, 1979.

——. *The New Testament as Canon: An Introduction*. Minneapolis: Fortress, 1985.

——. *Old Testament Theology in a Canonical Context*. Minneapolis: Fortress, 1985.

——. "The *Sensus Literalis* of Scripture: An Ancient and Modern Problem." In *Beiträge zur Alttestamentliche Theologie: Festschrift für Walther Zimmerli zum 70. Geburtstag*, edited by Herbert Donner, Robert Hanhart, and Rudolf Smend, 80–93. Göttingen: Vandenhoeck and Ruprecht, 1977.

——. "Speech-Act Theory and Biblical Interpretation." *Scottish Journal of Theology* 58:4 (2005): 375–92.

——. *The Struggle to Understand Isaiah as Christian Scripture*. Grand Rapids: Eerdmans, 2004.

Clark, Elizabeth A. *History, Theory, Text: Historians and the Linguistic Turn*. Cambridge: Harvard University Press, 2004.

Collins, John J. *The Bible after Babel: Historical Criticism in a Postmodern Age*. Grand Rapids: Eerdmans, 2005.

——. *Encounters with Biblical Theology*. Minneapolis: Fortress, 2005.

Cone, James H. *A Black Theology of Liberation*. 40th anniversary ed. Maryknoll, NY: Orbis, 2010.

——. *God of the Oppressed*. Rev. ed. Maryknoll, NY: Orbis, 1997.

Congar, Yves. *The Meaning of Tradition*. Translated by A. N. Woodrow. San Francisco: Ignatius, 2004.

Congdon, David W. *The Mission of Demythologizing: Rudolf Bultmann's Dialectical Theology*. Minneapolis: Fortress, 2015.

——. "The Word as Event: Barth and Bultmann on Scripture." In *The Sacred Text: Excavating the Texts, Exploring the Interpretations, and Engaging the Theologies of the Christian Scriptures*, edited by Michael Bird and Michael Pahl, 241–65. Piscataway, NJ: Gorgias, 2010.

Cooper-White, Pamela. "Intimate Violence against Women: Trajectories for Pastoral Care in a New Millennium." *Pastoral Psychology* 60:6 (2011): 809–55.

Cornell, Collin. "Are Greg Boyd and I Reading the Same Old Testament?" *The Christian Century*, 27 October 2017. Online at https://www.christiancentury.org/review/books/are-greg-boyd-and-i-reading-same-old-testament.

Cramer, David, Jenny Howell, Jonathan Tran, and Paul Martens. "Scandalizing John Howard Yoder." *The Other Journal*, 7 July 2014. Online at https://theotherjournal.com/2014/07/07/scandalizing-john-howard-yoder/.

Crisp, Oliver D. *Analyzing Doctrine: Toward a Systematic Theology*. Waco: Baylor University Press, 2019.

———. "Robert Jenson on the Pre-existence of Christ." *Modern Theology* 23:1 (2007): 27–45.

Croasmun, Matthew. *The Emergence of Sin: The Cosmic Tyrant in Romans*. New York: Oxford University Press, 2017.

Crumpton, Stephanie M. *A Womanist Pastoral Theology against Intimate and Cultural Violence*. New York: Palgrave Macmillan, 2014.

Cullmann, Oscar. "The Tradition." In *The Early Church: Studies in Early Christian History and Theology*, edited by A. J. B. Higgins, 59–99. London: SCM, 1956.

Cumin, Paul. "Robert Jenson and the Spirit of It All: or, You (Sometimes) Wonder Where Everything Else Went." *Scottish Journal of Theology* 60:2 (2007): 161–79.

Cunningham, Mary Kathleen. *What Is Theological Exegesis? Interpretation and Use of Scripture in Barth's Doctrine of Election*. Valley Forge, PA: Trinity Press International, 1995.

Daniélou, Jean. *Prayer as a Political Problem*. Edited and translated by J. R. Kirwan. Providence: Cluny, 2020.

Davidson, Ivor J. "In Memoriam: John Webster (1955–2016)." *International Journal of Systematic Theology* 18 (2016): 360–75.

———. "John." In *Theological Theology: Essays in Honour of John B. Webster*, edited by R. David Nelson, Darren Sarisky, and Justin Stratis, 17–36. New York: T&T Clark, 2015.

Davies, Philip R. *Whose Bible Is It Anyway?* 2nd ed. New York: T&T Clark, 2004.

Davis, Ellen F. *Opening Israel's Scriptures*. New York: Oxford University Press, 2019.

Davis, Ellen F., and Richard B. Hays, eds. *The Art of Reading Scripture*. Grand Rapids: Eerdmans, 2003.

Davison, Andrew. *Why Sacraments?* Eugene, OR: Cascade, 2013.

Dawson, John David. *Christian Figural Reading and the Fashioning of Identity*. Berkeley: University of California Press, 2001.

De La Torre, Miguel A. *Genesis*. Louisville: Westminster John Knox, 2011.

DeHart, Paul J. *The Trial of the Witnesses: The Rise and Decline of Postliberal Theology*. Malden, MA: Blackwell, 2006.

Dias, Elizabeth. "Pope Defrocks Theodore McCarrick, Ex-Cardinal Accused of Sexual Abuse." *New York Times*, 16 February 2019. Online at https://www.nytimes.com/2019/02/16/us/mccarrick-defrocked-vatican.html.

Doerksen, Paul G. *Beyond Suspicion: Post-Christendom Protestant Political Theology in John Howard Yoder and Oliver O'Donovan*. Eugene, OR: Wipf & Stock, 2009.

Dorrien, Gary. *The Barthian Revolt in Modern Theology: Theology without Weapons*. Louisville: Westminster John Knox, 2000.

———. *Kantian Reason and Hegelian Spirit: The Idealistic Logic of Modern Theology*. Malden, MA: Blackwell, 2012.

Duby, Steven J. *God in Himself: Scripture, Metaphysics, and the Task of Christian Theology*. Downers Grove, IL: IVP Academic, 2019.

Dulles, Avery Cardinal. *Models of the Church*. Exp. ed. New York: Image, 2002.

East, Brad. "Befriending Books: On Reading and Thinking with Alan Jacobs and Zena Hitz." *Mere Orthodoxy*, 23 November 2020. Online at https://mereorthodoxy.com/befriending-books-reading-thinking-alan-jacobs-zena-hitz/.

———. "The Church and the Spirit in Robert Jenson's Theology of Scripture." *Pro Ecclesia* 28:3 (2019): 278–300.

———. *The Doctrine of Scripture*. Eugene, OR: Cascade, 2021.

———. "God and All Things in God: The Theology of John Webster." *Mere Orthodoxy*, 20 August 2018. Online at https://mereorthodoxy.com/john-webster/.

———. "The Hermeneutics of Theological Interpretation: Holy Scripture, Biblical Scholarship, and Historical Criticism." *International Journal of Systematic Theology* 19:1 (2017): 30–52.

———. "The Jesus of History and the Gods of Natural Theology." *Los Angeles Review of Books*, 19 November 2020. Online at https://lareviewofbooks.org/article/the-jesus-of-history-and-the-gods-of-natural-theology/.

———. "John Webster, Theologian Proper." *Anglican Theological Review* 99:2 (2017): 333–51.

———. "Must Theologians Be Faithful? A Question for Volf and Croasmun." *Resident Theologian* blog, 24 October 2019. Online at https://www.bradeast.org/blog/2019/10/must-theologians-be-faithful-question.html.

———. "Reading the Trinity in the Bible: Assumptions, Warrants, Ends." *Pro Ecclesia* 25:4 (2016): 459–74.

———. "An Undefensive Presence: The Mission and Identity of the Church in Kathryn Tanner and John Howard Yoder." *Scottish Journal of Theology* 68:3 (2015): 327–44.

———. "What Are the Standards of Excellence for Theological Interpretation of Scripture?" *Journal of Theological Interpretation* 14:2 (2020): 149–79.

———. "What Is the Doctrine of the Trinity For? Practicality and Projection in Robert Jenson's Theology." *Modern Theology* 33:3 (2017): 414–33.

Ebeling, Gerhard. *The Word of God and Tradition: Historical Studies Interpreting the Divisions of Christianity.* Translated by S. H. Hooke. Philadelphia: Fortress, 1968.

———. *The Problem of Historicity in the Church and Its Proclamation.* Translated by Grover Foley. Philadelphia: Fortress, 1967.

Eitel, Adam. "The Resurrection of Jesus Christ: Karl Barth and the Historicization of God's Being." *International Journal of Systematic Theology* 10:1 (2008): 36–53.

Elie, Paul. "Confronting Flannery O'Connor's Racism." *Commonweal*, 12 August 2020. Online at https://www.commonwealmagazine.org/confront-facts-oconnor.

———. "How Racist Was Flannery O'Connor?" *The New Yorker*, 15 June 2020. Online at https://www.newyorker.com/magazine/2020/06/22/how-racist-was-flannery-oconnor.

———. *The Life You Save May Be Your Own: An American Pilgrimage.* New York: Farrar, Straus and Giroux, 2003.

———. "What Flannery Knew." *Commonweal*, 17 November 2008. Online at https://www.commonwealmagazine.org/what-flannery-knew.

Ens, Gerald. *Boundaries Thick and Permeable: Towards a Faithful and Vulnerable Ecclesiology with Yoder, Coles, and Merleau-Ponty.* Waterloo: Zwickau, 2014.

Ephrem the Syrian. *Hymns.* Translated by Kathleen E. McVey. The Classics of Western Spirituality. New York: Paulist, 1989.

Farkasfalvy, Denis. *A Theology of the Christian Bible: Revelation, Inspiration, Canon.* Washington, DC: Catholic University of America Press, 2018.

Farrow, Douglas, David Demson, and Joseph Augustine DiNoia. "Robert Jenson's *Systematic Theology*: Three Responses." *International Journal of Systematic Theology* 1:1 (1999): 89–104.

Farrow, Ronan. "From Aggressive Overtures to Sexual Assault: Harvey Weinstein's Accusers Tell Their Stories." *The New Yorker*, 10 October 2017. Online at https://www.newyorker.com/news/news-desk/from-aggressive-overtures-to-sexual-assault-harvey-weinsteins-accusers-tell-their-stories/.

Ferguson, Everett. *The Church of Christ: A Biblical Ecclesiology for Today.* Grand Rapids: Eerdmans, 1996.

———. *The Rule of Faith: A Guide.* Cascade Companions. Eugene, OR: Cascade, 2015.

Fischer, Zachary. *Preparing the Way for a Theological Theology: The Development and Explication of John Webster's Central Theological Principles.* Aschendorff: Münster, 2020.

Florovsky, Georges. *Bible, Church, Tradition: An Eastern Orthodox View.* Vol. 1 of *The Collected Works of Georges Florovsky.* Belmont, MA: Nordland Publishing Company, 1972.

Flynn, J. D. "Daniel Vanier, and What Comes Next." *Medium*, 7 March 2020. Online at https://medium.com/@jdflynn/daniel-vanier-and-what-comes-next-fb9a3250a234.

Ford, David F. *Barth and God's Story: Biblical Narrative and the Theological Method of Karl Barth in the Church Dogmatics.* 1985. Reprint, Eugene, OR: Wipf & Stock, 2008.

Ford, David F., and Graham Stanton, eds. *Reading Texts, Seeking Wisdom: Scripture and Theology.* Grand Rapids: Eerdmans, 2003.

Fortune, Marie M. *Sexual Violence: The Unmentionable Sin.* New York: Pilgrim, 1983.

Fowl, Stephen E. *Engaging Scripture: A Model for Theological Interpretation.* 1998. Reprint, Eugene, OR: Wipf & Stock, 2008.

———. *Idolatry.* Waco: Baylor University Press, 2019.

———. *The Story of Christ in the Ethics of Paul: An Analysis of the Function of the Hymnic Material in the Pauline Corpus.* Sheffield: JSOT, 1990.

———. *Theological Interpretation of Scripture.* Eugene, OR: Cascade, 2009.

———, ed. *The Theological Interpretation of Scripture: Classic and Contemporary Readings.* Malden, MA: Blackwell, 1997.

Francis de Sales, St. *The Catholic Controversy: St. Francis de Sales' Defense of the Faith.* Translated by Henry Benedict Mackey. 1886. Reprint, Charlotte, NC: TAN, 1989.

Frei, Hans W. "The Doctrine of Revelation in the Thought of Karl Barth,

1909–1922: The Nature of Barth's Break with Liberalism." PhD diss., Yale University, 1956.

———. *The Eclipse of Biblical Narrative: A Study in Eighteenth and Nineteenth Century Hermeneutics*. New Haven: Yale University Press, 1974.

———. *The Identity of Jesus Christ: The Hermeneutical Bases of Dogmatic Theology*. 1974. Reprint, Eugene, OR: Wipf & Stock, 1997.

———. "The 'Literal Reading' of Biblical Narrative in the Christian Tradition: Does It Stretch or Will It Break?" In *The Bible and the Narrative Tradition*, edited by Frank McConnell, 36–77. New York: Oxford University Press, 1986.

———. "Scripture as Realistic Narrative: Karl Barth as Critic of Historical Criticism." In *Thy Word Is Truth: Barth on Scripture*, edited by George Hunsinger, 49–63. Grand Rapids: Eerdmans, 2012.

———. *Types of Christian Theology*. Edited by George Hunsinger and William C. Placher. New Haven: Yale University Press, 1992.

Frey, Jennifer A. "Don't Cancel Flannery O'Connor." *First Things*, 29 July 2020. Online at https://www.firstthings.com/web-exclusives/2020/07/dont-cancel-flannery-oconnor.

Fryer, Gregory P. "Remembering My Teacher Robert W. Jenson." *Pro Ecclesia* 27:3 (2018): 259–62.

Fulkerson, Mary McClintock. *Places of Redemption: Theology for a Worldly Church*. New York: Oxford University Press, 2007.

Gallagher, Daniel. "The Obedience of Faith: Barth, Bultmann, and *Dei Verbum*." *Journal for Christian Theological Research* 10 (2005): 39–63.

Garrow, David J. "The Troubling Legacy of Martin Luther King." *Standpoint*, 30 May 2019. Online at https://standpointmag.co.uk/issues/june-2019/the-troubling-legacy-of-martin-luther-king/.

Gathercole, Simon. "Pre-existence, and the Freedom of the Son in Creation and Redemption: An Exposition in Dialogue with Robert Jenson." *International Journal of Systematic Theology* 7:1 (2005): 38–51.

Gaventa, Beverly Roberts, and Richard B. Hays, eds. *Seeking the Identity of Jesus: A Pilgrimage*. Grand Rapids: Eerdmans, 2008.

Gavrilyuk, Paul L. *The Suffering of the Impassible God: The Dialectics of Patristic Thought*. New York: Oxford University Press, 2004.

Gerhard, Johann. *On the Nature of Theology and Scripture*. Translated by Richard J. Dinda. St. Louis: Concordia, 2006.

———. *On Sacred Scripture, On Interpreting Sacred Scripture, Method of Theological Study*. Translated by Joshua J. Hayes. Edited by Benjamin T. G. Mayes. St. Louis: Concordia, 2017.

Gignilliat, Mark S. *Karl Barth and the Fifth Gospel: Barth's Theological Exegesis of Isaiah*. New York: Routledge, 2009.

Gilkey, Langdon. "Cosmology, Ontology, and the Travail of Biblical Language." *Journal of Religion* 41 (1961): 194–205.

Goossen, Rachel Waltner. "'Defanging the Beast': Mennonite Responses to John Howard Yoder's Sexual Abuse." *The Mennonite Quarterly Review* 89 (2015): 7–80.

——. "Mennonite Bodies, Sexual Ethics: Women Challenge John Howard Yoder." *Journal of Mennonite Studies* 34 (2016): 247–59.

Gordon, Joseph K. *Divine Scripture in Human Understanding: A Systematic Theology of the Christian Bible*. Notre Dame: University of Notre Dame Press, 2019.

Gould, Stephen Jay. *Rocks of Ages: Science and Religion in the Fullness of Life*. New York: Ballantine, 1999.

Green, Chris E. *The End Is Music: A Companion to Robert W. Jenson's Theology*. Eugene, OR: Cascade, 2018.

Green, Joel B. *Practicing Theological Interpretation: Engaging Biblical Texts for Faith and Formation*. Grand Rapids: Baker Academic, 2011.

Greene-McCreight, Kathryn E. *Ad Litteram: How Augustine, Calvin, and Barth Read the "Plain Sense" of Genesis 1–3*. New York: Peter Lang, 1999.

Gregory of Narek. *The Festal Works of St. Gregory of Narek: Annotated Translation of the Odes, Litanies, and Encomia*. Translated by Abraham Terian. Collegeville, MN: Liturgical, 2016.

Gregory, Eric. *Politics and the Order of Love: An Augustinian Ethic of Democratic Citizenship*. Chicago: University of Chicago Press, 2008.

Griffith, David. "Flannery O'Connor Didn't Care If You Liked Her Work." *Church Life Journal*, 29 June 2020. Online at https://churchlifejournal.nd.edu/articles/flannery-oconnor-didnt-care-if-you-liked-her-work/.

Griffiths, Paul J. *Christian Flesh*. Stanford: Stanford University Press, 2018.

——. *Decreation: The Last Things of All Creatures*. Waco: Baylor University Press, 2014.

——. *Intellectual Appetite: A Theological Grammar*. Washington, DC: Catholic University of America Press, 2009.

——. "On Radner's *Time and the Word*." *Pro Ecclesia* 27:3 (2018): 300–306.

——. *The Practice of Catholic Theology: A Modest Proposal*. Washington, DC: Catholic University of America Press, 2016.

——. *Religious Reading: The Place of Reading in the Practice of Religion*. New York: Oxford University Press, 1999.

———. *Song of Songs*. Brazos Theological Commentary on the Bible. Grand Rapids: Brazos, 2011.

———. "Which Are the Words of Scripture?" *Theological Studies* 72 (2011): 703–22.

Gritsch, Eric W. *Martin Luther's Anti-Semitism: Against His Better Judgment*. Grand Rapids: Eerdmans, 2012.

Gunton, Colin E. *The Christian Faith: An Introduction to Christian Doctrine*. Malden, MA: Blackwell, 2001.

———, ed. *Trinity, Time, and Church: A Response to the Theology of Robert W. Jenson*. Grand Rapids: Eerdmans, 2000.

Guth, Karen V. "Doing Justice to the Complex Legacy of John Howard Yoder: Restorative Justice Resources in Witness and Feminist Ethics." *Journal of the Society of Christian Ethics* 35:2 (2015): 119–39.

———. "Moral Injury and the Ethics of Teaching Tainted Legacies." *Teaching Theology & Religion* 21 (2018): 197–209.

Hahn, Scott W., and Benjamin Wiker. *Politicizing the Bible: The Roots of Historical Criticism and the Secularization of Scripture 1300–1700*. New York: Herder & Herder, 2013.

Hahn, Scott W., and Jeffrey L. Morrow. *Modern Biblical Criticism as a Tool of Statecraft (1700–1900)*. Steubenville, OH: Emmaus, 2020.

Hall, David D. *The Puritans: A Transatlantic History*. Princeton: Princeton University Press, 2019.

Harnack, Adolf von. *What Is Christianity?* Rev. ed. Translated by Thomas Bailey Saunders. New York: G. P. Putnam's Sons, 1908.

Harrison, Peter. *The Bible, Protestantism, and the Rise of Natural Science*. New York: Cambridge University Press, 1998.

———. *The Territories of Science and Religion*. Chicago: University of Chicago Press, 2015.

Hart, David Bentley. *In the Aftermath: Provocations and Laments*. Grand Rapids: Eerdmans, 2009.

Harvey, Barry. *Baptists and the Catholic Tradition: Reimagining the Church's Witness in the Modern World*. 2nd ed. Grand Rapids: Baker Academic, 2020.

Harvey, Lincoln. *Jesus in the Trinity: A Beginner's Guide to the Theology of Robert Jenson*. London: SCM, 2020.

Harvey, Van A. *The Historian and the Believer: The Morality of Historical Knowledge and Christian Belief*. Toronto: Macmillan, 1966.

Hatch, Nathan O. *The Democratization of American Christianity*. New Haven: Yale University Press, 1989.

Hauerwas, Stanley. "Begotten, Not Made: The Grammar of the Incarnation." *ABC Religion and Ethics*, 4 January 2017. Online at http://www.abc.net.au/religion/articles/2017/01/04/4600040.htm.

———. *A Better Hope: Resources for a Church Confronting Capitalism, Democracy, and Postmodernity.* Grand Rapids: Brazos, 2000.

———. *Christian Existence Today: Essays on Church, World, and Living in Between.* Grand Rapids: Brazos, 1988.

———. *A Community of Character: Toward a Constructive Christian Social Ethic.* Notre Dame: Notre Dame University Press, 1981.

———. *Hannah's Child: A Theologian's Memoir.* Grand Rapids: Eerdmans, 2010.

———. "In Defense of 'Our Respectable Culture': Trying to Make Sense of John Howard Yoder's Sexual Abuse." *ABC Religion & Ethics*, 18 October 2017. Online at https://www.abc.net.au/religion/in-defence-of-our-respectable-culture-trying-to-make-sense-of-jo/10095302.

———. *In Good Company: The Church as Polis.* Notre Dame: University of Notre Dame Press, 1995.

———. *Matthew.* Brazos Theological Commentary on the Bible. Grand Rapids: Brazos, 2006.

———. "Only Theology Overcomes Ethics; or, Why 'Ethicists' Must Learn from Jenson." In *Trinity, Time, and Church: A Response to the Theology of Robert W. Jenson,* edited by Colin Gunton, 252–68. Eugene, OR: Wipf & Stock, 2011.

———. *The Peaceable Kingdom: A Primer in Christian Ethics.* Notre Dame: Notre Dame University Press, 1983.

———. *Unleashing the Scripture: Freeing the Bible from Captivity to America.* Nashville: Abingdon, 1993.

———. *Without Apology: Sermons for Christ's Church.* New York: Seabury, 2013.

———. *Working with Words: On Learning to Speak Christian.* Eugene, OR: Wipf & Stock, 2011.

Hauerwas, Stanley, Chris K. Huebner, Harry J. Huebner, and Mark Thiessen Nation, eds. *The Wisdom of the Cross: Essays in Honor of John Howard Yoder.* Eugene, OR: Wipf & Stock, 1999.

Hauerwas, Stanley, and William H. Willimon. *Resident Aliens: Life in the Christian Colony.* Nashville: Abingdon, 1989.

Hays, Richard B. "The Future of *Christian* Biblical Scholarship." *Nova et Vetera* 4 (2006): 95–120.

———. *The Moral Vision of the New Testament: Community, Cross, New Creation: A Contemporary Introduction to New Testament Ethics.* San Francisco: HarperSanFrancisco, 1996.

———. *Reading with the Grain of Scripture*. Grand Rapids: Eerdmans, 2020.

Healy, Nicholas M. *Church, World, and the Christian Life: Practical-Prophetic Ecclesiology*. New York: Cambridge University Press, 2000.

———. *Hauerwas: A (Very) Critical Introduction*. Grand Rapids: Eerdmans, 2014.

———. "Practices and the New Ecclesiology: Misplaced Concreteness?" *International Journal of Systematic Theology* 5 (2003): 287–308.

Hector, Kevin W. *Theology without Metaphysics: God, Language, and the Spirit of Recognition*. New York: Cambridge University Press, 2011.

Heggen, Carolyn Holderread. "Sexual Abuse by Church Leaders and Healing for Victims." *The Mennonite Quarterly Review* 89 (2015): 81–93.

Hendreckson, David. "Monuments Can Be Destroyed, but Not Forgotten." *Christianity Today*, 9 September 2020. Online at https://www.christianitytoday.com/ct/2020/september-web-only/cut-stone-confederate-monuments-ryan-newson.html/.

Henry, James Daryn. *The Freedom of God: A Study in the Pneumatology of Robert Jenson*. New York: Lexington/Fortress Academic, 2018.

Hill, Wesley. Review of *The Domain of the Word*, by John Webster. *International Journal of Systematic Theology* 18:1 (2016): 118–20.

Hinlicky, Paul R. "How Theological Exegesis Disrupts Theological Tradition." *Harvard Theological Review* 114:1 (2021): 143–57.

———. "Theology after the Death of God." *Marginalia Review of Books*, 26 April 2019. Online at https://marginalia.lareviewofbooks.org/theology-after-the-death-of-god/.

Hitz, Zena. *Lost in Thought: The Hidden Pleasures of an Intellectual Life*. Princeton: Princeton University Press, 2020.

Holmes, Stephen R. "Radicalizing the *Communicatio*: Jenson's Theology in Confessional Lutheran Perspective." In *The Promise of Robert W. Jenson's Theology: Constructive Engagements*, edited by Stephen John Wright and Chris E. W. Green, 131–40. Minneapolis: Fortress, 2017.

Hughes, Richard T. *Reviving the Ancient Faith: The Story of Churches of Christ in America*. Abilene, TX: Abilene Christian University Press, 2008.

Hunsinger, George. *Disruptive Grace: Studies in the Theology of Karl Barth*. Grand Rapids: Eerdmans, 2000.

———. *How to Read Karl Barth: The Shape of His Theology*. New York: Oxford University Press, 1993.

———. "The Mediator of Communion: Karl Barth's Doctrine of the Holy Spirit." In *The Cambridge Companion to Karl Barth*, edited by John Webster, 177–94. New York: Cambridge University Press, 2000.

———. "Robert Jenson's *Systematic Theology*: A Review Essay." *Scottish Journal of Theology* 55:2 (2002): 161–200.

———, ed. *Thy Word Is Truth: Barth on Scripture*. Grand Rapids: Eerdmans, 2012.

———. "Truth as Self-Involving: Barth and Lindbeck on the Cognitive and Performative Aspects of Truth in Theological Discourse." *Journal of the American Academy of Religion* 61 (1993): 41–56.

Hunter, James Davison. *To Change the World: The Irony, Tragedy, and Possibility of Christianity in the Late Modern World*. New York: Oxford University Press, 2010.

Hunter-Bowman, Janna L. "Stanley Hauerwas's Response to John Howard Yoder's Legacy of Abuse is All About Yoder." *The Christian Century*, 26 October 2017. Online at https://www.christiancentury.org/blog-post/guest-post/opportunity-stanley-hauerwas-missed.

Jacobs, Alan. *Breaking Bread with the Dead: A Reader's Guide to a More Tranquil Mind*. New York: Penguin, 2020.

———. *A Theology of Reading: The Hermeneutics of Love*. Boulder, CO: Westview, 2001.

Jeanrond, Werner. *Text and Interpretation as Categories of Theological Thinking*. Translated by Thomas J. Wilson. New York: Crossroad, 1988.

———. *Theological Hermeneutics: Development and Significance*. New York: Crossroad, 1991.

Jeffrey, David Lyle. *Luke*. Grand Rapids: Brazos, 2012.

Jenkins, Philip. *The Next Christendom: The Coming of Global Christianity*. 3rd ed. New York: Oxford University Press, 2011.

Jennings, Willie James. *Acts*. Louisville: Westminster John Knox, 2017.

———. *The Christian Imagination: Theology and the Origins of Race*. New Haven: Yale University Press, 2010.

Jenson, Blanche. "You Shall Love the Lord with All Your Mind." *Pro Ecclesia* 27:3 (2018): 248–54.

Jenson, Robert W. *Alpha and Omega: A Study in the Theology of Karl Barth*. New York: Thomas Nelson & Sons, 1963.

———. "Can Ethical Disagreement Divide the Church?" In *The Morally Divided Body: Ethical Disagreement and the Disunity of the Church*, edited by Michael Root and James J. Buckley, 1–11. Eugene, OR: Wipf & Stock, 2012.

———. *Canon and Creed*. Louisville: Westminster John Knox, 2010.

———. "Christ in the Trinity: *Communicatio Idiomatum*." In *The Person of*

Christ, edited by Stephen R. Holmes and Murray A. Rae, 61–69. New York: T&T Clark, 2005.

———. "D. Stephen Long's *Saving Karl Barth*: An Agent's Perspective." *Pro Ecclesia* 24 (2015): 131–33.

———. *Essays in Theology of Culture*. Grand Rapids: Eerdmans, 1995.

———. *Ezekiel*. Brazos Theological Commentary on the Bible. Grand Rapids: Brazos, 2009.

———. *God after God: The God of the Past and the God of the Future as Seen in the Work of Karl Barth*. 1969. Reprint, Minneapolis: Fortress, 2010.

———. "The Hauerwas Project." *Modern Theology* 8 (1992): 285–95.

———. "Hermeneutics and the Life of the Church." In *Reclaiming the Bible for the Church*, edited by Carl E. Braaten and Robert W. Jenson, 89–106. Grand Rapids: Eerdmans, 1995.

———. "The Holy Spirit." In *Christian Dogmatics*, edited by Carl E. Braaten and Robert W. Jenson, 2:105–85. Philadelphia: Fortress, 1984.

———. "How Does Jesus Make a Difference?" In *Essentials of Christian Theology*, edited by William C. Placher, 191–205. Louisville: Westminster John Knox, 2003.

———. "How the World Lost Its Story." *First Things* 36 (1993): 19–24.

———. "It's the Culture." *First Things*, May 2014, 33–36.

———. "Jesus in the Trinity." *Pro Ecclesia* 8 (1999): 308–18.

———. *The Knowledge of Things Hoped For: The Sense of Theological Discourse*. New York: Oxford University Press, 1969.

———. *A Large Catechism*. 2nd ed. Delhi, NY: ALPB, 1999.

———. "Once More the *Logos Asarkos*." *International Journal of Systematic Theology* 13 (2011): 130–33.

———. "On the Authorities of Scripture." In *Engaging Biblical Authority: Perspectives on the Bible as Scripture*, edited by William P. Brown, 53–61. Louisville: Westminster John Knox, 2007.

———. *On the Inspiration of Scripture*. Delhi, NY: ALPB, 2012.

———. *On Thinking the Human: Resolutions of Difficult Notions*. Grand Rapids: Eerdmans, 2003.

———. "A Reply." *Scottish Journal of Theology* 52:1 (1999): 132.

———. "Reversals: How My Mind Has Changed." *The Christian Century*, 20 April 2010. Online at https://www.christiancentury.org/article/2010-04/reversals.

———. Review of *Barth's Moral Theology*, by John Webster. *International Journal of Systematic Theology* 2 (2000): 119–21.

———. Review of *On Christian Theology*, by Rowan Williams. *Pro Ecclesia* 11:3 (2002): 367–69.

———. "Scripture's Authority in the Church." In *The Art of Reading Scripture*, edited by Ellen F. Davis and Richard B. Hays, 27–37. Grand Rapids: Eerdmans, 2003.

———. "A Second Thought about Inspiration." *Pro Ecclesia* 13 (2004): 393–98.

———. "Some Riffs on Thomas Aquinas's *De ente et essentia*." In *Theological Theology: Essays in Honor of John B. Webster*, edited by R. David Nelson, Darren Sarisky, and Justin Stratis, 125–30. New York: T&T Clark, 2015.

———. *Song of Songs*. Interpretation: A Bible Commentary for Preaching and Teaching. Louisville: Westminster John Knox, 2005.

———. *Story and Promise: A Brief Theology of the Gospel about Jesus.* Philadelphia: Fortress, 1973.

———. "The Strange New World of the Bible." In *Sharper Than a Two-Edged Sword: Preaching, Teaching, and Living the Bible*, edited by Michael Root and James J. Buckley, 22–31. Grand Rapids: Eerdmans, 2008.

———. "A Theological Autobiography to Date." *Dialog* 46 (2007): 46–54.

———. *Theology as Revisionary Metaphysics: Essays on God and Creation.* Edited by Stephen John Wright. Eugene, OR: Wipf & Stock, 2014.

———. *A Theology in Outline: Can These Bones Live?* Transcribed, edited, and introduced by Adam Eitel. New York: Oxford University Press, 2016.

———. "Toward a Christian Doctrine of Israel." *CTI Reflections* 3 (2000): 2–21.

———. "Toward a Christian Theology of Judaism." In *Jews and Christians: People of God*, edited by Carl E. Braaten and Robert W. Jenson, 1–13. Grand Rapids: Eerdmans, 2003.

———. "The Triune God." In *Christian Dogmatics*, edited by Carl E. Braaten and Robert W. Jenson, 1:79–191. Philadelphia: Fortress, 1984.

———. *The Triune God.* Vol. 1 of *Systematic Theology*. New York: Oxford University Press, 1997.

———. *The Triune Identity: God According to the Gospel.* Philadelphia: Fortress, 1982.

———. *The Triune Story: Collected Essays on Scripture.* Edited by Brad East. New York: Oxford University Press, 2019.

———. *Unbaptized God: The Basic Flaw in Ecumenical Theology.* Minneapolis: Fortress, 1992.

———. *Visible Words: The Interpretation and Practice of Christian Sacraments.* Philadelphia: Fortress, 1978.

———. *The Works of God.* Vol. 2 of *Systematic Theology*. New York: Oxford University Press, 1999.

Jenson, Robert W., and Carl E. Braaten, eds. *Christian Dogmatics.* 2 vols. Philadelphia: Fortress, 1984.

Jenson, Robert W, and Eric W. Gritsch. *Lutheranism: The Theological Movement and Its Confessional Writings.* Philadelphia: Fortress, 1976.

Jenson, Robert W., and Eugene B. Korn, eds. *Covenant and Hope: Christian and Jewish Reflections: Essays in Constructive Theology from the Institute for Theological Inquiry.* Grand Rapids: Eerdmans, 2012.

———. *Plowshares into Swords? Reflections on Religion and Violence.* Efrat, Israel: Center for Jewish-Christian Understanding and Cooperation, 2014.

———. *Returning to Zion: Christian and Jewish Perspectives.* Efrat, Israel: Center for Jewish-Christian Understanding and Cooperation, 2015.

John Damascene, St. *Exposition of the Orthodox Faith.* Translated by S. D. F. Salmond. In vol. 9 of *The Nicene and Post-Nicene Fathers,* Series 2. Edited by Philip Schaff and Henry Wace. 1899. Reprint, Peabody, MA: Hendrickson, 2012.

Johnson, Elizabeth A. *She Who Is: The Mystery of God in Feminist Theological Discourse.* New York: Crossroad, 2002.

Johnson, Luke Timothy. *Constructing Paul.* Vol. 1 of *The Canonical Paul.* Grand Rapids: Eerdmans, 2020.

———. "The Crisis in Biblical Scholarship." *Commonweal,* 3 December 1993, 18–21.

———. *The Real Jesus: The Misguided Quest for the Historical Jesus and the Truth of the Traditional Gospels.* San Francisco: HarperSanFrancisco, 1996.

———. *The Writings of the New Testament: An Interpretation.* 3rd ed. Minneapolis: Fortress, 2010.

Johnson, Luke Timothy, and William S. Kurz. *The Future of Catholic Biblical Scholarship: A Constructive Conversation.* Grand Rapids: Eerdmans, 2002.

Jones, Serene. *Trauma and Grace: Theology in a Ruptured World.* 2nd ed. Louisville: Westminster John Knox, 2019.

Jowett, Benjamin. "On the Interpretation of Scripture." In *Essays and Reviews,* 330–433. London: Parker, 1860.

Kähler, Martin. *The So-Called Historical Jesus and the Historic Biblical Christ.* Translated by Carl E. Braaten. Philadelphia: Fortress, 1964.

Kantor, Jodi, and Megan Twohey. "Harvey Weinstein Paid Off Sexual Harassment Accusers for Decades." *New York Times,* 5 October 2017. Online at https://www.nytimes.com/2017/10/05/us/harvey-weinstein -harassment-allegations.html/.

Kelly, J. N. D. *Early Christian Doctrines*. Rev. ed. San Francisco: Harper and Row, 1978.

Kelsey, David H. *Eccentric Existence: A Theological Anthropology*. 2 vols. Louisville: Westminster John Knox, 2009.

———. *Human Anguish and God's Power*. New York: Cambridge University Press, 2021.

———. *Proving Doctrine: The Uses of Scripture in Modern Theology*. 1975. Reprint, Harrisburg, PA: Trinity Press International, 1999.

Kereszty, Roch A. *The Church of God in Jesus Christ: A Catholic Ecclesiology*. Washington, DC: Catholic University of America Press, 2019.

Kerr, Nathan R. *Christ, History, and Apocalyptic: The Politics of Christian Mission*. Eugene, OR: Cascade, 2009.

Kilby, Karen. *God, Evil, and the Limits of Theology*. New York: T&T Clark, 2020.

Kinzer, Mark S. *Post-Missionary Messianic Judaism: Redefining Christian Engagement with the Jewish People*. Grand Rapids: Brazos, 2005.

Kline, Peter. "Participation in God and the Nature of Christian Community: Robert Jenson and Eberhard Jüngel." *International Journal of Systematic Theology* 13:1 (2011): 38–61.

Köbler, Renate. *In the Shadow of Karl Barth: Charlotte von Kirschbaum*. Translated by Keith Crim. Louisville: Westminster John Knox, 1987.

Koontz, Gayle Gerber, "Seventy Times Seven: Abuse and the Frustratingly Extravagant Call to Forgive." *The Mennonite Quarterly Review* 89 (2015): 129–52.

Krall, Ruth. *The Mennonite Church and John Howard Yoder*. Vol. 3 of *The Elephants in God's Living Room*. 2013. Online at https://ruthkrall.com/downloadable-books/the-elephants-in-gods-living-room-series/volume-three-the-mennonite-church-and-john-howard-yoder-collected-essays/.

Kruger, Michael J. *The Question of Canon: Challenging the Status Quo in the New Testament Debate*. Downers Grove, IL: IVP Academic, 2013.

Lawson, Stephen D. "The Apostasy of the Church and the Cross of Christ: Hans Urs von Balthasar on the Mystery of the Church as *Casta Meretrix*." *Modern Theology* 36:2 (2020): 259–80.

Lee, Sang Hoon. "Toward an Understanding of the Eschatological Presence of the Risen Jesus with Robert Jenson." *Scottish Journal of Theology* 71:1 (2018): 85–101.

———. *Trinitarian Ontology and Israel in Robert W. Jenson's Theology*. Eugene, OR: Pickwick, 2016.

Legaspi, Michael C. *The Death of Scripture and the Rise of Biblical Studies.* New York: Oxford University Press, 2011.

——. "What Ever Happened to Historical Criticism?" *Journal of Religion & Society* 9 (2007): 1–11.

Leithart, Peter J. *Deep Exegesis: The Mystery of Reading Scripture.* Waco: Baylor University Press, 2009.

——. *Defending Constantine: The Twilight of an Empire and the Dawn of Christendom.* Downers Grove, IL: IVP Academic, 2010.

——. *The End of Protestantism: Pursuing Unity in a Fragmented Church.* Grand Rapids: Baker Academic, 2016.

Levenson, Jon D. *The Hebrew Bible, the Old Testament, and Historical Criticism: Jews and Christians in Biblical Studies.* Louisville: Westminster John Knox, 1993.

Levering, Matthew. *Christ and the Catholic Priesthood: Ecclesial Hierarchy and the Pattern of the Trinity.* Chicago: Hillenbrand, 2010.

——. *Christ's Fulfillment of Torah and Temple: Salvation According to Thomas Aquinas.* Notre Dame: University of Notre Dame Press, 2002.

——. *An Introduction to Vatican II as an Ongoing Theological Event.* Washington, DC: Catholic University of America Press, 2017.

——. *Mary's Bodily Assumption.* Notre Dame: University of Notre Dame Press, 2015.

——. *Participatory Biblical Exegesis: A Theology of Biblical Interpretation.* Notre Dame: University of Notre Dame Press, 2008.

——. *Scripture and Metaphysics: Aquinas and the Renewal of Trinitarian Theology.* Malden, MA: Blackwell, 2004.

——. "The Scriptures and Their Interpretation." In *The Oxford Handbook of Catholic Theology,* edited by Lewis Ayres and Medi Ann Volpe, 42–54. New York: Oxford University Press, 2019.

Levy, Ian Christopher. *Introducing Medieval Biblical Interpretation: The Senses of Scripture in Premodern Exegesis.* Grand Rapids: Baker Academic, 2018.

Lind, Millard C. *Yahweh Is a Warrior: The Theology of Warfare in Ancient Israel.* Scottdale, PA: Herald, 1980.

Lindbeck, George. "Barth and Textuality." *Theology Today* 43 (1986): 361–76.

——. *The Nature of Doctrine: Religion and Theology in a Postliberal Age.* Philadelphia: Westminster, 1984.

——. "Postcritical Canonical Interpretation: Three Modes of Retrieval." In *Theological Exegesis: Essays in Honor of Brevard S. Childs,* edited by

Christopher Seitz and Kathryn Greene-McCreight, 26–51. Grand Rapids: Eerdmans, 1998.

———. "Scripture, Consensus, and Community." In *Biblical Interpretation in Crisis: The Ratzinger Conference on Bible and Church*, edited by Richard John Neuhaus, 74–101. Grand Rapids: Eerdmans, 1989.

———. "The Story-Shaped Church: Critical Exegesis and Theological Interpretation." In *Scriptural Authority and Narrative Interpretation*, edited by Garrett Green, 39–52. Philadelphia: Fortress, 1987.

Lindsay, Mark R. *Barth, Israel, and Jesus: Karl Barth's Theology of Israel*. Aldershot: Ashgate, 2007.

Long, D. Stephen. "My Church Loyalties: Why I Am Not Yet a Catholic." *The Christian Century*, 28 July 2014. Online at https://www.christian century.org/article/2014-07/my-church-loyalties.

Long, Thomas G. *1 & 2 Timothy and Titus*. Louisville: Westminster John Knox, 2016.

Longenecker, Richard N. *Biblical Exegesis in the Apostolic Period*. 2nd ed. Grand Rapids: Eerdmans, 1999.

Louth, Andrew. *Discerning the Mystery: An Essay on the Nature of Theology*. New York: Oxford University Press, 1983.

Lubac, Henri de. *Medieval Exegesis: The Four Senses of Scripture*. Vol. 1. Ressourcement: Retrieval and Renewal in Catholic Thought. Translated by Mark Sebanc. Grand Rapids: Eerdmans, 1998.

Luther, Martin. *D. Martin Luthers Werke. Kritische Gesamtausgabe*. 73 vols. Weimar: Herman Böhlaus Nachfolger, 1883–2009.

MacDonald, Neil B. *Karl Barth and the Strange New World within the Bible: Barth, Wittgenstein, and the Metadilemmas of the Enlightenment*. Carlisle: Paternoster, 2000.

Mangina, Joseph L. *Karl Barth on the Christian Life: The Practical Knowledge of God*. Issues in Systematic Theology. New York: Peter Lang, 2001.

Markus, R. A. *Saeculum: History and Society in the Theology of St. Augustine*. 2nd ed. New York: Cambridge University Press, 1989.

Martens, Paul. *The Heterodox Yoder*. Eugene, OR: Cascade, 2012.

Martens, Paul, and David Cramer. "By What Criteria Does a 'Grand, Noble Experiment' Fail? What the Case of John Howard Yoder Reveals about the Mennonite Church." *The Mennonite Quarterly Review* 89 (2015): 171–93.

Martin, Dale B. *Sex and the Single Savior: Gender and Sexuality in Biblical Interpretation*. Louisville: Westminster John Knox, 2006.

Mathewes, Charles. *A Theology of Public Life*. New York: Cambridge University Press, 2007.

McBride, Jennifer M. *The Church for the World: A Theology of Public Witness*. New York: Oxford University Press, 2012.

McClendon, James Wm., Jr. *Doctrine*. Vol. 2 of *Systematic Theology*. Nashville: Abingdon, 1994.

——. *Ethics*. Vol. 1 of *Systematic Theology*. Rev. ed. Nashville: Abingdon, 2002.

——. "John Howard Yoder, One of Our Own (1927-1997)." *Perspectives in Religious Studies* 25 (1998): 21-26.

——. *Witness*. Vol. 3 of *Systematic Theology*. Nashville: Abingdon, 2000.

McCormack, Bruce L. "The Being of Holy Scripture Is in Becoming." In *Evangelicals and Scripture: Tradition, Authority, and Hermeneutics*, edited by Vincent Bacote, Laura C. Miguélez, and Dennis L. Okholm, 55-75. Downers Grove, IL: IVP, 2004.

——. "Historical Criticism and Dogmatic Interest in Karl Barth's Theological Exegesis of the New Testament." In *Biblical Hermeneutics in Historical Perspective*, edited by Mark S. Burrows and Paul Rorem, 322-38. Grand Rapids: Eerdmans, 1991.

——. *Karl Barth's Critically Realistic Dialectical Theology: Its Genesis and Development 1909-1936*. Oxford: Clarendon, 1995.

——. *Orthodox and Modern: Studies in the Theology of Karl Barth*. Grand Rapids: Baker Academic, 2008.

McDonald, Lee Martin. *The Biblical Canon: Its Origin, Transmission, and Authority*. 3rd ed. 1995. Reprint, Peabody, MA: Hendrickson, 2007.

McFadyen, Alistair. *Bound to Sin: Abuse, Holocaust, and the Christian Doctrine of Sin*. New York: Cambridge University Press, 2000.

McFarland, Ian A. "The Body of Christ: Rethinking a Classic Ecclesiological Model." *International Journal of Systematic Theology* 7 (2005): 225-45.

——. *The Divine Image: Envisioning the Invisible God*. Minneapolis: Fortress, 2005.

——. *In Adam's Fall: A Meditation on the Christian Doctrine of Original Sin*. Malden, MA: Blackwell, 2010.

——. *The Word Made Flesh: A Theology of the Incarnation*. Louisville: Westminster John Knox, 2019.

Milbank, John. *Being Reconciled: Ontology and Pardon*. New York: Routledge, 2003.

——. *The Word Made Strange: Theology, Language, Culture*. Malden, MA: Blackwell, 1997.

Milbank, John, Catherine Pickstock, and Graham Ward, eds. *Radical Orthodoxy: A New Theology*. New York: Routledge, 1998.

Miller, Ike. *Seeing by the Light: Illumination in Augustine's and Barth's Readings of John*. Downers Grove, IL: IVP Academic, 2020.

Miller-McLemore, Bonnie J. ed. *The Wiley Blackwell Companion to Practical Theology*. Malden, MA: Blackwell, 2014.

Moberly, R. W. L. *The Bible in a Disenchanted Age: The Enduring Possibility of Christian Faith*. Grand Rapids: Baker Academic, 2018.

———. *The Bible, Theology, and Faith: A Study of Abraham and Jesus*. New York: Cambridge University Press, 2000.

Molnar, Paul D. *Divine Freedom and the Doctrine of the Immanent Trinity*. 2nd ed. New York: T&T Clark, 2017.

———. Review of *Systematic Theology*, vol. 1: *The Triune God*, by Robert W. Jenson. *Scottish Journal of Theology* 52:1 (1999): 117–31.

Moore, Stephen D., and Yvonne Sherwood. *The Invention of the Biblical Scholar: A Critical Manifesto*. Minneapolis: Fortress, 2011.

Morgan, Robert. "*Sachkritik* in Reception History." *Journal for the Study of the New Testament* 33:2 (2010): 175–90.

Morgan, Robert, with John Barton. *Biblical Interpretation*. New York: Oxford University Press, 1988.

Morris, Wesley. "Cliff Huxtable Was Bill Cosby's Sickest Joke." *New York Times*, 26 April 2018. Online at https://www.nytimes.com/2018/04/26/arts/television/cosby-show-african-americans.html.

———. "How to Think about Bill Cosby and 'The Cosby Show.'" *New York Times*, 18 June 2017. Online at https://www.nytimes.com/2017/06/18/arts/television/how-to-think-about-bill-cosby-and-the-cosby-show.html.

———. "The Morality Wars." *New York Times Magazine*, 3 October 2018. Online at https://www.nytimes.com/interactive/2018/10/03/magazine/morality-social-justice-art-entertainment.html.

Morris, Wesley, and Rembert Browne. "The Bill Cosby Issue: Processing the Fall of an Icon." *Grantland*, 21 November 2014. Online at https://grantland.com/hollywood-prospectus/bill-cosby-rape-allegations-the-fall-of-an-icon/.

Morrow, Jeffrey L. *Pretensions of Objectivity: Toward a Criticism of Biblical Criticism*. Eugene, OR: Pickwick, 2019.

———. *Theology, Politics, and Exegesis: Essays on the History of Modern Biblical Criticism*. Eugene, OR: Pickwick, 2017.

Muller, Richard A. *Holy Scripture: The Cognitive Foundation of Theology*. Vol. 2 of *Post-Reformation Reformed Dogmatics*. Grand Rapids: Baker, 1993.

Murphy, Francesca Aran. *God Is Not a Story: Realism Revisited*. New York: Oxford University Press, 2007.

Nation, Mark Thiessen. *John Howard Yoder: Mennonite Patience, Evangelical Witness, Catholic Convictions*. Grand Rapids: Eerdmans, 2006.

Nelson, R. David, Darren Sarisky, and Justin Stratis, eds. *Theological Theology: Essays in Honour of John B. Webster*. New York: T&T Clark, 2015.

Neuhaus, Richard John, ed. *Biblical Interpretation in Crisis: The Ratzinger Conference on Bible and Church*. Grand Rapids: Eerdmans, 1989.

Newman, St. John Henry. *An Essay on the Development of Christian Doctrine*. 6th ed. 1888. Reprint, Notre Dame: University of Notre Dame Press, 1994.

Newsom, Carol A., and Sharon H. Ringe, eds. *Women's Bible Commentary*. Exp. ed. Louisville: Westminster John Knox, 1998.

Newson, Ryan Andrew. *Cut in Stone: Confederate Monuments and Theological Disruption*. Waco: Baylor University Press, 2020.

Niebuhr, H. Richard. *Christ and Culture*. San Francisco: HarperSanFrancisco, 2001.

Noble, Paul R. *The Canonical Approach: A Critical Reconstruction of the Hermeneutics of Brevard S. Childs*. New York: Brill, 1995.

———. "The *Sensus Literalis*: Jowett, Childs, and Barr." *The Journal of Theological Studies* 44:1 (1993): 1–23.

Novak, David. "Theology and Philosophy: An Exchange with Robert Jenson." In *Trinity, Time, and Church: A Response to the Theology of Robert W. Jenson*, edited by Colin Gunton, 42–61. Eugene, OR: Wipf & Stock, 2011.

Nugent, John C. *The Politics of Yahweh: John Howard Yoder, the Old Testament, and the People of God*. Eugene, OR: Cascade, 2011.

Ochs, Peter. "A Jewish Reading of *Trinity, Time and the Church: A Response to the Theology of Robert W. Jenson*." *Modern Theology* 19 (2003): 419–27.

———. "Robert W. Jenson: The God of Israel and the Fruits of Trinitarian Theology." In *Another Reformation: Postliberal Christianity and the Jews*, 63–91. Grand Rapids: Baker Academic, 2011.

O'Donnell, Angela Alaimo. "The 'Canceling' of Flannery O'Connor?" *Commonweal*, 3 August 2020. Online at https://www.commonwealmagazine.org/cancelling-flannery-oconnor.

———. *Radical Ambivalence: Race in Flannery O'Connor*. New York: Fordham University Press, 2020.

O'Donnell, Karen, and Katie Cross. *Feminist Trauma Theologies: Body, Scripture, and Church in Critical Perspective*. London: SCM, 2020.

O'Donovan, Oliver. *The Desire of the Nations: Rediscovering the Roots of Political Theology*. New York: Cambridge University Press, 1999.

———. "The Moral Authority of Scripture." In *Scripture's Doctrine and Theology's Bible: How the New Testament Shapes Christian Dogmatics*, edited by Markus Bockmuehl and Alan J. Torrance, 165–75. Grand Rapids: Baker Academic, 2008.

Oppenheimer, Mark. "A Theologian's Influence, and Stained Past, Live On." *New York Times*, 11 October 2013. Online at https://www.nytimes.com/2013/10/12/us/john-howard-yoders-dark-past-and-influence-lives-on-for-mennonites.html.

Origen. *On First Principles*. 2 vols. Edited and translated by John Behr. New York: Oxford University Press, 2017.

Paddison, Angus. *Scripture: A Very Theological Proposal*. New York: T&T Clark, 2009.

———. "Theological Exegesis and John Howard Yoder." *Princeton Theological Review* 14 (2008): 27–40.

Paddison, Angus, ed. *Theologians on Scripture*. New York: Bloomsbury, 2016.

Pannenberg, Wolfhart. "A Trinitarian Synthesis." *First Things*, May 2000, 49–53.

Park, Joon-Sik. *Missional Ecclesiologies in Creative Tension: H. Richard Niebuhr and John Howard Yoder*. New York: Peter Lang, 2007.

Parler, Branson L. *Things Hold Together: John Howard Yoder's Trinitarian Theology of Culture*. Harrisonburg, VA: Herald, 2012.

Peeler, Amy L. B. *You Are My Son: The Family of God in the Epistle to the Hebrews*. New York: T&T Clark, 2015.

Pelikan, Jaroslav. *Acts*. Grand Rapids: Brazos, 2005.

———. *The Christian Tradition: A History of the Development of Doctrine*. 5 vols. Chicago: University of Chicago Press, 1971–1989.

Perrin, Nicholas, and Richard B. Hays, eds. *Jesus, Paul, and the People of God: A Theological Dialogue with N. T. Wright*. Downers Grove, IL: IVP Academic, 2011.

Pierce, Madison N. *Divine Discourse in the Epistle to the Hebrews: The Recontextualization of Spoken Quotations of Scripture*. Society for New Testament Studies Monograph Series 178. New York: Cambridge University Press, 2020.

Pitts, Jamie. "Anabaptist Re-Vision: On John Howard Yoder's Misrecognized Sexual Politics." *The Mennonite Quarterly Review* 89 (2015): 153–70.

Ployd, Adam. *Augustine, the Trinity, and the Church: A Reading of the Anti-Donatist Sermons*. Oxford University Press, 2015.

Polet, Jeffrey. "The Problem of Eric Gill." *Local Culture* 2:1 (2020): 46–55.

Poling, James Newton. *Understanding Male Violence: Pastoral Care Issues*. Danvers, MA: Chalice, 2003.

Preus, J. Samuel. *Spinoza and the Irrelevance of Biblical Authority*. New York: Cambridge University Press, 2001.

Preus, Robert. *The Inspiration of Scripture: A Study of the Theology of the 17th Century Lutheran Dogmaticians*. St. Louis: Concordia, 1957.

Radner, Ephraim. *The End of the Church: A Pneumatology of Christian Division in the West*. Grand Rapids: Eerdmans, 1998.

———. *Hope among the Fragments: The Broken Church and Its Engagement of Scripture*. Grand Rapids: Brazos, 2004.

———. *Time and the Word: Figural Reading of the Christian Scriptures*. Grand Rapids: Eerdmans, 2016.

Rae, Murray A. *History and Hermeneutics*. New York: T&T Clark, 2005.

Rahner, Karl. *Inspiration in the Bible*. Translated by Charles H. Henkey. New York: Herder & Herder, 1961.

Rambo, Shelly. *Resurrecting Wounds: Living in the Afterlife of Trauma*. Waco: Baylor University Press, 2017.

———. *Spirit and Trauma: A Theology of Remaining*. Louisville: Westminster John Knox, 2010.

Ransby, Barbara. "A Black Feminist's Response to Attacks on Martin Luther King Jr.'s Legacy." *New York Times*, 3 June 2019. Online at https://www.nytimes.com/2019/06/03/opinion/martin-luther-king-fbi.html.

Ratzinger, Joseph (Benedict XVI). *Church, Ecumenism, and Politics: New Endeavors in Ecclesiology*. Translated by Michael J. Miller et al. San Francisco: Ignatius, 2008.

———. *God's Word: Scripture, Tradition, Office*. San Francisco: Ignatius, 2008.

———. *Jesus of Nazareth*. 3 vols. San Francisco: Ignatius, 2007–2012.

———, ed. *Schriftauslegung im Widerstreit*. Freiburg: Herder, 1989.

———. *The Word of the Lord: Verbum Domini*. Post-Synodal Apostolic Exhortation. English translation online at http://www.vatican.va/content/benedict-xvi/en/apost_exhortations/documents/hf_ben-xvi_exh_20100930_verbum-domini.html.

Reed, Adolph, Jr. Review of Richard J. Herrnstein and Charles Murray's *The Bell Curve*. In *Left Hooks, Right Crosses: A Decade of Political Writing*. Edited by Christopher Hitchens and Christopher Caldwell, 63–79. New York: Thunder's Mouth/Nation, 2002.

Reimer, A. James. "Theological Orthodoxy and Jewish Christianity: A Personal Tribute to John Howard Yoder." In *The Wisdom of the Cross: Essays in Honor of John Howard Yoder*, edited by Stanley Hauerwas, Chris K. Huebner, Harry J. Huebner, and Mark Thiessen Nation, 430–48. Eugene, OR: Wipf & Stock, 1999.

Reno, R. R. "Biblical Theology and Theological Exegesis." In *Out of Egypt: Biblical Theology and Biblical Interpretation*, edited by Craig Bartholomew, Mary Healy, Karl Möller, and Robin Parry, 385–408. Grand Rapids: Zondervan, 2004.

Reventlow, Henning Graf. *The Authority of the Bible and the Rise of the Modern World*. Translated by John Bowden. Minneapolis: Fortress, 1985.

———. *From Late Antiquity to the End of the Middle Ages*. Translated by James O. Duke. Vol. 2 of *History of Biblical Interpretation*. Atlanta: Society of Biblical Literature, 2009.

———. *From the Enlightenment to the Twentieth Century*. Translated by Leo G. Perdue. Vol. 4 of *History of Biblical Interpretation*. Atlanta: Society of Biblical Literature, 2010.

———. *Renaissance, Reformation, Humanism*. Translated by James O. Duke. Vol. 3 of *History of Biblical Interpretation*. Atlanta: Society of Biblical Literature, 2010.

Rogers, Eugene F., Jr. *After the Spirit: A Constructive Pneumatology from Resources outside the Modern West*. Grand Rapids: Eerdmans, 2005.

———. *Sexuality and the Christian Body: Their Way into the Triune God*. Malden, MA: Blackwell, 1999.

Rogers, Jack B., and Donald K. McKim. *The Authority and Interpretation of the Bible: An Historical Approach*. 1979. Reprint, Eugene, OR: Wipf & Stock, 1999.

Rook, Russell D. *Rhyming Hope and History: Theology and Culture in the Work of Robert Jenson*. Eugene, OR: Wipf & Stock, 2011.

Rosato, Philip J. *The Spirit as Lord: The Pneumatology of Karl Barth*. New York: T&T Clark, 1981.

Roth, John D., ed. *Constantine Revisited: Leithart, Yoder, and the Constantinian Debate*. Eugene, OR: Pickwick, 2013.

Runia, Klaas. *Karl Barth's Doctrine of Holy Scripture*. Grand Rapids: Eerdmans, 1962.

Sanders, Fred. *The Triune God*. New Studies in Dogmatics. Grand Rapids: Zondervan, 2016.

Sanneh, Lamin. *Disciples of All Nations: Pillars of World Christianity*. New York: Oxford University Press, 2008.

——. *Whose Religion Is Christianity? The Gospel Beyond the West*. Grand Rapids: Eerdmans, 2003.

Sarisky, Darren. *Reading the Bible Theologically*. New York: Cambridge University Press, 2019.

——. *Scriptural Interpretation: A Theological Exploration*. Malden, MA: Wiley-Blackwell, 2012.

——. "What Is Theological Interpretation? The Example of Robert W. Jenson." *International Journal of Systematic Theology* 12:2 (2010): 201–16.

Sarisky, Darren, ed. *Theology, History, and Biblical Interpretation: Modern Readings*. New York: Bloomsbury, 2015.

Scarsella, Hilary. "Not Making Sense: Why Stanley Hauerwas's Response to Yoder's Sexual Abuse Misses the Mark." *ABC Religion & Ethics*, 30 November 2017. Online at https://www.abc.net.au/religion/not-making-sense-why-stanley-hauerwass-response-to-yoders-sexual/10095168.

Scarsella, Hilary, and Stephanie Krehbiel. "Sexual Violence: Christian Theological Legacies and Responsibilities." *Religion Compass* 13:9 (2019): https://doi.org/10.1111/rec3.12337.

Schlesinger, Eugene R. "Trinity, Incarnation, and Time: A Restatement of the Doctrine of God in Conversation with Robert Jenson." *Scottish Journal of Theology* 69:2 (2016): 189–203.

Schmemann, Alexander. *The Eucharist: Sacrament of the Kingdom*. Translated by Paul Kachur. Crestwood, NY: St. Vladimir's Seminary Press, 1987.

——. *Of Water and the Spirit: A Liturgical Study of Baptism*. Crestwood, NY: St. Vladimir's Seminary Press, 1974.

Schmidt, Simon P. *Church and World: Eusebius's, Augustine's, and Yoder's Interpretations of the Constantinian Shift*. Princeton Theological Monograph Series 237. Eugene, OR: Pickwick, 2020.

Schneiders, Sandra M. *The Revelatory Text: Interpreting the New Testament as Sacred Scripture*. 2nd ed. Collegeville, MN: Liturgical, 1999.

Schooping, Joshua, ed. *The Holy Standards: The Creeds, Confessions of Faith, and Catechisms of the Eastern Orthodox Church*. Olyphant, PA: St. Theophan the Recluse, 2020.

Schreiner, Thomas R. *Interpreting the Pauline Epistles*. Grand Rapids: Baker Academic, 1990.

Schüssler Fiorenza, Elisabeth. *Bread Not Stone: The Challenge of Feminist Biblical Interpretation*. Boston: Beacon, 1985.

——. *In Memory of Her: A Feminist Theological Reconstruction of Christian Origins*. 10th anniv. ed. New York: Crossroad, 1994.

Schwartz, Yishai. "A Living Memory: Amalek, Forgetting, and the Lessons of Jewish Memory." *Comment*, 12 March 2020. Online at https://www.cardus.ca/comment/article/a-living-memory/.

Schweitzer, Albert. *The Quest of the Historical Jesus*. Translated by W. Montgomery. 1906. Reprint, Mineola, NY: Dover, 2005.

Schwöbel, Christoph. "The Creature of the Word: Recovering the Ecclesiology of the Reformers." In *On Being the Church: Essays on the Christian Community*, edited by Colin Gunton and Daniel W. Hardy, 110–55. Edinburgh: T&T Clark, 1989.

Seitz, Christopher R. *Convergences: Canon and Catholicity*. Waco: Baylor University Press, 2020.

Selinger, Suzanne. *Charlotte von Kirschbaum and Karl Barth: A Study in Biography and the History of Theology*. University Park, PA: Pennsylvania State University Press, 1998.

Sertillanges, A. G. *The Church: A Comprehensive Study in Ecclesiology*. 1922. Reprint, Providence, RI: Cluny, 2020.

Sheehan, Jonathan. *The Enlightenment Bible: Translation, Scholarship, Culture*. Princeton: Princeton University Press, 2005.

Sholl, Brian K. "On Robert Jenson's Trinitarian Thought." *Modern Theology* 18:1 (2002): 27–36.

Sider, Alexander. *To See History Doxologically: History and Holiness in John Howard Yoder's Ecclesiology*. Grand Rapids: Eerdmans, 2011.

Silliman, Daniel, and Kate Shellnutt. "Ravi Zacharias Hid Hundreds of Pictures of Women, Abuse during Massages, and a Rape Allegation." *Christianity Today*, 11 February 2021. Online at https://www.christianitytoday.com/news/2021/february/ravi-zacharias-rzim-investigation-sexual-abuse-sexting-rape.html.

Slee, Nicola. *Fragments for Fractured Times: What Feminist Practical Theology Brings to the Table*. London: SCM, 2020.

Smith, Christian. *The Bible Made Impossible: Why Biblicism Is Not a Truly Evangelical Reading of Scripture*. Grand Rapids: Brazos, 2011.

Smith, James K. A. *Awaiting the King: Reforming Public Theology*. Grand Rapids: Baker Academic, 2017.

———. *The Fall of Interpretation: Philosophical Foundations for a Creational Hermeneutic*. 2nd ed. Grand Rapids: Baker Academic, 2012.

Smith, Mitzi J., ed. *I Found God in Me: A Womanist Biblical Hermeneutics Reader*. Eugene, OR: Cascade, 2015.

Smith, Wilfred Cantwell. *What Is Scripture? A Comparative Approach*. Minneapolis: Fortress, 1993.

Sommer, Benjamin D. *Revelation and Authority: Sinai in Jewish Scripture and Tradition.* New Haven: Yale University Press, 2015.

Sonderegger, Katherine. *The Doctrine of God.* Vol. 1 of *Systematic Theology.* Minneapolis: Fortress, 2015.

———. *That Jesus Christ Was Born a Jew: Karl Barth's "Doctrine of Israel."* University Park, PA: Pennsylvania State University Press, 1992.

Soto Albrecht, Elizabeth, and Darryl W. Stephens, eds. *Liberating the Politics of Jesus: Renewing Peace Theology through the Wisdom of Women.* New York: T&T Clark, 2020.

Soulen, R. Kendall. *The God of Israel and Christian Theology.* Minneapolis: Fortress, 1996.

Spencer, Archie J. *The Analogy of Faith: The Quest for God's Speakability.* Downers Grove, IL: IVP Academic, 2015.

Spinoza, Baruch. *Theological-Political Treatise.* Edited by Jonathan Israel. Translated by Michael Silverthorne and Jonathan Israel. New York: Cambridge University Press, 2007.

Stanglin, Keith D. *The Letter and Spirit of Biblical Interpretation: From the Early Church to Modern Practice.* Grand Rapids: Baker Academic, 2018.

Stanley, Brian. *Christianity in the Twentieth Century: A World History.* Princeton: Princeton University Press, 2018.

Steinfels, Peter. "John H. Yoder, Theologian at Notre Dame, Is Dead at 70." *New York Times,* 7 January 1998. Online at http://www.nytimes.com/1998/01/07/us/john-h-yoder-theologian-at-notredame-is-dead-at-70.html.

Suzukamo, Leslie Brooks. "E-mail Address Led Police to U Professor." *St. Paul Pioneer Press,* 29 July 2001. Online at https://emmalabs.com/news/5213.html.

Swain, Scott R. *The God of the Gospel: Robert Jenson's Trinitarian Theology.* Downers Grove, IL: IVP Academic, 2011.

———. *Trinity, Revelation, and Reading: A Theological Introduction to the Bible and Its Interpretation.* New York: T&T Clark, 2011.

Sweeney, Douglas A. "Ratzinger on Scripture, Tradition, and Church: An Evangelical Assessment." In *Joseph Ratzinger and the Healing of the Reformation-Era Divisions,* edited by Emery de Gaál and Matthew Levering, 349–71. Steubenville: Emmaus Academic, 2019.

Sykes, Stephen W., ed. *Karl Barth: Centenary Essays.* New York: Cambridge University Press, 1989.

———, ed. *Karl Barth: Studies of His Theological Method.* New York: Clarendon, 1979.

Tanner, Kathryn. *Christ the Key*. New York: Cambridge University Press, 2009.

———. *God and Creation in Christian Theology: Tyranny or Empowerment?* 1988. Reprint, Minneapolis: Fortress, 2005.

———. *Jesus, Humanity, and the Trinity: A Brief Systematic Theology*. Minneapolis: Fortress, 2001.

———. "Scripture as Popular Text." In *Theology and Scriptural Imagination*, edited by L. Gregory Jones and James J. Buckley, 117–36. Malden, MA: Blackwell, 1998.

———. "Theology and the Plain Sense." In *Scriptural Authority and Narrative Interpretation*, edited by Garrett Green, 59–78. Philadelphia: Fortress, 1987.

———. *Theories of Culture: A New Agenda for Theology*. Minneapolis: Fortress, 1997.

Tapie, Matthew A. *Aquinas on Israel and the Church: The Question of Supersessionism in the Theology of Thomas Aquinas*. Eugene, OR: Pickwick, 2014.

Taylor, Derek W. *Reading Scripture as the Church: Dietrich Bonhoeffer's Hermeneutic of Discipleship*. Downers Grove, IL: IVP Academic, 2020.

Thiemann, Ronald. "Response to George Lindbeck." *Theology Today* 43 (1986): 377–82.

Thomas Aquinas, St. *The Aquinas Catechism: A Simple Explanation of the Catholic Faith by the Church's Greatest Theologian*. Manchester, NH: Sophia Institute, 2000.

———. *Summa Theologica*. 5 vols. Translated by the Fathers of the English Dominican Province. Notre Dame: Christian Classics, 1948.

Thompson, Mark D. "The Generous Gift of a Gracious Father: Toward a Theological Account of the Clarity of Scripture." In *The Enduring Authority of the Christian Scriptures*, edited by D. A. Carson, 625–43. Grand Rapids: Eerdmans, 2016.

———. "Witness to the Word: On Barth's Doctrine of Scripture." In *Engaging with Barth: Contemporary Evangelical Critiques*, edited by David Gibson and Daniel Strange, 168–97. New York: T&T Clark, 2009.

Thurian, Max, ed. *Churches Respond to BEM*. Vol. 6. Geneva: World Council of Churches, 1988.

Tietz, Christiane. *Karl Barth: A Life in Conflict*. Translated by Victoria J. Barnett. New York: Oxford University Press, 2021.

———. "Karl Barth and Charlotte von Kirschbaum." *Theology Today* 74:2 (2017): 86–111.

Tonstad, Linn Marie. *Queer Theology*. Eugene, OR: Cascade, 2018.

Torrance, T. F. "The Legacy of Karl Barth (1886–1986)." *Scottish Journal of Theology* 39 (1986): 289–308.

Townes, Emilie, ed. *A Troubling in My Soul: Womanist Perspectives on Evil and Suffering.* Maryknoll, NY: Orbis, 1993.

Treier, Daniel J. *Introducing Evangelical Theology.* Grand Rapids: Baker Academic, 2019.

———. *Introducing Theological Interpretation of Scripture: Recovering a Christian Practice.* Grand Rapids: Baker Academic, 2008.

———. "What Is Theological Interpretation? An Ecclesiological Reduction." *International Journal of Systematic Theology* 12:2 (2010): 144–61.

Trible, Phyllis. *Texts of Terror: Literary-Feminist Readings of Biblical Narratives.* Minneapolis: Fortress, 1984.

Troeltsch, Ernst. *The Absoluteness of Christianity and the History of Religions.* Translated by David Reid. Richmond, VA: John Knox, 1971.

———. "Historical and Dogmatic Method in Theology." In *Religion in History,* translated by James Luther Adams and Walter F. Bense, 11–32. Minneapolis: Fortress, 1991.

Turner, Denys. *Eros and Allegory: Medieval Exegesis of the Song of Songs.* Kalamazoo, MI: Cistercian, 1995.

Turretin, Francis. *First Through Tenth Topics.* Vol. 1 of *Institutes of Elenctic Theology.* Translated by George Musgrave Giger. Edited by James T. Dennison Jr. Phillipsburg, NJ: P&R Publishing, 1992.

Tushnet, Eve, ed. *Christ's Body, Christ's Wounds: Staying Catholic When You've Been Hurt in the Church.* Eugene, OR: Cascade, 2018.

Vanhoozer, Kevin J. *Biblical Authority after Babel: Retrieving the Solas in the Spirit of Mere Protestant Christianity.* Grand Rapids: Brazos, 2016.

———. *The Drama of Doctrine: A Canonical-Linguistic Approach to Christian Theology.* Louisville: Westminster John Knox, 2005.

———. "Expounding the Word of the Lord." In *The Theology of Benedict XVI: A Protestant Appreciation,* edited by Tim Perry, 66–86. Bellingham, WA: Lexham, 2019.

———. *Is There a Meaning in This Text? The Bible, the Reader, and the Morality of Literary Knowledge.* Grand Rapids: Zondervan Academic, 2009.

Vanhoozer, Kevin J., with Craig G. Bartholomew, Daniel J. Treier, and N. T. Wright, eds. *Dictionary for Theological Interpretation of the Bible.* Grand Rapids: Baker Academic, 2005.

Villegas, Isaac Samuel. "The Ecclesial Ethics of John Howard Yoder's Abuse." *Modern Theology* 31 (2021): 191–214.

Volf, Miroslav. *After Our Likeness: The Church as the Image of the Trinity*. Grand Rapids: Eerdmans, 1998.

———. *Captive to the Word of God: Engaging the Scriptures for Contemporary Theological Reflection*. Grand Rapids: Eerdmans, 2010.

Volf, Miroslav, and Matthew Croasmun. *For the Life of the World: Theology That Makes a Difference*. Grand Rapids: Brazos, 2019.

Ward, Pete, ed. *Perspectives on Ecclesiology and Ethnography*. Grand Rapids: Eerdmans, 2012.

Ware, Timothy (Kallistos). *The Orthodox Church: An Introduction to Eastern Christianity*. 3rd ed. New York: Penguin, 2015.

Warfield, B. B. *The Inspiration and Authority of the Bible*. Edited by Samuel G. Craig. Philadelphia: P&R Publishing Company, 1967.

———. *The Significance of the Westminster Standards as a Creed*. New York: Charles Scribner's Sons, 1898.

Warner, Megan, Christopher Southgate, Carla A. Grosch-Miller, and Hilary Ison, eds. *Tragedies and Christian Congregations: The Practical Theology of Trauma*. New York: Routledge, 2020.

Warnock, Raphael G. *The Divided Mind of the Black Church: Theology, Piety, and Public Witness*. New York: New York University Press, 2014.

Watson, Francis. "The Bible." In *Cambridge Companion to Karl Barth*, edited by John Webster, 57–71. New York: Cambridge University Press, 2000.

———. "Does Historical Criticism Exist? A Contribution to Debate on the Theological Interpretation of Scripture." In *Theological Theology: Essays in Honor of John B. Webster*, edited by R. David Nelson, Darren Sarisky, and Justin Stratis, 307–18. New York: T&T Clark, 2015.

———. *Text, Church, and World: Biblical Interpretation in Theological Perspective*. Grand Rapids: Eerdmans, 1994.

Weaver, Alain Epp. "Missionary Christology: John Howard Yoder and the Creeds." *The Mennonite Quarterly Review* 74 (2000): 423–39.

Webster, John. *Barth*. 2nd ed. New York: Continuum, 2004.

———. "Barth, Karl." In *Dictionary for Theological Interpretation of the Bible*, edited by Kevin J. Vanhoozer with Craig G. Bartholomew, Daniel J. Treier, and N. T. Wright, 82–84. Grand Rapids: Baker Academic, 2005.

———. *Barth's Ethics of Reconciliation*. New York: Cambridge University Press, 1995.

———. *Barth's Moral Theology: Human Action in Barth's Thought*. Grand Rapids: Eerdmans, 1998.

———. "Canon and Criterion: Some Reflections on a Recent Proposal." *Scottish Journal of Theology* 54 (2001): 67–83.

——. *Christ Our Salvation: Expositions and Proclamations*. Edited by Daniel Bush. Bellingham, WA: Lexham, 2020.

——. *Confessing God: Essays in Christian Dogmatics II*. New York: T&T Clark, 2016.

——. "Courage." In *Virtue and Intellect*, vol. 2 of *God without Measure: Working Papers in Christian Theology*, 87–102. New York: T&T Clark, 2016.

——. *The Culture of Theology*. Edited by Ivor J. Davidson and Alden C. McCray. Grand Rapids: Baker Academic, 2019.

——. "David F. Ford: *Self and Salvation*." *Scottish Journal of Theology* 54 (2001): 548–59.

——. "The Dignity of Creatures." In *The God of Love and Human Dignity: Essays in Honour of George M. Newlands*, edited by Paul Middleton, 19–33. New York: T&T Clark, 2007.

——. "Discovering Dogmatics." In *Shaping a Theological Mind: Theological Context and Methodology*, edited by Darren C. Marks, 129–36. Burlington, VT: Ashgate, 2002.

——. *The Domain of the Word: Scripture and Theological Reason*. New York: T&T Clark, 2012.

——. "Ecclesiocentrism: A Review of *Hauerwas: A (Very) Critical Introduction*." *First Things*, October 2014. Online at https://www.firstthings.com/article/2014/10/ecclesiocentrism.

——. "The Goals of Ecumenism." In *Paths to Unity: Explorations in Ecumenical Method*, edited by Paul Avis, 1–12. London: Church House Publishing, 2004.

——. *God and the Works of God*. Vol. 1 of *God without Measure: Working Papers in Christian Theology*. New York: T&T Clark, 2016.

——. *The Grace of Truth*. Edited by Daniel Bush and Brannon Ellis. Farmington Hills, MI: Oil Lamp, 2011.

——. *Holiness*. Grand Rapids: Eerdmans, 2003.

——. *Holy Scripture: A Dogmatic Sketch*. New York: Cambridge University Press, 2003.

——. "ὑπὸ πνεύματος ἁγίου φερόμενοι ἐλάλησαν ἀπὸ θεοῦ ἄνθρωποι: On the Inspiration of Holy Scripture." In *Conception, Reception, and the Spirit: Essays in Honour of Andrew T. Lincoln*, edited by J. Gordon McConville and Lloyd K. Pietersen, 236–52. Eugene, OR: Wipf & Stock, 2015.

——. "'In the Society of God': Some Principles of Ecclesiology." In *Perspectives on Ecclesiology and Ethnography*, edited by Pete Ward, 200–222. Grand Rapids: Eerdmans, 2012.

——. "Introduction." In *The Oxford Handbook of Systematic Theology*, edited by John Webster, Kathryn Tanner, and Iain Torrance, 1–15. New York: Oxford University Press, 2007.

———. "Karl Barth." In *Reading Romans through the Centuries: From the Early Church to Karl Barth*, edited by Richard Bauckham, Daniel R. Driver, Trevor A. Hart, and Nathan MacDonald, 69–94. Grand Rapids: Brazos, 2009.

———. "Lambeth: A Comment." *Pro Ecclesia* 8:2 (1999): 143–46.

———. "Ministry and Priesthood." In *The Study of Anglicanism*, edited by Stephen Sykes, John Booty, and Jonathan Knight, 321–32. Rev. ed. Minneapolis: Fortress, 1998.

———. "Perfection and Participation." In *The Analogy of Being: Invention of the Antichrist or the Wisdom of God?*, edited by Thomas Joseph White, OP, 379–94. Grand Rapids: Eerdmans, 2011.

———. "Perfection and Presence: 'God with Us' According to the Christian Confession." Kantzer Lectures, 2007. Online at https://henrycenter .tiu.edu/kantzer-lectures-in-revealed-theology/past-lectures -publications/john-webster-perfection-presence/.

———. "The Promise and Prospects of Retrieval: Recent Developments in Dogmatics." *Common Places* blog, 20 November 2014. Online at http://zondervanacademic.com/blog/common-places-the-promise -and-prospects-of-retrieval-recent-developments-in-dogmatics/.

———. "Systematic Theology after Barth: Jüngel, Jenson, and Gunton." In *The Modern Theologians: An Introduction to Christian Theology since 1918*, edited by David Ford with Rachel Muers, 249–64. 3rd ed. Malden, MA: Blackwell, 2005.

———. "Theology after Liberalism?" In *Theology after Liberalism: A Reader*, edited by John Webster and George P. Schner, 52–61. Malden, MA: Blackwell, 2000.

———. "*Ut Unim Sint*: Some Cross-Bench Anglican Reflections." In *Ecumenism Today: The Universal Church in the 21st Century*, edited by Francesca Aran Murphy and Christopher Asprey, 29–43. Burlington, VT: Ashgate, 2008.

———. *Virtue and Intellect*. Vol. 2 of *God without Measure: Working Papers in Christian Theology*. New York: T&T Clark, 2016.

———. "What Is the Gospel?" In *Grace and Truth in the Secular Age*, edited by Timothy Bradshaw, 109–18. Grand Rapids: Eerdmans, 1998.

———. "'Where Christ Is': Christology and Ethics." In *Virtue and Intellect*, vol. 2 of *God without Measure: Working Papers in Christian Theology*, 5–28. New York: T&T Clark, 2016.

———. "Witness to the Word: Karl Barth's Lectures on the Gospel of John." In *The Domain of the Word: Scripture and Theological Reason*, 65–85. New York: T&T Clark, 2012.

———. *Word and Church: Essays in Christian Dogmatics*. Edinburgh: T&T Clark, 2016.

Webster, John, ed. *The Cambridge Companion to Karl Barth*. New York: Cambridge University Press, 2000.

Webster, John, and George P. Schner, eds. *Theology after Liberalism: A Reader*. Malden, MA: Blackwell, 2000.

Wells, Samuel. *Improvisation: The Drama of Christian Ethics*. Grand Rapids: Brazos, 2004.

Werntz, Myles. *Bodies of Peace: Ecclesiology, Nonviolence, and Witness*. Minneapolis: Fortress, 2014.

West, Traci C. *Wounds of the Spirit: Black Women, Violence, and Resistance Ethics*. New York: New York University Press, 1999.

White, Thomas Joseph. *The Incarnate Lord: A Thomistic Study in Christology*. Washington, DC: Catholic University of America Press, 2017.

White, Thomas Joseph, ed. *The Analogy of Being: Invention of the Antichrist or the Wisdom of God?* Grand Rapids: Eerdmans, 2011.

Wiebe, Joseph R. "Fracturing Evangelical Recognitions of Christ: Inheriting the Radical Democracy of John Howard Yoder with the Penumbral Vision of Rowan Williams." In *The New Yoder*, edited by Peter Dula and Chris K. Huebner, 294–316. Eugene, OR: Wipf & Stock, 2010.

Wilken, Robert Louis. *John Chrysostom and the Jews: Rhetoric and Reality in the Late 4th Century*. Eugene, OR: Wipf & Stock, 1983.

Williams, A. N. *The Architecture of Theology: Structure, System, and Ratio*. New York: Oxford University Press, 2011.

———. "The Parlement of Foules and the Communion of Saints: Jenson's Appropriation of Patristic and Medieval Theology." In *Trinity, Time, and Church: A Response to the Theology of Robert W. Jenson*, edited by Colin Gunton, 188–200. Eugene, OR: Wipf & Stock, 2011.

Williams, D. Newell, Douglas A. Foster, and Paul M. Blowers, eds. *The Stone-Campbell Movement: A Global History*. St. Louis: Chalice, 2013.

Williams, Delores S. *Sisters in the Wilderness: The Challenge of Womanist God-Talk*. Maryknoll, NY: Orbis, 1993.

Williams, Rowan. *Christ on Trial: How the Gospel Unsettles Our Judgement*. Grand Rapids: Eerdmans, 2003.

———. *Christ the Heart of Creation*. New York: Bloomsbury Continuum, 2018.

———. *On Christian Theology*. Malden, MA: Blackwell, 2000.

———. *Why Study the Past? The Quest for the Historical Church.* Grand Rapids: Eerdmans, 2005.

———. *Wrestling with Angels: Conversations in Modern Theology.* Edited by Mike Higton. Grand Rapids: Eerdmans, 2007.

Wilson, Jessica Hooten. "How Flannery O'Connor Fought Racism." *First Things*, 24 June 2020. Online at https://www.firstthings.com/web-exclusives/2020/06/how-flannery-oconnor-fought-racism.

———. "O'Connor and Race." *First Things*, August 2020. Online at https://www.firstthings.com/article/2020/08/oconnor-and-race.

Winner, Lauren F. *The Dangers of Christian Practice: On Wayward Gifts, Characteristic Damage, and Sin.* New Haven: Yale University Press, 2018.

Winship, Michael P. *Hot Protestants: A History of Puritanism in England and America.* New Haven: Yale University Press, 2019.

Wittman, Tyler. "John Webster (1955–2016): Reflections from One of His Students." *The Gospel Coalition*, 1 June 2016. Online at https://www.thegospelcoalition.org/article/john-webster-reflections-from-one-of-his-students.

Wolterstorff, Nicholas. *Divine Discourse: Philosophical Reflections on the Claim that God Speaks.* New York: Cambridge University Press, 1995.

Wood, Donald. *Barth's Theology of Interpretation.* 2007. Reprint, New York: Routledge, 2016.

Wood, Susan K. *Spiritual Exegesis and the Church in the Theology of Henri de Lubac.* Grand Rapids: Eerdmans, 1998.

Woodbridge, John D. *Biblical Authority: A Critique of the Rogers-McKim Proposal.* Grand Rapids: Zondervan, 1982.

Work, Telford. *Living and Active: Scripture in the Economy of Salvation.* Grand Rapids: Eerdmans, 2001.

Wright, N. T. *Collected Essays.* 3 vols. Grand Rapids: Zondervan Academic, 2020.

———. *History and Eschatology: Jesus and the Promise of Natural Theology.* Waco: Baylor University Press, 2019.

———. *The New Testament and the People of God.* Vol. 1 of *Christian Origins and the Question of God.* Minneapolis: Fortress, 1992.

———. *The New Testament for Everyone.* 18 vols. Louisville: Westminster John Knox, 2001–2011.

———. *Scripture and the Authority of God: How to Read the Bible Today.* New York: HarperOne, 2011.

———. *Surprised by Scripture: Engaging Contemporary Issues.* New York: HarperOne, 2014.

Wright, Nigel Goring. *Disavowing Constantine: Mission, Church, and the Social*

Order in the Theologies of John Howard Yoder and Jürgen Moltmann. Paternoster Theological Monographs. 2000. Reprint, Eugene, OR: Wipf & Stock, 2006.

Wright, Stephen John. *Dogmatic Aesthetics: A Theology of Beauty in Dialogue with Robert W. Jenson*. Minneapolis: Fortress, 2014.

Wyschogrod, Michael. *Abraham's Promise: Judaism and Jewish-Christian Relations*. Edited by R. Kendall Soulen. Grand Rapids: Eerdmans, 2004.

Yoder, John Howard. *Anabaptism and Reformation in Switzerland: An Historical and Theological Analysis of the Dialogues Between Anabaptists and Reformers*. Edited by C. Arnold Snyder. Translated by David Carl Stassen and C. Arnold Snyder. Kitchener, ON: Pandora, 2004.

———. "Armaments and Eschatology." *Studies in Christian Ethics* 1 (1988): 43–61.

———. "Biblical Roots of Liberation Theology." *Grail* 1 (1985): 54–74.

———. *Body Politics: Five Practices of the Christian Community Before the Watching World*. Scottdale, PA: Herald, 1992.

———. *Christian Attitudes to War, Peace, and Revolution*. Edited by Theodore J. Koontz and Andy Alexis-Baker. Grand Rapids: Brazos, 2009.

———. *The Christian Witness to the State*. 1964. Reprint, Scottdale, PA: Herald, 2002.

———. "Could There Be a Baptist Bishop?" *Ecumenical Trends* 9 (1980): 104–7.

———. *Discipleship as Political Responsibility*. Scottdale, PA: Herald, 1964, 2003.

———. "The Ecumenical Movement and the Faithful Church." In *Radical Ecumenicity: Pursuing Unity and Continuity after John Howard Yoder*, edited by John C. Nugent, 193–222. Abilene, TX: Abilene Christian University Press, 2009.

———. *The End of Sacrifice: The Capital Punishment Writings of John Howard Yoder*. Edited by John C. Nugent. Harrisonburg, VA: Herald, 2011.

———. "Ethics and Eschatology." *Ex Auditu* 6 (1990): 119–28.

———. "Exodus and Exile: The Two Faces of Liberation." *Cross Currents* 23 (1973): 297–309.

———. *For the Nations: Essays Public and Evangelical*. Grand Rapids: Eerdmans, 1997.

———. *The Fullness of Christ: Paul's Vision of Universal Ministry*. Elgin, IL: Brethren, 1987.

———. *He Came Preaching Peace: Bible Lectures on Peacemaking*. Scottdale, PA: Herald, 2004.

———. "Historiography as a Ministry to Renewal." *Brethren Life and Thought* 42 (1997): 216–28.

———. "Is There Historical Development of Theological Thought?" In *Radical Ecumenicity: Pursuing Unity and Continuity after John Howard Yoder*, edited by John C. Nugent, 223–35. Abilene, TX: Abilene Christian University Press, 2009.

———. *The Jewish-Christian Schism Revisited*. Edited by Michael G. Cartwright and Peter Ochs. Grand Rapids: Eerdmans, 2003.

———. *Karl Barth and the Problem of War and Other Essays on Barth*. Edited by Mark Thiessen Nation. Eugene, OR: Cascade, 2003.

———. "Meaning after Babble: With Jeffrey Stout beyond Relativism." *Journal of Religious Ethics* 24:1 (1996): 125–39.

———. *Nevertheless: The Varieties and Shortcomings of Religious Pacifism*. Rev. ed. Scottdale, PA: Herald, 1992.

———. *Nonviolence: A Brief History*. Edited by Paul Martens, Matthew Porter, and Myles Werntz. Waco: Baylor University Press, 2010.

———. "On Christian Unity: The Way from Below." *Pro Ecclesia* 9 (2000): 165–183.

———. "On Not Being Ashamed of the Gospel: Particularity, Pluralism, and Validation." *Faith and Philosophy* 9 (1992): 285–300.

———. "On Not Being in Charge." In *War and Its Discontents: Pacifism and Quietism in the Abrahamic Traditions*, edited by James Patout Burns, 74–90. Washington, DC: Georgetown University Press, 1996.

———. *The Original Revolution: Essays on Christian Pacifism*. Scottdale, PA: Herald, 1971.

———. *A Pacifist Way of Knowing: John Howard Yoder's Nonviolent Epistemology*. Edited by Christian E. Early and Ted G. Grimsrud. Eugene, OR: Cascade, 2010.

———. *The Politics of Jesus: Vicit Agnus Noster*. 2nd ed. Grand Rapids: Eerdmans, 1974, 1992.

———. *Preface to Theology: Christology and Method*. Edited by Stanley Hauerwas and Alex Sider. Grand Rapids: Brazos, 2002.

———. *The Priestly Kingdom: Social Ethics as Gospel*. Notre Dame: University of Notre Dame Press, 1984.

———. "Primitivism in the Radical Reformation: Strengths and Weaknesses." In *The Primitive Church in the Modern World*, edited by Richard T. Hughes, 74–97. Urbana and Chicago: University of Illinois Press, 1995.

———. *Radical Christian Discipleship*. Edited by John C. Nugent, Andy Alexis-Baker, and Branson L. Parler. Harrisonburg, VA: Herald, 2012.

———. *Real Christian Fellowship*. Edited by John C. Nugent, Branson L. Parler, and Heather L. Bunce. Harrisonburg, VA: Herald, 2014.

———. Review of *Liberation and Change*, by Gustavo Gutiérrez and Richard Shaull. *Theology Today* 36 (1979): 128.

———. *Revolutionary Christian Citizenship*. Edited by John C. Nugent, Branson L. Parler, and Andy Alexis-Baker. Harrisonburg, VA: Herald, 2013.

———. *Revolutionary Christianity: The 1966 South American Lectures*. Edited by Paul Martens, Mark Thiessen Nation, Matthew Porter, and Myles Werntz. Eugene, OR: Cascade, 2011.

———. *The Royal Priesthood: Essays Ecclesiastical and Ecumenical*. Edited by Michael G. Cartwright. Scottdale, PA: Herald, 1994, 1998.

———. *Theology of Mission: A Believers Church Perspective*. Edited by Gayle Gerber Koontz and Andy Alexis-Baker. Downers Grove, IL: IVP Academic, 2014.

———. *To Hear the Word*. 2nd ed. Eugene, OR: Cascade, 2010.

———. *The War of the Lamb: The Ethics of Nonviolence and Peacemaking*. Edited by Glen Stassen, Mark Thiessen Nation, and Matt Hamsher. Grand Rapids: Brazos, 2009.

———. *What Would You Do? A Serious Answer to a Standard Question*. Rev. ed. Scottdale, PA: Herald, 1992.

———. *When War Is Unjust: Being Honest in Just-War Thinking*. 2nd ed. Eugene, OR: Wipf & Stock, 1996.

———. "The Wider Setting of 'Liberation Theology.'" *The Review of Politics* 52 (1990): 285–96.

Young, Frances M. *The Art of Performance: Towards a Theology of Holy Scripture*. London: Darton, Longman and Todd, 1990.

———. *Biblical Exegesis and the Formation of Christian Culture*. New York: Cambridge University Press, 1997.

Young, Stephen. "Love the Scholarship but Hate the Scholar's Sin? 'Himpathy' for an Academic Pedophile Enables a Culture of Abuse." *Religion Dispatches*, 24 June 2020. Online at https://religiondispatches.org/love-the-scholarship-but-hate-the-scholars-sin-himpathy-for-an-academic-pedophile-enables-a-culture-of-abuse/.

Yuen, Alfred H. *Barth's Theological Ontology of Holy Scripture*. Eugene, OR: Pickwick, 2014.

Zimmerman, Earl. *Practicing the Politics of Jesus: The Origin and Significance of John Howard Yoder's Social Ethics*. Scottdale, PA: Herald, 2007.

Index of Authors

Index of Subjects

agency: divine *vs.* human/church, 49, 81, 84–85, 89–94, 96–98, 119, 163, 260, 272–75, 323–25; of Scripture, 48–49, 88n80
Allen, Richard, 34
Ambrose, St., 72n11
apostolic church, 251
apostolic mission, 173, 228, 285–86
apostolic succession, 33, 34, 306
Augustine, St., 31n64, 70, 72n11, 74n18, 95, 155, 157, 159, 191, 194, 220, 234, 261n15, 274n44, 287, 288; *De Doctrina Christiana*, 95
authority of Christ, 56–58, 61
authority of the church: dogmatic and interpretive, 130–35, 155–56, 169–71, 260–61, 283, 285, 297–98, 318, 327, 331–32; as subordinate to Scripture, 55–61, 87–89, 114–15, 117–22, 283, 295–96
authority of Scripture: church as subordinate to, 55–61, 87–89, 114–15, 117–22, 283, 295–96; moral, 148–49; as provisional, 121, 284
authorship and origins of Scripture: communal context, 211–12; dual, emphasis on humans/church, 130, 260, 272–73, 323, 324–25; dual,

emphasis on the divine, 4, 81–82, 84–85, 89–92, 119, 310, 323–24; dual, equal emphasis on humans and the divine, 174, 273–75; God as both author and character in narrative, 137; Holy Spirit's role in, 81–82, 91, 143–44, 164–65, 174, 310, 323–24; wholly by humans/church, 321–22. *See also* canon and canonization

baptism, 63, 155, 246
baptist tradition: church-as-vanguard typology, 311–16; overview, 34–35, 36–37; Yoder's alignment with, 197, 223, 240
Barth, Karl, 39–66; on apostolic church, 251; on authority of Scripture, 54–61, 134–35n44; exegetical method, 39, 61, 62–64, 255; Jenson as student of, 24, 31n64; legacy, 8, 253–56; on nature of Scripture, 47–54; reception of, in light of moral failings, 192; on reconciliation, 50n24, 110; on revelation, 42–45; on Scripture as mediated revelation, 45–46, 51; theology of Scripture, overview, 61–62, 64–66, 253; and TIS origins, 18, 31–32;

Index of Scripture References